Chicano Theater

Themes and Forms

Bilingual Press/Editorial Bilingüe

Studies in the Language and Literature of United States Hispanos

General Editor
Gary D. Keller

Managing Editor
Karen S. Van Hooft

Editorial Board
Ernestina N. Eger
Joshua A. Fishman
Francisco Jiménez
William Milán
Amado M. Padilla
Raymond V. Padilla
Eduardo Rivera
Richard V. Teschner
Guadalupe Valdés
Juan Clemente Zamora

Address
Bilingual Review/Press
Hispanic Research Center
Arizona State University
Tempe, AZ 85287-2702
(602) 965-3867

Chicano Theater,
Themes and Forms

WITHDRAWN

Jorge A. Huerta

Bilingual Press/Editorial Bilingüe
TEMPE, ARIZONA

ISBN: 0-916950-26-3
Printed simultaneously in a softcover edition. ISBN: 0-916950-25-5

Library of Congress Catalog Card Number: 81-68425

PRINTED IN THE UNITED STATES OF AMERICA

Second Printing, October 1990

Cover design by Christopher J. Bidlack

Photo of author by Diane Sherlock

The author wishes to express his appreciation to the teatros and photographers who so graciously permitted the use of their photos in this book.

Acknowledgments

I am indebted to all of the dedicated cultural workers represented in this book and to the many who are not. This study can only be the first of many, for I discovered as I wrote that there is still much more to be said, and to those who do not appear in this volume, I thank you for your patience and understanding.

I am grateful to my friends and colleagues who guided me along the way, pointing out my errors with constructive criticism. Warm and heartfelt abrazos to Ricardo Romo, Francisco Jiménez, Nicolás Kanellos, Mary Lamprech, George Woodyard, and a very special hug to Frantisek Deak, without whose guidance this volume would not have been possible. To Edith Fisher, for all her support and help, gracias. To my many students over the years, young and eager minds who always questioned, I am continually thankful. My warmest gratitude to my editor, Karen Van Hooft, for her interest and patience. A special word of appreciation to my typists, Sandra Inzunza, Sofía Cebrero, and Linda Pishalski.

This book would not have been possible without a grant from the National Chicano Council on Higher Education, administered by Dr. Arturo Madrid, as well as the support of the Committee on Research of the University of California at San Diego. To Professor William R. Reardon, who guided me and made my graduate studies meaningful, a note of thanks.

Finally, I would like to thank my family, my mother and father, Elizabeth and Jorge, and my sisters Tencha, Raquel, Naomi, Carmen, and Betty—you all taught me how to love, to care, and to be aware of injustices throughout the world.

To my wife, Ginger,
and to my sons,
Ronald and Gregg

TABLE OF CONTENTS

Introduction   1

Chapter 1   *In Fields and Factories: The Worker's Struggle*

    Luis Valdez Goes to Delano   11
    The *Acto*   14
    Of Masks and Moralities: *Las dos caras del patroncito*
       and *La quinta temporada*   18
    The Urban Struggle: *El hombre que se convirtió en perro*   27
    A "Super-Acto": *Los pelados*   36

Chapter 2   *The Search for Identity: What is a Chicano?*

    No More Melting Pot   47
    Cucarachas on the Walls and Vendidos in the Closet: *The*
       Shrunken Head of Pancho Villa   49
    How to Buy a Used Mexican: *Los vendidos*   60
    Is There No Choice?—*La víctima*   68

Chapter 3   *The Chicano in War at Home and Abroad*

    Remember the Alamo!   83
    Chicanos and the War in Vietnam: *Vietnam campesino*   86
    The Acto in Transition: *Soldado razo*   91
    A Veterano's Mito: *Dark Root of a Scream*   97
    The War at Home: *Manolo*   103

Chapter 4   *Back to the Barrio: Local Government and*
                Education

    The Politics of Learning   119
    A Symptomatic Acto: *The High School Counselor*   121
    Learning the ABC's: *No saco nada de la escuela*   129
    Who's to Blame?—*El alcalde*   134
    A Microcosm in a Docudrama: *Guadalupe*   140

Chapter 5   *Justice: On the Streets and In the Courts*

With Liberty and Justice For Some	155
Salsipuedes—Get Out If You Can: *Trampa sin salida*	161
Tampering With the Evidence: *Las many muertes de Richard Morales*	167
The Ultimate Pachuco: *Zoot Suit*	174

Chapter 6   *The Chicano and His Cosmos: Reaching for the Stars*

The Indigenous Roots of Chicano Theater	187
Northward to Aztlán	192
A Contemporary Myth: *Bernabé*	195
The Return of Quetzalcóatl: *La gran carpa de los rasquachis*	199
An Apocalyptic Vision: *El fin del mundo*	207

Afterword   *The Many Stages of the Revolution*

From the Temple to the Arena	215
Expanding the Perimeters	217
Securing the Resources	221
Keeping the Revolution on Stage	225

Notes

Introduction	227
Chapter One	227
Chapter Two	229
Chapter Three	230
Chapter Four	231
Chapter Five	234
Chapter Six	236

Bibliography   241

I. Pre-Columbian Period	242
II. Mexican Colonial Period	243
III. Aztlán Before 1965	245
IV. Teatro Campesino and Luis Valdez, 1965-70	248
V. Teatro Campesino and Luis Valdez, 1971-80	250
VI. *Zoot Suit*	253
VII. Other Teatros, General	256
VIII. Festivals	262
IX. Other Teatros, Reviews	264

Index   266

Opening scene of *Zoot Suit* by Luis Valdez, 1978; shown is Edward James Olmos as El Pachuco. *Photo: © Ricardo Martinez*

El Teatro Campesino performing *La gran carpa de los rasquachis,* c. 1975-76. *Photo: Teatro Campesino*

Teatro Obrero performing *Mímica del oprimido*, c. 1977; shown
are Lilly Delgadillo (L) and Evelina Fernández (R).
Photo: © *Ricardo Martínez*

El Teatro Campesino's Banda Calavera, c. 1967.
Photo: Teatro Campesino

El Teatro Campesino performing *El corrido*, which appeared on PBS in 1976. Shown are José Delgado (L), Socorro Cruz (R), and Félix Alvarez as Jesús Rasquachi. *Photo: Melvyn Richardson*

Teatro de la Esperanza performs *La victima* at the 8th Annual Chicano Theater Festival, 1977. Shown are José Saucedo and Rodrigo Duarte-Clark. *Photo: Peter Marshall*

INTRODUCTION

When I first began to investigate the theater of the Mexican American in 1970, I discovered that very little had been written about the current rise of Chicano theater groups, although there was a great deal of information about the Spanish religious folk theater of the Southwest. Prior to the founding of the Teatro Campesino in 1965, little attention had been paid to the Chicano's theatrical activity outside the church. It seemed that Chicanos were more interesting to historians and theater chroniclers as "folk" than as activists, and a search for records of political theater in the barrios had limited results. But with the rise of a political movement in the Chicano community in the late sixties and seventies, attention had to be given as well to political aspects of this activity, including the work of the many teatros, or theater groups, that began to follow in the wake of the highly successful Teatro Campesino.

The Teatro Campesino, or Farmworker's Theater, was founded by Luis Valdez, a native of Delano, California, the son of migrant farmworkers. Although another person might have attempted to do what he did with a group of striking farmworkers, it was Valdez who went to César Chávez and suggested that the incipient farm labor union sponsor a street theater to educate and entertain the farmworkers. It is doubtful that Valdez realized at the time just how momentous his charge or his influence would be; yet, by 1980, he and his group would be internationally recognized, and a national network of other Chicano theater groups would be expressing the hopes and dreams, frustrations and demands of the Chicano in all parts of the United States and beyond.

The Teatro Campesino became the symbol of the Chicano's theatrical expression, inspiring Chicanos all over the country to form other teatros dedicated to exposing the sociopolitical conditions of the Mexican-American community. The year 1965 became the point of departure for a veritable renaissance of cultural and political activity among Chicanos, motivating young and old to assert their identity in a society that had ignored them for generations. "The silent minority" would no longer acquiesce to the stereotypes and racial biases that plagued all aspects of the media but would, instead, fight for dignified representation on stage and film, in print and on the air. It took a particular cause (the striking farmworkers), a special atmosphere (the civil rights movement), and a growing political consciousness (the Chicano student movement) to give rise to a theatrical movement that continues to evolve in the 1980s.

One of the most important features of the evolution of Chicano theater is the fact that the teatros have not been spawned in geographically separated vacuums, but have enjoyed a certain amount of cross-feeding, exchanging ideas, techniques, and mutual concerns through a national network, TENAZ, *El Teatro Nacional de Aztlán*. The word "tenaz" means "tenacity," a symbol of the organization's determination to survive. Formed in 1971, TENAZ became an important arm of communication and coordination among the majority of teatros in the United States, including progressive Puerto Rican troupes on the East Coast and companies in Mexico, TENAZ' yearly festivals have brought together troupes from all parts of Latin America and Europe, as the teatros gather to share performances, workshops, and critiques. Originally motivated by the Teatro Campesino, TENAZ has been guided by various groups and individuals from throughout the United States and Mexico. The organization's major charge is to foster and promote the development of Chicano theater groups and playwrights. All of the groups and individuals represented in this book have been involved in TENAZ as leaders and participants, searching for their connection with other Chicano theater artists as they affirm their roles in their particular communities.

TENAZ has also kept in touch with its membership through various publications over the years, beginning with an informal publication entitled *El Teatro/El Tenaz* in 1970. This publication was originally produced by the Teatro Campesino, and when TENAZ was formed in 1971, it became the organization's communique, edited by members of Valdez' troupe. In the spring of 1973, the organization published the first of three magazine-style volumes entitled *Chicano Theatre One*. The following summer, *Chicano Theater Two* appeared, and the third issue came out in the spring of 1974. These publications contained articles about various groups, exercises, editorials, and *actos*. This short-lived but very valuable publication was followed by an informal newsletter, "TENAZ Talks Teatro," published quarterly by the present author beginning in 1978. Each of these efforts has served to keep the teatros abreast of the activities of the organization and its members. Looking back at this relatively young outgrowth of a need to assert a cultural and political identity, it is clear that Chicano theater was born of and remains a people's theater. As evidenced by this book, the themes and styles have varied, but the majority of Chicano theater groups and playwrights are addressing the issues they feel are important to their communities. And judging from the responses of those communities, it is safe to say that the people embrace the teatros and their dramatic expressions. Encouraged by the approbation of their popular audiences, teatros and playwrights have endured because of a determination to expose the many problems that plague the Chicano in this society. Often, the message is more important than the medium, and the developing groups, like the original Teatro Campesino, place politics above aesthetics, unfettered by considerations of Great Drama.

The majority of teatros remain people's theaters, rooted in an oral tradition that avoids formalized scripts because the plays are based on improvisations of the moment. Like any other popular movement, however, there have been those groups and individuals that have chosen to go beyond the basic street theater techniques, studying other aspects of world theater in an attempt to express the Chicano condition in other forms. These teatros and playwrights are usually the older practitioners of their craft, and they have evolved to the point of publishing their works and touring beyond their immediate communities, thus reaching a wider audience. Because published scripts are more accessible to the reader, the majority of the works discussed in this book have reached the printed page and represent the more successful theatrical expressions of the Chicano. These works also serve to demonstrate the diversity of issues dramatized from the earliest farmworker *actos* to the realistic play. Needless to say, the plays discussed here represent a small portion of the dramatizations being produced in barrios throughout the country.

By analyzing plays on varied topics relevant to the Chicano community, this book attempts to define Chicano theater, its major dramatists, and theater groups in an effort to reveal its diversity. Although Chicanos have inherited a long tradition of religious theatrical expression that spans centuries, the relatively recent rise of Chicano theater remains generally unknown to the average citizen, particularly outside of the barrio. What I once termed "the best kept secret in North American Theater" is no longer a secret, but it is certainly not a household word. Perhaps a study of this kind can help to inform the person who asks: "What is Chicano theater?"

Before immersing the reader in the several themes that serve as foci of this book, some definition of the term "Chicano" seems imperative. It is clear by now that Chicano theater addresses issues common to the Chicano, but just what *is* a Chicano as opposed to a Mexican American, Mexican, Hispanic, or Latino? More than anything, the term Chicano seems to identify a certain political consciousness, asserted with vigor especially after 1965. The etymology of the word is unclear, but most observers agree that "Chicano" came from the people themselves; it is a self-definition that denies both a Mexican and an Anglo-American distinction, yet is influenced by both. In essence, Chicanos assert that they are neither Mexican nor Anglo-American, employing a term that stems from barrio realities and linguistic patterns on this side of the Mexican border. The term has been in common usage for generations and is often employed to distinguish between the middle-class Mexican American and the working-class Chicano, a delineation that separates the so-called "assimilationist" from the political activist.[1] There are still many Americans of Mexican descent who see the term Chicano as "common" and indicative of a low-class status. As shown in Chapter Two, these Mexican Americans are often the butt of barrio humor that pokes fun at those who would try to "pass" within the dominant society. While Mexican Americans assert their "Americanness," Chicanos purposely distinguish themselves from Anglo-American culture, desperately hanging on to what they can of barrio culture. Very often, assimilated Mexican Americans look down their noses at this cultural assertion, content in their ability to "make it" in this society and contemptuous of "those Chicanos" who dare to be different.

Like any immigrant to this country, the Mexican American has often attempted to adopt the customs, mores, and standards of the dominant society. But, unlike any other "minority group," the Mexican American has witnessed a continual influx of citizens from the homeland as well as a centuries-long tradition of residence in the Southwest. In effect, as Luis Valdez puts it: "We crossed no ocean... No Statue of Liberty greeted our arrival in this country . . . We did not, in fact, come to the United States at all. The United States came to us."[2] I believe this concept is essential to understanding why the Chicano has attempted to hold on to his culture, his language, and his identity. With so many daily reminders of the Old Country surrounding him, the Chicano who lives in the barrio exists in a world that mingles aspects of both the Mexican and Anglo cultures. In the larger urban concentrations of Chicanos such as Los Angeles, Chicago, and San Antonio, to name a few, it is possible to live one's life without ever learning English. Spanish-language newspapers, radio, television and films remind the recent arrivals as well as the native sons and daughters that they have a heritage on the other side of a border and within this very nation.

Yet, with all this cross-feeding of Mexican customs in an Anglo-dominated society, the mixture has not always proved beneficial to all. Thus we find Chicanos calling Mexicans "T.J.'s," signifying Tijuana as their port of entry, and Mexicans calling Chicanos "pochos," an equally derogatory term. *"¿Por qué no hablan español?"* ("Why don't you speak Spanish?"), Mexicans will ask contemptuously, while Chicanos will condemn them for not communicating in English. Ideally, they would all speak both languages with facility, but this has not been the case to date. Millions of undocumented workers in this country live in a sort of demi-world, always cautious of being apprehended and deported. As members of the working class, many Chicanos have accepted the politicians' rhetoric about the "illegal alien threat," unaware of the fact that the undocumented workers contribute to the economy rather than detract from it.

And so there is a difference between the Chicano and the Mexican in terms of language, attitudes, social customs, and place of birth, but in the final analysis they are both members of the working class and share the same consequences of an insensitive society: poverty, alienation, exploitation in wars, manipulation by government, ignorance in the schools, and injustice in the courts—the several themes that Chicano theater has explored. While progressive playwrights, theater groups and political organizations have tried to foster a better line of communication between the Mexican and the Chicano, it must be understood that the two are not generally alike. Therefore I have followed the current trend, distinguishing between the Mexican and the Chicano when differences are important, but referring to the "Mechicano" as a symbol of both peoples, when distinctions are inappropriate. To the playwrights and teatros represented in this book, the Mexican and the Chicano share equally in their oppression, and most of the plays have attempted to educate their audiences in this regard. Thus, I will usually refer to the "Mechicano" as representative of all Spanish-surnamed peoples with a connection to Mexico, whether recent or historical.

One of the major distinctions between the Mexican and the Chicano is the language employed by each group. Generally, the more recent arrivals from Mexico speak little or no English, while most Chicanos usually speak both Spanish and English to varying degrees. The majority of the plays produced for audiences will reflect this linguistic particularity, employing a mixture of Spanish and English as well as *caló*, the language of the streets. Most teatros are composed of bilingual members who have discovered that their audiences delight in hearing their particular language re-created onstage. Barrio audiences are usually a mixture of Mexicans and Chicanos. Many Mexicans who do not speak English can understand it, and many Chicanos who do not communicate in Spanish can recognize the language of their parents, thus enabling these distinct groups to comprehend the messages conveyed. By addressing a bilingual public, teatros are asserting a very definite particularity that may arouse resentment among the non-bilingual members of the audience, especially the English speakers. Because of this, some groups will present their productions completely in one language and then the other; however, most teatros speak to their specific communities, in their own language.

Because the overwhelming majority of Chicano playwrights and theater groups are addressing the socio-politico-economic condition of the Mechicano, it is safe to say that Chicano theater is political theater. Departing from Luis Valdez' original intent of educating and entertaining, teatros and playwrights have followed the path of didactic drama. Any analysis of the major themes that have been dramatized must therefore include some sort of historical perspective as well as documentation about the veracity of the representations. Rather than start this book with a chapter on the historical development of Chicano theater, beginning with the earliest Pre-Columbian rituals and Spanish religious folk theater, each chapter contains a brief review of the precedents in order to remind the reader that Chicano theater has a history as well as a present. In some instances, the historical precedents reach back through centuries, while in others we have no records of productions that deal with the same themes. In all cases, the focus is on the outstanding examples of today's playwrights and teatros.

Looking at the many issues addressed in the plays in this book, it becomes apparent that one would have to be an anthropologist, sociologist, political scientist, linguist, and theologian to appropriately discuss the problems dramatized. But this is a book about theater, and hopefully I have not ventured too far afield in my attempt to add dimension. Documentation is noted where appropriate, and the reader is advised that most of the themes in this book are being studied by the appropriate social scientists, and further reading would usually verify the truth of the depiction. It is the intent of this book to expose the reader to the many problems plaguing the Mechicano community, not only as social documentary but, more importantly, as *theater*. By demonstrating how different playwrights and teatros have addressed similar themes in divergent ways, it is my intention to give the reader a better understanding of what Chicano theater is all about. Most especially, I would hope that the reader will learn something about the Chicanos by seeing how they visualize themselves, their different struggles, and their dramatizations of those struggles.

As this book was being written, it remained the first such attempt of its kind. Dissertations had been written on different aspects of Chicano theater, and several studies were evolving in the minds of Chicano graduate students in theater, but, essentially, this would be the first published book about the subject. This became, then, a major distinction and an overwhelming responsibility. The first book about Chicano theater? What do you say? What do you not say? Why should the reader be interested in this theme? Who will read the book? These and many other questions plagued me, and with the encouragement and advice of many friends in the field, I ventured forth, eager to share a subject that is very close to me. Too close? Perhaps. And yet, what true investigation of a subject can remain a cool, detached observation without losing some of its essential life—its energy and commitment to the topic? By addressing this book to the general reader, Chicano and non-Chicano alike, I have had to be perhaps too specific in some instances and possibly too general in others. The notes will guide the reader to further study of the various topics discussed.

A survey of the major dramas produced by teatros since 1965 reveals a thematic pattern that inspired the structure of this book. Each of the six chapters studies a particular theme and a number of dramatic works that have dealt with that theme. We begin with the worker's struggle because the Mechicano is a worker in this society, from fields to factories, contributing to the economy. As members of the working class, Mechicanos do not differ from any other workers, and the plays considered in the first chapter are relevant to any effort to organize laborers. Yet they are uniquely Chicano efforts, whether born of the *campesinos'* cause or adapted from a Latin American play about corporate dehumanization. The language, rhythms, and focus of all of the plays studied in this book capture the Chicano and the Mexican, not as totally distinct from any other member of the working class, but still dissimilar. The substance of the text will illuminate this question as it seeks a definition of Chicano theater.

Having explored in the first chapter three distinct examples of Chicano worker's theater, both rural and urban, the second chapter looks at the proverbial question: "What is a Chicano?" This complex question is not easily answered, and the plays that concentrate on the identity of the Chicano contrast the "sellout" with the revolutionary, the assimilationist with the activist, in an effort to reveal the complexities of cultural and political identity within the dominant society.

The third chapter focuses upon the Chicano as soldier, concentrating on the war in Vietnam and the Chicano's resistance to that conflict. While protest rallies raged throughout the country during that unwanted aggression in Southeast Asia, Chicanos, too, refused to be persuaded that their country was somehow the guardian of the economic and political system of Vietnam, and their theater reflects that skepticism. The plays in this chapter are significant reminders that the lessons learned from Vietnam will not be forgotten.

Chapter Four attempts to demonstrate that Chicanos are victims of both local government and the educational system, neither of which seems concerned with the educational or political advancement of the barrio. This chapter is perhaps the most diverse in its motifs; it shows how teatros from California to Indiana illustrate the educational and political repression that afflicts Mechicanos in the Southwest and even Puerto Ricans and Chicanos in the Midwest. Education is crucial to the economic advancement of the Mechicano, and the plays in this chapter are excellent dramatizations of how and why this group is still behind any other except Puerto Ricans and Native Americans in educational achievement.

The Mechicano has long been a victim of injustice at the hands of the police as well as the courts, and Chapter Five presents three distinct efforts to dramatize this fact. With national attention focused daily on the police brutality and killings in this country, these plays reflect the Chicanos' continued concern with this problem. Solutions are not easily suggested, but the conflicts are expressed and the playwrights and teatros ask their audiences to recognize a problem that few people can ignore.

The police violence and judicial antipathy discussed in the fifth chapter contrast with the final section, which looks at the Mechicano's spiritual theatrical heritage. This survey of the religious theater from Pre-Columbian times to the present is the most extensive examination of precedents, for this is the most enduring theatrical tradition in the barrio. The focus is on the Neo-Maya theater of Luis Valdez, since the thematic and dramatic evolution of the leading figure in Chicano theater cannot be ignored. The Afterword offers an overview of what has been accomplished to date and what remains to be fulfilled by Chicano playwrights and teatros.

By distinguishing among the various themes that issue forth from Chicano pens and stages, I can only hope to introduce the reader to the subject, mindful of the limitations of addressing a phenomenon that is not constant. Other themes remain to be explored by playwrights and teatros, individuals and collectives, as Chicanos continue to express a living testament to their own perseverance and determination. This book is only a beginning, and should not long remain the sole example of its kind, for there is much to be learned from studying a continually evolving movement, even as it makes its twists and turns. Sixteen years after the founding of the Teatro Campesino, and centuries after the inception of a ritual theater that has not been forgotten, the Chicano theater movement lives. This book is dedicated to the firm belief that Teatro Chicano will endure, as the Chicanos themselves have endured—confronted with struggle, yes, but armed with tenacity as well.

El Teatro Campesino performing huelga songs, c. 1965.
Photo: Teatro Campesino

Chapter One

IN FIELDS AND FACTORIES:
THE WORKER'S STRUGGLE

Luis Valdez Goes to Delano

It is the fall of 1965. Luis Valdez, a young Chicano whose experience in theater includes acting and playwriting, has come to Delano, California, to discuss the possibility of forming a farmworker's theater. He and a small group of striking farmworkers are meeting in a little pink house that is part of the union headquarters. Valdez talks for a while, but he knows that he will have to get the people themselves to demonstrate their situation. Speaking to the *campesinos* in a mixture of Spanish and English, Valdez urges members of his audience to step up in front of the others and show what happened in the strike that day. He has brought signs to hang around these "actors'" necks, identifying the characters, and asks for two volunteers to portray *huelgistas*, or strikers, and a third volunteer to play an *esquirol*, or scab. Everyone is reluctant to play the part of the despised strikebreaker, but finally a brave young farmworker says he'll do it.

"Now show us what happened today on the picket line," Valdez tells these three farmworkers, and immediately the two "strikers" begin yelling at the "esquirol," who good-naturedly shouts back at them. The other people in the room join in the fun and laugh and shout as they witness this rudimentary re-creation of their own experiences. Another person volunteers to take part; suddenly the room is filling up with people from nobody knows where, all laughing and having a good time. "I'll play the *esquirol* this time," offers an enthusiastic voice from the back of the room, and "I want to be the *huelgista*" emerges from another corner, as these tired but dedicated farmworkers begin to see themselves as the protagonists in a daily drama that had seemed theirs alone until this moment.

Valdez now triumphantly pulls out another theatrical device, a pig-like mask which is immediately identified by the jeering crowd as *El Patroncito*, the "boss" or grower. There, for all to see, is a face that could belong to no one else, and the people respond with glee at the prospect of seeing a portrayal of a despised figure—the wealthy grower who refuses to negotiate with the union. "Who wants to play *El Patroncito?*" asks the director, and the volunteers rush forward, eager to make their individual comments about the villain in their lives. Valdez chooses an energetic striker to don the mask, and as soon as he puts it on, the audience cheers in delight and disgust. The actor turns his head to face the audience, and the mask seems to come alive, sneering this way and that, drawing roars of laughter with every move. "Y'all stop that laughing!" he shouts at the crowd in a Texas drawl, and they love it.

With each improvisation of their daily struggles, these *campesinos* demonstrate to Valdez that there is a message to be dramatized and that the talent to dramatize it is in this room. Though he has just met them for the first time, Valdez knows these workers because he was born to a migrant farmworking family in this very town and first started picking the crops at the age of six. He is familiar with the hardships and trials of the migrant worker and remembers in these tired faces how his youth was spent, moving with the crops, interrupting his education until he finally earned a scholarship to San Jose State College. He knows the characters portrayed this evening, and he has come to Delano in the spirit of genuine involvement, not with an attitude of "Here's what *I* can do for you." Valdez and these incipient members of a farmworker's theater need each other. Valdez' vision of a theater that will speak of the Chicano and Mexican struggles in the fields is more than just a possibility—it has come alive this evening.

At the close of the first improvised session, the Teatro Campesino has been born. Not all of the people in the room will become members, for there are many responsibilities in the organization of a farmworker's union, but those that choose to get involved will become the collective authors of the Teatro's first *actos*: improvised scenes that present the realities of the struggle. The improvisations this evening are the seeds of what will follow; under Valdez' guidance, his group will explore the characters and situations that must be exposed in order to educate the farmworkers about the need for a union. There is an immediacy about the evening's improvisations.

These are not actors portraying characters from a playwright's pen; they are people expressing their own experiences by donning signs or masks and saying to their viewers: "Look, this is what happened to me on the picket line today. Do you think it's fair?" And the audience, composed of fellow strikers, responds with "No! It isn't fair, and we're going to do something about it: *¡Huelga!*" "*¡Huelga!*" (Strike) "*¡Ya basta!*" (We've had it!) are heard in this old pink house, as *campesinos* find a spirit of reinforcement and encouragement in the simple re-creations of their plight. Valdez has already had his first two plays produced at San Jose State College in 1964, and the playwright in him immediately recognizes the possibilities here for a series of short *actos* to evolve out of the daily improvisations in the fields and in the group's rehearsal space. The drama of a picket line, with strikers urging scabs not to cross the line as blank-faced sheriffs look on, waiting for violence to erupt, is an improvisation in itself, and Valdez knows that he has found a means of re-enacting this basic conflict for fellow *campesinos*. The symbolic victories over the grower or scab, as portrayed in this first session, may seem like vicarious triumphs at best, but in their truth-to-life they have a certain force that calls to mind the political theater of the 1930s in this country. All the people who have crowded into the house this evening return to their respective homes with spirits lighter than usual, for they have enacted the triumph of their cause and released some of their frustrations through the laughter aroused.

Long after the people have gone, Valdez is still thinking about his new venture. The overwhelming response of the people that evening has encouraged him beyond his greatest expectations; but will it really work? His first two plays were written to be performed in theaters, not fields. *The Theft* was a one-act about a young Chicano, and the full-length *The Shrunken Head of Pancho Villa* was a fantastical play whose action revolved around a farmworker family struggling for cultural and economic survival. *Shrunken Head* was written to include settings, costumes, and all the technical apparatus not found in the fields or on a flatbed truck. The success of the second play had given Valdez a good deal of confidence, and as he contemplated the events of this evening, wondering where they might take him, he looked back on his most recent theatrical experience and knew that his present venture would succeed.

Valdez had first heard about the Delano strike while working with the San Francisco Mime Troupe in the spring of 1965. He had joined the troupe in 1964 after a trip to Castro's Cuba in the summer of the same year. Both the trip to Cuba and the work with the Mime

Troupe led Valdez to Delano, for each had an important effect on the young Chicano, both politically and aesthetically. An early student activist, his impassioned speeches and charismatic appeal had won him passage on the first "Venceremos Brigade" to Cuba. While there, he saw the Castro revolution in action and was moved to proclaim "that we support Fidel Castro as the real voice of Latin America, declaring to the world with dignity that social justice must be given to Latin America."[1] Like other Chicanos in the burgeoning Chicano movement, Valdez saw himself and all Mexican Americans as part of Latin America and knew that he would fight for social justice "in the belly of the monster" at home.

The production of *The Shrunken Head of Pancho Villa* had encouraged Valdez to pursue a life in the theater, and after the trip to Cuba it seemed only natural to join the San Francisco Mime Troupe, which was under the political and artistic direction of Ron Davis. Though he only worked with the Mime Troupe for one year, Valdez learned a great deal about the group's style. He immediately realized that its bawdy, outdoor presentations would be very effective with farmworker audiences. At that time the Mime Troupe was in its sixth year of performing contemporary adaptations of Italian *commedia dell'arte* scenarios. The group's productions were characterized by the broad farce of the Italian originals, along with a political consciousness common to the progressive theaters of the period. The major influence of the Mime Troupe experience was the use of body language, masks, and the exaggerated actions necessary to overcome the noises surrounding the Troupe's outdoor performances in the parks of San Francisco. As Valdez watched the farmworker/actors that first evening in Delano, he could envision the gestures of the Mime Troupe and the struggle for social justice that they all shared. The improvisational nature of the *commedia dell'arte* style was ideally suited to Valdez' purpose, for no repertoire of farmworker plays existed. If he and his group had something to say, they would have to create their own statement.

The *Acto*

Before Valdez gave the designation of *acto* to the improvisations he and his group were collectively creating, he understood the importance of the form. Because he was working with non-theater people, he had to start with the basics of stage presence and had to educate his actors about stage directions, projection, and the bare essentials of a beginning acting class. He could not gather the people for a rehearsal and announce, "Today we'll work on blocking for scene two," for there was no scene two. There were farmworkers eager to develop theatrical statements about their condition, and there was the young, energetic Valdez, anxious to create effective learning pieces for his audience. Common goals with uncommon backgrounds somehow managed to develop into exciting, comic and poignant statements about the farmworkers' plight in 1965.

"We could have called them 'skits,' " relates Valdez, "but we lived and talked in San Joaquín Spanish (with a strong Tejano [Texan] influence), so we needed a name that made sense to the Raza."[2] In standard Spanish, *acto* means "an act, action" and can also be used in the theatrical sense for an "act" of a play. For Valdez' incipient troupe and all of the groups that later employed the form, the *acto* was and is a political statement, a declaration of dissatisfaction with the status quo. The *acto* is not a part of a larger theatrical piece, like an act of a play, but a complete statement in itself. But the label given to these improvised creations was not important; what they had to say was.

The *acto* is not a new form in the annals of world theater. Earlier examples of didactic theater include Bertolt Brecht's *lehrstucke*, or learning pieces,[3] and the agit-prop theater of revolutionary Russia, which influenced political theater in this country in the 1930s.[4] In the 1960s other political theater groups employed street theater techniques similar to the *acto* form that Valdez evolved. However, in bringing together the elements that constitute the *acto*, Valdez was stating that the Chicano, too, had issues to be expressed, and the *acto* was the most expedient form of bringing them to the public eye. From that first experience in the pink house with everybody wanting to take a turn at demonstrating his or her experience in the strike, the *acto* became the basic tool for dramatization. If there was anything unique about the *acto*, it was the fact that it addressed the concerns of the Mechicano in the language of the fields and barrios. The first *actos* dealt with the *campesino*'s problems, but with time the issues of concern to urban Mechicanos would become the inspiration for other scenarios.

It was a dual birth that night in Delano as farmworkers became actors and Valdez discovered that theater could be used to educate as well as entertain the striking *campesinos*. The name of the new troupe was as simple and direct as the problems shared by these one-time children of the sun who now found themselves working another man's land for paltry wages and a shorter life expectancy than the average citizen. "El Teatro Campesino," The Farmworker's Theater, became the cultural ambassador of the Chávez forces, creating *actos* and performing them for other farmworkers in an effort to get them to join the union. As the group developed its *actos*, Valdez began to synthesize the scope and purpose of these presentations. In 1971, he listed the following five goals of the *acto*:

> Inspire the audience to social action.
> Illuminate specific points about social problems.
> Satirize the opposition.
> Show or hint at a solution.
> Express what people are thinking.[5]

What distinguishes the *acto* from plays scripted by an individual playwright is its genesis: the *acto* is collectively created through improvisation based on the experiences of its participants. In the early stages of the Teatro Campesino's evolution, there was scarcely a distinction between the worker and the actor—the first became the latter in the Brechtian manner of a demonstrator telling an observer about an incident he was part of or had witnessed. In his poem "On the Everyday Theater," Brecht gave vivid examples of "The Theatre whose stage is the street":

> Look—the man at the corner re-enacting
> The accident.
> Thus he gives the driver at his wheel
> To the crowd for trial.
> Thus the victim, who seems old.
> Of each he gives only so much
> That the accident be understood
> Yet each lives before your eyes
> And each he presents in a manner
> To suggest the accident avoidable.
> So the event is understood
> And yet can still astound:
> The moves of both could have been different.[6]

Valdez and his fellow performer/demonstrators brought to life the theater whose stage was the fields. The daily conflicts that became the scenarios of early *actos* all had one solution in common: "Join the union." Because the members of the troupe were striking farmworkers themselves, Valdez' company made no pretense of creating Great Art. Nor did it have the time for such aesthetic dreams when members of the group could be called away at any moment to walk the picket lines or hand out leaflets in a field or get involved in any of the activities the fledgling union demanded. "In a Mexican way," wrote Valdez in 1966, "we have discovered what Brecht is all about. If you want unbourgeois theater, find unbourgeois people to do it."[7] He had also found the perfect form for getting those "unbourgeois people" to present their own realities, even as they lived them every day.

Anybody can create an *acto*. The basic improvisation needs two characters and a conflict, with information about who they are, where they are, and what they are doing. A group of farmworkers asked to demonstrate their cause should have no more difficulty improvising their grievances than a gathering of irate housewives seeking to lower taxes or textile workers anxious to give exposure to their problems. If the conflict is understood, the improvisation that follows will come naturally. The essential element needed for the creation of an *acto* is a conflict that can somehow be solved by its participants. An individual can write an *acto*, but it will not be the same as those that were collectively created by the Teatro Campesino under the guidance of Luis Valdez.

The Teatro Campesino published its first and only anthology of *actos* in 1971—a very important volume of representative works from its repertoire to that date.[8] No other teatro or individual playwright has published as effective and essential *actos* as appear in the Campesino's collection. Imitations abound, to be sure, and some other successful *actos* have been published. But few of the dramatic efforts that are now available in print approximate the quality of Valdezian *actos*. Perhaps the success of this creative genius' collaborations with his ever-evolving troupe is due to the fact that Valdez is a poet, playwright, actor and director who can see all of the elements necessary for effective theater and who can transpose those visions to the stage.

Soon after the newly formed Teatro Campesino began performing for the striking farmworkers, singing *huelga* songs and creating *actos* that demonstrated the goals of the striking *campesinos*, they were invited to perform at Stanford University. The Teatro seized the opportunity to present its program to the college crowd. Here was a chance to take the farmworkers' message into the cities, where the majority of their supporters would be found. It was also a paid performance, and the Union needed all the financial assistance it could get. The Teatro's performance was a success, and from that moment on the group began to tour campuses and churches, community halls and theaters throughout California. Valdez' raggle-taggle troupe of actors and singers portraying their own experiences amazed and touched audiences and moved them to donate what they could to the union coffers. In the spring of 1966, less than a year after its inception, the Teatro inspired Ralph Gleason of the *San Francisco Chronicle* to write: "It's vital, earthy, and vividly alive theater . . . an impressive demonstration of what can be done when men work together in a common cause."[9]

Shortly after he started working with his teatro, Valdez discovered that comedy was the troupe's predominant asset,

> . . . not from a satirical point of view, but from the fact that humor can stand up on its own . . . We use comedy because it stems from a necessary situation—the necessity of lifting the morale of our strikers. . . . This leads us into satire and the underlying tragedy of it all— the fact that human beings have been wasted in farm labor for generations.[10]

Valdez' broad sense of humor, coupled with the experiences of the other members of the teatro, enabled the playwright in him to select situations and devices that would draw a laugh from any crowd. In one of his first articles about the Teatro, Valdez wrote in *Ramparts*, in 1966: "El Teatro Campesino is somewhere between Brecht and Cantinflas."[11] The influences of both the great German playwright/ theorist and the superlative Mexican comedian pervade any analysis of Valdez' work, but most especially his early *actos*.

The four works to be discussed in this chapter owe their genesis to the early *actos* of the Teatro Campesino and also share in their intent: to expose the problems of the Mechicano worker. Mechicanos, long an important part of the work force in the United States, are working-class citizens proud of their contributions in fields and and factories and in every aspect of labor. Too often, the struggles of the worker have gone unnoted or ignored; the *actos* we will examine attempt to enlighten both the workers whose issues are being dramatized and interested observers who find themselves at a performance. The study begins with the early farmworker *actos* because these collective creations marked the birth of the contemporary Chicano theater movement and inspired other groups to follow their example and illustrate the workers' grievances.

Of Masks and Moralities:
Las dos caras del patroncito and *La quinta temporada*

When Valdez took that pig-like mask to Delano, he was certain of its effect on the audience as well as the actors. Under Ron Davis' direction, Valdez the actor had learned to bring a character to life through the use of a comic mask and the body movement necessary to animate the false face. He also understood that the mask was a form of protection for the wearer, separating him or her from the character assumed. Although the farmworkers were at first reluctant to portray the despised *esquirol*, shielded only by a paper sign hung around their necks, the comic mask offered another alternative, for it *hid* the real person behind the disguise. The instant anyone put it on, the howls of laughter showered the actor with a sort of approval, and he could relax, knowing that the spectators were not laughing at him but at what he represented. A swift move of the mask would bring the cartoon face to life and transform the person who wore it into another person—a character. One of the first improvisations with that mask evolved into the earliest *acto* to be published: *Las dos caras del patroncito* (The Two Faces of the Boss).[12]

Created in the early stages of the evolution of both the Teatro and the union, *Las dos caras del patroncito* is representative of the needs of that time. Striking and organizing were difficult tasks to begin with, but they were often made more difficult by the power of the growers and their unabashed flaunting of their wealth and materialistic strength. In an effort to combat this, Valdez and his actors created an *acto* in which the grower exchanges roles with his worker and discovers what it is really like to be at the bottom. It is an allegorical situation, based on the assumption that the grower's shedding of his mask will turn him into a worker while the real worker can simply don the guise of the grower, undetected by the grower's own hired guards. The lesson is simple: we are all alike when beneath materialistic shields. The exposition needed to demonstrate the conditions suffered by the worker simultaneously enlightens the audience as well.

Like each of the *actos* that followed it, *Las dos caras del patroncito* was created out of expediency. It could not be limited by cumbersome settings or the use of many props because it had to be as portable as the *huelgistas* themselves, prepared to scatter at a moment's notice. Often performed at the edge of the fields, the farmworker *actos* enjoyed an incredible realism in their settings. Because the action was usually related to the fields, references to the vast expanses of agricultural wealth had ironic impact on the strikers, who could see it all around them. Outside, on the ground or on a flatbed truck, the neophyte Teatro members often had to compete with blaring radios or honking cars, all calculated to discourage their theatrics and keep the interest of the scabs on their work. The very situation the strikers found themselves in was theatrical beyond imagination: a daily morning ritual in which the strikers would attempt to dissuade the strikebreakers from entering the fields as sheriff's officers stood in the background. Tension hung like leaden mist as strikers shouted at the scabs to join them and thus thwart the efforts of the growers. Many of the strikebreakers had been brought in from outside, and the majority were undocumented workers who could not afford to join the union due to the risk of deportation that hung albatross-like around their necks. In this type of atmosphere an *acto* had to be short, fast-paced and to the point if it was to get its message across.

From the very first line, *Las dos caras del patroncito* presents a great deal of information to the audience. The first character to enter the acting area is the *esquirol*, identified by the sign around his neck and carrying a pair of pruning shears. He tells us he has been brought to this ranch by his *patroncito*, all the way from Mexico. Immediately the audience knows that he is an undocumented worker, since the bracero program is no longer allowing growers to *legally* import cheap Mexican labor into the fields.[13] He is carrying the only prop necessary to identify his work—pruning shears—and he also tells us that his boss does not like to see him talking to strangers. More wonderful irony, for the strangers the growers did not want their workers talking to were the very strikers performing the *acto*, as well as their supporters watching the presentation. With a twenty-second monologue to the audience, a direct communication with them is established, breaking any pretense at theatrical realism.

As the *esquirol* begins to pantomime pruning the vines, we hear another character making the roaring sounds of a car, like a child playing, and the *patroncito* "drives" onto the acting area. He is wearing a sign and the pig-face mask that identifies him. The name *patroncito* is a Mexican way of demeaning a person of prominence, as it brings him down to human dimensions rather than elevating him to Olympian standards. Cantinflas is noted for these degrading references, which always rouse the audiences' laughter and the character's ire. In this *acto*, however, the grower is not aware of the joke. The ridiculous motions of driving a car further debase the grower, portraying him in child-like terms. The patroncito is chomping on a cigar, that symbol of capitalist power, and is carrying a whip. He also speaks with a Texas drawl:

> PATRONCITO: Good morning, boy!
> FARMWORKER: Buenos días, patroncito. *(His hat in his hands)*

PATRONCITO: You working hard, boy?
FARMWORKER: Oh, sí! Muy hard! *(He starts working furiously)*
PATRONCITO: Oh, you can work harder than that, boy. *(He works harder)* Harder! *(He works harder)* Harder! *(He works still harder)* Harder!
FARMWORKER: Ay, that's too hard, patrón!

The *acto* must be larger than life, with exaggerated movements and characters that create images the audience can relate to and think about. This opening is pure farce: exaggerated movements in the pantomiming of the work as the farmworker begins to double and triple his speed in an effort to please the grower. When he finally says "Ay, that's too hard, patrón!" the comic pace is stopped short, and there is a moment of pause for the audience to register what has just happened. The worker is no more than a machine to this pig-faced grower, who can turn him on, set his pace and stop him at will. Interestingly, in this dialogue, the farmworker has only used one word in English prior to the last line: "hard." While the grower speaks to the worker in English, the latter responds in Spanish until the boss demands too much. He can play the "dumb Mexican" only as long as he is not threatened, but when pushed he can communicate in the grower's language with ease. His entire opening monologue is given in English, but once the boss enters he assumes the passive, lowly worker role, and the audience sees itself in this social reality.

The *esquirol* knows his place in this relationship, and though he sometimes lets his true feelings come out, if they are not agreeable to the boss he quickly changes what he has said to please him. And his physical gestures are all calculated to demonstrate his subservient position. He kisses the boss's posterior and feverishly tries to polish his shoes. He gets so carried away with the shoes that a third, minor character, an ape-like policeman, comes running. He is stopped by the *patroncito* with: "Charlie! Charlie, no! It's OK, boy, this is one of my Mexicans! . . . Now you go back to the road and watch for union organizers" (pp. 10-11). The irony of watching an actor imitating an ape-like guard when the real "officers of the peace" were within in shooting distance created quite an effect.

The discussion between the grower and his strikebreaker is calculated to demonstrate the realities of the working conditions without a union contract. The grower has a false and myopic view of what it is like to be one of his workers and demonstrates his patronizing attitude toward them:

All my Mexicans love to ride in trucks! Just the sight of them barreling down the freeway makes my heart feel good; hands on their sombreros, hair flying in the wind, bouncing along happy as babies. Yesirree, I sure love my Mexicans, boy! (p. 10).

When the farmworker puts his arm around the grower after this last gush of emotion, the *patroncito* responds quickly: "I love 'em about ten feet away from me, boy." Their dialogue continues as the grower tries to explain to the worker why he is lucky not to have the responsibilities of a multi-million dollar agribusiness. To the grower, the Mexicans are fortunate with their "air conditioned cabins," free transportation, and beans and tortillas, while he has to suffer the "frustrations" of a luxury car, a house on the hill, a blonde, bikini-clad wife, and all of the expenses she incurs.

Suddenly, it occurs to the grower that he *can* trade places with the worker. At first the farmworker is reluctant to undergo this transformation, but he is persuaded by the *patroncito*, who sheds his sign, his cigar and whip, and then his coat. Upon assuming each of these outward symbols of the grower's position, the farmworker becomes more and more like his oppressor, but there is one thing missing: the mask. When the *patroncito* starts to remove his mask, the *campesino* howls in protest, but it is too late. Once the mask is removed, the farmworker says in amazement: "Patrón, you look like me!" When Luis Valdez and his younger brother Danny played the grower and the worker, they did indeed look alike, adding a wonderful comment to the action. Once the striker has put on the mask, his ultimate symbol of transformation, he *is* the *patroncito*.

At first, the real grower, now wearing the other character's sign and holding his pruning shears, enjoys the game and goes along with it, though he is obviously somewhat apprehensive. As the farmworker-cum-grower begins to list the things that belong to him and offers to pay less than the real grower had offered, the latter realizes he has gone too far and calls for help. Unfortunately for the *patroncito*, Charlie sees only the mask and takes the real grower away. As he is being dragged off, the grower shouts "Where's those damn union organizers? Where's César Chávez? Help! *¡Huelga!*" (p. 19). Once the other two have left the stage, the farmworker removes the pig mask and says to the audience:

> Bueno, so much for the patrón. I got his house, his land, his car— only I'm not going to keep 'em. He can have them. But I'm taking the cigar. Ay los watcho. See you later (p. 19).

And the *acto* is over.

For a moment, the farmworkers watching this *acto* could lose themselves in the illusion of the transformation, enjoying the joke and laughing at the antics of the characters with firsthand knowledge of what they were saying. The *patroncito's* patronizing and the strike-breaking farmworker's groveling are here presented as examples of what these two types represent. They are stereotypes of the grower-scab relationship, and the transformation they undergo is simply a humorous way of exposing them. But the deceit cannot last, we are told, because the farmworker does not keep any of the grower's material objects except for the cigar. What is more important to the *acto*—and to the strikers who are presenting it—is the information divulged and the solution offered: call for César Chávez!

The second *acto* in the Teatro Campesino anthology is *La quinta temporada* (The Fifth Season), created in 1966. This *acto* reflects the troupe's concern with another farmworker problem: the farm-labor contractor. Farmworkers call the labor contractor "coyote"; it is an appellation of scorn and hatred, for he is probably one of the most despised figures in agribusiness. The contractor is paid by the growers to gather cheap stoop laborers in the barrios and deliver them to the fields. While the workers toil under miserable conditions, the coyote sits in his air-conditioned truck reaping profits at the expense of the workers. The alternative to this procedure was the union hiring hall, a system that guaranteed the rights of the workers and controlled the rate of pay and security of a contract. In order to demonstrate most effectively the need for eliminating the coyote, the Teatro created a modern morality play with this *acto*, whose solution once again is "join the union."

La quinta temporada is a descendant of the Spanish *auto sacramental*, the Iberian version of the medieval mystery and morality plays that combined qualities of both, mingling biblical characters with mortals and with allegorical figures as well. An earlier, unpublished *acto*, *The Three Grapes*, had included allegorical portrayals of green, ripe, and rotten grapes, and for this next creation the troupe required the four seasons. In the tradition of the Church dramas, an idea becomes visual, and the audience is told in the simplest of terms what the problems are and how to go about gaining a solution. Perhaps a troupe accustomed to the trappings of a theater might blanch at the idea off representing each of the four seasons onstage, but for Valdez' unsophisticated thespians it was as simple as a sign, a word, and a shirt covered with imitation dollar bills. The *campesino* audiences understood the meaning of each season—summer rich with fruit and lean winter threatening any hopes of financial respite. Thus, when an actor walked onto the platform announcing

"I am summer," his hat and shirt covered with dollar bills, the audience recognized the significance of this allegorical figure.

Valdez explained the importance of the seasons to an interviewer in 1966:

> . . . I can remember my family going north toward the prune and apricot orchards. My image was of leaves and fruit clustered on the trees, and all of this turning into flows of dollar bills. When you see a ripe orchard or vineyard, the limbs boughing down they're so heavy with fruit, this is money. All you have to do is get up and stretch out your hand . . .
>
> It's a vision of paradise; you're going there—the promised land— you're getting there finally.
>
> Then reality creeps in again, and you end up with less money than you started with. But the dream is always there, the dream that you're going to get rich quick.[14]

It was that vision that must have inspired the early members of Valdez' troupe to portray the seasons with nothing more than a sign and varying quantities of dollar bills. Unashamed, without pretense, these unschooled actors held no inhibitions about who or what they were and could let their creative energies run rampant. Unsophisticated, yes, but very effective theater as well.

Like *Dos caras, La quinta temporada* begins with a humble farmworker addressing the audience. This time, however, he is from Texas and is looking for a job. He tells us he can pick any kind of crop, and he needs to send money back to his family. Again, direct communication with the audience sets the time and place and establishes the objective: "I need a job." Enter the coyote with a typical coyote howl and a flourish. Both characters wear signs identifying their social roles. The farm-labor contractor introduces himself as Don Coyote, which is also on his sign, and the audience of farmworkers knows immediately who and what he represents. The title *Don*, which is usually reserved for distinguished older men, is here used to ridicule the character and reveal his true stature.

In every *acto*, as in any play, the characters must have an objective, a goal. We have quickly discovered that the *campesino* needs employment, and we now learn that Don Coyote needs cheap laborers. This one farmworker from Texas becomes the symbol of all migrant workers, and he agrees to work for the contractor. Just then the grower enters, with a sign ("Patroncito") identifying him, along with his swagger, southern drawl, and the inevitable cigar. No mask this time. The grower asks his contractor if his summer crew is ready. When Don Coyote assures him that it is, the *patroncito* shouts for

Summer to come on. Summer enters, replete with a sign and wads of dollar bills on his shirt and hat, and begins to cross the stage slowly. As the actor playing Summer crosses the stage, the farmworker quickly takes as much money off his back as he can, stuffing it into his own back pockets. The coyote is right behind the farmworker, taking the money out of his pockets, and the grower follows the contractor, taking the money out of *his* rear pockets. It is a quick and graphic way of demonstrating what happens to the money a farmworker earns when working through a middleman.

At the end of the season, after Summer has passed, the farmworker goes to count his money but finds his pockets are empty. He sees that the contractor and grower are counting bills and demands that he be given what he has earned, but he is unable to persuade the other two that it is his money they are counting. "You know what's wrong with you?" the coyote asks the farmworker, and continues: "You're stupid. You don't know how to SAVE money" (p. 24). The *acto* does not develop this financial situation further or explain why the farmworker's hard-earned money does not last a season. But the important image has been made, and there is no time in this brief *acto* to detail the living conditions and other factors that have made it historically impossible for migrant workers to achieve other than a meager existence. What we see is that there are three characters with the same objective—"to earn a living"—and that the farmworker is thwarted in his efforts by the other two.

The contractor persuades the farmworker that Autumn has his money and that he will be able to get rich quick off Autumn's abundant crop. When Autumn enters, he is wearing somewhat fewer bills than the previous season, and the same stage business occurs. At the end of this season, the *campesino* again finds himself with nothing while the other two, after paying Winter, leave for cushy vacations in Acapulco and Las Vegas. The farmworker is left alone to face a lean Winter, personified by another actor wearing a sign, dressed in white, and tossing "snowflakes" about. Whereas the other two seasons represented income, Winter signifies expenses with no prospects for remuneration because there are no crops at this time of year. Though it does not snow in the San Joaquín valley, the white-clad apparition of Winter complete with snowflakes is a humorous touch that symbolizes the coldness of that season in the valley.

Time and the seasons pass quickly in this allegorical *acto*, and soon after Winter has begun to drop snow on the farmworker and generally mistreat him, Spring, a woman, enters, dressed in a lovely spring dress and strewing flowers in her wake. Winter stops to recognize the woman, not the season, with: "Mamasota, who are you?" (p. 28). "Mamasota" is a sexual remark, literally "big mama," which was obviously placed here for its humorous effect. But it should also be noted that this is the first woman we have seen in either *acto*. There were few women in the Teatro in the early stages, and the characters portrayed reflect that fact. Spring is undaunted by Winter's advances and gently asks the season to move along. Winter ignores her calm requests until she alters her composed facade and shouts: "Get the hell out of here!" This outburst surprises Winter and the audience, eliciting the laughter that is born of such unexpected ejaculations. This kind of comic effect, which is created by juxtaposing one characteristic with another, often occurs in Valdezian *actos*, jarring the possible complacency of the audience with surprise and laughter.

Once Winter has passed, Spring urges the abused *campesino* to fight for his rights. Oddly enough, there is no mention of Chávez, the union, or *huelga* as Spring persuades the farmworker to fight back. Spring, the symbol of resurrection, rebirth, and renewed vegetation offers hope to the farmworker both figuratively and literally, just as it did for the agrarian ancestors of these humble folk. The seed is planted—an idea in the mind of the worker—and when the *patroncito* enters demanding his summer crew, the coyote cannot persuade the *campesino* to go into the fields and pick the crops. Summer passes slowly by, as the grower rants and raves and the farmworker sits adamantly, saying he is on strike: *"Estoy en huelga!"* (p. 30). Summer is gone, and nobody has picked the crops, leaving both the contractor and grower empty-handed. When Autumn passes, the same occurs, and when Winter enters, the contractor and the grower are desperate. Winter's first line: *"¡Llego el lechero!* And my name ain't Granny Goose, baby" (p. 32) is once again a comic technique because of its surprise and also because of the juxtaposition of ideas. Dressed in white, the actor could pass for a milkman, and when he enters with "The milkman's here!" it is almost a parody of the *acto* itself. Then the reference to "Granny Goose," another figure that could be dressed in white, further ridicules the *acto*'s simplicity. When he demands money, we know that he is serious and that the comedy is over for the farmworker; but it has just begun for the grower and his lackey.

We have seen the seasons come and go without the crops being picked, and now that Winter is here, the grower's funds have been depleted. When Winter accosts the striking farmworker, the woman who played Spring returns as "The Churches," Summer returns as "The Union," and Fall is transformed into "La Raza." Together these three symbols of the outside support being given to the striking families ward off Winter's cold advances. Unable to affect the farmworker, Winter now attacks the grower, demanding more and more money as he sits on his shoulders, showering him with snowflakes. When the grower appeals to the farmworker and his allies, they shout, "Sign a contract!" until he relents and agrees to do so. The contractor fights for his life, begging the grower not to sign with the union, but it is too late. The triumphant forces and the defeated grower leave the stage and the coyote attempts to sneak off behind them but is caught by Winter. When the coyote argues that Winter has passed and cannot detain him, Winter realizes that he is the "fifth season" and turns his sign around to reveal the words SOCIAL JUSTICE. He kicks the contractor offstage and turns to the audience to remind them that only social justice can eliminate the "crooked contractor."

La quinta temporada is a classic of its genre. It is a modern morality play that successfully combines allegorical figures with representative character types and a particular conflict that has an obvious solution. The major problem, the abuses of the farm-labor contractor, is exposed in graphic terms, and the only solution to such practices is demonstrated by the victory of La Huelga. This acto has been performed innumerable times by many teatros, often in the fields as well as in the urban centers. Created in 1966, La quinta temporada can still be performed in the organizing struggles that continue to concern the United Farmworkers and other agricultural unions in the United States in the 1980s. Most importantly, however, the early actos of the Teatro Campesino inspired other Chicanos to form their own teatros, expressing their struggles for economic, cultural and political survival. Valdez' original troupe, composed of striking farmworkers, was the only teatro which could justifiably be termed a "worker's theater," but later groups continued to explore the problems faced by workers in urban as well as rural situations.

The Urban Struggle: *El hombre que se convirtió en perro*

Soon after the Teatro Campesino began touring college campuses and community centers in other parts of the country, enthusiastic observers were moved to initiate their own teatros. It was as if Valdez' company were sowing seeds of creativity wherever it performed, leaving behind it a renewed sense of pride in the Mexican/Chicano cultures and fostering excitement about the Chicano's theatrical abilities. No matter how simplistic the presentations or how unsophisticated the performance conditions, Chicanos witnessed Valdez' theater company with an unmatched appreciation. As the members of the Teatro sang their songs and performed their *actos*, the audiences could immediately relate to the conflicts portrayed, whether they had worked in the fields or not. Theater of any kind was rare in the barrios, and the people were delighted with Valdez' keen sense of theatrics.

One of the first teatros to form after the Teatro Campesino was its urban counterpart, the Teatro Urbano, founded in 1968 at San Jose State College. Like many other teatros that were yet to be born, the San Jose group was founded by Chicano students during demonstrations and walkouts protesting the lack of Chicano students and faculty on campus. The students had witnessed the effectiveness of Valdez' worker's theater, and they proceeded to create their own *actos* dramatizing their demands. Though the neophyte teatro members did not have a Luis Valdez to direct them and oversee the creation of their *actos*, expediency allowed for a certain lack of sophistication in performance style.

This was a time of student unrest throughout the nation, fueled by the anti-war efforts and magnified by the civil rights movement. When colleges and universities began actively recruiting minorities, unwary Chicanos found themselves in an alien environment, looking for peers and role models with whom they could relate. Just as the Teatro Campesino had accompanied the birth of César Chávez' farmworker movement, so too did student teatros become an integral part of most campus Chicano organizations.

The late sixties were important years for minority students, as Chicanos and Blacks began to demand admittance to institutions that were Anglo-dominated and not particularly interested in the problems of these members of society who had traditionally been excluded from the mainstream. Federal laws requiring greater representation of minorities in the schools helped initiate admittance of these students, as did the financial aid programs sponsored by Washington. Although the number of Chicanos admitted to colleges and universities in 1968 and 1969 was not large, many of those that did enroll became actively involved in recruitment programs and Chicano student organizations. Inspired by the civil rights movement and by the image of César Chávez, Chicanos began to give birth to the Chicano Movement on campuses and in the communities. In the summer of 1969, 3,000 young Chicanos met in Denver, Colorado, for the Chicano Liberation Youth Conference, and declared:

> With our heart in our hands and our hands in the soil, We Declare the Independence of our Mestizo Nation. We are a Bronze People with a Bronze Culture. Before the world, before all of North America, before all our brothers in the Bronze Continent, We are a Nation, We are a Union of free pueblos, We are Aztlán.[15]

The Nahuatl term *Aztlán* means "the land to the north; the land from whence we, the Aztecs, came." By adopting the Aztec name for the area north of Mexico, these Chicanos were proclaiming their political and cultural ties with Mexico, not Plymouth Rock. They looked to the culture of the Mexican, both past and present, in an effort to define themselves as different from the other immigrants who had crossed an ocean to become a part of the "melting pot." Chicanos understood that they were different from the Europeans who had blended into the society around them and knew that they would have to seek their own forms of political power and self-sufficiency. Education, to many, was the key to independence, and many university administrators did not know how to handle these dark-skinned Children of the Sun who refused to become a part of traditional education. In a plan for higher education which was formulated at Santa Barbara, California, and published as *El Plan de Santa Bárbara* in 1970, its collective authors wrote:

> . . . we take as our credo what José Vasconcelos once said at a time of crisis and hope: "At this moment we do not come to work for the university, but to demand that the university work for our people."[16]

Paralleling the advances of the Chicano student movement which began in 1968, teatros began to form as the cultural and theatrical arms of the evolving campus organizations. These groups were often committees of the student organizations, and like the early Teatro Campesino they were at the command of the parent group. Aesthetics were subordinated to politics as teatros rushed to create last-minute *actos* for campus demonstrations or community rallies. Since the majority of teatro members had little or no formal training in theater, their presentations were characterized by enthusiasm and energy without theatrical acumen. But neither they nor their audiences demanded much more than an energetic appeal during the early stages of the student movement. The mere presence of Chicanos on a platform portraying the heroes and villains in campus politics was sufficient to arouse cheers of approval from the activist audiences.

During the period of demands for more Chicano students, faculty, and staff on campuses, the teatros created *actos* that reflected those needs. Other themes concerned student issues such as the insensitivity of non-Chicano faculty and administrators and the culture shock of living in predominantly Anglo dormitories. Personal themes, such as what it meant to be a Chicano from the barrio, were dramatized as these student groups explored their roles in the overall scheme of things. Very often, since no single member of a troupe had the training to direct the *actos*, the members would collectively administer their artistic and political organization. Collectivity was a byword of the era, and inexperienced teatros thought that they could create their *actos* without an individual director to oversee the process and the performance. This somewhat naive attitude was never the case within the structure of the student political organizations that spawned the teatros, yet these neophyte thespians were expected to operate as collectives when none of them knew anything about theater.

In the early stages of the developing Teatro Movement, most of the groups were nothing more than part-time committees, getting together once or twice a week to write, rehearse, and perform an *acto*. The major bond between the teatro members was usually the political cause they shared, and this was sometimes not enough to bind the tenuous relationships that developed under the pressures of being students, politicians, and performers. Most of the groups that were born of campus politics in the late sixties did not survive more than two years, though individual members of some of the early troupes went on to join other groups or form new teatros.

Unlike other student groups of the period, however, the Teatro Urbano separated from the campus situation, and in 1970 it toured the Midwest under the direction of Luis Valdez' younger brother, Daniel. Teatro Urbano became the second teatro to leave California and present its versions of the Chicano experience on campuses and in communities outside of its immediate circumstance. By leaving the campus, the San Jose troupe was seeking the autonomy that the Teatro Campesino had achieved in 1967 when it left the ranks of the Chávez union to become an independent group. Writing about the San Jose troupe in 1970, Daniel Valdez described its members as "high school and barrio vatos [dudes] who have made teatro their way of life."[17] The group was devoted to dramatizing the need for politically aware Chicanos in positions of power as well as exposing the injustices of the police, courts, schools, and government agencies.

Daniel Valdez left the troupe after the midwestern tour, and some of the former members re-grouped to form another teatro for the San Jose area. They returned to the campus arena, which was where the Chicano movement was based at the time, and began to create *actos* that reflected the needs of a fledgling political movement. Before the group had found a name for itself, two of the original members, Manuel Martínez and Ed Robledo, wrote an *acto* about the ills of the Movement. In their allegorical situation, the Movement was portrayed as an old woman, whose only hope for renewed vigor was an infusion of "new blood."[18] The group's search for a name that would distinguish it from the somewhat definitive names of Campesino or Urbano, led to the general appellative, "El Teatro de la Gente," the Theater of the People.

When it was first formed, on September 16, 1970, Teatro de la Gente was composed of students from two urban campuses: San Jose City College and the State College where Luis Valdez had graduated. These sister campuses are located in the heart of California's second-largest Mechicano population, and the newly formed teatro recognized both the need for a group such as theirs and the challenge that lay ahead of them. By adopting the name they had, the members of the People's Theater had clearly assumed a didactic role in the overall struggle of the Mechicano community. Though they were still students, they looked forward to the day that they would become independent from the campus and create a cultural center in the manner of the Centro Campesino Cultural, which Luis Valdez had formed upon leaving the union. Certainly, the large Mechicano population of the area was in need of a cultural center, but more importantly, the Teatro de la Gente had proclaimed itself the theatrical voice of the people and would have to live up to its name.

Unlike most of the less sophisticated teatros sprouting throughout the country at the time, the San Jose group was directed by two young men who were drama majors at San Jose State. Both Adrián Vargas and Manuel Martínez recognized the need for formal study of theater, and this vision is probably responsible for the Teatro's aesthetic and political survival, for they co-directed the group for five years. Vargas completed his Master of Fine Arts degree in playwriting in 1975 and became the sole director of the teatro when Martínez left the group at the end of that year. Vargas has continued to guide the development of the teatro to the present. The group founded El Centro Cultural de la Gente in a storefront in downtown San Jose in order to offer performance space and workshops in art, music and teatro for the community. With a board of directors composed of active community members, the Centro began to reflect the needs of its constituents. The members organized performances by visiting theater groups as well as exhibits of Mechicano arts in their gallery/lobby. Because their performance space was small, they often took presentations to local schools, churches and campuses and began to tour the Southwest and Midwest in 1977. By 1977, members of the troupe became independent from the campus situation and succeeded in gaining local, state, and federal subsidies in order to pay their actors and staff. Though funding was minimal, the group had at long last achieved financial autonomy and could call itself a theater of "cultural workers." Over the years, the Teatro's presentations included *actos*, folk plays, myths, and dramatizations of popular Mexican *corridos* (ballads). Because the director was trained in playwriting, he often had a hand in the scripting of the group's works and found a major challenge when the Teatro produced Osvaldo Dragún's *El hombre que se convirtió en perro* (The Man Who Turned Into a Dog) in 1977. The teatro members had chosen this Argentine playlet because they felt it was a universal comment on the dehumanization of the worker by industrial society, but when they performed it for their public, the audiences were somewhat confused. "They wanted less symbolism," Vargas told this writer, "so we simplified it for our audiences."[19]

El hombre que se convirtió en perro is the last of three playlets collectively entitled *Historias para ser contadas*, which Dragún wrote and produced in 1957.[20] Each of the three "stories" depicts an aspect of humanity's helplessness in the face of social insensitivity fostered by capitalism, corruption and greed. The story of the man who becomes a dog is portrayed by three men and one woman, each taking several roles as the script requires, without changes of setting or costumes. The story is delivered by the characters as they tell about what happened to a friend when he could not find a job and was forced to become the factory watchdog. In a quickly changing series of scenes, the actors demonstrate the transformation of their friend as he assumes the characteristics of a dog in order to feed his wife and the child she is going to bear. The transformation is not a quick change from man to canine, and though the man attempts to find other employment and fight back, he is finally transformed and captured by the dogcatcher, in whose care he is presumably still living.

By presenting a playlet that dealt with the urban worker, the Teatro was recognizing its need to establish conditions that distinguished it from a farmworker's theater. Though the San Jose troupe was not composed solely of urban laborers directly off the assembly line, its members were generally of the working class and were familiar with the problems of the Mechicano labor force. When their public asked for a less symbolic message, the Teatro members immediately began to adapt Dragún's script to suit their needs. While the original script lasted fifteen minutes in production, the expanded version took one hour and fifteen minutes to perform. Building upon the basic situation given by Dragún, the teatro members improvised new scenes, adding character motivations and expanding situations already in the original or suggested by their investigations of the problem. Their predominant objective was to give the audience what it wanted: a reflection of the worker in industrialized San Jose.

Constantly aware of the Mechicano's working conditions, the teatro members focused on the local electronics industry, which employed many Mechicanos. Through research and personal experience, the actors/investigators discussed situations they wanted to explore, which the playwright/director would then script. Working together, the actors and the playwright helped each other in creating their final statement. With a company of actors at his disposal, the playwright could see where his script needed revisions and could also respond to suggestions from the actors. The process was successful in producing a truly Chicano form which owed its genesis to Dragún as well as to elements of the Valdezian repertoire and the imaginations of the creators.

To Dragún, the Teatro owed the basic situation. His brief script set the scene and lent itself very well to the adaptation. From the Valdezian repertoire, the group extrapolated the *acto* stereotypes and the use of music to enhance the story. The actors and the director/playwright contributed their own sense of theatricality, focusing on the vision necessary for a successful extension of the *acto* form. The group's political awareness made it possible for the piece to capture the essence of the dehumanization of the workers while building upon that foundation to create a message that was clear and simple. Anything that might have been left unstated in the original was defined in the adaptation so as to leave no question unanswered.

The Teatro's adaptation of this play demonstrated an effective means of creating scripts that were relevant to a particular community. Local companies were named within the dialogue, giving the audiences direct comments on their own surroundings. A strike was inserted in the action, reflecting current situations that the audience members knew of and perhaps were even experiencing themselves. Thus the Teatro went from a universal statement about the dehumanization of the worker to a particular comment about conditions in the local electronics industry. The workers' strike becomes a pivotal center of the action in this expanded version of the play, but it is not presented as the final solution as in the early *actos* of the farmworker struggle. Indeed, the Teatro's adaptation avoids giving any easy solution; it only reveals some of the corrupt machinations behind corporate decisions and labor disputes, without attempting to define a clear course of action for the workers beyond the strike. As was then happening in the San Jose area, in response to the strike in the play the company decides to relocate in Mexico.

While the Dragún play focuses on an individual worker, the Teatro's version broadens its picture to encompass other characters and situations as well. The company owner is portrayed as a farcical buffoon, reminiscent of the *patroncito* in so many *actos*. Rather than merely talk about the unemployment line, the Teatro gives its audience a reenactment of this debasing experience, demonstrating what it is like to be searching hopelessly for a job. The central figure's frustrations lead to his acceptance of the watchdog post, and when the factory workers go on strike, he is used to quell the demonstrations—another example of the co-optation he has succumbed to that is not in Dragún's script. Still, the major focus is on the man-cum-watchdog, and both plays end the same: the man remains a dog.

Teatro de la Gente's adaptation of the Dragún script marked an important step in the development of a Chicano dramaturgy. Unlike the farmworker *actos*, whose genesis had been promoted by the experiences of the worker/actors, this adaptation was based on a successful Latin American script combined with elaboration through the collective process. Members of the Teatro had to study the working conditions in the electronics firms as well as the economic circumstances that made it profitable for the companies to move to Mexico. The stereotypes of *El Patrón* and his unfortunate worker remain integral to the plot, and the transformation into a dog recalls the allegorical figures of the seasons in *La quinta temporada* or the role-reversal of *Las dos caras del patroncito*. Barrio audiences were not offended by these fantastic devices, as long as they were explicit in their meaning.

El hombre que se convirtió en perro incorporated a stylized narration, which Dragún's script suggests, and went beyond his vision to include *corridos* that added a distinctly Mexican flavor to particular scenes. When the main character gets drunk in the local *cantina* after he has taken the job of watchdog, he sings a woeful *corrido* with all the sentiment of that popular musical form. The song emerges from the action in a realistic fashion, yet the entire premise of the play is based on an extension of reality: that a man can become a dog. This mixture of realism and symbolism keeps the production interesting and enables the audience to get involved with the characters and their plight, no matter how far-fetched. The expansion of the plot and the increased number of actors is a necessary method of clarifying the issues and successfully creates a statement that is relevant to the contemporary urban worker.

As it progressed from a student group to a community-based theater company, Teatro de la Gente served as a model for other groups seeking independence from institutions of any sort. Like all of the other groups, this teatro's membership was in constant flux, with a core group of experienced leaders who maintained a sense of equilibrium. Vargas' troupe was one of the first to hold auditions for actors and showed a new sense of professionalism by holding a competition for entrance into the company in 1977. New members often came from other groups that could not offer the financial support Teatro de la Gente had generated. Though pay was minimal, it allowed the members to concentrate on the work of the Teatro without having to hold outside employment. Funds raised by touring helped support the group but, like any other theater company, Vargas' teatro was continually seeking new sources of income. A few of the members worked in positions that were related to the Teatro's objectives, such as part-time community service jobs, but the company's ability to support its members distinguished it from most small professional theater companies in the United States.[21]

Involved in the political and cultural activities of its community Teatro de la Gente reflects a well-defined purpose. As "cultural workers," its members wish to be viewed as respected, productive members of their community whose work can be of service. A direct example of the kind of service the group is able to render was seen in 1978 and 1979, when it was funded to write and produce a play about child abuse by a local government agency. An earlier piece, *El corrido de Juan Endrogado*, had attempted to investigate the drug scene in the barrio, exposing the dangers of drug abuse for local youths. After the group had toured with *El hombre que se convirtió en perro* in 1977 and 1978, it turned to an original script that the playwright/director had been working on for several years about an ex-offender who returns to his barrio and finds he is unable to cope with his existence. It was a new direction for the troupe, incorporating elements of realism and expressionism as it searched for a style of its own.

In 1979, Teatro de la Gente could be termed a teatro in transition, continually evolving as it sought its place in the local community of issues and the national community of artistic achievement. The group was still composed of youthful actors and actresses and was under the direction of a young man just approaching 30 who had been successful in holding together a theater company for several years. The director and the Teatro were very involved in the national coalition of Chicano theater companies formed in 1971, TENAZ, and helped give that organization a sense of direction and stability. If the original Teatro Campesino was a true worker's theater, composed of striking farmworkers intent on giving exposure to their cause, Teatro de la Gente can be termed a theater of workers whose purpose is to dramatize the problems of the working-class Mechicano in the fields or in the factories.

A "Super-Acto": *Los pelados*

Teatro Libertad, of Tucson, Arizona, is an example of a more recent group that did not evolve from a campus organization but instead began as a collective effort of students and members of the community at large in 1975. An earlier group, Teatro del Pueblo, had formed in 1970; it expressed the political movement in Tucson with *actos* that the Teatro Campesino had created.[22] When the Teatro del Pueblo disbanded, a cadre of students, activists, laborers and farmworkers created the Teatro Libertad in an effort to fill the void left by the dissolution of the first group. The new teatro solicited the aid of Barclay Goldsmith, a drama professor at a local community college, and under his guidance it began to collectively create productions that expressed the concerns of its members.

The Teatro's first major piece was entitled *Vacil '76*. It was an anti-Bicentennial statement that attempted to dispel the propaganda being promoted by the "Freedom Train," which was touring the country during the 1976 Bicentennial celebrations. The one-hour production was too elaborate to be an *acto*, with varied settings and costume changes for scenes that took place in different cars of the Freedom Train. A narrator in the form of a *calavera* (skeleton) was reminiscent of other groups' *actos*, but the production itself was one of the most spectacular produced to date by a Chicano theater group.

The plot follows three Chicanos, a Mexican undocumented

worker, and an Irish American, all of whom find themselves thrown together on the "Freedom Train." They are led to realize their common bonds as members of the working class by a sardonic, comical narrator in the guise of an old woman *calavera*. When performed in 1977 at the Eighth Annual Chicano Theatre Festival in San Diego, California, the production demonstrated a lack of training coupled with a very energetic and sincere manner of presentation. It was obvious that this teatro was new, though several of its members were in their thirties and therefore not as young as most neophyte teatro members.

Working under a very well-defined collective process, Teatro Libertad continued to create productions that went beyond the early *acto* style, yet maintained a naiveté and unsophisticated quality that recalled many aspects of the Teatro Campesino's early efforts. This was not a teatro composed of workers in a common cause, as was the Campesino, nor was it a troupe of individuals who had come together to create Chicano theater by leaving their other jobs, as had the members of Teatro de la Gente. Teatro Libertad was a combination of the two, composed of workers from different occupations who continued to make their livings and support their families in the non-theatrical world while coming together to form a teatro. Though some of the members were still students in 1978, most of them were members of the working class whose daily involvements on the job and in the community inspired their creative process.

In 1978, the Teatro created and produced a play entitled *Los pelados*, which they subsequently published the same year.[23] The term *pelado* means "plucked, bare or bald" in a literal translation, and it can also refer to one's social and economic status, indicating a person who is "nobody, penniless." One of the Teatro Campesino's most successful productions, *La gran carpa de los rasquachis* (The Great Tent of the Underdogs), revolved around the central figure of Jesús Pelado Rasquachi, a character in the tradition of Cantinflas. The term *rasquachi* is also indicative of a person or object of little means or value and is a colloquialism common in any barrio. By focusing their play on one Jesús Pelado and his wife Margarita, the Teatro was not so much imitating the Campesino as it was acknowledging the universal meaning of the term *pelado*.[24]

Like the Teatro de la Gente, the members of Tucson's teatro consider themselves "cultural workers." They are guided by a central committee and further informed by various committees devoted to finances, audience development, and artistic development. The creative process is divided into three broad categories: (1) documentation, (2) dialogue, and (3) delivery.[25] As indicated by the names of each phase, the group first documents situations it feels might make good theatrical statements; it then discusses the ideas brought back to the group, collectively decides what the focus of the play will be, and creates the production; finally, the group takes the production to its public. The second phase is perhaps the most involved, with many hours of discussion and clarification spent before the demanding task of turning thoughts into theater. In the group's words: "the focus is on local problems, which are then elaborated so as to speak to the Chicano community at large."[26]

The issues addressed in *Los pelados* focus on domestic problems brought about by the high cost of living, unemployment, and inadequate housing. It is a contemporary view of barrio life that is influenced more by the *acto* than by Ibsen. In a series of twelve quickly paced scenes, the audience is exposed to the troubles of Jesús and Margarita Pelado through a mixture of exaggerated techniques combined with very realistic situations. The main characters are realistically portrayed, but the secondary figures of Doña Chona, Margarita's mother, and Don Faustino, the landlord, are typical *acto* caricatures, portrayed for laughs and broad farcical humor. The setting consists of a stylized backdrop, which is continually altered by substituting plugs in the walls to indicate interior and exterior scenes as the case demands. Pictures of Kennedy and the Virgin of Guadalupe indicate the interior of the Pelado's house, but when removed, the openings in the backdrop can become a bank teller's window or the credit office at Sears. In one scene, characters from Margarita's imagination appear in the windows as she daydreams about a conversation with her employer and her husband's supervisor.

Writing about the dangers of what they term the "extended *acto*," Juan Bruce-Novoa and David Valentín ask: "How long can you look at yourself as an archetype or stereotype before you start wondering where your individualizing characteristics are?"[27] Though these critics are not referring to *Los pelados*, the question makes a valid point, one that will continually arise when assessing the effectiveness of many collective efforts. The typical *acto* is never more than thirty minutes long. *Los pelados*, which has many characteristics of the *acto* form, takes one hour to perform, yet it does not suffer the weaknesses suggested by Bruce-Novoa and Valentín. The production's success lies in its clever mixture of *acto* stereotypes and barrio realities that seem to balance one another. This collective creation might be termed a "super-*acto*," for its genesis is directly related to that Valdezian form that almost all teatros begin with, but which is effectively extended by the Teatro members.

Los pelados begins with a prologue to the main action entitled "*La boda del piojo y la pulga*" (The Marriage of the Louse and the Flea), taken from the song of the same name. The prologue sets the action into motion, introducing the characters, the barrio atmosphere, and Jesús' major objective for the next scene: to get a job as garbage collector. The first scene is characteristically entitled "El Test—Chuy [Jesús] Gets A Job," indicating the action that is to follow. In the Teatro's dramatization of the examination, "Chuy," as he is referred to in the script, is forced to compete with other applicants while the "Efficiency Expert" announces the progress of the contestants as if they were in the Kentucky Derby. The dehumanization has just begun, though the metaphor is not developed as in Teatro de la Gente's canine transformation. But the message is clear: Chuy will have to "work like a horse," as the saying goes. He gets the job, and the remainder of the play dramatizes the typical problems the young couple faces. When the landlord announces that he is selling their house, Margarita decides to go to work, ignoring her husband's objections. Their meager income is barely sufficient to cover their expenses and pressures mount as they try to make sense of their situation. Finally, after several scenes have elaborated upon the couple's problems, they decide to join a tenant's union, ending the play on a note of hope for the future.

Each scene is appropriately titled, indicating the action that is to follow. Early in the play Chuy's job as a garbage collector and Margarita's work as a housewife and mother are effectively compared to show that their labor is of equal importance. It is equally monotonous as well, and the title of the scene, "Se chingan los dos" (literally, "they fuck themselves," meaning "they work their asses off"), reveals the Teatro's attitude toward the couple's daily routine. The script calls for a stylized, dance-like representation of the pair's demanding work. The two parallel each other as he lifts a garbage pail and she picks up a pail of water, both using slow-motion movements calculated to demonstrate their common drudgery. Their dance of labor comes to a frozen halt, jarred back to reality by the baby's cries and a fellow worker calling for Chuy.

This moment of dream-like fantasy is quickly contrasted by the entrance of Margarita's mother, Doña Chona, who returns the play to normalcy, though her character is a caricature. She is a wonderful parody of a tight-fisted old lady who would rather part with a grandchild than a dime. Her character is revealed by her words and actions as she significantly clutches her purse and says: "*Yo gracias a mi Dios no les pido nada*" ("I, thanks to my God, don't ask you for anything"). The comedy introduced by Doña Chona and her male counerpart, Don Faustino, keeps the audience's attention while the seriousness of the theme is not forgotten.

Although the dialogues between the major characters can be termed realistic, the techniques of the *acto* are never too far in the background. Margarita works in a typing pool, once again exaggerating the work to demonstrate its monotony. She leaves work, paycheck in hand, and immediately crosses to an opening in the backdrop that becomes the bank teller's window. As she moves from window to window, paying her bills, her earnings are completely depleted, recalling the action in *La quinta temporada*, in which the farmworker picks the crops/money but is finally left with nothing. This scene graphically presents a universal situation that any household manager can relate to.

Los pelados successfully tells the story of a typical Mechicano working-class couple, their hopes, frustrations, and their decision to take action against at least one of the forces that control them: the landlord. By depicting the couple at home, at work, and in the company of their relatives and peers, this "super-*acto*" begins to develop its characters on a more than superficial level. By maintaining its joyful theatricality of exaggeration and farce, the production is perfectly suited for the performance conditions the Teatro usually encounters. The quickly changing scenes and visual images work well to keep the attention of the audience, while the mirror-image vignettes give the piece an indisputable barrio quality. The dialogue reveals a sensitivity to the language patterns of the barrio, and the interactions represented are given more than cursory attention.

Both the Teatro Libertad and its collective creation are important to a study of the evolution of Chicano theater, for the two are reflections of both past and present trends in Chicano theater companies and processes. While the original Teatro Campesino was guided by its political cause rather than aesthetic goals, and the Teatro de la Gente reflects the growing concern for artistic quality as well as political strength, the Tucson teatro is a rare example of a contemporary worker's teatro that is involved in more than one struggle. Unlike the growing number of troupes whose goal is to become full-time practitioners of theater, Teatro Libertad's members are committed to a part-time involvement in their teatro. Like any other teatro, the Tucson troupe is concerned with the sociopolitical struggles of its community and defines its role in those struggles through theatrical statements that are entertaining and educational. Time and the approbation of its audiences may encourage Teatro Libertad to seek a full-time status, remunerating its members so that they can leave their present employment. But for the moment, the group remains a model to other teatros that have yet to make that perilous transition.

There is a certain luxury in being a worker's theater, purposely didactic and admittedly unsophisticated. When Valdez' original troupe toured the United States denouncing the wealthy growers and upholding the admirable cause of the defenseless farmworkers, the Teatro Campesino was lauded as a true worker's theater. It was not compared to regional theater, professional productions, or even to the evolving street theaters of the late sixties. The other theatrical groups were either "professional," and therefore not comparable, or "radical students,"who probably came from upper-middle-class backgrounds and could not be considered in the same breath with the *campesinos* who sang and shouted as if their lives depended on it. Critics recalled the political theater of the thirties when writing about the early Teatro Campesino. And they were usually not prepared to evaluate those portions of the presentations that were in Spanish, for they were admittedly non-Spanish-speaking.

When the Teatro Campesino left the ranks of the union to seek its own identity and to nourish its artistic vision and craft, it entered the mainstream of most theatrical activity in this country. When the Teatro de la Gente "graduated" from the university and began to establish its financial independence, it too joined the major current. Before and after his success with *Zoot Suit* in Los Angeles in 1978-79, Valdez continued to impress his audiences and critics with his unique theatrical vision and the stamp he placed upon his internationally famous company. The group was the leading Chicano theater company and was also one of the few theater troupes of any kind to survive the sixties and continue to evolve. When Valdez began to explore indigenous myths and spiritual solutions, some critics demanded a return to the political activism of the union period, but none could offer aesthetic criticism on the basis of the Teatro's artistic achievement. In a word, the Teatro Campesino was professional and could be judged alongside any professional theater company in the nation.

By leaving the realm of campus politics and part-time theatrics, the Teatro de la Gente was also stepping into the current established by Valdez' troupe. No longer a student group, Vargas' teatro had to be judged as one of the hundreds of small professional theater companies that were active in all sectors of American society. Certainly, Teatro de la Gente did not aspire to the same goals as resident companies that catered to the middle-class palate. However, by declaring itself a full-time teatro, it separated itself from the other teatros that could not be evaluated using the criteria applied to the Campesino.

By mid-1980, the San Jose teatro had returned to a part-time status, with a core group of four paid actor/administrators and a surrounding pool of community talent. Vargas' troupe had gained a modicum of experience and expertise and remained one of the leading California troupes. With an academically trained artistic director and members who had studied theater seriously, Teatro de la Gente was still unlike most teatros and would be judged differently than groups such as Teatro Libertad. Though no longer full time, the San Jose teatro was still aspiring to professional standards and seeking admittance to a much more demanding artistic territory. These "cultural workers" would have to prove their worth wherever they performed, but especially in the larger arena of alternative theater groups.

Thus, Teatro Libertad could stand apart from the mainstream in 1979, declare itself a worker's theater, and ask to be judged on a different level than the professional groups. Members of the Teatro were upset when a local reporter referred to their group as being "at the amateur level" in 1978, for by the very nature of their work they could not be understood on the terms the writer employed.[28] Though the group was concerned with improving its theatrical techniques, it did not pretend to Broadway standards or what it termed "commodity theater." *Los pelados* spoke to its audience in their particular language, on their terms. Like so many of the troupes that had followed in the footsteps of the Teatro Campesino, Teatro Libertad had to be witnessed in its own territory to fully appreciate its impact. Drawing on the life breath of their audiences, these cultural workers took messages of hope and the challenge to work for social change to people who might otherwise never have witnessed a theatrical production of any kind. Very effective theater was being wrought by direct descendants of the early Teatro Campesino, fourteen years after Luis Valdez had ventured to his birthplace to found a farmworker's theater.

By 1980, fifteen years after Valdez began the Teatro Campesino, the vast majority of Chicano theater groups were either campus or community oriented, composed of students and workers whose nontheatrical involvements kept them from full-time participation in teatro. The period of a worker's theater committed to its cause rather than its craft had ended in 1967 when Luis Valdez had decided to separate from the daily demands of the fledgling Chávez union in order to create a more aesthetically astute company of actors. That difficult decision was only the first of many that the premier Chicano dramatist would have to make, and it signaled the trend that most of the other teatros would follow. There were other issues that Valdez and his troupe would investigate beyond the fields of agribusiness, and as they searched for themes to dramatize, so too did other teatros find a variety of causes to adapt for the stage. Though the problems of both the rural and urban Mechicano workers were as poignant in 1980 as they had been in 1965, the vast majority of Chicano theater companies could no longer be considered "worker's theaters," but rather theaters of cultural workers seeking their theatrical and political identities on the platforms of the barrios.

It is important to note that though the works discussed in this chapter cover a time span of thirteen years, each is directly indebted to the original *acto* format. None of these dramatizations of the worker's struggle is written in the realistic style; instead, they are exaggerated, broadly played attempts to bring people and problems to life. While the *actos* require no setting at all, the other two productions we have seen do not demand much in the way of backdrops, and therefore each of these pieces is very portable. The exaggeration of the acting style plays against the minimal settings, which only suggest a locale rather than attempting to duplicate it realistically. Audiences are asked to contribute to the creative process by filling in where the settings are indicative rather than explicit. There is a definite contrast between the bare stage of the *actos* and the backdrop of *Los pelados*, but the latter remains within the bounds of a theater of economy.

Each of these examples of a worker's theater reflects the financial poverty of the groups that have created them—collectives that have risen above fiscal needs to express in theatrical terms the urgency of their causes. Because these works can be performed on any platform, stage or empty space, they can be taken to the most remote barrios. In 1971 Luis Valdez wrote: "If the Raza will not come to the theater, then the theater must go to the Raza."[29] By creating works that could, indeed, be taken to the people, these teatros were not only continuing an artistic tradition but recognizing a political consideration as well.

To date, there have been no effective dramatizations of the worker's struggle using the social realist form. As can be seen by each of the productions in this chapter, special consideration has to be given to the performance conditions in the barrio: noisy children running about, people coming and going, and all manner of distractions. Psychological motivations get lost in the confusion, and only the broadest style can compete with the noises of a park on a Sunday afternoon. From *Las dos caras del patroncito* to *Los pelados*, it is clear that these works are dependent on a direct communication with a particular audience, though anybody should be able to understand the message. In each production there are clearly defined protagonists and antagonists, with no attempt to create a villain who has any redeeming features. The grower is no good, the manufacturer is a crook, and the landlord is a shyster just like the Pelados' employers. The villains are flat, but the heroes are not.

Because the works get longer as they progress from the first *acto* to *Los pelados*, we find that the heroes and heroines become more fully drawn. The singular victim of the campesino *actos*, the lonely farmworker who has left his family in Mexico or Texas, is replaced by a man with a wife in *El hombre que se convirtió en perro* and an entire family in the final production. As the themes expand to include problems beyond the fields or factories, domestic troubles sprout up in these teatros' attempts to hold a magnifying mirror up to other aspects of life. When Margarita and Jesús Pelado find themselves in domestic straits, however, their argument is not played in an exaggerated fashion because there is no farce to the situation as in a Punch and Judy bout. This brings to mind the Bruce-Novoa and Valentín questioning of the *acto* structure, for the realism of the domestic quarrel contrasts sharply with the caricaturesque scenes and seems to indicate that the play is straining at the conventions of the *acto* form.

As these four theater pieces progress, it is obvious that the brief Campesino *actos* are the least demanding in terms of character delineation. A sign, a mask, and certain gestures immediately define not only the character but his or her social role as well. But as the San Jose and Tucson groups attempt to develop the *acto* structure to include relationships beyond the worker/employer, they enter a more difficult medium. As an *acto*, or a super-*acto*, *Los pelados* can be quite effective, but as a realistic play this collective effort falls far short of the mark. The troupe understood the differences between social realism and the *acto* and thus did not fall into the common mistake of trying to re-create "reality" on stage. Eventually, Chicano playwrights may develop dramas in the tradition of social realism, but for the moment the *acto* and super-*acto* will define the problems of the Mechicano working class.

As the issues develop from rural to urban, the conflicts become more complex and not as easily solved. The strike is thwarted in *El hombre que se convirtió en perro* when the electronics firm elects to go to Mexico, and we do not know the outcome of the tenants' strike in *Los pelados*, though we can be certain that a tremendous struggle will ensue. Still, each of the works is true to Valdez' definition of what the *acto* should do: if not show a solution, at least hint at one. By moving from the particular (an actual farmworker's strike) to the general (a composite of electronic workers' strikes) and then back to the particular (a tenants' union), these works demonstrate how any problem can be dramatized, whether the actors/demonstrators are participants in the conflict represented or not. What is essential, however, is an understanding of the problems exposed, and each of these productions shows a very clear perception of the issues.

Although there may be no workers' teatros in the tradition of the original Teatro Campesino today, the *actos* and super-*actos* discussed in this chapter indicate a continuing commitment among the teatros to a theater that addresses the problems of the urban and rural workers as employees, as family members, and as honest, hard-working people fighting to keep their humble homes. The issues remain just as valid today as when they were first produced, and perhaps these works will inspire others like them. Any would-be teatros can learn a great deal from the evolution of the three groups discussed in this chapter; the most important lesson is that they must have the leadership, commitment and discipline of these early teatros if they are to succeed.

Teatro de la Gente performing *El hombre que se convirtió en perro*,
8th Annual Chicano Theater Festival, 1977. *Photo: Peter Marshall*

Chapter Two

THE SEARCH FOR IDENTITY: WHAT IS A CHICANO?

No More Melting Pot

Ultimately, there are few dramatic works by Chicano play-wrights or theater groups that are not in some way an assertion of a cultural or political identity. The three works discussed in this chapter, *The Shrunken Head of Pancho Villa, Los vendidos,* and *La víctima* are each expressly concerned with defining what it is to be a Chicano in the latter half of the twentieth century. By focusing on characters who deny their heritage and attempt to blend into the allegorical melting pot, the plays demonstrate what the Chicano should not be and indicate positive alternatives to such behavior. To the emerging playwrights and creators of these intentionally didactic dramas, the ideal characters exhibit a political awareness that suggests an active substitute to assimilation. Though the works vary in form and content, they all agree that Chicanos must take action against social injustice inside and outside the barrio as they seek their true identity.

If the politically active Chicano is the hero, the apolitical Mexican American is the villain. Since before the rise of the Chicano Movement, there have always been those Mexican Americans who believe that there is no discrimination against their kind and that if there has been it is the fault of the victims, not the perpetrators. These Mexican Americans have often "made it" in the Anglo world, and they feel that the political activists are renegades without a cause, unstable students or radicals who prefer words to work. The assimilated Mexican American is generally apathetic in the face of political unrest; often having left the barrio for the suburbs, he or she is content to say: "I made it, why can't they?" This insensitive attitude has frequently alienated the successful from the less fortunnate, prompting disparaging remarks from both sides of the economic spectrum. Mexican Americans who "escape" from the barrio are termed *vendidos*, or sellouts, and long before the rise of the Chicano Movement they became targets for parody and ridicule.

As Chicanos continued to search for their own identity after 1965, opinions about what constituted a "real Chicano" varied, but all agreed that they were *not* Anglo, though there might be some who aspired to that designation. If Chicanos were not Anglo, then the Mexican Americans who denied any links with barrio realities were anathema to those who sought a unique, non-WASP image. *"El Mexicano hacerse gringo, no puede ni quiere"* ("The Mexican can't become a Gringo; nor does he want to") sang barrio musicians during this period of reaffirmation, aiming their humor at the ever present *vendido*. The Chicano who attempted to be what he was not had always been the subject of satire in the barrio, and early twentieth-century performing troupes had presented sketches about these people who attempted to "pass."[1] The darker the actor's skin, the funnier the representation, for it was obvious that the character was fooling nobody but himself. No matter how emphatic the assertion, the *vendido* would never be accepted as "white."

When Valdez and his troupe left the Chávez union in 1967, their first major *acto* reflected their search for themes beyond the issues of the fields. Significantly titled *Los vendidos*, this *acto* was calculated to expose some of the humorous and unsavory characteristics of the assimilationist. *Los vendidos* carefully satirized the antithesis of the emerging Chicano: the Mexican American who attempted to hide his identity or reject his background and blend into the proverbial melting pot. That collective *acto* had been preceded by Valdez' first full-length play, *The Shrunken Head of Pancho Villa*, produced in 1964 while he was still a student. Valdez' script demonstrated an early interest in the Chicano's cultural survival, focusing on a family consisting of Mexican parents and their Chicano children. The latter range from a street youth-cum-revolutionary to an older son who disavows his heritage altogether and becomes the ultimate *vendido*.

In 1976, another teatro created one of the most significant attempts to define the Chicano within a historical and political context: *La víctima* (The Victim).[2] Collectively created by El Teatro de la Esperanza (The Theater of Hope), *La víctima* is a documentary that reflects the group's search for new forms as well as its concern for who and what the Chicano is in this society. *La víctima* traces a Mexican family from the time it leaves Mexico for this country during the Revolution of 1910 to the present. Based on documented fact about the immigrations and deportations of Mexicans, the piece mingles history with fiction to create the central figure of a Mexican American who becomes an immigration officer and believes that he must make the ultimate rejection of his culture, his heritage, and his identity to continue in his chosen profession.

From the play by Valdez and the *acto* created by his company, to a documentary created by a theater collective, the distinct forms are held together by a mutual cause. Each of the works discussed has been successful on the stage and has inspired its audiences to pause and reflect upon the messages delivered and the questions raised. The productions are all entertaining as well as enlightening, revealing a continuing awareness of the importance of a dramaturgy that goes beyond mere slogans or pamphleteering. Though the search for identity continues to the present and may never be too far removed from the public platform, the progression studied here reveals three diverse approaches to that enigmatic question: "What is a Chicano?"

Cucarachas on the Walls and Vendidos in the Closet: *The Shrunken Head of Pancho Villa*

Of Luis Valdez' four plays to be discussed in separate chapters of this book, *The Shrunken Head of Pancho Villa* is the most concerned with the identity of the Chicano. *Bernabé* is a contemporary myth that mingles indigenous deities with barrio characters in a search for cosmic revelation. *Dark Root of a Scream* is another modern mythical play that investigates the past and the present through a young Chicano who died in Vietnam. Finally, *Zoot Suit* recalls the Mechicanos of the 1940s and the discrimination they suffered at the hands of the media and the courts. Though each of the four plays investigates different aspects of the Chicano experience, the first focuses more on the inner workings of the family unit.

It is not surprising that Luis Valdez' first full-length play is about a Mechicano family, for each of the works he has created concerns a family in crisis. For Valdez, the family is the main source from which his dramaturgy must spring forward, searching for its identity or its purpose. It is the family that copes with the conflicts and confronts the problems generated by the society around it. That society is generally the Anglo-dominated world that remains on the periphery of his plays yet is most often responsible for the economic oppression his protagonists encounter. As with the farmworker *actos* discussed in Chapter One, the Chicano is also capable of betraying his own people, but it is ultimately the economic system that has the final power over the characters' lives.

Above all, Valdez' plays reflect a struggle for cultural survival. The initial search for identity in the first play will recur in each succeeding work, with certain character types returning in different forms. The youthful renegade, the *vato loco* or pachuco, is present in each of the plays and finds his ultimate personification as the narrator of *Zoot Suit*. While the first work sympathetically investigates the ubiquitous pachuco, it also concerns itself with the opposite type: the *vendido*. The subsequent dramas find their antagonists in other Chicano types or in those representatives of the system who continually oppress the Chicano. We will find Anglo policemen and Chicano racketeers, Catholic priests and racist judges, as Valdez depicts the forces that confront his characters.

History is also an important element in Valdez' dramaturgy, reflecting his concern with the Chicano's past as well as future. For Valdez, Chicanos must be aware of their history and must continually fight not only to preserve it but to portray it as it really was. His plays will never settle for school-book depictions of the Chicano's historical importance in this society, for those books have been written with "Manifest Destiny" in mind. Our playwright's mission is to set the record straight.

All of Valdez' plays are political. "To create art amidst this oppression," he told a TENAZ Director's Conference in 1971, "is to be political."[3] His art has never strayed from its original intent of showing the Chicano vis-à-vis the family, and in so doing it has not ignored the economic realities of the barrio. His families reflect the poorer echelons of Chicano society, not because there are no middle-class Chicanos, but because the poor are the people whose condition must improve. In his portrayal of the struggle for survival, it is the playwright's concern that his characters remain "culturally pure," even as they strive for economic progress. By exposing the situation of these impoverished families, Valdez is setting up a sociopolitical comment, for we cannot ignore their condition.

Thus we have a sense of community in each of Valdez' plays. His characters are not alone in their oppression but are members of a larger family called *La Raza*. His mothers become symbolic figures as they reflect the struggles of Mechicanas in crisis: they are the all-suffering members of their communities. The homes they occupy are warm, if very humble, and are extensions of any barrio household. Audiences can look at these dwellings and say "Yes, I've been there," for they know too well the cracking walls and rusty pipes re-created on stage. The old saying *"Mi casa es su casa"* ("My house is your house") becomes a summons in Valdez' plays that calls the audience in closer, saying "Don't be afraid, I know what it's like."

The characters who populate Valdez' stage are based on his acute observations of human nature in all its complexity, and if they are sometimes distorted or stereotypical it is because the playwright feels that these extensions of reality will best suit his purpose: to show how people can change, for better or for worse. Therefore the first family Valdez writes about becomes a dream-like vision, with attitudes and actions exaggerated beyond the commonplace in order to arouse the audience's imagination and interest. At times the lesson is clear; in other instances the audience members may have to decide for themselves the significance of the symbols.

In contrast to the symbolism that pervades the action of *The Shrunken Head of Pancho Villa*, the playwright calls for a musical slide presentation to precede the action—a history lesson which recognizes the fact that many in the audience do not know the true story of Pancho Villa's death. Though the characters in the play will later discuss the fabled revolutionary's life and times, this montage of slides and music evokes impressive images that will recur in the spectators' minds as the action unfolds. "We have a history," Valdez is telling his audience, "and this is only a small part of that tradition."

After informing us that Pancho Villa was ambushed in his car in 1920, the narration adds that his body was later disinterred and decapitated. The head was never found. The prologue concludes with the following: "This is the story of a people who followed him beyond borders, beyond death."[4] This is not the story of a family, the prologue tells us, but rather the story of a people. From the beginning, then, we know that these characters are representative of many Chicanos in Valdez' analysis of his people's condition.

This play is divided into five acts, the action taking place over a period of less than three years. It is a tale of survival, as we watch the Mexican parents attempt to keep their family of Chicano children together. Characters become the focus of the action, with dialogue created to move the story forward with humor and insight. The major action of the play is the transformation of two of the brothers, Joaquín and Domingo. These two represent opposite character types for Valdez; one is a *vendido*, the other a street youth who becomes a social bandit. Like so many of the later *actos*, the play's theme is unity, exploring various Mechicano types in its search for an answer to the loss of identity that Valdez feels is bred by acculturation.

Though the family loses its father to an ignoble death and a son abandons the family to become "Americanized," the family unit does not dissolve altogether. The daughter matures to resemble her mother, marrying a man who looks like her father, and the young couple has a baby whose physical uniqueness recalls the parents' first-born, Belarmino. Belo, as he is called, is only a head; he has no body, and when Joaquín returns from prison without a head at the end of the play, Valdez hints that an alliance between the bodyless head and the headless body will bring about the solution to the family's plight. The play ends on a note of hope but cannot offer easy answers to the problems posed. It is an interesting first work that has fascinated its audiences with its symbolism and the characterizations that Valdez creates so effectively.

Valdez' dramaturgy has always displayed an individuality and eclecticism that makes his style difficult to categorize. The opening scene is juxtaposed with the musical slide prologue as the playwright introduces us to this Mechicano family. As the curtain opens to reveal the living room of what appears to be a typical barrio dwelling, a guitar plays "La cucaracha," a popular song of the Mexican Revolution, and we find Pedro, the father, snoring on the couch. After the final note is heard on the guitar, Pedro shouts "Viva Villa!" in his sleep. This is followed by "the cry of a full-grown man" in the next room and a fierce rendition of "La cucaracha" from the unseen voice. The play begins with noises because sound is very important to the playwright. Speaking of this play in 1968, Valdez called attention to the importance of noise to the Mechicano and pointed out how street hawkers in Mexico represent the sounds that we do not hear in the United States. "That's because this society doesn't allow Mexicans to make noise. We're supposed to get off the streets, and stay at las cantinas and keep our mouths shut," Valdez told participants in a Radical Theatre Festival in San Francisco.[5] The opening scene of this play was a symbolic *grito* or shout of independence for the playwright as his script leapt with an audible vengeance onto the stage, declaring it his own.

Once we have been exposed to the sight and sound of the setting—the modest home and the rather loud snoring, shouting, and singing—Cruz, the mother, enters. We immediately see this woman as more Mexicana than Chicana, for she speaks with an accent and at times confuses words in English. It is important that she be the first character to speak for she is really the backbone of the family. She is also continually concerned about her son in the next room, always telling the others to be quiet lest they should disturb his sleep. The opening scene tells us that her husband is a man who drinks and lives in the past, purporting to have ridden with Pancho Villa. Since he is not young, and the action of the play takes place "fifty years after the Mexican Revolution," he could in fact have known Villa. His wife puts up with his references to the past with the resignation of any alcoholic's spouse. Her name means "Cross" in English and is symbolic of her station, for she is the standard-bearer for the family and also has her own cross to bear.

We discover another of Cruz's crosses in the character of her youngest son, Joaquín. He represents the Chicano who has lost his Mexican identity yet is not Anglicized either. He is a street youth who we discover has been released from jail the day before and who his sister calls a "lousy pachuco." He tells the others that he had a fight with a *gavacho* (Anglo) who called him "Pancho." "I wasn't looking for no trouble," he says. "I even take Pancho at first, which was bad enough, but then he call me a lousy Pancho, and I hit the stupid vato in the mouth." He has taken the term "lousy" literally and resents the inference. Like the cockroaches that will become important symbols of this family's plight, lice identify a certain social standing and are negative images that Joaquín loathes. When his mother asks him what troubles him so much, he responds: "The gavachos."

It is Joaquín, the youngest son of this family in flux, who represents the hope of the future, recalling the early California folk hero Joaquín Murieta, who also had his troubles with the "gavacho." Our contemporary Joaquín, unable to blend into the larger society, has already been in trouble with the authorities, but we see him as a good person who is a victim of injustice. Explaining to his father how he was falsely accused, Joaquín says, "Then there at the station the placa [police] give us all matches, and the one wis the short one was guilty. They catch me red-handed! But I didn't swipe no tires." He has spent the last year in jail and has returned to find his family on welfare, awaiting the arrival of his older brother, the "war veteran."

The first act is a quick succession of scenes that keep the action flowing. There are few discussions that last longer than two pages without another character coming on or going off. The dialogue is also quickly paced. The exposition is carefully situated to make the conversations interesting, and the typical Valdezian humor abounds, with double entendres and sibling insults that remind us of our own youth. The first lengthy discussion is between Joaquín and his father and reveals the son's character as well as the father's obsession with Villa. Pedro recalls the fact that Pancho Villa bought a "Chivi" when his favorite horse died and was subsequently ambushed while driving that car. Joaquín asks if Villa ran down "a lotta gavachos" in the car, adding the image: "Squashed 'em!" Joaquín's hatred of the Anglo is constantly present, and his last remark reminds us of the act of squashing a cockroach or a louse.

The discussion about Pancho Villa fascinates our young warrior of the streets and is the first step toward transforming Joaquín into the revolutionary he will become. All the while, the women are in the kitchen preparing beans and tortillas for Belarmino, the oldest son who has only been heard grunting, belching, and shouting from the other room. He is, it seems, eating them all out of house and home, a constant consumer of the family's meager provisions. All but the mother speak disparagingly about Belarmino, yet he is accepted as another burden on the family with the resignation common in the barrio.

The discussion about Villa is interrupted by the arrival of Mingo (as Domingo is called), whose entrance is marked by a certain departure from reality. The mother has just asked "Where's Mingo?" in an absent-minded fashion, and when Joaquín says "Not home from the war yet," Mingo appears at the front door with the line: "Anybody say war?" The all-too-well timed arrival suddenly sets things ajar, beginning the transformation from social realism into fantasy. Mingo is the first *vendido* in Valdez' dramaturgy: a cold materialistic ex-Marine whose major goal is to get the family "Americanized" and out of the barrio. When he announces that he has bought a new "Chivi," the allusion to Pancho Villa's last ride cannot be ignored. The American car was the Mexican revolutionary's death trap and we wonder if it will bring about the demise of this would-be "Mexican American."

The change of style that begins with the soldier's entrance is prompted by his almost stereotypical character. Mingo is on a different level of reality in this play, and his transformation into the ultimate sellout contrasts with Joaquín's conversion into a revolutionary. Both the pachuco and the *vendido* fascinate Valdez, but it is the latter who remains outside the bounds of conventional reality. The fact that Mingo does not remember his sister's name or even that he has another brother reveals the acculturation process begun in the Marines, but the overtness of this transformation cannot be termed a subtle change of character. Domingo foreshadows another *acto* villain, for he tells his family that he is going to get rich as a farm-labor contractor, thus combining the unsavory characteristics of both the *vendido* and the coyote. In his "Note on Style" preceding the play, Valdez states: "The play is not intended as a 'realistic' interpretation of Chicano life . . . [but contains] realistic and surrealistic elements working together to achieve a transcendental expression of the social condition of La Raza in Los Estados Unidos." The first act constructs the realistic framework for the audience to identify with and gradually begins its transformation just as the characters evolve. We are carefully introduced to the surreal just as one would walk slowly into a cold stream rather than take a quick, shocking leap. Speaking of the *actos* in 1970, Valdez remarked: ". . . we can only stay a step ahead of our audience, and it has to be a very easy step for them to make, or they won't make it. . . ."[6] He understood that axiom when he wrote *The Shrunken Head of Pancho Villa*, and he searched for a form that would best describe his vision of *La Raza's* plight.

When the second act opens it is three months later. Once again we are confronted with loud Mexican music when the curtain rises, but there is something strange about the walls. We look more closely and discover that they are speckled with red cockroaches of various sizes. The daughter, Lupe, is standing behind her father, delousing him as he sleeps. A white lace veil covers Belarmino's head on an old sofa in the corner, and when Lupe finds something on her father's head she exclaims, "Lousy cucaracha!" This is curious, for we think she is delousing him; yet she seems to have found a cockroach in his hair and she describes it as "lousy." For Valdez and other Chicano writers, the cockroach represents *La Raza* in its indomitable spirit and ability to survive against all odds. A cockroach that is "lousy" is a metaphor for a Chicano who is infested with lice and thus a member of the poorest class.

The setting, with its cockroach-covered walls, suggests the expressionism of the early twentieth century, with exaggerated settings and properties used to emphasize the forces that overpower characters in the plays. In Valdez' dramaturgy, the symbols do not overpower as much as they serve to underline images that are recognizable to the Chicano. When the mother tells her daughter to "Go water the beans," a barrio audience will immediately know what she means. Someone who is not familiar with the Mechicano kitchen may think the daughter is going to the garden to water plants, when she is simply being asked to add water to the pot of boiling beans. A Mechicano audience knows all too well that Lupe is looking for lice and is thus aware of the juxtaposition that occurs when she pulls out a cockroach. Someone who has never experienced the process of delousing would lose the effect. The cockroach metaphor becomes increasingly important as the play develops.

After adjusting to the visual image of cockroach-covered walls, we find that Lupe resents her bodyless brother, for she has to stay home to feed him. She uncovers the head for a moment, and we see that it is the face of a 30 to 35-year-old man with deep, dark expressive eyes and a large moustache. Since he cannot talk, he communicates in grunts and howls and with those all-encompassing eyes. His head is larger than normal, a full eighteen inches in diameter. Lupe is in the midst of deriding her brother for making her feel like a slave, a *negra*, when her boyfriend Chato enters saying, "Hi *negra*." Though he uses the term endearingly, it is tantamount to "blackie," and we discover that neither of these young, dark-skinned Chicanos wants to be considered "dark." They are not aspiring to the Anglo world like Mingo, but they are representative of the many Chicano young people who are ashamed of their skin color and who respond to media images of what is beautiful. Chato tells Lupe that people are talking about her brother, claiming that he is only a head, to which she responds, "You black *negro*! You dirty Mexican!" employing racist epithets to combat his tauntings. She, we discover, cannot speak Spanish, but Chato can. Lupe becomes a transitional character caught between the pachuco and the *vendido* syndromes, neither one nor the other, searching for her identity. When she denies the fact that her brother is a head, she in effect denies her very culture.

Mingo, the aspiring farm-labor contractor, announces that they are going to buy a new house in "Prune Blossom Acres." He has previously referred to his family as "defeated" and insists that they have to leave the barrio to improve their condition. The move to the new location would constitute the ultimate rejection of his cultural heritage, Valdez is telling us, for it is symbolic of the Anglo encroachment of the land since the Southwest was taken from Mexico. What used to be an orchard where this family once worked has been converted into a typical California tract of identical houses bunched closely together. Cruz does not want to move, however, because in the barrio she feels safe from people's reactions to her oldest son. She does not realize that even there the people are talking, for she claims, "In this barrio they don't care."

MINGO: I care!
CRUZ: And the gringos?

MINGO: Whatta you mean gringos?
CRUZ: Who else live in new houses?

The playwright carefully controls the fantastic aspects of the play, exposing the fact that Belo is only a head at the close of the first act without actually revealing the visage. Belo's head sits onstage in the second act, covered by a cloth. We see his face for a moment and are very much aware of his presence. In the third act, Valdez uncovers the head and places it prominently upstage center. Having prepared his audience for this surrealistic atmosphere, the playwright is ready to add to the complexity. It is during the crucial third act that Belo first speaks. The speechless head can talk, and he warns his younger brother Joaquín not to tell anyone that he is really the head of Pancho Villa. Belo chooses Joaquín for this revelation because he recognizes him as the only hope for the family's salvation, calling his identity a "political secret." When Joaquín enthusiastically tells his parents that Belo is really Pancho Villa, neither will believe him. Ironically, Pedro, who is continually referring to "Mi General Francisco Villa," does not accept Belo's head as that of the martyred revolutionary. The father represents the shattered hope of the Revolution, living on inebriated images of Mexico's true liberation. When the father dies, his hopes of a return to Mexico fade away with him, underlining the playwright's belief that the revolution is here and now.

Pedro is killed by a passing train, a symbol of the revolutionaries' transport in Mexico. Recalling the emotion of Pancho Villa's campaigns, Pedro had described the excitement that would greet his train, with people "climbing all over like lices." The image once again equates the poor with lice, and it is heightened by the old photographs that preceded the play—projections in black and white that caught the fervor of the moment and which the audience no doubt envisions in its mind. Though we do not see Pedro's death, the playwright calls up the sounds of the train passing and the progression from the railroad crossing bells to church bells; Belo then lets out a "sorrowful cry of death" and the scene blacks out. It is a poignant moment in a play that depends on character and language more than mournful emotions for its effect. The father's demise is soon overshadowed by the familial conflicts, for this is a play about life, not death.

Pedro's passing leaves Cruz in charge of the family, but she is helpless in the face of the poverty and dissolution of her brood. Lupe is pregnant out of wedlock, Joaquín is an ex-offender, and

Mingo is slowly denying not only his heritage but his family as well. Mingo wants his brother to join the Marines, while Joaquín berates him for not being "Chicano." Joaquín tells Mingo that he can never be what he really wants, "Gavacho," which emphasizes what the Chicano is *not* rather than describing what he should be. As the play progresses, the brothers' transformations are the central issue. Mingo finally leaves the family and Joaquín becomes a "social bandit."

The transformations are bilateral, climaxed by Joaquín's arrest and Mingo's collusion with the police. When the latter arrive, Mingo tells them he is "only a boarder in this house." He helps them capture Joaquín rather than assisting his brother, who has become a Chicano Robin Hood. In helping the police, Mingo comes to embody the idea of "law and order." Joaquín has organized his friends to steal food from the supermarkets to feed the poor, offering an active, if illegal, alternative to their poverty. In contrast, Mingo hoards his food in the refrigerator, unwilling to share it with his own family. Both are exaggerated expressions of what the playwright is underscoring: extremes that have real counterparts in society.

Food is a major image in this play, first as nourishment for Belo, then as the symbol of liberation through Joaquín's supermarket forays. By the fourth act everybody is clamoring for food: Mingo hoards it; the women constantly make beans and tortillas to feed Belo; Joaquín comes home with sacks of beans and flour; and the ever-present Belo eats anything that is put into his mouth. Food becomes more than physical nourishment; it is a symbol for energy, drive, and initiative. Mingo tells his mother that instead of spending money on "the head," he is going to spend money "where it counts: on self-improvement." Yet his self-improvement is only a conversion from a family orientation to selfish egocentrism. This early version of the *vendido* finds it very easy to deny even sustenance to his family and, in effect, to his people.

The final act takes place two years after the close of the previous act. It is winter again, and the walls are crawling with larger cockroaches than before. Lupe's baby is also just a head, and both she and her husband Chato have begun to resemble her parents in appearance and dress. History, it seems, is repeating itself. Paralleling the opening of the first act, they are waiting for Joaquín to arrive, released from prison. They are also awaiting a visit from the social worker. Belo has learned to talk and has become, in his mother's words, "the man of the house." "The head of the house," his sister responds, enjoying the pun.

When the social worker arrives, we recognize him as Mingo,

but when his mother runs to kiss him he tells her his name is Mr. Sunday and that though he once lived in a house very much like this one, it was "in another barrio . . . another town." Mr. Sunday now speaks some Spanish and is representative of those Mexican Americans who claim to be interested in helping "others less fortunate" while denying their own families as well as translating their names, for Domingo means Sunday in English. Mr. Sunday brings in a reformed Joaquín who is clean, well-dressed, and even taller, but who has no head. Lupe consoles her mother with: "He can still find a job in the fields. A man don't need a head to work there."

When Belo sees that muscular, headless body, he is delighted, and he asks someone to place him on top of Joaquín's shoulders. But Cruz tells her children that neither Belo nor the new baby will get this body as she leads Joaquín into another room. All go to bed, leaving Belo to tell the audience:

> . . . Sooner or later, the jefita gots to come across wis Joaquín's body. All I need is to talk sweet when she give me my beans, eh? In other words, organize her. Those people don't even believe who I am. Tha's how I wan' it. To catch 'em by surprise. So don' worry, my people, because one of this days Pancho Villa will pass among you again. Look to your mountains, your pueblos, your barrios. He will be there. Buenas noches.

Belarmino *is* the head of Pancho Villa, just as he is the hope for the future or the oppression of the present. This fantastic head represents the characters' ability to help themselves if they recognize the challenge. That challenge, in Belo's words, is to organize. As long as Cruz refuses to accept the fact that her oldest son is only a head, she must feed him beyond endurance. Her blindness is further emphasized when she sees Joaquín's headless body and refuses to combine it with Belo's head. When Belo says he has to organize her, he is speaking of La Raza as a whole, for which Cruz has become the archetype. She is more than the symbol of motherhood; she is all Mechicanos.

Belarmino represents the symbolic head of the Mechicano people as they have become under the yoke of Anglo-dominated society. The bodyless head typifies the disunity among the Mechicanos and their inability to see that their condition would change if they could get organized. It will not be through Mexican-American social workers, Chicano Robin Hoods, or even "50,000 vatos on horses and Chivis" that the Mechicano will find social justice, but in his own home. Just as Cruz refuses to accept the fact that she and her family are oppressed by the economic system around them, neither will she recognize the fact that her son is only a head. When she acknowledges the true nature of her family's condition, Valdez is telling us, she will have liberated herself from that internal colonialism that keeps the Mechicano in his subservient place.

For Valdez, the family is the hope for the future; it is the cradle of birth, maturation, death, and rebirth. The family he has dramatized in this play is also representative of the larger microcosm called the barrio. Valdez points to the barrio itself for the answers, underlining the premise that Mingo's total assimilation is a rejection of the heritage and culture of the community that nurtured him. Mr. Sunday's cold, deliberate denial of his family's basic needs paints a very negative picture of the sellout type. In contrasting the socially conscious Joaquín with Mr. Sunday, Valdez obviously favors the young warrior's determination to help his people. As a farm-labor contractor we see Mingo cheat his workers of their pay, and we also observe his selfishness in the home. But Joaquín's enthusiastic shoplifting earns him the respect of the people and the retribution of the establishment. When he returns from prison "reformed," he has no head and is therefore speechless; yet Belo knows that his mother will eventually combine the strong youthful body with the mind that is aware of its history and understands that its people are oppressed.

Given its use of fantasy and of symbols that are sometimes simplistic and sometimes obscure, *The Shrunken Head of Pancho Villa* is not easily interpreted. What is very clear, however, is Valdez' attitude toward the ubiquitous *vendido*. The playwright condemns those Chicanos who attempt to deny their culture and offers as an alternative the combination of Joaquín's youthful strength and Belo's tradition of revolution. Though the youngest son has been supposedly "rehabilitated," the playwright leaves his audience with the impression that he can still be helped. The power of the people is stronger than the institutions that attempt to suppress active resistance, Valdez tells us, and only time will reveal how long it will take for the people to put the necessary forces together.

How to Buy a Used Mexican: *Los vendidos*

The Teatro Campesino left the state of California for its first national tour in the summer of 1967. The troupe performed on campuses, in union halls, and in civic auditoriums to publicize the Huelga and generate much-needed funds for the union's treasury. On the east coast, the Teatro performed in New York's Village

Theater, the Newport Folk Festival, and travelled to Washington, D.C., to perform for the Senate Sub-Committee on Migratory Labor. The group was bringing national recognition to the strike and the boycott and was also broadening its horizons. Articles about its program of *actos* and songs appeared in major newspapers and journals, reflecting the impact the group had wherever it performed.[7] For many the group recalled the radical theater of the thirties, when political theater in this country had reached its apex. The Teatro was seen as something of a novelty, for it was obvious that these actor-singers were not professional but rather, *real* farmworkers. And they had left the fields to tell about their struggle with vitality, talent, and raw persuasion. Audiences were moved from coast to coast.

It was after that first national tour that the Teatro decided to leave Delano and the union. It was not an ideological difference that motivated the separation, but the need to become a full-time theater, unencumbered by the daily demands of a struggling labor union. Valdez had to ask himself if he could really accomplish his goals with a sometime troupe, or if the Teatro Campesino could become a major force in the wider spectrum of the burgeoning Chicano Movement. He knew that the majority of Mechicanos were not farmworkers, and he also knew that there were many more issues that needed to be expressed onstage. He wanted to grow, and his actors needed to expand their performance capabilities as well. The union kept them from achieving that goal.

In September of 1967 the Teatro Campesino left Delano and moved to the small rural community of Del Rey, 65 miles from the Chávez headquarters. It was still the Farmworker's Theater, and it would never abandon its rural roots as it began an odyssey that would eventually take it to a permanent home in San Juan Bautista, California. The first move was rather cautious, not too far away, but separated enough to give the Teatro a sense of being on its own. The group rented an old store-front, quickly converted it into a performance area, and began to offer classes in guitar and art, while also organizing teatro workshops that soon led to rehearsals and performances. No longer tied solely to the cause of the farmworker, the Teatro began searching for means of expressing some of the other issues confronted by the Mechicano. The third *acto* in its anthology reflects the group's search for identity and is a major statement about the problem of assimilation and acculturation. It is entitled, quite simply, *Los vendidos* (The Sellouts) and was created in 1967.[8]

Los vendidos has probably been produced by more teatros than any other *acto*. It is another definition of who and what the Mechicano should *not* be, and in its simple form and comic style it is a classic of the genre. All that is required of a setting is a large sign, placed to the side of the acting area, that reads "HONEST SANCHO'S USED MEXICAN LOT AND MEXICAN CURIO SHOP." When the *acto* opens, we find Honest Sancho busily dusting what appear to be three mannequins but are actually live actors, each dressed differently and identified by a sign hung around his neck. Moving from right to left we first see the "revolucionario," dressed to look like a revolutionary of the Pancho Villa era; center stage is a "pachuco," wearing the typical clothes of the street youth; and on the left we see a "farmworker" in humble clothes and ragged hat. Sancho's first lines are to the "dummies," as he energetically asks them: "*Bueno, bueno, mis monos, vamos a ver a quien vendemos ahora, ¿no?*" ("Well, well, my little dummies, let's see who we'll sell today, eh?") (p. 36). Upon completing this statement, he turns to the audience and addresses it directly. The signs have told us where and who the characters are, and Sancho's first dialogue illustrates his objective for us: sell a Mexican today.

We ask ourselves "How can you *sell* a Mexican?" But there is not much time to ponder this for Sancho goes on to explain to us that he used to be a farm-labor contractor but has managed to go into business for himself. Now we know. He has experience selling Mexicans, for that is what the contractor does. All he needs now is a customer. A bell rings offstage, and in comes a dark-skinned woman in business clothes, looking like a typical secretary. She greets this man who has sold Mexicans before with "Good Morning, I'm Miss *Jim*enez—" and before she can continue, Sancho says enthusiastically: "Ah, una Chicana! Welcome, welcome, Señorita Jiménez" (p. 36). She has introduced herself as JIM-enez (with Anglo-accented pronunciation), and he responds with the proper Spanish, in contrast to her acculturated dialect. For those in the audience who have not caught this social comment, Miss Jiménez corrects the proprietor, repeating her name and emphasizing the "Jim."

Here, in the person of this brown-faced woman, we confront our first sellout. Mechicano audiences who first hear her say her name might be a bit reticent about laughing, not knowing if this is the actress or the character, but as soon as they are shown that this is the teatro's statement, the laughter is released with knowing glee. Everybody has at least one *vendido* in the family, and here, onstage for all to see, is a living example of this well-known type. The Chicano audience recognizes Miss JIM-enez and waits to see what other characteristics she will display that are like cousin John or Aunt Clara. It is one thing to mispronounce the Spanish language if you are a Chicano, for most people know that Chicanos do not usually take formal training in the tongue. But to mispronounce your name and then emphasize the mispronunciation is another fault altogether. Miss JIM-enez has interested us, and we are eager to find out who and what she is.

Miss Jiménez tells Sancho that she has come to buy a Mexican because she works in the governor's office and they need a "brown face" for a luncheon. The governor mentioned is Ronald Reagan, and the reference to a token Mexican was as familiar in the late sixties as it is today. Now we know the problem: sell a Mexican/buy a Mexican. We wonder if this representative from Reagan's office will be satisfied with one of the three models on hand. When the secretary says she is looking for someone who will be hardworking, Sancho immediately takes her to the farmworker model. She examines this rather rustic-looking "dummy" with moderate interest and comments that he does look durable. Sancho has described this model as if he were describing a used car, and we realize that he is really that familiar face on late-night television trying to interest us in a 1975 Dodge. Yet this is what seems to be a real human being, and we are forced to realize that, in truth, we *can* be bought and sold and have been all our lives. This situation is not as ridiculous as it may seem, for the metaphor is revealed and we laugh at the concept, even as we realize its verity.

The comedy in this *acto* is perhaps what makes it so popular to perform and to see produced. As Sancho lists the characteristics of this farmworker, he is making a social comment on the exploitation of the *campesino* and reminding us of the stereotypes we might hold about the migrant worker. When Miss Jiménez asks if he is economical, Sancho assures her that he is "the Volkswagen of Mexicans," and we laugh at the allusion. The more he tells her, and us, about the farmworker, the more we realize that these people really are treated as machines, important only for the cheap labor they provide. When Sancho tells his customer that the farmworker does not speak English, she knows this is not her model. Besides, she was really looking for something "more sophisticated." "Sophisti-que?" Sancho asks, playing the "dumb Mexican," and she answers simply, "An urban model." Anyone who knows the barrios of the cities turns immediately to the central figure, the pachuco, anxious to see and hear what Sancho will tell us about this one as he directs her to Johnny Pachuco.

Los vendidos is the first *acto* collectively created by the Teatro Campesino that explores the character of the pachuco. This figure will reappear in later works as Valdez explores the enigmatic *vato loco*, as he is also termed. *Vato* means guy or dude in the vernacular of the streets, but "crazy dude" does not define the character as well as his own definition of himself: a *vato loco*, somehow making it through this *vida loca* (crazy life), though all odds are against him finding a way out. Johnny Pachuco is a generalization of the pachuco and must remain so within the context of this *acto* about generalizations. There cannot be a deep and searching study of a character in less than twenty minutes, for that is not the purpose of the *acto* form. We listen to see how Miss Jiménez will react to this "model."

Johnny, Sancho tells us, does everything necessary to survive in the city. He steals, carries a knife, dances, resists arrest, and makes an excellent scapegoat. We can lay the blame for all our ills on this one figure of the pachuco and rest assured that it is he who makes it difficult for other, decent Mexican Americans to succeed. These characteristics are not too pleasing to Miss Jiménez, but when Sancho offers her a chance to kick him, she reluctantly accepts and soon discovers what a pleasure it is. She begins to kick the model with such enthusiasm that she has to be pulled away by Sancho. Remembering that the major flaw with the farmworker was his inability to speak English, Sancho tells her that Johnny is bilingual. Johnny struts downstage a few paces, affecting the particular walk of the pachuco, and then suddenly stops, turns to the audience and delivers "Fuck you!" to their faces. Audiences love this surprise, but Miss Jiménez is aghast, which makes the comment even more humorous. In response to the secretary's shock, Sancho assures her that this language was "learned in your school" (p. 40). A later *acto* will explore the relationship between the pachuco and the educational system, but for the moment we can only pause and reflect on what Sancho has just said. So this is what the pachuco learns in school, remembering later the significance of the outburst.

Further descriptions of the pachuco from Sancho reveal the fact that he is economical, smokes marijuana, sniffs glue, and has an inferiority complex. When Johnny demonstrates how well he steals by grabbing Miss Jiménez' purse and running, she exclaims: "We can't have any *more* thieves in the State Administration" (p. 42), and the comment is complete. Just as we expected, this model does not please the exacting Miss Jiménez, and she asks to see another.

Groping for a stereotype, she asks for someone "more romantic," calling to mind the Latin lover mystique. The only model left on the floor is the *revolucionario*, pot belly and all, and we laugh as Sancho directs the customer to him.

Sancho and Miss Jiménez spend the least amount of time with this model, briefly reminding us that it can be seen in all sorts of Western movies and even in a television commercial. The model asks: "Is there a Frito Bandito in your house?"—a direct reference to the "Fritos" commercial that showed a cartoon "Bandito" invading homes to steal Fritos corn chips. When Sancho informs his customer that this model was made in Mexico, it is obvious that he will not do. "He has to be Mexican, but American," she insists, and is about to leave when Sancho tells her he has just what she wants in the back room. She agrees to wait, and is pleasantly surprised when Sancho leads his latest model, Eric García, into the shop. Eric is dressed in a business suit, wears horn-rimmed glasses, and boasts an American flag in his lapel. His sign reads: "Mexican-American." He is, in fact, the male counterpart to Miss Jiménez, and she is delighted. He is charming, speaks well, and will even eat Mexican food on "certain ceremonial occasions." When asked to give a political speech, Eric says just what the typical *vendido* says about the Mexican: "He's stupid" (p. 46).

Of course, this model is perfect for Miss Jiménez' purposes, and after reluctantly paying $15,000 for him, she snaps her fingers for him to follow her. Instead he goes berserk, yelling revolutionary slogans in Spanish. She does not understand the language and continues to try coaxing him out, until he turns to the other "models," bringing them to life, and they all confront her threateningly, causing her to run out in desperation. Once Miss Jiménez has left, the "models" stretch their arms and legs, tired of having stood there immobile for such a long time, and we notice that Sancho is now frozen in his place, the wad of money in his hand. Sancho, it turns out, is the real puppet, and the others are making money, "ripping off the man," by selling phony Mexicans. One of the models carries Sancho to the back room for an oil job, and they all leave for a party, the money being divided between them.

The surprise ending is a clever device, and the premise would be fine except that there is no purpose for the deception other than to earn these four young men some money. The problems exposed in this *acto*, unlike the earlier farmworker pieces, are not as easily solved. This *acto* is dealing with attitudes, presenting characteristics of the four types but focusing on the farmworker, pachuco, and sellout. We discover a little about how these people think, survive, and what their attitudes toward each other are. The character most exposed is the Mexican American, as personified by Eric and Miss Jiménez, and though there can be no quick or facile solutions to their syndrome, their attitudes are at least revealed. Members of the audience who share some of the sentiments of the Mexican American might reconsider what they feel and be a bit more sensitive to their Mechicano brothers and sisters. The *acto* is often produced by high school groups, and the young people often find themselves re-evaluating their attitudes about calling themselves Chicanos, Mexican Americans, or Mexicans after studying this simple statement.

When *Los vendidos* was videotaped by KNBC in Los Angeles for broadcast in 1973, Valdez altered the ending significantly. In the televised version, we discover that the operation is masterminded by a soft-spoken scientist (played by Valdez) whose models do go with their buyers and who are being placed in every major center of Mechicano population. One day soon, these "Mexican-Americans" will become Chicanos and defend the rights of their people rather than fight against them. This solution is much more interesting, and the symbolic "used Mexican lot" can be interpreted to mean an employment agency or perhaps the university, from whose halls a number of Chicanos are entering the work force.

Looking at the title again, we find that *Los vendidos* can also mean "those who have been sold." If we consider this literal translation of the title, we find that it applies to all of us, for there are few who can say they have not been bought or sold by somebody or something. The farmworker model has clearly been purchased by the growers and their henchmen; the pachuco is the perfect scapegoat for the police as well as for Mexican Americans, who find great pleasure in "kicking" him; the *revolucionario* has been purchased by Hollywood too many times; and the Eric Garcías of the community are numerous. Even Miss Jiménez, the supposed purchaser, has been bought and sold by the state government. Both of these Mexican Americans have been co-opted by their employers because as token Mexicans they do not cause any trouble and they give credence to the attitude that "anybody can make it." They thus rid themselves of any responsibility for the condition of other members of La Raza. The only reason Eric does not change his last name to Smith is that his skin color reveals his true identity; so he will, for the moment, ride the tide of tokenism, accepting a meaningless "face-in-the-crowd" position.

Through a fantastic situation, an allegory, *Los vendidos* makes its audiences stop and ask themselves if they have been bought too. During an early performance of this *acto* in Del Rey, a man in the audience called Valdez out and asked: "What are you insulting me for?" Valdez saw that the man was drunk and was also carrying a knife, and he replied: "What, it's just a skit about a sell-out Mexican-American." "Well, I'm not a sell-out," the man insisted. Valdez quickly assured him: "Well, shit, we didn't even say it was you."[9] Perhaps the man in question was not a sellout, but his response indicates that he was genuinely affected by the *acto* and may have found the characters of Miss Jiménez and Eric too close for comfort. Valdez avoided possible violence, forcing the man to question his own motives, when he told him that this *acto* could apply to anybody, not necessarily to him. After that, it was the man's responsibility to reassess his attitudes and take a closer look at the real-life counterparts to the *acto*'s "models."

Los vendidos does not offer ready-made solutions like the previous worker's *actos* discussed in Chapter One. By placing recognizable stereotypes on the stage and telling the audience a little about each one, this *acto* simply suggests the possibility of change. Certainly, attitudes can change, but there is also the feeling here that the farmworker's situation can improve, that the pachuco might be better understood and helped to cope with his particular problems, and that the media might be forced to abandon the negative stereotypes of the Mexican. In fact, the television "Frito Bandito" commercial was eventually discontinued due to pressure from Chicanos actively opposing the negative stereotype—evidence that change, however slow, *is* possible. The revised version of the *acto* relied on the transformation of the many "Mexican-American models" that were being placed throughout the nation to bring about the changes necessary to improve the Chicano's condition, thus indicating that their transformation would spur society's. This is a much more effective ending than the original and points out the major flaw in the *acto*'s initial rendering.

When *Los vendidos* was produced by El Teatro de la Esperanza in 1971, the group noted the politically weak ending and altered it slightly by having the youths decide that the money they had just received would be used to build a community center. The troupe felt that even though the *acto* was fantastic, its basis in truth demanded more than a mere party as its conclusion. Because the *acto* is critical of Chicanos rather than Anglos, some audience members felt that *Los vendidos* should not be presented for non-Chicanos and should remain instead a sort of "in-house" *acto* that did not need public exposure. It was acceptable for Chicanos to laugh at the foibles of their own kind, they felt, but they did not like to see others enjoying the racial humor. Since the majority of those who witnessed the Santa Barbara troupe were Chicanos, the group did not attempt to keep anybody out of the auditorium. They were interested, however, in the response of the real *vatos* in the audience when Johnny Pachuco came forward and were relieved to find that the street youths were delighted. One young man even offered to assist the actor playing the pachuco in affecting the walk peculiar to his type. "It's OK the way you do it," he said by way of preface, "but it should be like *this*." Both the actor and the young man from the audience enjoyed working together to improve the characterization.

Los vendidos demonstrated to Valdez and his troupe that Chicanos like to see themselves reflected onstage, even if critically exposed. They also learned that the "Mexican Americans" were seldom in the audience to see themselves presented, for their politics kept them away from Chicano rallies and other functions that were the settings for teatro performances. With the passing of the years this *acto* would reach thousands of people, and the response would always be positive, for it was based on Valdez' keen sense of his people's characteristics and his wonderful comic vision. The sellout type would return to strut on Valdez' stage, as well as in other playwrights' and teatros' visions, reminding their audiences that the Mr. Sunday, Eric García, and Miss Jiménez type is never too far removed.

Is There No Choice?—*La víctima*

El Teatro de la Esperanza began in 1969 as a student group at the University of California at Santa Barbara, under the name of Teatro Mecha. The original teatro was a committee of the student organization known as M.E.Ch.A., which is the acronym for *Movimiento Estudiantil Chicano de Aztlán* (Chicano Student Movement of Aztlán); it had chapters throughout California and in other parts of the Southwest. The present author went to Santa Barbara to direct Teatro Mecha in the fall of 1970. When it became apparent that the student organization intended to keep a tight rein on the Teatro, the director and six of the members formed Teatro de la Esperanza in June of 1971. The separation was not a difficult choice to make, for it was a question of either continuing with campus politics or choosing community involvement through a Chicano center—then in its infancy—called La Casa de la Raza, located in the Santa Barbara barrio. La Casa de la Raza offered the newly formed troupe autonomy and performance space, thereby giving the students from the university a place in the community that they could call their own. The alliance proved fruitful to both organizations, and the Teatro is still a very important component of what has become one of the outstanding Chicano community centers in the Southwest.

The first summer in La Casa, the Teatro mounted a production consisting of three *actos* by the Teatro Campesino: *La quinta temporada, The Militants*,[10] and *Los vendidos*. These *actos*, which had proven very popular on the campus, were equally successful in the Teatro's new little theater. Audiences loved the satire of each piece and were impressed by the messages conveyed. The group's first summer in the Casa led to a succession of performances and workshops over the years as the Teatro mingled "Town and Gown," functioning as a student group but based in the community. After tours of the surrounding areas, the Teatro next produced three original scripts that had been written by the director's students at the university. The following year, another bill of *actos* and plays was presented by the Teatro as it developed its own themes and forms. The most popular of these works were published by the group in 1973 in the second anthology of its kind, one following in the tradition of the Teatro Campesino's first collection.[11]

In January 1974, the Teatro began an investigation of a neighboring town that had been the subject of a report to the U.S. Commission on Civil Rights. The result of the investigation became the Teatro's first docudrama, *Guadalupe*, which premiered in May of that year. This effort, to be discussed in Chapter Four, was the product of interviews, research, and improvisations; these led to a production consisting of thirteen scenes connected by musical narration and introductory statements that made sociopolitical comments on the action. With the success of *Guadalupe*, the director and his wife, who was the business manager and musical director, chose to leave the group, confident that the members were prepared to continue without them. The Santa Barbara troupe had gained a strong reputation with *Guadalupe*, and a core number of members who had graduated in 1974 was eager to concentrate on Teatro activities.

At this juncture the Teatro decided to direct itself collectively. Four of the remaining eight members had earned their bachelor's degrees in drama and the others had worked with the group for at least two years, gaining a certain amount of training under the original directors. Two of the drama majors, José Saucedo and Joey

García, were selected to handle the overall administration of the Teatro, but all agreed that artistic direction would be a group process. When García left the troupe in the fall of 1975, the members voted to become totally collective, making all decisions as a group. This was not an easy task, and members later confided that it would have been much easier to let one person make the majority of decisions. Nevertheless, the group learned a great deal about itself and its ability to survive no matter how great the personal conflicts. Together, the members decided to expand the documentary technique and based their next collective creation, *La víctima*, on a fictional family and its evolution. The fictitious plot is underscored by documented facts about the mass deportations of Mexicans from this country that began in the early 1920s.

The group chose the theme of deportation because of the "illegal alien scare" that was then permeating the media and because of the concurrent deportation of thousands of undocumented workers, who were being blamed for the ills of the economy. The Teatro's goal was to demonstrate its belief that the mass repatriations were political maneuvers and that a curtain of misrepresentations had made a scapegoat out of the Mexican. The group's research began with an analysis of Franz Fanon's *The Wretched of the Earth*[12] and Albert Memmi's *The Colonizer and the Colonized*,[13] both of which speak of an internal colonialism that the Teatro felt was relevant to the Chicano experience.[14] "We're trying to show the Chicano public that they are scapegoats for capitalism," the members told this author in 1976, reflecting a Marxist analysis of Chicano history, which the group had begun to study.

After reading Fanon and Memmi, the Teatro divided itself into study groups, each group focusing on a particular period in the history of the Mechicano since the Mexican-American War. They found that the mass repatriations of Mexicans coincided with the economic recessions in this country beginning in the 1920s. "Why not focus on a particular family from the time it first comes to the U.S.?" a member suggested, and the group agreed to follow a family through three generations in order to show its audiences the particular form of discrimination the Mexican has inherited. Each member was assigned a certain number of scenes to script, based on improvisations the group had experimented with in daily sessions. After several weeks of discussion, improvisation, scripting, and more discussion and changes, *La víctima* had its premiere at the University of California at San Diego on Cinco de Mayo (May 5—the date commemorating the struggle against the French-imposed rule of

Emperor Maximilian), 1976. Though the creation was still a work-in-progress, the audience that night was totally enthralled. The story was clear, the characters well-defined, and the impact of the final scene was momentous. After the initial success of *La víctima*, the troupe continued to rework the piece, responding to audience suggestions and to their own sense of artistic integrity. The structure remained the same, but the group altered scenes within the play to clarify issues or objectives that were not intelligible to the spectators. The Teatro toured *La víctima* throughout he Southwest in 1977 and performed the piece in Manhattan in 1978 on its way to international theater festivals in Poland, Yugoslavia and Sweden.

Continuing the practice established in *Guadalupe*, the actors in *La víctima* never left the stage, sitting at the sides of the acting area like members of a team watching their teammates in action. Six of the eight actors played at least two characters each, and minimal costume or property changes were used to distinguish one character from another. The actors playing the two central characters did not take any other roles. The performers donned another hat or shirt to denote a change of character or another historical period while sitting on the sidelines, thus becoming demonstrators who never disappeared from the audience's view and eliminating any sense of "theatrical magic" or suspense. These changes were not distracting because the audience's attention was well focused on the action of each scene. The production was designed to tour theaters or lecture halls, and therefore the setting was minimal, with chairs and benches serving a number of purposes. A simple folding table functioned as a desk or a kitchen table, depending on the scene in which it was used. Because the actors did not leave the stage, a backdrop was not necessary, and the production was usually played in front of a bare wall or whatever nondescript curtains were available. The group purposely directed the audience's attention to the acting area and to the characters involved in the action.

The action of *La víctima* runs continuously, without intermission, and lasts ninety minutes. Although there are no act breaks during performance, the Teatro divided the script into five acts and fifteen scenes. Each scene is preceded by a "quote" or comment delivered from both sides of the acting area in Spanish and English. Placards labelling the scenes are also placed at the side, emphasizing the documentary format. These comments frame the action of the following scene, giving the group's political analysis of what is to happen or suggesting reasons for the actions taken by the characters. A comment such as "President Hoover promises to rid the country of Mexicans" illustrates the temper of the period and reveals some of the attitudes displayed publicly by politicians and the media. Following the tradition begun by the Teatro Campesino and its use of the *corrido* technique, the separate scenes are often introduced by a musical narration that moves the action forward, explaining the passing of time or a change of setting. The group wrote new lyrics to popular *corridos*; this served to draw attention to the narration as those familiar with the tunes listened to the new words.

Because much of the action takes place in Mexico or within a family that would speak mostly Spanish even in this country, the group chose to present *La víctima* mainly in Spanish. This deliberate choice was necessary to achieve a certain amount of verisimilitude, but, as a result, those in the audience who were not totally bilingual could not grasp the full meaning of the piece. Even the musical narration was sung in Spanish because the *corrido* style does not adapt well to translation. "We tried translating some of the lyrics," said a member of the troupe, "but it just didn't work. It sounded stilted and forced." The group hoped that the bilingual comments preceding each scene would help clarify the action, but these were not sufficient. Unlike the *acto*, whose physical action clearly defines what is happening onstage, *La víctima* depends on the dialogue, and both the monolingual Spanish and English-speaking auditors felt neglected.

La víctima moves swiftly from scene to scene as it follows Amparo Villa from her first crossing to this country during the 1910 Revolution to the present. The focus of the piece is on Amparo and her son Samuel, who is lost at the train station during a mass repatriation and who grows up in the United States in an adoptive family. Amparo represents Samuel's national heritage, which he is forced to deny when he becomes an officer for the Immigration and Naturalization Service. Neither of these central characters is an *acto* stereotype, for their personalities are well defined by scenes that illustrate their psychological motivations. We get to know these people well and can relate to them as human beings who are caught in a complex set of circumstances.

After setting their props and costumes in place, visiting with members of the audience, and generally being themselves rather than "actors," the demonstrators gather at the center of the stage for the Prologue. The three shawled women kneel in a semicircle and recite the words of the prologue in Spanish, as if saying a rosary, while the men stand at the sides and deliver the same words in English so that all in the audience can understand them:

El Chicano es una víctima	The Chicano is a victim
de una sutil y compleja	of a subtle and complex
forma de opresión,	form of oppression,
que se distingue de	which differs from
formas tradicionales,	traditional forms,
pero que resulta en	yet results in the
lo mismo: La explotación	same end: The exploitation
de un grupo, para el	of one group, for the
beneficio de otro.	benefit of another.[15]

Each line is delivered first in Spanish, then in English, in rhythm to the rosary-like chanting of the women; all of the actors complete the last line of the Prologue in unison and then declare: "*El Teatro de la Esperanza presenta La víctima.*" A guitarist at the side begins to strum the music to "*El Corrido de Rosita Alvirez*" as actors either join him at the side, sit down, or form the opening tableau of Amparo's family waiting for the train.

The musical narration informs the audience that it is about to see the story of what happened to the poor who fled Mexico in 1913. After the song, the "quote" explains that during the Mexican Revolution over 370,000 Mexicans were admitted legally into the United States and that, combined with illegal entries, Mexicans entering during this period totalled over 750,000 people. Once the narration has been delivered in both languages, the tableau comes to life and we meet Amparo's family, huddled in the desert darkness while waiting for the train to the north. Amparo is the youngest of this family's children, and she tearfully waves goodbye to her home as the train approaches. It is a tender scene that demonstrates the difficult decision the family had to make in beginning its search for a peaceful existence far from civil war and daily uncertainties.

While the first scene is totally in Spanish, the second takes place in 1920, when Amparo has become a young lady and has acquired some English. The setting is a community dance, and we meet Amparo's friend Lupita, who is attempting to sound "American" by affecting a mixture of Spanish and English. When Amparo asks Lupita if she looks good, Lupita answers: "In my opinion, *es que todo está en su* right place" (". . . everything's in its right place"). Dressed like flappers of the era, the girls' language and behavior draws amused laughter from the audience, for they reflect today's linguistic patterns in the barrio as well as that of the past. By portraying the girls as "flappers," the characters are placed in a context that reminds the audience that the Mexican has a historical presence in this country.

The first two scenes demonstrate the conventions and structure of the ensuing play, spanning years within a single narrative song and methodically pointing out the evolution of the major figures, Amparo and Samuel. As the first scenes progress, we find that Amparo has married Juan, who works for the railroad. They have a son, Samuel, and she is expecting a second child when Juan loses his job and decides to take his family back to Mexico. After the birth, Amparo is seen at the train station, where she gets separated from Samuel as the train slowly pulls away. Guitar strums and a train whistle represent the imaginary train Amparo is standing on, searching for her son, who is at the opposite side of the stage. She shouts "¡Mijo!" ("My son") as he cries "¡Mamá!" and everyone freezes an impressive tableau that captures the pathos of the moment and leaves the audience stunned.

Once the mother and son have been separated, the plot line assumes a dual pattern, focusing on each of them separately in order to demonstrate the developments in their lives. Sam grows up and proposes to his girlfriend Clara on the eve of his recruitment into the Army, bound for Korea. Once again, another historical period is recaptured, with these two Chicano youths from the fifties going through the post-adolescent motions of courting. Both Sam and Clara are likeable characters, eager to start a life of their own upon his return. In basic training, Sam learns to "kill the communists" as his sergeant indoctrinates him with a patriotic fervor that will manifest itself in his later profession.

The final scenes in the play take place several years after Sam and Clara have married, and we find him well established in his position as an officer of the INS. Their only child, Janie, is a college student who does not like what her father does for a living. The development of Sam's character, of his employment, and of his family circle is paralleled by the evolutions in Amparo's family in Mexico. Amparo's other two children, Antonia and Meño, have come to the United States to work, and when their father passes away, they smuggle their mother back into this country. She has never forgotten the trauma of losing her son at the train station and returns reluctantly to the country that "stole my first-born child." There is a strike at the factory where Antonia and Meño work and Amparo joins her children on the picket line. The INS conducts a raid on the factory, and all the Mexicans, including Amparo, are arrested.

Sam is responsible for the factory raid and finds himself interrogating Amparo, who tells him that the same forces he now works for separated her from her child many years ago, "when you were still a boy." Though she never calls Sam her son, there is the distinct feeling that she knows who he is. The coincidence is too much for him and he orders her removed from his sight. The final scene follows quickly after the traumatic moment in which Sam refuses to acknowledge his mother. He and his wife are in bed, and he awakens in a sweat, calling out "I hate you!" to the image of Amparo at the opposite side of the stage. He suffers a mixture of guilt and hatred for his decision, as his wife attempts to comfort him and Amparo recites the words to a folksong she had taught him as a child:

Cuando lejos te encuentres de mí;	When you find yourself far from me;
Cuando quieras que esté yo contigo;	When you want me to be by your side;
Piensas en todo el amor que te di;	Think of all the love that I gave you;
Y dirás que esté yo contigo.	And you'll say that I'm here yet beside you.

The actors freeze for a moment, Sam on the floor at his wife's feet, looking very much as he did when he was left on the train platform, and his mother staring straight ahead, a look of deep sorrow on her face. The guitars begin to strum, and the actor/demonstrators gather for the closing song, which reminds the audience that the struggle still continues and will only be successful if they recognize the conditions that perpetrate these injustices. The focus of the message is on Sam, who serves as an example of what can happen to anyone.

Sam has become more than the *vendido* represented in so many *actos*; he is a man who breathes and talks and suffers for his choices. His dedication to his employment is like his military indoctrination, and he can see no other way to combat the "illegal alien problem" than he could the "communist threat" he fought against in Korea. He sincerely believes in what he is doing and demonstrates those human qualities that make us pause and reflect on what he must be going through. When he shouts "Mamá" at the close of the play, he demonstrates his need for the identity he had forgotten until the incident in the interrogation. Sitting upright in her chair, his mother asked him why he did this sort of work, questioning his motives as they had never been before, and when she reminded him of his separation from his mother so many years ago, he could take no more and ordered her return to Mexico.

La víctima is moving because of the characters presented and the situations that unfold about them. The dual plot line comes together in a manner that is highly improbable, yet not impossible:

these are the extraordinary circumstances that make a drama larger than life. When asked why Sam could not recognize his mother and keep her with him, the Teatro members explained that they felt a "happy ending" would shatter the dramatic effect of the present conclusion. "He has to send her away," a member told this author, "because she represents all that he has attempted to deny throughout his career with the INS." In becoming an officer of the INS, Sam becomes a "Migra," the colloquialism used to identify these agents by the community that despises them so much. Readily recognizable in any barrio, the image of the Migra immediately arouses hatred and suspicion, for Chicanos and Mexicans know all too well the humiliation of being confronted on the streets or in their homes and asked for their papers.

Perhaps because he is so human, Sam arouses both the ire and the sympathy of the audience. Certainly, few can forgive him his ultimate act of rejection toward his mother, even though he is not certain that she really is his mother. Amparo's knowledge of the man's youth is too accurate for coincidence, though Sam chooses to believe that she cannot be the woman who bore him. It is that very choice that illustrates the character's human weakness and the extremes that his profession demands of him. If Sam can deport his own mother, no one is safe from his rejection. To the audience, it is one thing to be an Anglo Migra—that is expected—but to be a Chicano caught up by the rhetoric of the period is unforgivable.

Sam's daughter Janie represents the only hope for the future in this work, for it is she who has gained a social conscience and is actively involved in campus and community politics. Even though her father has been symbolically bought by his profession, Janie may become an effective activist when she graduates from college and helps lead the struggle for social justice. Clara is caught between her love for her husband and a certain amount of sensitivity about what he does—her subconscious awareness that his work is loathsome. In the original version Clara was painted as a social climber who encouraged her husband not to regret his actions. She was a cold, calculating woman whose character aroused no sympathies and whose influence over her repentant husband made him seem extremely weak and ineffective. By becoming more sympathetic to her daughter's objections while still struggling with the fact of her husband's job, Clara provides a needed contrast to both her husband and her daughter. Like so many wives and mothers, she is caught in the middle.

Curiously, both Antonia and Janie were played by the same

actress, underscoring the role of the activist woman in both families. The women work for social justice and are actively involved; the men have to be pushed. Meño finally joins the picket line, and he is undoubtedly deported along with his mother, for he has crossed illegally. In contrast, Antonia, who was born in the United States, is a citizen and remains. Though there is no attention drawn to this fact, a Mechicano audience knows very well how the system of deportations has separated families because of technicalities of birth. The Teatro chose not to comment any further upon the fates of Sam's brother and sister, focusing instead on his central counterpart, Amparo.

La víctima represents a rather unique development in Chicano theater, for it is one of the more successful creations to have come from a group process. Written and directed by the Teatro members, this work reflected the troupe's artistic discipline in performance and impressed many observers as a major achievement. A long-time activist and critic, Raúl Ruiz, witnessed *La víctima* during the Eighth Annual Chicano Theater Festival in 1977 and commented that only once before had he seen a festival audience respond as enthusiastically as it did that night: during the Teatro's presentation of *Guadalupe* in 1975. "Sam makes us all uncomfortable," wrote Ruiz, "not because we are all INS agents, but because he is so much like all of us as a son and father."[16] Ruiz was most pleased with the acting, which he felt was "superb," and with the serious nature of the work. Reacting to the many other teatros he had witnessed, Mr. Ruiz exulted: "We finally have a plot," referring to other efforts that have gotten lost in "stilted postulations of political rhetoric."

In Poland and Yugoslavia, *La víctima* could not be very well understood by audiences who spoke neither English nor Spanish. The introductory quotes were translated into the languages of each country, and translations of the lyrics were also included, but for most audiences this was insufficient. One Polish critic was impressed by the group's creation and felt that it "was firmly rooted in their own reality and smacked of truth."[17] A Spanish critic who saw the production at the Belgrade International Theatre Festival commented that the group's collective work combined aesthetic and didactic processes and did not ignore the fact that its audiences were "de corta formación intelectual" (of a limited intellectual formation).[18] The reviewer was notably impressed with the Teatro's craftsmanship and commended its political purpose.

During the European tour of 1978 the Teatro found its most enthusiastic audiences in Sweden. "They all speak and understand

English," José Saucedo commented to this writer, "and they were fascinated by the bilinguality and the politics." After having performed in the two Slavic countries with varying degrees of success, the Teatro members were relieved to discover that the Swedes could understand English and set about translating as much as they could to accommodate their audiences. Exiled Latin Americans in that country also found their way to the Teatro's performances and were thrilled to find that this group of Chicanos was expressing itself in their language. "After experiencing audiences that didn't understand anything besides the plot-line that had been translated for them," Estella Campos confided, "it was wonderful to hear responses from the auditorium."

El Teatro de la Esperanza became the second Chicano theater group to cross the Atlantic, following closely after the Teatro Campesino's third tour to the Continent. The Valdez troupe had performed *actos, corridos*, and the spectacular *Gran carpa de los rasquachis* in several European countries, and it was time for another teatro to demonstrate its own style and content. Wherever either group performed, it became a cultural and political ambassador for Chicanos, and the members were surprised to discover how much interest there was in their culture and its problems in the United States. Many Europeans had read about the continual influx of Mexicans to the United States, and *La víctima* revealed the politics behind the repatriations that the State Department would have preferred ignored.

The progression from *The Shrunken Head of Pancho Villa* to *La víctima* is a reflection of the continuing search by Chicano playwrights and teatros for themes and forms that effectively speak of the Chicano experience. Valdez' play is significant for its use of surrealistic elements within a realistic structure, and it remains one of the few Chicano plays to explore this form. The Teatro Campesino's *acto* is a classic of the genre, demonstrating a technique that does not require years of training to perform successfully even though it is the product of a collective creative genius. Teatro de la Esperanza's contribution is important for its uniqueness, standing out as a singular example of the documentary form. All of these works are the products of a thorough understanding of theater, which is imperative for a creation to have an impact on its audience.

La víctima represents Teatro de la Esperanza's attempt to "demystify" the theatrical experience, to eliminate the feeling that the actions being portrayed are happening as if behind a fourth wall. The presentational style and the lack of symbolism are concerted efforts to leave the audience with a clearly defined message. Although the Teatro discovered that its audiences could not be deterred from getting emotionally involved in certain scenes, it fought against any possible compacency by freezing the action and inserting a comment and by structuring the work in episodes, constantly reminding the audience that it was in a theater.[19] Both the actor playing Sam and the actress playing Amparo portrayed only those characters, from childhood onward. This use of adults in children's roles exemplified the Teatro's attitude that the actors were really *demonstrating* their characters. The audience accepted a full-grown man portraying a five-year-old Sammy because of the nature of the presentation. The actor played the child as if he really were that little boy, confused by the disappearance of his friends, and the humor in his innocence was magnified by the straightforward characterization. "This is how it was," the Teatro tells its audience, and the people look and listen.

Of the three productions in this chapter, *The Shrunken Head of Pancho Villa* requires the most technical support. From the setting to the costumes, makeup, lighting, and sound effects, Valdez' play reflects the student's typical fascination with all the paraphernalia of the theater. Belarmino's head is a designer's challenge, as are the cockroach-covered walls and the headless Joaquín. In his surreal vision, the young playwright called for all the magic of the theater and employed it well for his purposes while avoiding a flamboyance that could have been distracting. Valdez' first full-length play is representative of his fascination with spectacle, for each of his works calls for a certain amount of theatricality, leading up to the spectacle of *Zoot Suit*.

There is one element of spectacle common to both the Valdez and Esperanza scripts that never appears, yet has an influence upon the action of each: the train and its tracks. Early in *The Shrunken Head of Pancho Villa* we learn that the family lives close to the railroad tracks, and we accept this as a true reflection of reality, for most barrios can be found close to and "on the wrong side of" the tracks. To Pedro, the father, the train is reminiscent of the revolutionaries clamoring to go to the front with their leader, Pancho Villa, and represents his dream of fighting for a peace that he never found in this country. The train becomes the symbol of his escape, and when he is crushed by this mechanical monster it becomes his executioner as well. Pedro's train ride leads only to the afterlife.

The first scene of *La víctima* takes place at the side of the tracks, with the father telling his son to put his ear to the ground and listen for the coming train that will take them to their supposed freedom.

The train approaches, and the family rushes to stop it with their lanterns; they are frozen for an instant as the scene comes to an end, capturing these people with their hearts so full of hope. When Amparo becomes a young lady, the men around her talk about working for the railroad, and when we find her married, it is the railroad company that has dismissed her husband, forcing them to return to Mexico. Pedro's vision of people jumping on the revolutionary train (in Valdez' script) contrasts with the scene in *La víctima* that so vividly presents the mother's separation from her child as the train slowly pulls away. Frozen on a bench that elevates her above the others as if she were on a train, Amparo's ride delivers her to never-ending torments.

The use of train whistles and the rhythmic sounds of a train passing, while never actually attempting to re-create that train onstage, demonstrate the power of the audience's imagination. Each of the three works in question relies on the audience's willingness to accept certain conventions and become a part of the creative process along with the actors. Audiences accept Belarmino's grunting, belching head and try to relate it to what they see within the walls of Cruz's home and what they imagine to be in the playwright's mind. When Honest Sancho tells his public that he is about to sell a Mexican, the public laughs and watches carefully to see how this is done. When asked to believe that a train whistle on an empty stage can represent a family's escape from revolutionary Mexico, the audience accepts and travels through three generations willingly, unconcerned that two stacked benches do not really resemble the cab of a truck or that a 25-year-old-man is portraying a five-year-old boy.

The focus in each of these pieces is on the characters and their actions, and because they are created with a determined sense of who and what they represent, the audiences can believe in them, watch them grow, follow their changes, and leave the presentation with a sense of having participated in more than an evening of theater. Though each of the works invites the audience to fill in where the script has left some room for expansion, the *acto* depends most heavily on the auditors' ability to add their own observations. Each of the types represented in *Los vendidos* has its counterpart in every auditorium, and Mechicano audiences delight in seeing themselves re-created onstage, even if the treatment is critical. "You know," said someone to a member of the Teatro de la Esperanza, "I have a brother who is an immigration officer. I wish he could see this *obra* (work)." To which the actress could only reply, "We do too." It is the hope of the creators of each of these dramatic efforts that as many people as possible can see their work, especially the *vendidos*.

El Teatro Campesino performing *Los vendidos*, c. 1967; shown
is Luis Valdez as "Sancho." *Photo: Teatro Campesino*

Chapter Three

THE CHICANO IN WAR
AT HOME AND ABROAD

Remember the Alamo!

It is the summer of 1975, on the closing day of the Sixth National Chicano Theater Festival, as tourists gather around a local Chicano theater group on the steps of the legendary Alamo, curiously awaiting their performance. Most have come to this historic site not to witness a theater group, but to relive a moment in history that has been converted to legend by historians and Hollywood. The shout, "Remember the Alamo!" means a battle lost but a war gained and the beginning of Anglo-American domination over the Southwest. This is where Travis, Bowie, and Crockett met their deaths, and to most of the people entering the aged structure, these men were true American heroes. But to the Teatro de los Barrios, San Antonio's Chicano theater collective which was formed in 1970, the Alamo represents another falsification of the truth. The group's play, *El Alamo: Our version of what happened*, was written by Héctor González, a member of the troupe, and it premiered in 1973. Based on a historical event, *El Alamo* is still an important theatrical statement whose message is not diminished by time. It recalls the circumstances that enabled the United States to annex the entire Southwest and reminds Mechicanos that they have been involved in many battles for their homeland and their freedom.

Long before the Battle of the Alamo, the Mechicano's ancestors were fighting for other causes and creating theatrical pieces that dramatized historic battles and victorious coups. The New Mexicans, whose heritage of religious theater has been well documented by historians, also promoted a secular theater that was designed to demonstrate their superiority over any foes. *Los comanches* dramatized the Spanish defeat of the Comanches around 1777-79 and was performed on horseback,[1] undoubtedly influenced by another popular equestrian spectacle, *Los moros y los cristianos*. The latter work dramatized the Spanish expulsion of the Moors and was one of the first Spanish dramas to be performed in the New World.[2] Like its predecessor, *Los comanches* glorifies the Spaniards and paints a very negative picture of the enemy.

Another New Mexican drama with a military theme is entitled *Los tejanos* (The Texans). It was also written to present the New Mexicans as superior to their foes—in this case the Texans. Written between 1841 and 1846, *Los tejanos* tells of the New Mexican defeat of a Texan expedition to New Mexico in 1841.[3] This play, which portrays the Texans as ignorant racists whose only motivation is their hunger for wealth and power, curiously foreshadows by several generations the *actos* of the current Chicano repertoire. The leader of the Texans, General McLeod, tries to bribe an Andalusian with the promise that, "you will be taken to Texas at my expense and there we will get you a job with a good salary." This line has found its way into many an *acto* portraying a wealthy grower or manufacturer dangling visions of economic grandeur before the eyes of hungry immigrants. Because the New Mexicans had created an insular community of their own, even the Mexicans are portrayed as inferior in this script, and of course the New Mexicans win the day.

Los tejanos and *Los comanches* are the only surviving New Mexican manuscripts from what might be termed the Mechicano's Theater of War before the present century. Present-day historians have uncovered records of Mexican travelling troupes that performed plays based on historic Mexican battles and toured with these productions to cities in the Southwest during the late 1800s and early 1900s.[4] Thus, San Antonio's Teatro de los Barrios had its precedents when the members decided to dramatize a battle that meant so much to them. To the Teatro, and to many other Chicanos, the Alamo represents the beginning of Anglo racism and discrimination against the Mechicano. The legends that arose from that battle fostered an attitude that Mexicans were cowards, drunks, liars, and thieves, while the superior Anglos were brave soldiers who fought to the end. In the words of Rodolfo Acuña, noted Chicano historian, "This stereotyping . . . served as a rationalization for later aggression against Mexico and the Anglo's mistreatment of the Chicano. It is also significant," Acuña continues, "that the Spanish-surnamed 'defenders' within the Alamo conspicuously have been omitted from the roll call of Texas heroes."[5]

El Alamo is written in a format that allows ten actors to portray
different personages.[6] The dialogue is a kind of choral poetry in
which the actors recite the narration either in unison, in pairs, or
in any number of combinations as they jump in and out of characters
and situations that elaborate their version of what happened at the
Alamo in 1836. When not in the action, the actors, who are dressed
in identical dark shirts and pants, stand at the rear of the acting
area with their backs to the audience. The script takes less than
twenty minutes to perform and is thus unbroken in its flow from start
to finish. Without sets, free of props and expensive accoutrements
that could have been a part of such a spectacle, the actors simply portray moments in the lives of the Anglo-Americans who became im-
mortalized in that famous battle in order to demonstrate what most
history books have chosen to ignore about the "heroes" and their
motives.

El Alamo is an indictment of the doctrine of Manifest Destiny
and compares expansionist theory to imperialism as it has been
practiced throughout the centuries. Focusing on the Anglo takeover
of Texas, the Teatro's position is that both the theory of Manifest
Destiny and the men who died for its achievement represented the
interests of robbers, assassins, liars, and politicians. The play presents James Bowie as an entrepreneur who had sold slaves and dealt
in land swindles before going to Texas in search of silver mines. Davy
Crockett is portrayed as an Indian-hater who killed natives for sport;
William Travis is shown to have abandoned his wife and children,
allowing a slave to be convicted of killing a man whom he himself
had shot. The Mexicans are shown to be unprepared and ill-equipped
against superior weapons, yet they are victorious until a few days
later, when Sam Houston's forces ensure the independence of Texas.

Through narrative and brief dialogues between the major figures
in the story, Teatro de los Barrios presented what it felt was Truth
as opposed to the fiction that had been created around their local
landmark. Possibly because most of the dialogue was in Spanish,
some observers lost interest and went inside the adobe walls that
afternoon in 1975, but there were those who stayed behind to see for
themselves what this street theater was trying to say. For many the
information presented was new; the media had successfully constructed such inviolable myths around the Anglo-Americans that
their lurid pasts or evil deeds had effectively been erased from mem-
ory. But for most Mechicano audiences, *El Alamo* represented the
growing awareness that their people were and are brave soldiers
and just as willing to die for honorable causes as the Hollywood

heroes. This was an even more important message in 1975, when the wounds from the latest war were very close to barrio realities, as Vietnam veterans searched for a place in the society for which they had fought. Between the time of the Alamo and Southeast Asia, the Chicano had participated in two World Wars and several "conflicts," but none had prompted the reaction of the activists like Vietnam. To politicized Chicanos, the war in Southeast Asia was an unjust cause, and their theater attempted to define the reasons why.

While the early New Mexican scripts and the more recent *El Alamo* dramatized victorious battles, the works discussed in this chapter focus on the war in Vietnam and its effect on La Raza and on the individual soldier who is the ultimate victim. *Vietnam campesino* is a typical *acto* that exposes some of the machinations behind the war and demonstrates that the *campesinos* in the United States are no different from the peasants in Southeast Asia. While this *acto* gives a broad picture of the effects of the war on both sides of the Pacific, the next, *Soldado razo*, focuses on the death of a Chicano soldier. These two *actos* by the Teatro Campesino lead naturally to a play by Luis Valdez entitled *Dark Root of a Scream*. Valdez' play focuses even more sharply on an individual victim of the war and tells its audience about the soldier who did not have to die. These three poignant statements about the horrors of the war and the unnecessary deaths are contrasted with the final play to be discussed, *Manolo*, by Rubén Sierra. Sierra's play follows a Chicano veteran who returns to his barrio alive, but whose addiction to heroin makes his survival of the war meaningless.

From satire to pathos, each of the theatrical statements in this chapter was born of a desire to stop the war when it was happening and the need to remind the audience that the battles may have ended, but the struggle continues.

Chicanos and the War in Vietnam: *Vietnam campesino*

On August 29, 1970, thousands of Chicanos marched in East Los Angeles to protest the war in Vietnam and the disproportionate number of Chicanos who were dying in that distant conflict.[7] The National Chicano Moratorium was the largest demonstration of anti-war sentiment in the Chicano community and brought thousands of people onto the streets to express their discontent. This was a war that few people understood, and when the people rallied together it seemed that here, at last, was an issue which would unite

La Raza. Unfortunately, the Los Angeles County Sheriff's Department was ready for violence at home, and the riot squad successfully turned the demonstration into a tear gas and rock-throwing melee that left several people wounded and jailed and transformed a *Los Angeles Times* newspaper reporter, Rubén Salazar, into a Chicano martyr. The rest, of course, is history. The people there blamed the officers, the officers blamed the people, but one fact was irrevocable: Chicanos were not being fooled about the war anymore.[8]

Luis Valdez had long been an opponent of the war in Vietnam, and both his personal politics and the growing opposition to the war led to the creation of two important *actos: Vietnam campesino* in 1970 and *Soldado razo* (Buck Private) in 1971. Together these two works show the *acto* in transition from the episodic form of the earlier piece to the singular action of *Soldado razo. Vietnam campesino*'s five episodes are designed to illustrate different points about the war and the Chicano's relationship to it. It carries the *acto* conventions to the extreme, as the action jumps from place to place, and even continent to continent, without apologies. The usual slapstick and farce is intermingled with allegorical figures, and just when we think the *acto* might turn into a dramatized lecture, it is saved from this distraction by a new scene or another action. No excuses or explanations are necessary, as each scene demonstrates the action taking place without the least self-consciousness. Each of the five episodes in *Vietnam campesino* is given a title that immediately defines its purpose. The first scene, "The Military-Agricultural Complex," portrays the machinations devised by agribusiness and the military-industrial complex to defeat the lettuce boycott promoted by the United Farmworkers Union. The Teatro had by this time separated from the Union, but the problems of the *campesino* would always be a major theme for Valdez' troupe. Humble farmworkers again become the protagonists in this *acto*, although they here represent all Mechicanos, whether rural or urban. Scene One establishes the major villains: Butt Anglo, the grower, and General Defense. Together, these buffoon-like characters expose "the real enemy." The general and the grower are almost God-like in their ability to manipulate the situation to suit their needs. By portraying them as clowns, the Teatro is ridiculing the institutions they represent, while keeping the audience's attention on what they are doing.

The second scene in this *acto* illustrates what its title implies: "Pesticides in the Fields." The use of deadly poisons to dust the crops becomes the central issue causing the farmworkers to go on strike. Domestic and international conflicts are juxtaposed in this *acto* in an effort to draw parallels between the problems of the *campesinos* in this country and the peasants in Southeast Asia. When the farmworkers refuse to work, the succeeding scene, "The Farmworker and the Draft," clearly illustrates how the poor and the minorities are being drafted while the rich are able to seek asylum in college. Scene Four, "Vietnam campesinos," continues to draw the analogy between the Vietnamese and the Mechicanos, and just when the *campesinos* begin to empathize with the Vietnamese, the general orchestrates the final scene, "The Chicano at War," which shows how the death of a Chicano in Vietnam can arouse the anger and hatred of his family toward the Vietnamese. At the conclusion of this *acto*, the dead soldier and *campesinos* on both sides of the ocean rise and tell the audience: "The fight is here, Raza! ¡En Aztlán!" (p. 130).[9]

Vietnam campesino requires no setting and can be performed anywhere. Characters speak directly to the audience, including them in the situation while urging them to think about what is transpiring. In order to avoid giving a mere catalogue of issues, the *acto* carefully builds the action as it illustrates how the forces represented by the grower and the general work hand in hand to benefit each other. Like stand-up comedians, the two discuss the fact that the Pentagon helped the growers during the grape boycott by buying grapes and sending them to the boys overseas. Now that lettuce is being boycotted, the general is reticent to buy it:

GENERAL: Can it pal, we can't use em. What's a GI or a Marine going to do with lettuce?
BUTT: Make salads?
GENERAL: In the middle of the jungle, in the rice paddies? Up in a chopper? With grapes, we could at least make raisins (p. 109).

Butt suggests that the boys can smoke the lettuce, and the general is persuaded to buy it. "The boys will smoke anything over there these days," he says, and the two agree on one million dollars for the sale.

The back-scratching antics of the grower and the general are exaggerated to the extreme in typical, farcical theatrics, drawing attention to their covert connivings through overt physical actions. While the one instructs the other on how to go about fooling the American public, he is also revealing these concepts to the audience. When the general attempts to demonstrate how the Pentagon installed a puppet regime in Vietnam, he calls out the character of Don

Coyote, who is dressed to look like President Diem, with strings attached to his "master." The parallels between the farm-labor contractor and the puppet government leader in Vietnam are made very apparent by exaggerating the connection. The audience is forced to see the real-life counterparts and events in a new light, reassessing their faith in what the government has been telling them.

Visual images are very important in any *acto*, and *Vietnam campesino* is rife with ideas transformed into pictures. The crop-dusting sequence is dramatized by having the grower's son, Little Butt, come onstage with a toy airplane in his hands, like a child playing. He whirls his miniature model of an airplane around the stage, making the sounds of the motor as he "dusts the crops." A farm-worker audience will know what the image represents, but others may not, and the character tells the audience who he is and what he is doing. An idea is transformed into an action, although this time it is miniaturized rather than made larger than life. The technique works, however, and when this boy's "job" is done, Don Coyote is left blinded.

The farce in this *acto* is reserved for the first four scenes and is centered around the villains rather than the heroes. Don Coyote is that same bungler we have seen in the previous farmworker *actos*, and *campesino* audiences love to see him ridiculed on stage. When the coyote is blinded, he looks for his workers and thinks he is kicking one of them, but he is really attacking his employer. The physical abuse that each gives the other is calculated to elicit the audience's laughter. The comic effect is also achieved by well-constructed timing and building to the moment of climax. In order to persuade both his contractor and his farmworkers that Don Coyote is not blind, the grower waves money in front of his face:

> BUTT: Look here, can you see this ten dollar bill?
> DON COYOTE: No, señor.
> BUTT: How about this twenty?
> DON COYOTE: Just barely.
> BUTT: And this fifty?
> DON COYOTE: It's more clearer.
> BUTT: This ought to clear it up good. A one hundred dollar bill!
> DON COYOTE: Patroncito, I can see again! *(He grabs the money)* (p. 114).

Of course, the audience and the *campesinos* on stage know that he has been blinded by the pesticides, but the lesson is clear: bribery works on both sides of the Pacific Ocean.

The allegorical figure of "The Draft" is employed in the tradition of the earliest *actos*, portraying an institution in order to make a point. The Draft is a shrouded figure who does not speak but moves silently toward his "victims," wearing a death mask that leaves no doubt about what he ultimately represents. Little Butt is able to hide between his father's legs and is immediately enrolled in the nearest college for refuge, but the Chicano farmworker is drafted by the shrouded figure, who pantomimes casting a fishing rod at him and catching him. Though the image is somewhat ludicrous, the boy's helplessness is underscored as he is thrown offstage by the all-powerful Draft. When the young Chicano is killed by a Vietnamese on one side of the stage, his parents at the opposite side react with horror, and the vastness of their separation in time and space is reduced to a few feet, once again illuminating in the simplest of terms a momentous event.

Like the crop dusting, which is a form of genocide, the killing of Vietnamese is reduced to visual terms. When the Chicano soldier is ordered to burn a Vietnamese farmworker's hut, he ignites a small model of a peasant dwelling. Economical considerations and fire laws aside, this miniaturized incineration is probably more effective than the burning of a life-sized hut. It is a wonderful example of how a street theater can effectively portray an idea of tremendous magnitude in explicit and seemingly child-like terms. Both the Vietnamese and the Chicano are the victims of this war, however. After the hut is ignited, the action goes into slow motion and the soldier is shot and killed. While Chicano *campesinos* are being killed in the fields of agribusiness with pesticides, Chicanos and Vietnamese are being exterminated in Vietnam as Little Butt drops "bombs" of deadly lettuce on both sides of the Pacific. Contaminated lettuce is correlated with the weapons of extermination in Southeast Asia, and the audience cannot ignore the comparison.

This simple *acto* shows quite clearly that Chicanos, as members of the working class, were drafted and that the sons of the wealthy were able to avoid conscription. Ralph Guzmán wrote during this period that Chicanos joined the armed forces because of economics, status, and in an effort to prove their Americanism in a society that had always found them "suspect."[10] Guzmán also pointed to the fact that few Chicanos were finding refuge from the military in institutions of higher education, as were the more affluent members of the dominant society. Though the Chicano in this *acto* attempts to hide from the Draft, he is "hooked" and cannot avoid eventual combat duty. He becomes representative of the soldier who remains anony-

mous, for we do not get to know him very well in this brief dramatization. We do know that the creators of this collective *acto* perceive his death as useless.

What begins with farcical, exaggerated characterizations and
situations ends with a somber tone of dignified silence, as if out of
respect for the many Chicanos who did not return from the war alive.
The topic of the war and the many unnecessary deaths that barrio
families had to endure was a difficult theme to dramatize, and the
Teatro chose the *acto* form to present its message. This is the first
acto in the Teatro Campesino's anthology that deals with the subject of death, and while it characteristically pokes fun at the general
and the grower, it cannot hide its emotion. *Vietnam campesino* treats
a subject that is too real to be kept in the realm of farce, and the *acto*
is an ingenious combination of pathos and comedy. The solemn ending foreshadows the next and final *acto* in the Teatro's collection,
the serio-tragic *Soldado razo*.

The Acto in Transition: *Soldado razo*

Soldado razo was first presented during the Chicano Moratorium on the War in Vietnam in Fresno, California, in April of 1971.
The seriousness and singularity of purpose in this work make it different from the previous *actos* by the Teatro Campesino. It calls to
mind Brecht's premise that suspense should be avoided by immediately giving the audience the situation as well as the outcome, so that
there can be no uncertainty about what will happen. The death-like
specter of The Draft from the previous *acto* is here transformed into
the figure of Death itself: a singing, laughing, sardonic narrator who
glides in and out of the story he is telling us and is a constant reminder
of the central figure's fate. In skull-face mask and black shroud, La
Muerte immediately sets the mood by jovially informing us that we
are about to hear the story of the *Soldado razo*, the Buck Private,
who met his death in Vietnam not too long ago. Though there is no
need for a setting or a backdrop, this is the first *acto* that requires
some furniture for an interior setting. However, the majority of props
are pantomimed in this economical presentation, which typically
focuses on the characters and their actions. There is never any question of where the scene is taking place, for La Muerte tells his audience where they are. The narrator keeps the action flowing from the
central figure's home to the bus station and, finally, to Vietnam.
This *acto* has more Spanish than any of the Teatro Campesino's

previous works, with the family scenes mostly in Spanish and the narration and Johnny's dialogue usually in English. Johnny is the soldier whose demise we are about to witness, but not before La Muerte has an opportunity to show him to us as a living human being whose humanity is common to all of us. La Muerte never leaves the stage and is continually commenting on the action, determined that all in the audience should understand the message. It is he who reminds us that Chicanos went to war because they felt it the manly thing to do, often urged on by the sentiments of their own families. La Muerte even tells us what the characters are thinking by speaking their thoughts as they mouth the words. While Johnny and his mother embrace, La Muerte comments:

> ¡Orale! Qué picture de tenderness, ¿no? Pero watcha la jefita. Listen to what she's thinking. Ahora sí, mijo es hombre. Se mira tan simpático en ese uniforme. (Right on! Isn't that a picture of tenderness? But pay attention to the mother. Listen to what she's thinking. Now my son's a man. He looks so handsome in that uniform.) (p. 132).

The mixture of Spanish and English in the first line is humorous, always causing laughter in the audience, and the lines that follow are meant to be introspective, urging members of the audience to re-evaluate their opinions about the same issues. "Do you think this way?" La Muerte is asking us, and enjoys the comment. He has already told us that Johnny will die, and his continual reminders that we might have influenced this young man's desire to go to war press us to reconsider our attitudes toward uniforms and masculine endeavors. Throughout the *acto* there is the feeling that Johnny is as much a victim of Mechicano attitudes about manhood, machismo, and the need to assert one's masculinity as he is a tool of the War Machine.

In a particularly long monologue, during which Johnny is walking to his girl friend's house, the young Chicano expresses his fears and hopes for himself and his girl. La Muerte has introduced this sequence by telling us that Johnny is thinking, and the monologue is then delivered as if in the character's mind. Johnny reveals a certain apprehension that he may not come back alive, and La Muerte continues the dialogue with the audience by adding: "*Loco pero no pendejo, ¿eh?* (Crazy, but not stupid, eh?). He knew the kind of funeral he wanted and he got it" (p. 133). As he speaks to us, this cynical version of the Grim Reaper applies white makeup to Johnny's face, telling us not to worry: he is simply getting the character ready for what is to come. As Johnny leaves the stage to go to his girlfriend's house, La Muerte sets the new scene, pointing to the interior of the home and introducing the father.

La Muerte continues to comment upon the characters and their thoughts as we listen to what the mother, father, and little brother think about Johnny's future. Nobody wants to talk about death, of course, and the figure of man's mortality enjoys demonstrating to the audience how this humble family thinks. As soon as Johnny arrives with his girlfriend Cecilia, the family sits down at an imaginary table, pantomiming the eating of the dinner. In order to inform the spectators about what is being eaten so that they will not be distracted by the pantomime, the characters refer to the food, identifying each course. While the group eats and continues the usual small talk, La Muerte relates what each person is thinking. The brother provides a bit of comic relief with quips about "Colonel Sanders' tamales," and so does the father with his obvious disdain for the boy, whom he continually tells to shut up. All the while, La Muerte calmly applies more white makeup to Johnny's face. The climax of this scene is the couple's announcement of their engagement, with hugs and warm congratulations all around. Everybody is excited about the impending wedding, and La Muerte revels in the knowledge that it will never happen.

Before Johnny and Cecilia leave for a party, she tells his family that her parents have lent them their car for the evening. The father is pleased and tells his son that he must have made a good impression on her family, to which Cecilia replies: "He sure did. They say he's more responsible now that he's in the service" (p. 141). La Muerte immediately says to the audience: "Did you hear that? Listen to her again," and she repeats the line exactly as before. "Así me gusta!" (That's how I like it!) shouts La Muerte, and the point has been emphatically made. To some observers this might seem a simplistic technique, hardly necessary if the audience is paying attention to the dialogue, but the deliberate pointing is never overdone and has an impact. An important consideration that most professional theater groups have little or no experience with is the presence of children in the audience. The figure of La Muerte is quite theatrical and can hold a child's attention for a while, but if the little ones are uninterested, their energies turn to other children, running and screaming in the aisles. If any character can renew the children's interest it is La Muerte, and his unexpected interjection may serve to quiet them and allow the audience to grasp the full meaning of Cecilia's line. There is no farce in this *acto* as it draws to a close, and it is therefore a much more difficult piece to perform in a community situation with the ever-present children.

On the eve of Johnny's departure, our eternal narrator once again sets the scene. He describes the bus depot and its occupants and makes a typical call for passengers, adding the appropriate sound effects. When Johnny goes to buy his ticket, La Muerte becomes the man behind the ticket counter, and asks:

MUERTE: Where to?
JOHNNY: Vietnam. I mean, Oakland.
MUERTE: Round trip or one way?
JOHNNY: One way.
MUERTE: Right. One way. *(Applies more make-up)* (p. 143).

Though Johnny has asked for a one-way ticket to Vietnam, he does not realize the ramifications of the request, while the audience is relentlessly reminded of his coming doom. After tearful goodbyes and innocent anticipation of the soldier's safe return, La Muerte is left alone to ponder the reasons for Johnny's actions: "He didn't want to go and yet he did. It never crossed his mind to refuse" (p. 144). A survey of how many Chicanos fled the country or refused to go to Vietnam would reveal a very small percentage, particularly in comparison to the overwhelming numbers of Chicanos who were drafted or voluntarily enlisted. La Muerte's comment might have caused at least a few young men to stop and think about their actions and was a glaring indictment of what seems to be a cultural drive toward proving valor and achieving recognition through the armed forces.

The final scene recalls the trans-Pacific setting of *Vietnam campesino* as Johnny sits and writes a letter in Vietnam and his mother mirrors this activity on the other side of the stage in the United States. While the son writes, he recites his letter aloud in English, and his mother responds in Spanish, as if she were writing to him as well. Johnny is now in full battle gear, and his face is a skull mask as he tells his mother about the horrors of war. He relates a recent nightmare in which he carried out orders to kill a family of Vietcong and then saw that their faces were those of his own family back home, recalling the implications in *Vietnam campesino*. Just as Johnny is intensely asking his mother to tell his friends what it is really like in Vietnam, La Muerte fires a shot at his head and he slumps over, dead. The mother screams without looking at her son, and now a solemn Muerte concludes the *acto* by describing in very brief, almost clinical detail how the soldier's body lay in the field for two days before being placed in a freezer for shipment home. During this epilogue, the other characters file past the body and form a circle around it as taps is played, and the *acto* is over.

Soldado razo is the most emotionally appealing of the Teatro Campesino's *actos*, and whenever it was performed there were few dry eyes in the auditorium. Inevitably, there were members of the audience who had suffered the loss of a family member in the war, and this poignant reminder touched emotional wounds that were still fresh. The final tableau of the family gathered around the dead soldier's body as taps was played was calculated to arouse the sympathy of the audience as well as its anger. Though the technique of eliminating all suspense during the course of the action had a Brechtian flavor, the final scene could never allow the audience to remain cool and detached as the German theorist might have wanted. Even though La Muerte continually reminded the audience that Johnny was going to die and that his demise might have been avoided, the audience could not help but get caught up in the emotions of the final scene. The dead soldier's wake onstage spread its impact beyond the curtain line to embrace the men, women, and children in the auditorium, and they all felt the loss.

The complexity of the war in Vietnam had been touched upon in *Vietnam campesino*, leaving the troupe to dramatize here the emotional destructiveness of that unwanted conflict. While liberal intellectual journals such as the *Saturday Review* continually condemned the war and radical magazines such as *Ramparts* cried out for revolution at home, the vast majority of working-class Mechicanos shared the majority opinion that "Uncle Sam" knew what he was doing and that communism had to be stopped no matter what the cost. The minorities who were the unwitting fodder for the War Machine had little choice, belonging to a culture that had continually fought for its masculine identity in the face of racism and economic oppression. Few Chicano sons would have been able to face their fathers, many of whom were veterans of World War II or Korea, if they had evaded their "duty" in the armed forces. There were a few Chicanos who were able to gain asylum in the universities, but thousands found themselves on the front lines. The only way to combat this basically emotional syndrome, Valdez felt, was with emotions.

In her excellent study of the Teatro Campesino, Betty Diamond concludes the following about *Soldado razo*: "The tears so overwhelm the analysis of the war that the effect of the acto is, I suspect, to provide an emotional release rather than the desired motivation to action."[11] Diamond acknowledges the *acto*'s continual attempt to objectify the action through the commentaries of La Muerte, yet she is troubled by the emotional conclusion. Perhaps a greater understanding of the Mechicano psyche would reveal the fact that the emotional release of this *acto* would lead to action. The real problem, perhaps, was the nature of the action to be taken. There was no Union to join, no lettuce or grapes to boycott. There was only confusion, frustration, and anger as the people most touched by the war groped for some sort of normalcy at home. When performed on university campuses, this *acto* was greeted with shouts of approval and vicarious understanding, for before the draft was abolished students were the most active opponents of the war. When presented in the barrios as an exclamation point to an anti-war rally, once again this *acto* was applauded for its message and appeal. But the major question remains: How many Chicanos did not go to war because of *Soldado razo*'s message? The question is impossible to answer.

It is clear, however, that when *Soldado razo* was presented by the Teatro Campesino as well as other teatros throughout Aztlán, it impressed Mechicanos and non-Hispanics alike. During a run at Los Angeles' Inner City Cultural Center in the fall of 1971, this *acto* moved Dan Sullivan to write:

> Tragedy - comedy - realism - surrealism—the sketch put all the elements of the theater to work at once, without once seeming forced or arty or false-primitive.
>
> Agit-Prop Theater? I guess so, if we need a definition, but equally close to 'Everyman' and the great medieval chronicles. Something very complicated and very simple and very rare is going on . . .[12]

And so it was. History and the passage of time have given us the knowledge of the war's outcome, and we are now left to deal with the hundreds of thousands of young men whose lives were immeasurably altered by the experience. In its time, during the heat of battle both at home and abroad, *Soldado razo* made its statement against the war and demonstrated to the world that there were Chicanos who were not content to follow blindly in the wake of national hysteria. It was a vital statement, full of the anger and trauma of the moment, as it urged Chicanos to say "No" to the government and refuse to fight. At a time when the mass media were churning out pro-war messages, *Soldado razo* offered a different, more courageous statement to the barrios and concluded that he who refused to follow blindly was the braver man. Though placed in the context of a particular war, this *acto* may be revived when the poor and minorities are once again called up to fight the "threat of communism" in the future.

A Veterano's Mito: *Dark Root of a Scream*

The simple, silent procession past the dead soldier's body in the final scene of *Soldado razo* has become a wake in the living room of Quetzalcóatl Gonzales, another casualty of the war in Vietnam, in *Dark Root of a Scream*. Having participated in the collective creation of *Vietnam campesino* and *Soldado razo* as the Teatro Campesino's statements against the war, Valdez complemented and extended those *actos* with a very moving play which he terms a "*mito*," or myth. To Valdez, the *acto* portrays the Chicano through the eyes of man, while the *mito* sees the Chicano "through the eyes of God."[13] *Dark Root of a Scream* continues where *Soldado razo* left off; it is the playwright's attempt to synthesize the earthly with the spiritual, the present with the past. The previous *acto* had begun with La Muerte's sardonic introduction, telling the audience what was going to happen and then narrating the action as it moved to its inevitable conclusion. *Dark Root of a Scream* begins with the *acto*'s emotional ending, and through exposition it tells us who and what the dead soldier represented. Like the constant pull of the positive and negative forces that propel a molecule, this play moves forward as it reaches to the past, bringing the two forces together in a stunning climax.

Unlike any of the *actos*, this play depends a great deal upon its setting. The surreal interior of *The Shrunken Head of Pancho Villa* and the stylized setting of *Bernabé*[14] come together in this work to form a pyramid whose different levels represent the Chicano's progression from the earthly to the spiritual. At opposite ends of the base of the pyramid are two settings: a street scene and the interior of a living room. Rising behind these two settings is the pyramid itself, which changes as it ascends from a composition of "iron and the hard steel of modern civilization—guns, knives, automobile parts; others reveal a less violent, more spiritual origin—molcajetes [Mexican stone mortars], rebozos [shawls], crucifixes, etc."[15] These earthly objects blend into indigenous symbols as the pyramid rises, crowned with conches, jade, and feathered serpent heads. The lighting is a very important element in this production, accenting the progression from the materialistic to the transcendental as it blends from brightness at the base to darkness at the crest. Although this is not indicated in the published script, in a 1971 production of this play the lighting shifted from the street to the wake as the dialogue undulated from one side to the other.[16] Though the play can be produced without a complex lighting plan, the 1971 production benefited greatly from the spectacle.

From the beginning of this play, with its symbolic setting, the audience is aware that it is witnessing a non-realistic vision. The curtain rises on the fantastic setting and the two tableaux of characters at the base of the pyramid. Stage left is the wake, with a priest, an older woman, and a young woman. These three are entering through a curtained doorway, and they freeze as the action immediately shifts to the street scene and the three *vatos* who draw our attention. The youths are typical pachucos in their dress and demeanor, but their faces are made up to look like their nicknames: Gato (Cat), Lizard, and Conejo (Rabbit). These sobriquets echo the barrio custom of giving someone a name that fits his or her character (such as "Smiley") or physical features (such as "Negro"). The makeup and costumes of the three youths reflect their animal characteristics and recall indigenous attitudes toward their animal types. Lizard is a sexual animal, snake-like and obsessed with the physical. Gato is cunning and evil, the major antagonist in this play. Conejo is kind, softhearted, yet the wisest of the three. He is the main connection with the dead soldier whose body lies in the metal coffin at the wake, and like his sister, who we will presently meet, Conejo defends the fallen warrior.

In what is a meticulously planned and well-timed technique, the action shifts from side to side, as would a serpent—the major motif of this play about a Chicano named Quetzalcóatl, or feathered serpent. The undulating rhythm is at first slow, then builds to a point where the dialogue of the two separate scenes is melded into what seems a single conversation. This duality of scenes and dialogue is a metaphor for the redeemer-figure, Quetzalcóatl, for the feathered serpent represents the coming together of the earthly—the serpent—and the heavenly—the quetzal bird. Whereas *Bernabé* brings back the Aztec Sun God, a symbol of that people's militaristic society, this play recalls his opposite force, the kindly Quetzalcóatl, giver of life and symbol of divine transcendence over the mundane. Valdez is here discovering ancestral philosophies, and he finds a sharper focus in this play as he creates a modern *mito* that compares the god and culture hero Quetzalcóatl with a contemporary Chicano leader who was also named Quetzalcóatl. *Dark Root of a Scream* is basically a history lesson, but the premise on which it is based creates a fascinating drama.

While *The Shrunken Head of Pancho Villa* was constantly moving forward with crises and continual entrances and exits of characters, *Dark Root of a Scream* is much more dependent upon the past to move the action forward. It is the story of the dead soldier, and his past is recalled by the characters in the two scenes as they discuss his life. What could become a boring biography is kept interesting by Valdez' constant use of colorful, witty dialogue and the contrast of the two settings. The opening lines, delivered by Lizard, are: "Come on, ese, let's toke up" (p. 80), immediately identifying these other-worldly characters as contemporary *vatos*, smoking that ever-present symbol of their defiance, marijuana. Their dialogue tells us who they are and the fact that they knew the dead soldier, nicknamed Indio. We learn that Conejo's sister was Indio's girlfriend, and the scene shifts suddenly to the opposite side of the stage where the priest is saying, "That's it, easy does it, Señora Gonzales. No sense in getting hysterical about these things" (p. 80).

The priest, we discover, is not Hispanic, though he does speak Spanish when he communicates with the mother. His opening remarks establish him as somewhat cold, an outsider who feels that he knows what is best for his barrio parish. Though he speaks the language, he obviously has little understanding of the people. The first four scenes are brief encounters with the characters that establish the situation and the major objective: to mourn the dead soldier. However, the true mourners are the mother, the girlfriend, Dalia, and her brother, Conejo. The attitudes of the other three range from the indifference of the priest to the hostility of Gato. The Valdezian family in crisis is reduced to a suffering mother-figure who has lost everybody: her husband and her three sons. The first son died in World War II, the second in Korea, and the last lies in a coffin beside her. Now the mother is left with mere extensions of her son: Dalia and Dalia's brother, who was his friend. The family has, in effect, crumbled, and we find these vestiges of a once-proud people in verbal combat with the others to protect the image of the dead Chicano.

At the beginning of Scene IV, the mother finds blood dripping from the flag draped over the coffin. This discovery makes her think that her son is alive in the coffin, and she shouts "¡Mi hijo está vivo!" (My son is alive!), foreshadowing the major premise of the play: Quetzalcóatl lives. She faints from the stress of this discovery, and the action shifts quickly to the next scene on the street. In the following scene the dialogue begins to alternate between settings and characters. At first the transition is subtle. The boys are discussing another dead soldier whose body had already begun to reek of death at his funeral, and Gato remarks: "I bet Indio smells like that." Immediately the scene shifts to the wake, where the priest offers the stricken mother a cloth soaked with alcohol and says: "Here, madre, smell this" (p. 83). Though the numbering does not change to Scene VI, the focus remains on the wake rather than the street. Scene VI switches back to the street, and we continue to learn about Indio's past. Once again, in Scene VIII, the dialogue fuses, this time as if the two conversations were identical.

The boys discuss Indio's given name, and Conejo says, "Quetzalcóatl, the feathered serpent," to which the priest adds: "Quetzalcóatl Gonzales. What a name for an American soldier. I wonder what it means? The first part, of course. Everyone knows what Gonzales means" (p. 85). Conejo then answers the question as if he had been asked by one of the *vatos*. The conversations have become one now, and though the characters are separated in time and space, their discussion clarifies the differences in objectivity about the dead soldier. Scene IX illustrates the different levels of communication between the characters as Conejo and Dalia answer questions for the priest and Lizard:

PRIEST: How did Indio come to have a name like that?
CONEJO: His father name him that.
PRIEST: Oh yes, his father. How did his father—?
DALIA: He was a teacher in Mexico.
CONEJO: His name was Mixcóatl—Cloud-serpent.
PRIEST: I see. A nationalist, eh?
LIZARD: So what, man? Over here he was a wetback, a farm laborer just like everybody else.
PRIEST: A political exile, no doubt.
CONEJO: He knew a lot about Mexican history. Quetzalcóatl used to be a god for the Indians a long time ago.
LIZARD: Sure, man, the Apaches (p. 85).

Both the priest and Lizard hold attitudes toward Indio and his culture that are bred of ignorance and insensitivity: the priest representing the Church's apathy toward indigenous cultures and the street youth indicative of another form of cultural bias. Lizard can only think of "Apaches" when the image of an Indian comes to his mind, the product of John Wayne movies and television stereotypes. Lizard's line is also an example of Valdez' juxtaposition of the serious with the sardonic, the ridiculous with the sublime. Like many immigrants to this country, Indio's father left his country an educated man, only to become another common laborer.

As the scenes evolve and the dialogue continues to undulate from one group to the other, the discussion centers around the god Quetzalcóatl, the Toltec leader named after him, and the Chicano named after both.[17] Valdez does not bother to distinguish between the myths surrounding the Toltec leader Ce Acatl Topiltzin Quetzalcóatl and the god after whom he was named, for the central theme is the parallel between the indigenous figure, whether god or man, and his contemporary incarnation. It is Valdez' intent to draw comparisons between the indigenous myth and the Chicano *mito* and his characters describe the corresponding qualities of each. Like the indigenous figure, Indio did not like war and human sacrifice and had worked to stop street violence and restore the Chicanos' pride in their heritage and culture. Indio was a contemporary leader who was drafted in the prime of his cause, a victim of the racism the priest accused him of. This juxtaposition is interesting, for the audience knows that it is the priest, not the Chicano, who is basically racist in his inability to comprehend the youth's motives for trying to help his people.

In an interesting parallel, Indio was betrayed by the priest and Mexican Americans in his parish who did not allow him to use the church hall for meetings, just as Quetzalcóatl was tricked by evil priests who caused his downfall. The legendary figure was deceived by Tezcatlipoca, who got him drunk and then forced him to see himself as he really was in a mirror. Shamed, Quetzalcóatl fled on a raft of serpents, promising to return. When Indio got drafted, he consulted with the priest about what to do. The priest tells Dalia: "He was considering fleeing the country, but he knew he'd never be able to return as a community leader." To which Gato responds in the other scene: "Big community leader." That draft notice showed him to his face who he was, like a mirror" (p. 90). By drawing contemporary parallels to ancient themes and symbols, Valdez succeeds in educating his audience about the past and the present. The main theme of *Soldado razo*, which attributed the soldier's basic willingness to go to war to societal pressures, is reflected here again, but the dynamics become much more complex than in the *acto*.

The *vatos* decide to go to the wake after Gato and Lizard have a scuffle. Gato is clearly the other's superior, and the emotional climax of the threatened knife fight is comically dissipated by lizard's cocky strut offstage after he has composed himself. Lizard's exit is juxtaposed with the priest's next line: "Now we will pray," as the scene shifts back to the wake and the requiem for the dead. The three youths appear at the door and clumsily enter the service. Gato sits by Dalia and attempts to get fresh with her, while the priest chants "Quetzalcóatl, your humble servant," and the others repeat "Bless him Señor" (p. 94). The service is halted when the youths repeat "Your humble *serpent*" and the priest discovers Gato's lascivious advances toward Dalia. Pandemonium breaks loose; the priest rushes out for the police with Lizard close behind him. Gato tells Conejo to try and stop him, and the intensity builds until the mother lets out a blood-chilling wail and attacks Gato. This stops Gato; then, as the mother sobs over her son's coffin, Lizard enters dressed in the priest's cassock.

Once again there is a mixture of pathos and the grotesque as Lizard tells the others that the priest is running down the streets "in his shorts" (p. 96). Suddenly he notices the mother and Dalia at the coffin; they have discovered more blood dripping onto the floor. As the boys decide who is going to open the coffin, the mother steps up to it and pulls up the lid. Conejo looks in and says, "It's . . . feathers!" Lizard reaches in and pulls out "a brilliant headdress of green feathers and a cloak of Aztec design" (p. 97). He puts these vestments on and asks: "How do I look, ese?" as drums begin to beat in the background. They all look toward the coffin, and Lizard, looking very much like an Aztec priest atop a ceremonial pyramid, reaches into the casket, pulls out something, and lifting it in his hands screams: "Indio's heart! (p. 98). The stage directions tell us that "the heart gives out light in the descending darkness," and the play ends.

In the 1971 production mentioned above, the scrim behind the pyramid dissolved, revealing the silhouette of the mythical Quetzalcóatl in his indigenous costume, looming above everything as the heart emitted a pulsating light in Lizard's hands. Just as he had promised, Quetzalcóatl had returned. In his review of that production, Dan Sullivan asked: "Is that a dead soldier or a dead god lying under the American Flag in the funeral parlor? If a dead god, is he dead forever? If a dead soldier, need there be others?"[18]

Sullivan recognized Valdez' genius in this production and noted that his plays "seem to spring from a far more comprehensive view of life than most Americans can manage without confusion." His question reflected that complexity, for unlike *Soldado razo*, *Dark Root of a Scream* evoked many images and called upon its audiences to go back and forth in time and space just as the action had. According to Valdez' *mito*, that bleeding, pulsating heart must be likened to the Sacred Heart of Jesus, which represents eternal life, not death. The light that emantes from the heart is energy; therefore it lives, and so too does Quetzalcóatl.

In the opinion of this author, *Dark Root of a Scream* remained for several years Valdez' finest dramatic achievement, but ironically it was seldom produced. The cost of an adequate production was inhibitory and the playwright also told this writer that he felt the work was not yet complete. The spectacle required is also difficult to produce and would be virtually impossible to tour to the usual barrio locations. Within a few years the war ended, causing the play to lose its topical impact. Because most Chicano theater groups attempt to produce works that speak to the immediate issues affecting the barrio, this play has not been produced since the war ceased. Still, *Dark Root of a Scream* is an excellent example of the Valdezian *mito* that addresses a current issue even as it explores ancient and universal concepts. It is a short play, yet it is such a gripping tale that it leaves its audiences immersed in its themes, engrossed by its premise.

The War at Home: *Manolo*

Manolo was first produced in 1976 by Teatro Quetzalcóatl and directed by the playwright, Rubén Sierra. Teatro Quetzalcóatl was a group that Sierra and his students formed in 1975 at the University of Washington in Seattle. Originally, the director and several of the actors had been members of the university's first student troupe, Teatro del Piojo (Theater of the Louse), which was formed in 1970.[19] Sierra had entered the graduate program in the School of Drama at the university in 1972 and had immediately begun working with the original student teatro. After completing his Master of Arts degree in directing in 1974, he joined the faculty of the School of Drama and continued to direct non-Chicano plays for the school, while also directing the Teatro del Piojo. After forming the new teatro, Sierra and his students decided to produce *Manolo*, which he had been writing since he was an undergraduate at St. Mary's University in Texas. Though the play is the product of the author's creativity, Sierra also credits the members of his teatro with contributing to its final development.

"We created a lot of it as we went along," Sierra told an interviewer in 1976, and continued: "Both the cast and I were eager to find out how the story turned out, and we discovered that together as we worked."[20] The playwright/director and the cast were also receptive to their audiences' responses and altered the script in early performances before touring with the play in the Southwest in August of 1976. Like so many other teatros, the Seattle troupe assisted its playwright by enabling him to see his characters and hear his dialogue. But, unlike the majority of student groups, Teatro Quetzalcóatl was directed by a person who was trained in theatrical production and whose experience as a director of a variety of plays broadened his understanding of theater. Most of the members of the Teatro were not drama majors, and the responsibility for the finished product lay heavily on the director. As any director who has worked with inexperienced actors knows, Sierra had to spend much of his time in rehearsals teaching the cast to act. But the 1976 tour proved very successful with barrio audiences, introducing most of the enthusiastic observers to their first realistic play.

While many teatros have collectively created *actos* about the drug problem in the barrio, *Manolo* is the first realistic play to dramatize this important theme.[21] It is also the only play in the Chicano repertoire that combines the drug situation with the problems faced by a Vietnam veteran. Unlike the other works discussed in this chapter, *Manolo* brings its protagonist home alive and forces the audience to face issues that are as real today as they were when the war was in progress. By creating characters that are based on a realistic observation of the barrio yet are not the typical *acto* stereotypes, the playwright has given us people who seem to live and breathe as we do. The characters are all in their teens and twenties with the exception of one person who is thirty-five. Young actors portraying these roles do not have to reach too far beyond their own experiences in order to re-create characters who invite the audience to listen to what they have to say.

The playwright calls for a flexible setting that relies a great deal on lighting to change locales.[22] The action shifts from Manolo's apartment to exteriors "somewhere in the barrio," leaving the choice of where several scenes take place up to the director and designer. Though the situation and the characters represent attempts to portray reality on stage, the basic setting is simple and not at all realistic. Because the production that Teatro Quetzalcóatl toured had to be economical and adaptable to any situation, it only required platforms of varying heights and sizes to delineate locales within the script. But *Manolo* could be designed to indicate more than the playwright has suggested in his production notes, employing a selective realism that would include partial walls and furniture appropriate to the particular settings. Several scenes take place outside, on the street or wherever the director chooses, and these outdoor locales can also be designed to offer some sort of definition of setting. Sierra has written a realistic script that focuses on the characters rather than the spectacle, though the two can still be combined successfully by a good designer.

Manolo is divided into three acts and several scenes that trace the final days of the protagonist after whom the play is titled. Sierra has created an interesting plot line that focuses on Manolo's efforts to free himself of the drug addiction he acquired in Vietnam. The play is a very sympathetic analysis of Manolo's pathetic condition, and it creates a central figure who is worthy of our attention because he is so human. Manolo is not portrayed as totally good but rather as a young man who finds himself caught in a situation that frustrates him, angers him, and finally destroys him. His self-pity removes him from the category of the saccharine hero who can do no wrong, reminding us that most people would respond in the same manner. He is a fighter, but his struggle must come to an end in Sierra's portrait of this neglected subject.

The play begins peacefully on the streets of the barrio just before Manolo leaves to fight for his country—another barrio draftee who cannot say "No." The first scene stands in sharp contrast with the following action of the play; it is a prologue that serves to give the audience an image of the central character before he returns from the war addicted to heroin. It is a brief scene, free of the tension that pervades the remainder of the work. The major thrust of the scenes that follow in the first act is to give the necessary exposition about Manolo and his situation. His addiction is presented as an internal struggle that is aggravated by the character of Louie, his boyhood friend who is now the local pimp-turned-pusher. Louie is the personification of evil, urging Manolo to sell drugs for him to support his habit. Manolo staunchly refuses to have anything to do with this despicable figure, though his addiction is a daily hell. This is again a play of character and action, presenting a succession of events that continually complicate the plot and move the action forward. By the end of the first act, Louie has been reported killed and Manolo's best friend, Domingo, is arrested as a suspect in the murder. The act ends with a nightmare, which is Manolo's daily torment as he injects himself with heroin.

The second act reveals Manolo as a major suspect in Louie's murder. A Chicano policeman, Sergeant Jiménez, is introduced as the barrio narcotics officer who is not liked by the young people but who is bent on finding a large quantity of heroin that Louie apparently hid before his death. The location of the heroin and the identity of Louie's murderer become the motivating questions in this act as Louie's thugs harass Manolo's young friends and Jiménez interrogates Manolo and berates him for being a "junkie." Manolo decides that he must end his addiction and goes into withdrawal with the help of his girlfriend Teresa and her brother Domingo. He survives three days of agony and is on the road to recovery when Louie's thugs once again come looking for him in his apartment. They have just begun to threaten Teresa and Domingo when Jiménez enters and sends them on their way. The two young people leave to find Manolo, and as the policeman looks out the window at the barrio, Louie enters and shoots him. Standing over Jiménez' body, the resurrected demon quips: "Next I get Manolo," and the second act is over.

The third and final act reveals the fact that Louie had arranged his own "death" in order to go underground in search of the heroin that Jiménez was also anxious to locate. Manolo tells his friends that he has found the heroin in a hiding place only he and Louie knew about and mailed it to Jiménez to ward off temptation. Louie knows that only Manolo could have found the drugs and arranges to meet with his former friend in order to make a deal. The final scene pits Manolo and his friends against Louie and his stooges, and when a struggle ensues, Louie shoots Manolo. Manolo's friends manage to overtake their adversaries, but Manolo lies dying on the street as the scene comes to an end. An epilogue follows in which Manolo's friends soberly discuss the turn of events that brought about their friend's death.

The mood of the epilogue recalls the first scene in which we met the promising young protagonist. Manolo's "spirit" appears behind Teresa as she sits alone; remembering the Manolo she had fallen in love with as a little girl. Though she cannot hear him, the "spirit" looks down at Teresa and says: "*Te quiero con toda mi vida y con toda mi alma*" ("I love you with all my heart and soul") (p. 109). This rather sentimental conclusion leaves the audience with a feeling of tenderness and is a gentle reminder of the once proud Chicano who loved his barrio and his people. Yet the realities of the barrio are not altered by Manolo's ephemeral love. Either Louie and his cohorts will return, or another drug pusher will move in to take their place. Life, however squalid, will go on.

The playwright has set this play in three distinct locales: the streets of the barrio, Manolo's apartment, and Manolo's mind. These three areas encompass the protagonist's world and the author explores them in order to fully elaborate upon his character. The play opens and closes on the street because the author sees the barrio as the necessary proving ground for his characters. The unspecified locations within the barrio become essential to the action, like another character, making each a microcosm of its own. Throughout the play, characters refer to their physical surroundings and the mood of the environment. Listening to the sudden quiet of the night after Louie's thugs have attempted to rape one of the girls, Domingo comments: ". . . not a sound, *ni un perro* (not even a dog)" (p. 81). It is as if the barrio itself has responded to the near tragedy with a motherly calm that suggests supernatural forces.

By making references to the environment, Sierra's characters inform the audience of the time of day and the mood of the scene. After spending three harrowing days with Manolo during his first withdrawal, Teresa looks out the window; when Manolo asks her: "See anything interesting outside?" she responds "*Nada.* Just some passing cars and some *niños* playing kick the can" (p. 91). It is a brief reference, another reminder that these characters are not alone but are part of a community. Though we do not see the children or even hear them, their presence is constantly felt as part of the neighborhood. Just before Louie kills him, we see Jiménez looking out the same window in Manolo's apartment and sighing, "*Ay, qué barrio éste*" ("What a place this barrio is") (p. 95), once again making reference to the surroundings.

Manolo's apartment is the only interior setting the playwright takes us to, and it is unlike any of the other places the characters inhabit. There is no description of the setting, but there is the distinct feeling that it is very modest and very sparse. This is a place in which Manolo sleeps, injects himself with heroin, and suffers physical torture as he combats his addiction. In the stage directions, the playwright describes only "a platform" upon which Manolo is sleeping and the presence of the window that looks out on the barrio. This space becomes Manolo's rehabilitation quarters and Jiménez' murdering ground, and the rather nondescript quality of the area serves to underline the protagonist's inner and outer struggles. The window to the outside is also symbolic of the "window" into Manolo's mind that reveals the nightmares and visions that haunt him and illuminate his character. These apparitions are kept at a minimum and are purposely staged unrealistically, in a dream-like fashion, because they are glimpses of the past and present as perceived by the protagonist.

Manolo's first encounter with his psychiatrist, Dr. Shain, occurs after the opening scene, establishing both the character of the doctor and the form that Manolo's meetings with him will take. The scene is preceded by the sounds of warfare and soldiers marching to the words of "I want to be an airborne Ranger. . . . I want to live a life of danger. . . . I want to go to Vietnam" (p. 69). This transition in sound from the peacefulness of the first scene to the torment of the next is delivered in a blackout, allowing the audience's imagination to complete the picture. Because the action of the play is still moving forward in time, the transition and the first session with Shain are not flashbacks but "flash-forwards" through the years, moving quickly to the main action of the play which occurs at least two years after the opening farewell. Manolo's first dialogue with Shain sets the style for the next flashback, calling for separate spotlights on the two men, who do not speak to each other as in real life but look straight ahead from their positions at opposite sides of the stage. Shain appears on a platform upstage right, an area that becomes the window into Manolo's persona.

It is through the dialogues with the psychiatrist that Manolo reveals his human weaknesses. He has witnessed death in Vietnam and returned to find that both his mother and his brother, his only family members, are dead. The memories of death at home and abroad incessantly haunt Manolo, making his escape through heroin no less troubling, but possibly more understandable. In the first encounter with the psychiatrist Manolo tells him: "I keep having dreams . . . nightmares. Sometimes I wake up screaming . . . shaking all over like a scared little boy. I'm a grown man, but the little boy in me wants to keep coming out" (p. 70). In the psychiatrist's other appearance, he urges Manolo to discuss his addiction, but the young man refuses:

> SHAIN: Don't you want to rehabilitate yourself?
> MANOLO: Being a junkie suits me just fine.
> SHAIN: You like depending on drugs?
> MANOLO: What difference does that make?
> SHAIN: Do you or don't you?
> MANOLO: To tell you the truth, Dr. Shain, it doesn't really matter
>   any more.
> SHAIN: Can you remember when you had your first fix?
> MANOLO: No.
> SHAIN: Do you want to remember?
> MANOLO: Goddamit doc, quit asking me so many fucking questions!
>   (p. 87).

Dr. Shain's subsequent probings reveal Manolo's character, explaining some of the causes of his addiction if not supplying the answers to it.

The other "window" into Manolo's psyche is provided by his nightmare. After he has injected himself with heroin, the young Chicano falls into a tormented vision that manifests itself in specially lighted areas behind him. With music and the sounds of a storm to add to the mood, "Death" appears, beckoning to Manolo, followed by a couple waving the *huelga* (strike) flag of the farmworker's union. These symbols of death and struggle give way to the image of Teresa lovingly appealing to her man, silently pleading with him as she fades into darkness. Next a soldier appears, aiming his rifle at Manolo. Manolo tosses and turns on his bed as the final apparition materializes: two men with knives in their hands who slowly fight and finally kill each other as a strobe light flashes to heighten the dream-like quality of the vision. The moment the two are dead, the lights go out, and Manolo screams in agony as he awakens and calls out "*Dios mío . . .* dear God *ayúdame* (help me)!" (p. 78). There is no mystery to the meaning of the images; each appearance represents the important events in Manolo's life.

The spectre of death continually haunts the protagonist and is mentioned throughout the play, mostly by Manolo himself. "I can't seem to get away from death," he tells Domingo, "Everywhere I turn or go *la muerte* is waiting. . . . The barrio seems to call out my name *y me dice* (and says to me) 'Manolo, *tu tiempo* (your time) has come and you must die!' " (p. 75). The appearance of Death in his dream represents Manolo's fears as well as his desires, for he hates himself for what he is and for his inability to overcome his addiction. The vision of the soldier aiming a rifle at Manolo recalls how close he was to death in Vietnam and how he avoided dying there only to come home to a living hell in his barrio. The two men who kill each other may represent his brother in combat with Louie; Manolo knows that Louie killed his brother, although no one could prove it and Louie has gone unpunished. Or perhaps the two men represent Manolo's mortal combat with himself, for he knows that he is bringing about his own demise.

Contrasted with the images of death are the love of Teresa and the hope of the *huelga*, the only positive forces in Manolo's nightmare. Several references are made during the play to Manolo's earlier involvement in the barrio and the respect that everyone has for him. Sierra has chosen the symbol of the farmworkers' struggle, the red and black flag that has become synonymous with Chicano activism and perseverance, even though there is no reference to the characters as *campesinos*. This choice may have been due to the influence of the members of Teatro Quetzalcóatl, many of whom were from migrant families. But more importantly, the *huelga* flag is really the only symbol of the Chicano's political struggle that is universally understood. Even in the cities, Chávez' organizing efforts remain a constant source of pride and sympathy for the farmworker's plight, and Sierra's play reflects this reality.

Manolo's inner struggle is compounded by the forces that surround him, both good and evil. The corruption represented by Louie and his thugs is contrasted with Manolo's circle of friends: a group of likable young people who look up to him as their leader. Manolo shuns any responsibility now that he is an addict, but his friends continue to respect him because of what he used to be. It is obvious in Sierra's portrayal of Manolo that his protagonist loves his friends, yet his addiction overwhelms him and he can be quite insensitive to their needs. At times he is protective of his friends, but usually he is a very lonely figure, unable to respond to those around him. Sierra has created a complex figure in Manolo—a man who can be loving and kind as well as egocentric and self-pitying. Manolo was once a man of action, involved in a struggle to help his people, but he is now caught between his addiction and his hatred for Louie and all that he represents. He wants to help his friends but is sometimes unable to overcome his physical as well as psychological craving for heroin, and his friends suffer.

At times it might seem that the youths who support Manolo are too devoted to this shell of the man who used to be, but their attitude is characteristic of an adolescent adoration. To them Manolo can do no wrong, and even in his harshest moments they are understanding and accepting in a manner that bespeaks their need for a barrio leader. Though Manolo slaps one of the boys when he will not go home, the boy returns to help him, for he sees it as his responsibility. Manolo's friends believe in him more than he does, and their commitment becomes symbolic of the playwright's belief in the need for community understanding. Unfortunately, most adults might not have the same patience exhibited by Manolo's friends, and that becomes a major lesson in this play.

To avoid depicting Manolo's supporters as one-sided characters who have no purpose other than to follow their appointed leader, Sierra gives the youths distinctive qualities of language and behavior. From Joey Boy, the youngest of the lot, to Chano, the barrio bulletin who knows everything about the neighborhood, Sierra's juveniles are based on real-life counterparts in any barrio. Chano is the most colorful of Manolo's friends, a streetwise cat burglar who only steals from "them that gots" and "never hits the same place twice" (p. 69). Chano's dialogue is unique in its rhythms, a sort of Black-American "jive talk" that is often found in the barrios bordering black neighborhoods. "Come on bro," he tells Manolo, "I can see that you is *down* and a little jam might help you to find what happened to *up*" (p. 81). Domingo refers to Chano as a Joaquín Murieta, recalling the character of Joaquín in Luis Valdez' *Shrunken Head of Pancho Villa*, though this aspect of his character is not developed. Chano confidently tells Manolo: "I'm so fast when I steal a radio I leave the music behind" (p. 81).

Chano is the barrio realist, well aware of what it means to be addicted to drugs, though he seems to avoid them himself. When Manolo asks Chano to get him a "fix," he quickly agrees, without question. While the other people in Manolo's circle try to keep him from continuing his habit, it is the "hip" Chano who knows that this is an impossible goal. He goes for the heroin as if he were running to the corner store for an ice cream cone, for this is the reality of the drug culture. Chano knows many people and he knows how and where to get anything in the barrio. His character is contrasted with the idealists who surround Manolo, thus telling us that this man's habit is no fairy-tale affliction that can be wished away with a kiss.

Manolo is decidedly a male-dominated play, with only three females in a cast of twelve. The major female role is Manolo's girlfriend Teresa, who is a youthful counterpart of the all-suffering mother in other Chicano dramas. Teresa is an important part of Manolo's circle, but her role is limited to that of a patient, loving, and accepting woman whose life seems to revolve around "her man." She and her brother Domingo stay with Manolo during his three days of withdrawal, even though Manolo has shunned her because he is ashamed of what he has become. Sierra has thoughtfully avoided the romantic notion of having his protagonist decide to overcome his habit out of love for his girlfriend, but nonetheless Teresa's major objective throughout the play is to love Manolo and not much else. The other two girls are close friends who add a "feminine touch" to the situations and dialogue, but none of the women are prime movers in this drama of motion.

Standing to the side of the groups that surround Manolo is the narcotics officer, Jiménez. In an earlier version of the script, Sierra had portrayed this Chicano policeman as a friend of the youngsters, but the final version presents him as a common enemy to both Manolo's group and the thugs. Everybody in the barrio hates this Chicano policeman, although his determination to stop the drug problem seems a noble cause. Jiménez is the oldest character in the play; he is a hard-nosed cop who could have been scripted as an Anglo, but whom the playwright decided to portray as a Chicano. All policemen, whether brown, black, or white, are suspect in any barrio and Sierra's decision to make this policeman no exception was undoubtedly influenced by this general attitude. It is also a reflection of the playwright's intention not to make Jiménez the hero of the day— a martyred policeman who is mourned by all the barrio for his efforts. What may seem a callous disregard for what Jiménez is trying to do is in fact a very real picture of the barrio's distrust of all police officers.

It is the little boy in Manolo who escapes reality through drugs, ignoring the pleas of his friends until Jiménez forces him to accept responsibility for his actions. Jiménez taunts the former activist, reminding him that he can no longer help his people if he cannot help himself. Perhaps because he dislikes the policeman so much, Manolo decides that he must prove to everybody, but especially to Jiménez, that he *can* help himself. It is curious that these two men with equally fervent desires to rid the barrio of drugs cannot work together. Yet ultimately we discover that Manolo has mailed the heroin to Jiménez, signifying his acceptance of the narcotics officer's role in the drug eradication program. Though they never liked each other, Manolo does tell Domingo that he is sorry Jiménez had to die. Still, if Manolo decides to quit the habit because of Jiménez, the playwright does not allow the play to succumb to facile solutions, and Manolo's inner combat with heroin finds its overt counterpart in the character of Louie. It is Louie who opens yet another window into Manolo's mind as Sierra adds strokes to his broadening canvas.

Louie is the necessary evil in this play, for it is through his threats, temptations, and outright violence that the action moves forward. Even in his "death," Louie lives on in the characters of his flunkies, Bimbo and Tank, who continually harass the young people. These two thugs are the closest Sierra comes to stereotypes, and they can be interpreted as such, but they are ultimately flat because their counterparts in the barrio are flat. They have but one goal: to find the heroin, a drive that is only momentarily diverted by the possibility of raping one of the girls. Bimbo is a moronic type who grunts and growls rather than speaking, and Tank is another typical bully who must have set cats' tails on fire as a boy. Louie seldom appears without his cohorts, and the three constitute quite a triumvirate of evil.

It is the character of Louie that gives Manolo a tangible enemy, something or someone he can blame for the barrio's drug problems. Their relationship recalls Cain and Abel of the Old Testament, for they were once as close as brothers. Louie is a necessary adjunct to Manolo's conflict, for he represents what the drug addict most wants and what he hates more than anything as well. While Louie could reward his former friend with all the heroin he needs, Manolo staunchly refuses to have anything to do with the man who literally killed his real brother and is figuratively killing his other "brothers" in the barrio through drugs. Even when he sends Chano out for a fix, Manolo refuses to ask Louie for heroin because that would be the ultimate sign of deliverance to his enemy. The young veteran may be a drug addict, but he still has a moral code that eschews any association with the hateful Louie.

Manolo's moral code is tested in the final scene when Louie threatens to kill Domingo if Manolo does not take an injection of heroin that he obviously needs. Louie has the advantage in this cat-and-mouse game, for he and his friends are armed. He can see that Manolo needs a fix, and it is a very tense moment when the focus is on this pathetic figure as he looks weakly at the hated drug. Manolo says "Give it to me" (p. 106), but we do not know whether he is doing this to save his friend's life or because he can avoid the drug no longer. He has been struggling against his body's craving the entire evening, and his decision to take the drug is probably a combination of concern for the safety of his friend and his addiction. Sierra's play is too realistic a portrayal of drug addiction to suggest that Manolo could have overcome his habit so quickly. It is during this moment of weakness and nobility that Manolo is killed, just as he is about to receive the injection. Louie and his partners are apprehended, but not in time to avoid Manolo's death. The sacrifice of Manolo has brought about the downfall of these three devils and is an expiation that was necessary to return the barrio to its original peacefulness.

The calm that follows Manolo's demise may only be temporary, but it is the playwright's way of pointing to a brighter future, a time when drugs will no longer plague the Mechicano community. The spirit of Manolo, the casualty in life and death, permeates this and other barrios. Like Quetzalcóatl Gonzales in *Dark Root of a Scream*, Manolo returns after his death to assure the audience that his spirit will not die as long as there are those who care for him and struggle in his cause. The highly intense and climactic ending of the Valdez play contrasts sharply with this almost austere epilogue, though both serve to reassure the audience that hope is not lost. The palpitating, light-emitting heart of Valdez' play is replaced by a vision of the victim himself, a man whom we got to know through his words and deeds as well as what others said about him. Yet both plays exist for the same reason and successfully create appropriate atmospheres necessary to their purposes. Both of these vital young Chicanos died unnecessarily, and they were both victims of the war and of their own barrio and its attitudes.

Of the four works studied in this chapter, *Manolo* creates the most explicit picture of the barrio. Sierra's play is the only one to bring its major character back to the barrio alive, though tenuously, and it is through the interactions of the characters that the audience learns about the environment that surrounds them. It is also the only full-length play of the four, which permits the audience more time with its characters and consequently an opportunity to know them better. As in the other works, it is the war that brings about the protagonist's downfall, though in Sierra's play the evil represented by Louie does the actual killing. In spite of the fact that he struggles against the forces that entrap him, Manolo must die, for he cannot live as a drug addict. Ultimately, Sierra is telling his audience that Manolo had no choice after he became addicted to heroin in the service. His fourteen months in the rehabilitation center did not cure him, and while those who love him try to help, he cannot help himself in the end. This is a very unidealized portrayal of a drug addict who refuses to succumb to a happy ending. Although the play is rife with emotional appeals and sentimental circumstances, it is finally a naturalistic picture of a very real problem.

Sierra's script indicates that the action of *Manolo* can take place in any barrio in the Southwest. The dialogue is mostly in English, with scatterings of Spanish or "Spanglish" to give a barrio flavor to the language; thús the play is actually not limited by linguistic regionalisms. For some observers there may be too much English dialogue, but for non-Spanish-speaking audiences *Manolo* is a refreshing contrast to a work such as Teatro de la Esperanza's *La víctima*, which is almost entirely in Spanish. Each of the characters has his or her own particular dialect, ranging from the rather Americanized language of the women to the different degrees of street-talk used by the men. Sierra has obviously taken great care to translate most of what the characters might have been expected to say in Spanish into English, while maintaining enough Spanish to reflect realistic barrio dialogue. If a character gives a line completely in

Spanish, the response will be in English and will define the previous line, carefully clarifying the character's intent.

The barrio life that Sierra re-creates in his play is a curious mixture of peaceful strolls and dangerous encounters with Louie and his cohorts, and it reflects the very real paradoxes of the typical Chicano neighborhood. The characters are very much at home in their own community, but the threat of danger is always at hand. The most hated symbols in the play's barrio are the drug pusher and the Chicano policeman, though the officer becomes a savior of sorts when he stops the two hoodlums from harming Domingo and Teresa. By the close of the play, both Jiménez and the drug pushers are gone, but there is no indication that they will not be replaced immediately by others who will be just as unwanted.

Domingo and Teresa represent the hope for the future, as the playwright puts forth the common premise that the Chicano must help himself. There is no Valdezian mother to represent the matriarch or symbolic family thread in this play, but instead Sierra offers the symbol of brother/sister as his redeemer figures. The Valdezian family that surrounded the soldiers in the scripts discussed previously in this chapter is here replaced by Manolo's close circle of friends: the broader family of the barrio. This barrio family includes the antagonists represented by the three hoodlums and the policeman, who are notably Chicano and not Anglo. This realistic picture reminds the audience that evil knows no racial distinctions and avoids a simplistic portrait of "good Chicanos" versus "bad Anglos."

The only Anglo in the play is Dr. Shain, who tries to help his patient but is incapable of succeeding. The psychiatrist represents the entire Army and the government bureaucracy that perpetrated the war, which are significantly non-Chicano, once again laying the burden of responsibility on the dominant society. As in the other works in this chapter, the War Machine is the ultimate culprit, although Manolo also blames the barrio pushers for perpetuating the evils of the war at home. Unlike *Vietnam campesino*, which suggested a military drug involvement in Southeast Asia during the war, Sierra does not indicate where Louie obtains his heroin. Granted, this play is not intended to expose this controversial issue, but there might have been mention of it to spark the audience's imagination and interest. While Louie is more than a street peddler, he is still beholden to someone at a higher level for his supply of the barrio quota.

As the play progresses, the incidents increase in number in

typical melodramatic fashion. The audience is made aware of events that have happened offstage as well as actually seeing incidents such as the two killings transpire before their eyes. From the serenity of the first scene to the final shooting, this is an eventful drama, as prescribed by standard guides to the well-made play. But because this work is constructed in the melodramatic mold, it is always on the verge of falling over the precipice into mediocrity. There is nothing unique about the playwright's vision, and the unfolding events are almost predictable; still, there is a certain atmosphere about the play that lifts it above the usual *acto* or drug-related works that are so common in the barrios. There is a versimilitude in the language of the characters that is so real as to be clichéd, yet it is an honest reflection of the way such people would speak. Typical barrio types are all there: the girlfriend, the best friend, the drug pusher/pimp, the kids—all born of a very acute observation of the barrio and its rhythms. The movement from scene to scene, the music, and concern for the characters help to keep the attention of the audience riveted to the stage.

Manolo is well focused on its major action and central character, exposing some of the conflicts of drug addiction while maintaining an interesting sequence of events. The characters are generally well delineated, and their words and actions are realistically presented. The playwright skillfully creates a major antagonist who is a personification of evil yet truly human, avoiding an *acto*-like, allegorical devil figure that would be out of place in this realistic play. *Manolo* is one of the few successfully written and produced realistic Chicano plays that has been published to date, and it merits the attention of any study of serious Chicano drama.

The four works discussed in this chapter represent a chronological and structural progression from the *acto* to realism, which parallels a significant trend in the development of many Chicano theater groups. As teatros have evolved over the years, their search for theatrical forms has always begun with the *acto* and then usually progressed through some kind of *mito*, the expressionistic play, and culminated with a realistic vision of the barrio. As the teatros and playwrights in this chapter have attempted to dramatize their impressions of the war in Vietnam and their concerns with it, the dramatic works created have been uniquely their own, though they have all focused on the individual soldier. It is important to remember that the first three works were written during the actual conflict, and the fourth play was begun during the height of the war but completed after the troops had returned home. Similarly, the first three pieces culminate with the soldier's death in Vietnam, while the final play never leaves the barrio and its protagonist is murdered in his own neighborhood.

As the works progress from the *acto* to the play, the focus shifts as well. *Vietnam campesino* exposes the "War Machine," as represented by the grower and the general. A Chicano soldier dies in Vietnam, but so do other *campesinos* on both sides of the Pacific. This *acto*'s subject is directly related to the year in which it was created, a time of efforts to escalate the war in Southeast Asia and attempts to quell the dissidents at home. *Soldado razo* is centered around the private, Johnny, and his immediate family and fiancée. His tragedy is universal; he is an individual caught in a war that he has realized is unjust. But he is unable to alter the course of fate. His revelation is accompanied by his death in an emotional climax to a serious *acto*. Both of these *actos* were the products of a collective creativity fueled by current events and continuing efforts to inform the public about the war. Brief and expedient, *Vietnam campesino* and *Soldado razo* served an important purpose in their time.

Valdez' *Dark Root of a Scream* was also written during the war, and while the focus is on an individual soldier, Quetzalcóatl Gonzales, it is a *mito* that creates a broader picture of the Chicano's indigenous culture and beliefs as personified by the dead soldier. Whereas the first *acto* indicted the United States government for the deaths of Chicanos in Vietnam, and the second intimated that the soldier might have refused to go had it not been for Mechicano attitudes about the masculine image, this play blames the general disunity of the Mechicanos for the death of its protagonist. Valdez' play recalls historical/mythical figures in an effort to demonstrate that Chicanos do not have to die in the war. By juxtaposing and mingling the past with the present, *Dark Root of a Scream* urges its audience to find the answer to internal conflicts in an understanding of indigenous philosophy coupled with an analysis of the forces behind the war. The focus is on a dead soldier whom we never see but whose every breath is evident in the discussions about him. His palpitating heart denies his death and offers hope for those who follow him.

The final play was completed after the war had ended and was in effect compelled to focus on the veteran in his own barrio, alive. But while the previous *actos* lay the blame for the soldiers' deaths flatly on the government, and the Valdez script created a mythological hero of its protagonist, Sierra's play left the war behind his protagonist physically while never allowing him to forget it emotionally. Though we are not told what Manolo's contributions to the barrio were, as in the case of Indio, we do know that he was an activist who can now struggle no longer. His defeat is based on a war-related drug addiction but is also tied to the circumstances that surround the deaths of his mother and brother. In the previous works, it is the mother who mourns her son's death; in Sierra's play it is the son who mourns the passing of his family.

Although death abounds in each of the four works and is the center of the action in each, there is never a feeling that all hope is lost. Typical of most Chicano drama, these works are not defeatist, but rather they indicate the Chicano's will and determination to survive. The very reason for the creation and production of these anti-war statements was to educate the public in order to bring about change. Though the characters in each piece may have thought they had no choice, the *actos* and plays all tell their audience that they do have a choice. Each of the sacrifices represented by the fallen soldiers is a symbol of the belief that the audience can learn from their example and, hopefully, not make the same mistakes. As the war in Vietnam passed into recent history, so too did the *actos* and plays that dramatized that conflict, but the final play reminds us that the struggle is not over.

Chapter Four

BACK TO THE BARRIO: LOCAL GOVERNMENT AND EDUCATION

The Politics of Learning

Chicano activists in both academic and community circles have long been aware of the educational inadequacies and lack of political representation in the barrios. Studies abound with statistics about discrimination in the schools as well as in their surrounding communities; the inevitable conclusion is that the Mexican American has always been a second-class citizen. Addressing the issue of education in the barrio, Rodolfo Acuña maintains that the "mission of Anglo-American public schools was not to educate, or to create social consciousness, but to condition the newcomer as well as the majority of citizens to accept corporate society."[1]

By referring to both the forces of education and the corporate structure, Acuña's statement summarizes the attitudes expressed by the four works in this chapter. The first two *actos* focus on education alone, the third on local government, and the fourth is a docudrama that addresses both these issues to create a well-rounded criticism of the treatment of the Mechicano in this society. The four works all agree: there is need for a great deal of improvement on all fronts.

Many studies have been conducted about the educational achievement of the Chicano, and the resulting information has surprised no one from the barrio. In a word, the Chicano has not been educated in the schools. During the recent years of the Chicano Movement, scholars have revealed the fact that Spanish-surnamed people are well below the national average in levels of scholastic achievement and in many cases are lower than any other group.[2] In a statement to the U. S. Senate Committee on Executive Reorganization in 1969, Martin G. Castillo reported: "There is a 2.1-year to 5-year education completion gap between the Anglo population and the Spanish-surnamed population . . . Something must be done to narrow this gap if our people are to survive in this society."[3] Though this information came as no real shock to Chicanos, who had long been alienated by the educational system, the published research provided documentation for those who wanted to bring about progressive change.

The evidence was in, and it became obvious that education was the vital key to the improvement of the Chicano's socioeconomic condition. As has already been noted in reference to the rise of teatros,[4] the Chicano student movement was beginning to make its presence known in 1969 as incipient scholar/activists redefined the nature of the university student. For a few, usually middle-class Mexican Americans, a college degree was an expected goal, but for the majority of barrio residents that prospect had never seemed attainable. Studies had also concluded that the economic level of Spanish-surnamed people was imposed by their lack of education, placing the majority of Mechicanos firmly in the culture of poverty. Until federal financial aid programs made it possible for Chicanos to attend the university, the monetary burden often made advanced degrees impossible.

Without adequate education or employment, the inhabitant of the barrio is faced with the same conditions any member of the lower class is heir to: substandard housing, unemployment, broken homes, crime and violence. As the progression of works in this chapter will reflect, the student teatros first defined themselves within the structure of the educational process and later explored the dynamics of the local political forces in the barrio. This study therefore begins with a simple *acto* about a Chicano high school student who wants to go to college but whose desire is thwarted by his counselor. This is a very frequent *acto* in teatro repertoires, and reveals an all-too-common practice among educators. Based on several variants the author has encountered in barrios throughout the country, this *acto* may be categorically titled: *The High School Counselor*.

The introductory *acto* is followed by a three-part, extended *acto* created by the Teatro Campesino, appropriately titled: *No saco nada de la escuela* (I Don't Get Anything Out of School). This *acto* progresses from grammar school through high school and on to college, examining the treatment of students from various ethnic and economic backgrounds by racist, insensitive teachers. It is as much an examination of the acculturation/socialization process as it is an indictment of the educational system, for the *acto* contrasts the teachers' attitudes towards Chicano, Black and Anglo students.

The *acto* that follows was written by the Teatro Desengaño del Pueblo (Theater of Enlightenment), under the direction of its founder, Nicolás Kanellos. Entitled *El alcalde* (The Mayor), this midwestern view of local politics has a general theme that can be produced in any barrio while treating a problem that is peculiar to its geographic location: conflicts between the different Hispanic groups that populate the Midwest. This teatro is significant for its multiracial composition, being one of the few that includes Chicanos, Puerto Ricans and Anglos. Though there are regional distinctions, Teatro Desengaño del Pueblo illustrates a common bond with other groups throughout the country.

El alcalde leads naturally to the next piece, a docudrama that examines all of the sociopolitical forces manifested in a particular microcosm: the rural community of Guadalupe, California. Entitled *Guadalupe* after the barrio that inspired it, this effort was collectively created by Teatro de la Esperanza of Santa Barbara, California. *Guadalupe* indicts the schools, the growers, the politicians, the Church, and the police as institutions that maintain a feudal economy amidst vast agricultural wealth.

Tracing the treatment of Mechicanos from childhood to maturity, the four pieces in this chapter attempt to dispel what some have termed the "American Dream" and to urge the audience to combat the forces that uphold the status quo. Each of the dramatic works is based on personal experience as well as documented fact, and all are valid reflections of past and present conditions. Whereas the works in the previous chapter examined an international conflict brought about by national priorities that seemed unchangeable, the present efforts bring the problems to the very doorstep of the barrio, demonstrating that change, however gradual, is possible.

A Symptomatic Acto: *The High School Counselor*

It was "High School Recruitment Day" at a midwestern university, and the two hundred Chicanos from the surrounding communities were gathered in an auditorium to hear the featured speaker. The speaker was the director of a teatro on the West Coast, and he had been invited to address these high school students and inspire them to go to college. Born and raised in East Los Angeles, this Chicano knew the problems faced by the Mexican-American student in California but had not yet discovered the dynamics of the midwestern Chicano experience. So far from their homeland, many of the Mexicans who migrated to the Midwest eventually found employment in industries there and settled in urban centers; others continued to work in agricultural communities throughout the area. Some maintained a sense of culture through community organizations, the Church, and local fiestas and Mexican dances. Others bowed to the melting-pot theory and assimilated as best they could, even changing their names if need be to get ahead. The students in the auditorium that day represented the broad spectrum of Chicanos from the area and would soon discover how much they had in common with other students like them in the Southwest.

After briefly describing Chicano theater to these students, the speaker asked if anyone in the room had ever seen a teatro. Several people raised their hands, but the majority of the students had never witnessed an *acto* or any other form of the Chicano's theatrical expression. Rather than describe an *acto* for these young people, the speaker demonstrated different characters from early Teatro Campesino *actos* such as *La quinta temporada*, calling their attention to the broad style of acting and the exaggerated situations. The speaker then gave a one man performance of *Los vendidos*, jumping from character to character, assuming the character of each "model" and demonstrating for the delighted audience how another teatro had created its comment about the "sellout." The spectators understood the *vendido* syndrome and responded with the laughter of recognition that so often accompanies this *acto*.

The students were now warmed up, and the speaker saw that it was time for them to create their own acto. "All right," he said to them, "now it's time for *you* to create an *acto*." Nervous laughter from the young people and adults, for few had ever seen a teatro, much less performed for a group of strangers. "What's the first thing you have to have for an *acto*?" he asked, testing their attention to what he had pointed out earlier. "A problem," whispered a girl near the front of the stage. "A what?" he asked, putting his hand to his ear to let her know that she would have to speak louder. "A conflict!" shouted a braver student from the other side of the auditorium. "Good," the speaker said, "you get an 'A' for the day! Now, somebody give me a problem." Silence. "Oh," the speaker said with a hint of sarcasm in his voice, "I see. You all don't have problems in Michigan." Laughter from the audience. "Well, what about school. Do you have any problems in school?" More laughter from the auditorium from both teachers and students. "I thought so," said the speaker with a grin, satisfied that they were getting ready to commit themselves.

The speaker had lectured about Chicano theater in many parts of the Southwest and had worked with college-level teatros in the Midwest, but this was the first time he had encountered a room full of high school students in Michigan. From earlier experiences he had observed that a large majority of Chicanos in college had been advised by their teachers or counselors not to attend a university. That had been his personal experience in the late fifties, but he had not expected the same pattern from educators in the early seventies. Yet everywhere he went, he found that conditions had not improved for the Chicano high school student. Realizing that this room contained a sample of Chicano students from different parts of the state, as well as a few teachers, counselors, and parents, the speaker decided to take the plunge and ask the question:

"How many of you," he asked rather slowly, "were told by a teacher or counselor not to go to college?" Both he and the audience were astounded by the response. Almost every hand in the auditorium went up. There were a number of schools represented in that room, and this fact exacerbated the issue, for the problem was not limited to one location. The reactions of shock or surprise turned to laughter, followed by a certain sense of indignation about the issue. Here, then, was a Problem with a capital P, and the speaker knew he had the ingredients for an *acto*. This was a situation everyone in the room could relate to, even the counselors, for they were obviously not suspect, having taken their students to a program of this nature. Now the speaker had to see if anyone would volunteer to step up to the stage and improvise this common complaint.

"Well," he said, with a look of satisfaction on his face, "I see that this is something you can all relate to." Laughs and grumbles from the auditorium let him know that they were ready for collective action. "Which one of you would like to demonstrate for the rest of us how this happened to you?" A young Chicana near the back of the auditorium quickly raised her hand, and her friends applauded her with glee. "Great! Come on up here, and we'll find you a partner." "You mean I have to go up on the stage?" she asked in shock, causing everybody to react with amusement at her innocence. "Well, it's a lot easier to see you when you're up here than down there," he answered with a smile, continuing: "Come on, you can do it." Everybody applauded the young woman, glad that they were not she, and she reluctantly rose and walked up to the stage. When she reached the platform, all were silent in anticipation of what would follow.

"What's your name?" he asked her, and she whispered: "Carmen." "Can you all hear her?" he said to the quiet auditorium, which resounded with shouts of "No!" "The first thing you have to do when you're in an *acto*," he said, as much to her as to the audience, "is be heard." Giggles from the girl, who then addressed her peers and stated: "My name is Carmen." "Wonderful," the speaker said, confident that Carmen would do just fine. "Now, Carmen needs a partner. Who would like to be her partner?" Several boys in the front row raised their hands eagerly, until the speaker reminded them: "I mean up here, on the stage." All but one quickly lowered their hands. "I see there's one brave Chicano among you," the speaker said wryly, "so come on up." Generous applause from the audience for this act of courage, and a few catcalls from his circle of friends.

As soon as the young man reached the stage he announced loudly and clearly, "My name is Mike," before the speaker could verbalize the obvious question, and the audience responded to the boy's aplomb with appreciation. "Good. Do either of you know each other?" the speaker asked the two, to which they responded negatively. "OK," the speaker continued, "here we have two brave people who have volunteered to come up here and demonstrate an *acto* for you." Looking at both of them, he then asked, "Have either of you been told you should not go to college by a counselor?" Nods of affirmation. "Good. Now, one of you will demonstrate a student, which you really are, and the other will demonstrate a counselor, which you really aren't. Got it?" Nods of affirmation from the two. Looking at the audience the speaker then asked for the characters' objectives, and a student announced: "She's the student, and she wants to go to college, and he's the counselor, and he doesn't want her to go because . . ." Interrupting her, the speaker said, "Fine, but we don't want them to know anything more than their objectives, OK? That way, they will have to improvise their own situation." To the two volunteers: "Mike, grab that chair and pretend that you are in your office, and Carmen, you come in to see him." The speaker then stepped to the side of the stage, focusing on the two students.

"What am I doing?" Mike asked the speaker. "Whatever you think counselors do in their office," he answered. "It's your *acto*." Mike then grabbed another chair, placed it in front of him as if it were his desk, put his feet on the "desk," and feigned sleeping. Shouts of approval from the delighted crowd. Already, the young man had made a social comment on the character he was playing, and the audience loved it. Carmen had to keep from laughing, but she bit her lip and crossed over to the young man, who was snoring away, and said, "Mister White." It was a typical name for a Chicano to give a teacher, and the audience reacted accordingly, but "Mr. White" remained asleep. "Mr. White!" she said more sternly, and then pulled on the young man's feet, causing him to fall off his chair. There was no stopping these two young people or the crowd, which was enjoying every word and action before them.

After getting himself up off the floor, "Mr. White" said: "Uh, oh, hello María (pronounced Mar-EYE-ah), what can I do for you?" "My name is Carmen, Mr. White. Don't you remember?" "Oh, yes, of course. But you know, you all *do* look alike." Boos and hisses from the audience. "Now, what can I do for you?"

"I want to go to college, Mr. White."

"You do, eh? What for?"

"What do you mean, what for? I want to be a teacher and help my people, that's what for." Applause from the students.

"Well, I think that's out of the question, María—I mean Carmen. Your people don't belong in college. Now about this homemaking class I want you to enroll in: that's what you Mexicans all need. You know, lots of babies, and all that." Mr. White carefully outlined typical stereotypes about the Chicana, telling his advisee that it was his responsibility to see that she be trained as a good housewife, "for that is what all good Mexican-American women should be."

"But I want a career," Carmen insisted, to which the quick-witted young actor responded: "Well, how about being a maid? You need good homemaking techniques for that." "I don't wanna be a maid!" she shouted, but "Mr. White" was oblivious. "Well, how about a waitress?" he asked, clearly enjoying his role and his own comment upon the situation. At this point the young lady looked at the speaker, and asked: "What do I do now?" with a look of total exasperation on her face. "*Mátalo!*" ("kill him!") exhorted someone from the audience, and the applause and laughter were unleashed with the fury born of any frustrating cause. After the laughter had died down, the speaker looked at the girl and asked: "What is your objective?" "To go to college," she answered firmly. "OK. Is Mr. White here going to help you do that?" he asked. "No." "Then what are you going to do about it?" Pause. "Now continue the scene, and see what you will do in this given situation. He's obviously not here to help you, so do what you have to do." The two stepped back into the *acto.*

"Now see here, Carmen," said "Mr. White" with a tone of disgust. "I am trying to help you."

"Well I don't want your kind of help, Mr. White. And I'm gonna go where I can find someone who *can* help me. There was a recruiter from the University of Michigan here last week, and I heard they wanted Chicanos and Chicanas over there, so good bye!" And she stormed out of the "office" accompanied by thunderous applause and stomping feet. This instant *acto* was an immediate success and was very reminiscent of what Luis Valdez had done that first night in 1965 in the old pink house in Delano. Here was a group of people with a common problem and the desire to overcome it. The student became the hero and the counselor the villain, paralleling the farm-worker/*patroncito* scenario of years before, as the audience members demonstrated for each other how to deal with the situation.

"Now there you have one situation and a solution," the speaker pointed out, "but let's reverse the roles and see what Carmen and Mike can do with it. The objectives are the same for each character, but now Carmen is the counselor and Mike is the student." Carmen then sat down at the "desk" and pretended to be reading something, when Mike knocked on an imaginary wall. "Come in," she said, then looked down her nose at the student and remarked with disdain, "Oh, it's you again. What do you want now?" "Can I sit down?" Mike humbly asked, at which point the speaker called out "Freeze!" At first the students did not know what he meant, but soon they realized that he was asking them to stand still and stop the *acto*. They froze in position, Mike in a humble, bent-over posture, and Carmen sitting grandly behind her imaginary desk, peering down her nose at him.

Looking at the audience, the speaker explained: "The reason I stopped them was to point out the social gestures each of the people has taken . . . gestures which immediately define certain things about these characters. What do you see?" A student in the audience called out: "He's too shy. He has to be stronger, or he'll never get what he wants." "What about the counselor?" the speaker asked the audience in general. "She's good!" and "That's what Miss so-and-so is like" came from different corners of the auditorium. "Good," continued the speaker, "her character is well-defined and immediately tells us a lot about her attitude towards this poor humble student." Then, in turning to Mike, he advised: "But Mike, here, is not forceful enough, and we will have trouble believing him or accepting his determination. You're not asking for an ice cream cone; you're asking for your life."

The two started the scene again, and this time Mike projected his own personality, full of vitality and determination. As the speaker expected, the excuses were different, this time the counselor advising the boy to take wood shop or metal shop classes or "run on the track team . . . don't they call you 'Speedy Gonzales?' " Carmen was in tune with the situation and gave her partner a dose of his own punishment as she relished the role of "stupid racist counselor." After a typical list of reasons why Mike should not go to college, including his poor grades, the high cost of an education, and other prevalent attitudes, Mike exclaimed: "Listen, you old bag, I ain't gonna listen to you! There's a meeting down to the school board tonight, and I'm gonna organize all the Chicanos to be there and get you busted!" And he too triumphantly walked out of the "office" as the audience applauded.

This second successful *acto* led to others from the students, who were now raising their hands in greater abundance, eager to demonstrate their solutions or re-create confrontations they had experienced in their own schools. With the crowd sufficiently animated, the speaker asked for other conflicts that could be dramatized, and the imaginations of the audience members began to flow with ease. The other situations were varied, but the speaker was most impressed with the high school counselor scene because it demonstrated the efficacy of such an *acto* wherever there were Chicano students.

From California to Michigan, Seattle to San Antonio, teatros were creating and presenting *actos* that expressed the frustrations of the Chicano high school student. The titles varied, and some were never given names, but the themes remained the same: keeping the Mechicano out of college. In some versions the counselor sent the male student to wood shop, metal shop, even plastic shop, tracking him into a vocation that required manual skill. "You Mexicans work so well with your hands," the counselor would tell his advisee, totally ignoring the student's interests. During the height of the war in Vietnam, some *actos* had the counselor enlist the males in the Army, telling them: "Just think of it: you'll see the world and be serving your country too." Of course, the students never took the counselor's advice and left the office in search of someone who could help rather than hinder their goals. "I'm gonna go to the EOP office at Cal State," the student would say, leaving an exasperated counselor to ponder what he or she had done wrong.

Whereas some of these *actos* presented the counselor as a blatant racist, others took a rather sensitive view of his or her objectives and gave the character a sincere desire to help the student. Certainly, a skilled craft is not a profession to be scorned, but at a time when

Chicanos were trying to break away from the image of only being "good with their hands," college was the obvious direction to take. Though many Chicanos enrolling in institutions of higher learning had come from barrio high schools and some required special admission programs, studies showed that they succeeded as well as the majority Anglo students, challenging the theory that they were lowering the standards of the university with their presence.[5]

In a fascinating study of militancy among Chicano high school students, Parker Frisbie prefaced his findings with the following: "Perhaps too often social scientists have imposed their own meaning on a situation and have failed to hear what the groups most directly involved have to say."[6] It is doubtful that any of the students in that auditorium in Michigan, or in any of the schools the speaker went to, had any knowledge of sociological studies dealing with their problems, yet the high school counselor *acto* invariably reflected what the academicians were discovering through their scientific research. Most importantly, this *acto* fit Valdez' early definition of the form already mentioned[7] and was able to offer a solution: go to college. Certainly, not everybody in that auditorium would enroll in a university, and many might not graduate, but the *acto* demonstrated another possibility to a people who had been given few options in the past.[8]

The High School Counselor deals with only one aspect of the educational process as it affects the Mexican-American student. The counselor's insensitivity and racism are exposed for all to see, and the positive alternative is always demonstrated. But because this *acto* focuses on the counselor role, it does not present a picture of the teachers' attitudes towards the Mechicano students in the classroom, especially at the primary levels. Studies have revealed that early childhood education is a crucial step in any student's life and perhaps even more vital for the Mechicano child. Thus, *The High School Counselor* is a reflection of a problem that has deeper roots, factors that are elaborated upon in the next *acto* and the concluding docudrama. For a look at the Mechicano student from elementary school through college, we turn to the Teatro Campesino's timely *No saco nada de la escuela* as we ponder the question raised by students and teatros throughout the country: "Why don't I get anything out of school?"

Learning the ABC's: *No saco nada de la escuela*

When it separated from the Chávez forces in 1967, the Teatro Campesino moved to Del Rey, California, and became a non-profit corporation under the administrative title of Centro Campesino Cultural (Farmworker's Cultural Center). The Centro Campesino Cultural would be the governing body under which the Teatro and other components Valdez envisioned would function. When the group moved to Fresno in January of 1969, its larger objectives became a closer reality. The Teatro occupied space in a church until October of the same year, when it rented a store-front Mexican restaurant and converted it into the new Centro. It was during this year that the Centro produced its first film, *I am Joaquín*, adapted from the poem by Rodolfo González.[9] Originally, the group had included a reading of González' poem accompanied by music and slides in its touring repertoire, and it elected to make the film in order to generate much-needed revenue from rentals and sales. Other films would follow as the Centro Campesino Cultural expanded into motion picture, publishing, and recording components.

Though the Teatro's repertoire still included farmworker *actos* in 1969, the group's relocation to Fresno was accompanied by a change in the composition of the troupe. Valdez had been hired to teach courses in Chicano Theater at Fresno State College, and his group became a student teatro, composed of some of his students.[10] Just as his first group had reflected the problems of the *campesino*, and the separation from the union had precipitated a search for identity, the move to Fresno inspired an investigation of the Chicano in the schools. The product of that investigation is significantly titled *No saco nada de la escuela*, which the Teatro members referred to as *No saco*. *No saco* is one of the longest actos in the Teatro's anthology; it follows five students from their first day in elementary school through college graduation.[11] True to the form of the *acto*, there is no attempt at subtlety here; every comment is as straightforward as a report card. However, in this case the schools are being judged, and they fail miserably. The major premise of *No saco* is to expose the racism and hypocrisy of the educational system in this country and its lack of sensitivity to the needs of the Chicano student.

Because of its length, *No saco* is divided into three scenes, each connected by the students whom we follow from school to school. Each of the scenes is really an *acto* in itself and could conceivably stand alone with little alteration. But together the three episodes in this *acto* create a broadly drawn caricature of student-teacher and student-student relations in the schools as it tries to discover why the Chicano does not get anything out of school. All that is needed to place the characters in the school settings are classroom desks that can serve for each of the three segments. The students remain the same, though they grow older before our eyes, and the teachers can either be played by the same actor or actress or by different members of the company. Masks are sometimes employed to add to the *commedia* quality of the *acto* and give it its most comfortable milieu.

The first scene opens with the sounds of elementary school children playing and laughing. The children enter, and we see that the adult actors are portraying youngsters of different backgrounds. There are two Anglo children, Flo and Abe; a Black boy, Malcolm; and two Chicanos, Moctezuma and Francisco. The atmosphere of farce is immediately noted, as these full-grown "children" run and play in typically exaggerated fashion. The contrast in cultures is made obvious when one of the children notes that Flo has a Black boyfriend and Flo quickly denies having anything to do with him. While the children are aware of their differences, they are still rather innocent; it is through the teacher's ideas and proddings that their innocence is brought to a startling end. The teacher is portrayed as an ugly old woman wearing a white mask and carrying an oversized pencil. She uses the pencil more as a weapon than a tool, emphasizing her militaristic stance and attitude. She has no name, this representative of so many others like her, and though she is being laughed at, her character is born of the actors' bitter memories of early schooling. Both the grammar school teacher and the high school instructor in the second scene are portrayed as being militaristic, reminding us that this *acto* was created during the war in Vietnam. Their combativeness was equated with the idea that the United States' involvement in Southeast Asia was colonialistic, and both their characters and that of Abe remind us of the war at home.

The elementary school sequence lays the groundwork for what is to follow. We see the teacher's obvious discrimination and its effect on the children. This first part gives the audience two extremes in the assimilation process in the characters of Francisco and Moctezuma. Using her oversized pencil to prod him, the teacher forces Moctezuma to change his name to the more Anglicized "Monty." This task completed, the assimilation process has begun for another Chicano child. It is not so easy with Francisco because he does not speak English. Rather than attempt to help the child, the teacher simply does not pass Francisco to the next grade; thus he has begun the road to alienation and defeat. Upset at the news that he is not passing, Francisco tells Monty: "Entonces dile a tu teacher que coma chet!" ("Then go tell your teacher to eat shit!") (p. 74). It is significant that one of the first English words spoken by Francisco is "shit." We are reminded of the comment in *Los vendidos* that the pachuco learned his language "in your schools."

Always reflecting their reality, the teatro members created characters out of their own experiences. It is not strange, therefore, that the rich Anglo student should be the son of a grower. An urban teatro might have made him the son of a doctor or a banker, but in this *acto* the symbol of the ruling class looms overhead in the form of the grower's son, Abraham. In elementary school Abe was a snot-nosed cry-baby; in high school his neck has acquired a strange reddish tint and he reminds us of a Nazi recruit. His girlfriend Florence is less obnoxious, but she is still unable to accept "those Chicanos." When she gets together with Monty, it is because he has by now denied his heritage entirely and might as well be white.

The female form of the assimilationist enters the high school sequence in the person of Esperanza. Also loath to call herself Mexican, she prefers the nickname Hopi, from the English translation of *esperanza*, "hope." When asked if she is Mexican, Hopi responds: "No, my parents were, but I'm Hawaiian" (p. 78). Perhaps this is what *Los vendidos'* Miss Jiménez was like in high school, we muse. Francisco has turned into a pachuco, as might be expected, and is only important to the school as its star baseball player. He is tolerated because of this athletic ability, not because of *who* he is, and he finally drops out of school.

The college scene opens with Francisco, broom in hand, asking a professor if he can enroll in college. The graphic reality of what is left for Chicano dropouts is here presented, and Francisco is not allowed to enroll.[12] This final scene is the longest of the three, perhaps because the members of the troupe were then in college and could collectively create more material dealing with their immediate experiences. The main point here is to inform the members of the audience that they too can go to college if they assert themselves. After the Black student Malcolm has forced his way into college, Francisco follows suit and demands equal rights. This is a simple demonstration of "Chicano Power" as it was seen then, and the *acto* may have influenced less militant Chicanos to demand more openings for Chicano students. An unfortunate reflection of the historical reality is that Francisco is only allowed to matriculate when he brandishes his rifle.

What is demonstrated in each of the three segments is that in order to succeed in the schools, the students have to repeat what the teacher wants and nothing else. It is the old "regurgitation" method once again, and the teatro uses the best means it has to illustrate its point. When the teachers ask their students to recite their "ABC's," they are graded according to their ability to repeat the American Dream. Francisco and Malcolm are continually degraded by the teachers because they reflect their own heritage, not that of Middle America. They do not relate to the professor's book of "American Knowledge"; when the book is opened we find that all it contains is a large dollar sign.

The sad reality is that many of this country's minorities have been taken in by the materialistic products of this society and do, indeed, go after the almighty dollar. In asking for the admission of more Chicanos to the colleges, the Teatro is demanding the same benefits any other group gains from higher education, not the least of which is more money. Ideally, Chicano college graduates would return to their respective barrios and contribute to their betterment. Monty, however, chooses to join the *vendidos*, and he obtusely follows "Nixon" offstage, prepared to become another "brown face in the crowd." He takes Nixon's symbolic "white bag" and becomes a part of the proverbial "melting pot," lost to his own people.

In a notably quick transition, Hopi regains her identity and becomes Esperanza again. In typical *acto* fashion, no real explanation is given, just the fact that she can change. The script notes that she walks like a pachuca, the female counterpart of Francisco. At that point in the Chicano Movement the street youth were being romanticized as the *real* Chicanos, and this metamorphosis in Hopi was necessarily extreme. In reality, there are few pachucos or pachucas in college; some Chicanos on the campuses may have been street youth, but a distinct adjustment is made when they become college students.

Once the doors of the imaginary college are opened to more Chicano students in *No saco*, they immediately plan a party. This penetrating comment about the Chicano college student is still valid and will draw a laugh of recognition from any student group. Once again the Teatro's mirror is held up to nature in order to demonstrate certain weaknesses. Francisco reminds the group that they are there to learn about their culture and history, not simply to have a good time. Significantly, when asked who will teach them the actors point to the audience and say: "Our own people!" (p. 94). The *acto* ends with a rousing song, and another American institution has been challenged.

In a period when bilingual programs were the rare exception, one of the major premises of *No saco* was that the Mechicano's use of Spanish was being turned against him in the schools. Francisco and Monty become the central figures of this piece as we watch them placed on two opposite tracks: the one destined for failure and the other for success in the dominant society. From the beginning, Francisco is degraded and held back for his use of Spanish while his counterpart Moctezuma is quickly indoctrinated by being forced to reject his name. Francisco's "ABC's" are a reflection of his sensitivity to his culture; Monty's are calculated to reflect what he knows the teachers want to hear. Even in high school, though he is now bilingual, Francisco's use of Spanish is his downfall, for the teacher cannot understand him and fails him on the spot.

The transformations that Francisco and the other Chicanos go through give this *acto* a dual purpose, for it examines the question of identity discussed in the second chapter of this book even as it examines the educational process. Clearly, the schools are very important tools in the assimilation process, and it becomes apparent in *No saco* that the sellout characters seen in Chapter Two are the products of this system. While *Los vendidos* introduced us to the pachuco syndrome in passing, *No saco* illuminates some of the possible reasons for such behavior. The Americanization of Moctezuma is classic in its directness, as he is literally prodded by the giant pencil-cum-bayonet into repudiating his own name, the symbol of his indigenous heritage. An *acto* for puppets entitled *La conquista de México* (The Conquest of Mexico)[13] precedes *No saco* in the Teatro's anthology, and it gives a deeper significance to the use of the name Moctezuma since it presents the ill-fated Aztec ruler as a despot who brought about his people's downfall. In effect, the Aztec emperor accepted the Spaniards as gods and denied his people, just as the contemporary Monty worships the Anglo and his way of life. We can imagine Monty walking off the stage and into *Los vendidos* as Eric García.

No saco does not attempt to present academically researched postulates but rather is the product of a collective analysis of personal experiences in the schools at all levels. Just as *The High School Counselor* is the creation of its participants' encounters with a certain situation in high school, so too is *No saco* to be viewed as the result of its creators' analyses. It is no accident that the characters point to the audience when asked who will teach them, for this was the dominant theme of the Chicano Movement in 1969. After demonstrating the unpleasant teachers at each level, the characters in the *acto* can look to none other than the community members for guidance and support. When people who have been planted in the audience go up on stage to join the actors for the finale, it is hoped that others will also make a stand, as if at a revival meeting. Thus the audience is reminded that its fervent spirituality can be transformed into political action.

No saco found enthusiastic audiences wherever it was performed, for it brought to life a certain aspect of the Chicano experience that few had escaped. Whether those in the audience related more to Francisco or Monty, Hopi or Esperanza, there were few who did not believe the characters and situations presented. Certainly, there was much more that needed to be said, but this three-part *acto* exposed the mood of the period in a way that could not be ignored. The vitality of the *acto*, with its exaggerated characterizations and biting satire, left its audiences with a lot to think about and a definite course of action to take. By looking to the community for its teachers, the *acto* was declaring its own people to be the leaders and models; the traditional teachers became the "culturally deprived."

While *No saco nada de la escuela* attempts to demonstrate why so many Chicanos do not succeed in the schools and to suggest solutions, the next *acto* treats other issues that have an impact on education and lays them on the mayor's desk. *El alcalde* focuses on local politics as another of the people's concerns, demonstrating how a midwestern teatro confronted inequities in its surrounding barrios. It is another example of the varied ways in which teatros throughout the United States expose local problems. We leave the politics of education for an encounter with the politics of corruption before seeing the two combined in the final docudrama of this chapter.

Who's to Blame?—*El alcalde*

There are several reasons for including *El alcalde* (The Mayor) in this study. This brief *acto* is the product of urban conditions in the Midwest, an area of the United States long ignored in studies of the Mexican American since most investigations focus on the Southwest. *El alcalde* was collectively created by Teatro Desengaño del Pueblo of Gary, Indiana, under the direction of Nicolás Kanellos, one of the leading scholars of Chicano and Puerto Rican theater in the United States. Kanellos' teatro was unique for its multi-ethnic composition as well as the broad range of ages of its members—from children to adults. As a Chicano-Puerto Rican-Anglo teatro, Desengaño del Pueblo differed from the majority of Chicano theater groups, yet it was continuing a theatrical activity in the Gary-East Chicago area that had begun with the first migrations of Mexicans into the area more than half a century before.[14]

El alcalde is actually a transitional *acto* within this chapter, for it leaves the teachers and counselors of the previous *actos* to address the bureaucrats who make the policies, represented by the mayor's office. Each of the works in this chapter expresses the attitude that the schools are only part of a much broader set of conditions responsible for the plight of the Mechicano in this society. While *The High School Counselor* and *No saco nada de la escuela* blame the educators and the schools, *El alcalde* takes its audience to City Hall and illustrates another possible solution to the educational problems of the Latino community. Because this acto is the product of conditions in the Midwest, it addresses nationalistic differences between the Chicanos and the Puerto Ricans—an issue that southwestern teatros do not have to deal with—thus adding another dimension to its purposes. In order to understand the atmosphere that spawned this *acto*, let us turn for a moment to the historical circumstances that led to the creation of a bilingual teatro in Gary, Indiana.

Large numbers of Mexicans began to migrate to the Midwest after 1910, attempting to find economic security in the steel mills and other industries as well as in agricultural enterprises throughout the area. So far from their homeland, these people sought to preserve what they could of their culture. For some that culture was expressed through a theatrical tradition that recalled the professional stage of Mexico City. In his seminal article about the Mechicano's theatrical activities in northwest Indiana, Kanellos emphasizes the fact that the immigrants were active in the Church and in mutual aid societies, institutions that have been instrumental in maintaining the theatrical tradition that continues to the present.[15] Responding to stereotypes that have described the Mechicanos as ignorant, uncultured, and unaware of theater as an art form, Kanellos describes five different companies that were active by 1920 in Gary and East Chicago, Indiana.[16]

Although the participants in the early Spanish-language plays did not earn their living in the theater, Kanellos notes that the productions were nonetheless of a professional quality, to judge from contemporary accounts. Some of the directors and actors were Mexican expatriates who had been involved in the professional theater in Mexico City, and their expertise contributed to the quality of the presentations. The repertoires consisted of religious dramas as well as contemporary Mexican plays. These companies had devoted followers and are still remembered by members of the older generation in the area.

Prior to the 1950s, the majority of Spanish-surnamed people in northwest Indiana were of Mexican origin, and the theatrical activity revolved around the Mexican barrios. But during the 1940s Puerto Ricans began to arrive, altering the composition of the barrios and bringing another theatrical tradition with them. Again, their theater was connected to the churches, but these were Puerto Rican Baptist congregations, not Roman Catholic as in the Mechicano community. Members of several Puerto Rican Baptist churches began producing plays during the period from 1956 to 1965, mostly on religious subjects, though secular dramas were also produced in the later years.[17]

When Nicolás Kanellos arrived in Gary in 1972 to teach Spanish literature at Indiana University Northwest, it seemed only natural that this Puerto Rican who had worked in Texas with the Teatro Chicano de Austin would found the first Chicano-Puerto Rican teatro. While a graduate student at the University of Texas, Kanellos had co-directed and acted with the Austin teatro and gained a great deal of experience in the teatro form. The Austin group presented *actos* like most of the other student groups around the country, and it represented an integral part of the Chicano Movement in its home state.[18] Though the Austin group no longer exists, several of its members have continued to work in teatro, joining other groups throughout the country. One of its most important graduates is the director of Teatro Desengaño del Pueblo.[19]

Inspired by the Chicanos' popular theater and informed by his knowledge of classical Spanish theater, Kanellos founded his Midwestern teatro in order to address sociopolitical issues that the community felt were pressing. Gary is a steel mill town, an urban area with a constant haze of smoke spewing from the huge furnaces in the nearby foundries. "You can tell you're in Gary," the locals tell visitors in the winter, "by the black snow." Transported from the clear skies and warm weather of Austin, Kanellos not only found black snow in Gary, but a Spanish-speaking community that needed organizing. In Austin he had been outnumbered by the Mechicanos who, of course, are the majority of Spanish-surnamed people in Texas. In Gary, however, this Puerto Rican from New Jersey found that there were large pockets of both *Riqueños* and Chicanos whom he could rally together by instituting a form of theater that would inspire collective creativity and social action.

Kanellos gathered students from his urban campus together with community members and their children, and these people from varied cultural backgrounds began to improvise situations that could be performed as *actos* before a public eager for a theater that expressed its needs. Kanellos began to understand the nature of Gary's Latino theatrical tradition when the daughter of a woman who had acted in one of the companies before the Depression joined the Teatro. Another member of the company had gained considerable experience in the Puerto Rican Baptist productions mentioned earlier. Thus were brought together the Spanish-language theaters of the past and the present.

El alcalde was one of the first *actos* to be created by the Teatro, and the group published it as a collective creation in 1973.[20] In typical *acto* fashion, *El alcalde* is played on an empty stage with one chair situated upstage right. Both the stage and the chair are empty when Raza Leader No. 1 comes on and addresses the audience. The other members of the cast are in the auditorium, as if they were auditors, not actors, and one by one they join the first actor as he calls out political slogans. *"¡Tenemos que organizarnos!"* ("We have to organize ourselves!") he shouts, and a woman repeats this from the audience. *"¡Tenemos que unirnos!"* ("We have to unite!"), the speaker continues, and the woman agrees and beckons the others to join them on stage. Nobody moves, and the woman calls out, "Hey, everybody!" to which the others respond in unison, *"¿Qué pasa?* What's wrong?" repeating the same line in English for those who do not understand the Spanish. The chorus of voices is referred to as the *pueblo* (community), and it represents the collective desires of the people as they respond mechanically to the calls for unity and an end to oppression. Suddenly a little girl in the crowd shouts out "I want a Latin teacher!" and the *pueblo* responds: "*Sí*, teacher." A teenager calls out "We want Latin counselors!" and the *pueblo* affirms the demand. "Stop urban renewal!" another woman shouts, and a little girl cries out: "I want *aguacate* (avocado) for lunch!" The demands thus listed, the people decide to go to the mayor for results.

The people march to the empty chair, chanting slogans as they go. When they reach the stage, they are stopped by Raza Leader No. 1, who reminds them that they have to go through the "proper channels." "Ohhh," the people respond in wonderment, and they are impressed to see that this leader has a petition ready for their signatures. As he had expected, the people elect him to deliver the petition, and he runs over to the mayor's office and finds him asleep in his chair. After the mayor has received the petition, he recognizes a political asset in this man and appoints him head of the Water Department. The leader is elated at this prospect and quickly changes into a dog, barking and urinating in canine fashion. The mayor places a dog mask on him and puts a leash around his neck, telling him "There's just one string attached, and here it is." Before sending his political appointee back to the community, the mayor gives him two small bones and sends him on his way while continuing to hold onto the long leash (p. 4).

When the leader returns to the other side of the stage, he eagerly announces: "Do I have some goodies for you!" The people are at first thrilled, but when they see that the two bones are meaningless, they begin to discuss their grievances. They realize that their children are being mistreated in the schools, put into special education classes, and failed in Spanish because the teacher is a *güerita* (Anglo), so they decide to go back to the mayor's office. The leader has been sitting at the mayor's side, like a dog, and he is prepared for them when they arrive with a renewed vigor. Rather than let them state their demands, the leader lists each one for them as if he were a political activist, mentioning bilingual education, Chicano and Puerto Rican Studies, Latin teachers and counselors, and other complaints that he knows they have. After each item, the people shout "Yes!" building emotionally to the leader's solution: "Well, ruff-ruff, all you have to do, ruff-ruff, is vote for the mayor in the next election" (p. 6).

The people are angered and frustrated by the leader's unsatisfactory suggestion, and they elect another leader, No. 2, to go see the mayor. No. 2 arrives full of the same political fervor as the first leader, and the mayor quickly drafts him as his new "community representative" because he is Mexican and the other was a "lazy Puerto Rican." The mayor gives this new leader a seat on the City Council as well as other worldly treasures such as a new Cadillac. No. 2 is thrilled and willingly accepts the dog mask and the leash that go along with his new assignment. He returns to the eager community to tell them he has a big bone for himself and a little bone for them: a teacher's aide. As soon as he has tossed the bone into the crowd a Puerto Rican and a Mexican fight over it, and the now divided groups run off the stage in opposite directions.

After a moment, a little girl comes onto the stage crying, for she has been bitten by a rat. A woman enters and discovers what has happened, and others join her as they realize that they have to unite against the mayor's office if they expect any changes. They all gather around the mayor and give him a swat with a newspaper after each demand is listed again. Their final pleas are for *"RESPETO, RES-PETO, RESPETO!"* as they lead the mayor offstage like a dog, chanting "C'mon, boy, C'mon, boy," thus concluding the *acto*.

The use of the dog mask and the attribution of animal character-istics are reminiscent of the earliest farmworker *actos*, as is the actors' exaggeration of the characters to get the point across. The dog image clarifies the relationship between City Hall and its so-called community representatives, for the leash is attached at all times to both the dog and the mayor. By grouping the community members as one *pueblo*, the *acto* demonstrates how easily the crowd is swayed, parodying political rallies and the vociferous responses of a public that is too easily led by rhetoric and political slogans. This is a reflection of itself that the community may not want to accept; it is made even more condemnatory when the two nation-alities divide over the "bone." The Puerto Ricans call the Mexicans "Wetbacks" and the Mexicans respond with "Green bananas" in a scenario that is familiar in relationships between the Latino cultures. The fact that the Puerto Ricans call themselves "Latins" indicates their recognition of a cultural difference, for they would no sooner want to be identified as Mexicans than the Mexicans would want to be called *Riqueños*.

Although the two groups agree on their demands, they cannot agree on who will get the bones until they are brought back to the harsh reality of the urban barrio by the little girl who has been bitten by a rat. This shock unites them once again, and the people are then able to march on City Hall and "beat" the mayor into submission. It is a symbolic solution, this physical abuse, but it is clearly a pos-sibility if the citizens join together in their effort to effect change for the better. They take the leader's suggestion that they vote for the mayor if they want to see some changes, and they thus demon-strate to all that a united front has power.

Curiously, while the Teatro Desengaño del Pueblo was creating its statement about community corruption and political runarounds in a midwestern city, a small rural community in California was be-ing investigated by the California Advisory Committee to the U.S. Commission on Civil Rights. Originally intended as a probe of the educational system, the Advisory Committee's report turned into an indictment of every aspect of the power structure in the town of Guadalupe. From the schools to the streets, the fields to the Church, an oppressive system of economic domination had corrupted Guada-lupe. This rural microcosm was unique in one way alone: the inequi-ties were documented by the federal government. *El alcalde* presents a quick, incisive view of local community problems that exist in any barrio. As an *acto* it succeeds in raising a voice of concern and demonstrating a positive course of action. The concluding work in this chapter examines what happened to a group of citizens who decided to take action against their oppressors and to demand what Puerto Ricans and Chicanos in Gary were also seeking.

A Microcosm in a Docudrama: *Guadalupe*

El Teatro de la Esperanza created its first docudrama, *Guadalupe*, in 1974, inspired by a government report about a nearby agricultural town of the same name.[21] Guadalupe has a population of approximately 3,000 people, of which over eighty percent are Spanish-surnamed. The town had achieved statewide recognition in 1973 when the California State Advisory Committee to the United States Commission on Civil Rights published a report entitled *The Schools of Guadalupe . . . A Legacy of Educational Oppression*. The report concluded that the Mexican-American children in the Guadalupe school district "have not received an adequate education, nor have they been encouraged to believe in their own worth as students and potentially successful Americans."[22] Though the focus of the report was on the schools, it substantiated the fact that Guadalupe was a microcosm of any Mechicano barrio, rural or urban. From the oppression of the small group of wealthy growers who owned the fertile land to the teachers' brutality and insensitivity, the broad range of problems confronting all Mechicano communities was evident in Guadalupe.

Guadalupe is an hour's drive from the Teatro's home of Santa Barbara, the county seat, and local coverage of the turmoil in Guadalupe drew the group's attention. The Teatro members proceeded to investigate all of the problems in the town, researching newspaper articles and court reports while also conducting interviews with members of the community. After reviewing the wealth of documented material, the Teatro improvised scenes dealing with the problems exposed in their research: the schools, drugs, the Church, the police, and the repressive tactics used by the power structure to quell any efforts to improve living conditions in the town.

From the inception of the study, events and facts fell into place as the people of Guadalupe told of their experiences with school officials, the growers, and the police. Even the parish priest fit perfectly into the Teatro's mold. He revealed himself in a sermon the group attended by telling his congregation of humble farmworkers that "Those of you who follow César Chávez or join his union will go directly to Hell!" The priest was a Spanish missionary who had been in Guadalupe for over forty years, perpetuating the almost feudal system that enabled the growers to have a cheap pool of labor constantly available by keeping the workers at bay through every means possible.

The Teatro based its scenario on the efforts of a group of parents who had attempted to oppose the repressive system and were effectively quieted by the city fathers in a well-planned community confrontation. Aware that the parents were mounting a platform of demands to the school officials, the school board invited a well-known *vendido* to speak at a town meeting. This living symbol of the *acto* stereotypes often spoke for the John Birch Society, condemning César Chávez, the Chicano Movement, and anything that opposed the ultra-right-wing politics of his organization. His rhetoric was typical, loaded with "Red Scare" tactics, and he often caused a great commotion when he appeared before a politically aware public. The organizers of the meeting knew this and used this controversial figure to create a situation they could take advantage of.

As expected, the speaker was shouted off the stage by angry parents, and three weeks after the meeting ten individuals who were active in the United Farm Workers, the Parents' Committee, or both were arrested *by mail* and charged with disturbing the peace. It was eventually discovered that one of the defendants was not at the meeting, and charges against him were dropped. Of the nine persons remaining, none was found guilty of disturbing the peace, seven were found guilty of disturbing a public meeting, and two were found not guilty of either charge. Sentences ranged from 45 days in the county jail to two years probation. The city fathers had succeeded in putting a stop to the organizing efforts of the parents and the union. People feared for their jobs and the welfare of their children and were therefore restrained. The Teatro saw this series of events as an excellent model for a documentary that would expose the universality of Guadalupe's situation.

After the initial period of investigation and improvisation, the Teatro members began to script individual scenes. These traced the development of the Parents' Committee and demonstrated the various means by which the people of the town were subjugated. All of the events were based on fact and inspired by the many interviews the company conducted with those most active in the committee and the union. Because drugs were a problem in this barrio, a subplot involving a Chicano heroin addict who eventually "sells" his wife for a fix paralleled the development of the Parents' Committee. The character of the addict was a composite based on actual persons and was added to demonstrate one of the more prevalent alternatives to the schools that had failed so many of the young people in the town.

Five months after the Teatro began its investigation and collective writing of the documentary, the group premiered it on Cinco de Mayo of 1974 in Santa Barbara. Because of the media coverage of events in Guadalupe, most Santa Barbarans were aware of the situation, but the dramatization of the people's plight added a new perspective to their perceptions of the case. In discussions with the audiences after each performance, the Teatro asked for criticisms and comments, eager to find out if their point had been well-taken. Throughout the eighteen months that the group toured with the production from Santa María to San Antonio, even travelling to Mexico City and rural parts of that country, the responses were always positive. In thirteen scenes introduced by political comments and traditional *corridos* set to new lyrics, the Teatro educated as it entertained, always emphasizing the idea that the events portrayed were happening in "any barrio, USA."

The Teatro continued to alter the script after the director and his wife left the group at the end of 1974, and the production was adapted for a thirty-minute episode of National Educational Television's "Visions" series in 1975. During the group's summer tour of Mexico in 1974, it had taped a ninety-minute special for Mexico's national television station, and combined with the NET production, *Guadalupe* reached a greater audience than most teatros can expect in a lifetime. Hailed by some observers as a milestone in Chicano theater, *Guadalupe* remains a singular representative of the documentary form and may serve as an example to other teatros.

In its final version, *Guadalupe* begins exactly like *El alcalde*: a lone speaker is on the stage, addressing the audience. Behind him there is a simple muslin backdrop with the name of the Teatro written across it, or perhaps only the rear wall of the stage. The bare stage is framed by two benches facing each other at opposite sides of the acting area. The benches are sprinkled with items of clothing, hats, and other paraphernalia that the actors will later use to portray the various characters. Packing crates at each side of the apron frame the acting area and provide the stations for the two musicians at either side of the action. The speaker is Marcos Cortez, a fictitious name based on the notorious Mexican American called in by the

Guadalupe School Board. He rushes onto the stage and angrily shouts for guards to be placed at each door. This creates a tense atmosphere as the audience is jolted to attention, for there is no dimming of the houselights to silence the crowd. Cortez introduces himself and fatuously explains that he is here to "tell the truth behind the Chicano Movement."[23] It is immediately apparent that this man is defending the teachers, not the students, and he next addresses a woman in the crowd, taunting her with his arrogance.

The scene is a re-creation of the night that sparked the court proceedings in Guadalupe, but the audience does not really know this yet. The eleven remaining members of the company are seated throughout the auditorium, and some call out to the speaker, expressing anger and frustration at what he is saying. Sometimes actual members of the audience join in the retorts to the speaker, but generally they watch and listen carefully, interested to see how this debate will end. In an effort to stop the proceedings, the actors portraying the actual people involved begin to shout "¡Viva César Chávez!" and urge the audience to join them in drowning out the detested speaker. Once the entire audience is caught up in the chanting, a drumbeat freezes the actors and halts the voices; then two actors announce (first in Spanish, then in English): "This parent-teacher meeting took place on March 16, 1972, in Guadalupe, California. The following events led up to this meeting." All of the actors then gather on the stage to sing the opening song in Spanish. They encourage the audience to weigh the issues that will be presented, for they are based on fact and are happening everywhere. The lyrics were written by two of the group's members and set to the music of a Latin American folk cantata, "Santa María de Iquique."[24]

After the slow, deliberate music of the opening song, two of the actors deliver a brief quote to set the mood: "A forty-year resident of Guadalupe says: 'We live in a concentration camp.' " A guitar strums the opening chord of a popular *corrido*, "Valentín de la Sierra," and the actors are quickly transformed into farmworkers picking the crops. Though the music is familiar, the lyrics tell of the people of this town, their grievances, their differences, and their lifestyle. Between verses the characters discuss what is being said in the song while they work the rows of imaginary tomatoes. This scene introduces the major figures in the documentary and establishes the problems that will be exposed. We meet the future leader of the yet-to-be-formed Parents' Committee, Señor Moreno, and an active mother, Virgie, as well as the local gossips, Pompis and Fruti. The two musicians at the side sing of the animosities between Chicanos and the Mexicans; this is followed by two actors illustrating those differences by arguing over the derogatory term used by Mexicans to describe a Mexican American: *pocho*. Each verse of the song goes on to define another problem and is followed by the actors demonstrating or discussing that problem. We next hear about the situation in the schools and see Virgie telling her son Frankie that he should go to school, to which he replies: "I don't like that place. They treat me bad over there and they make me feel stupid."

As the song continues and the workers keep picking the crop, the discussion turns to the need for unionization as well as the fact that the local priest does not support the Chávez forces. Following a verse about the collusion between the *migra* (the INS) and the growers, one of the workers shouts: "Ahí viene la migra!" ("Here comes the Migra!") in order to scare the undocumented workers and reveal their constant wariness about being deported. Virgie and her son discuss the drug problem, letting the audience know that this also plagues Guadalupe, and the last verse exhorts the audience to unite if they are to succeed in bringing about change. Moreno tries to interest a Mexican worker in joining the union, but the latter refuses because he is going back to Mexico after the season ends. A whistle blows and both the workday and the scene are over. In a few minutes, through musical narrative and dramatized dialogue, the entire spectrum of Guadalupe's problems has been presented, and the audience members have been urged to see how the problems are addressed in this re-enactment of a real situation.

From the beginning of *Guadalupe*, certain theatrical conventions are established. The opening scene is portrayed as if Marcos Cortez were a real speaker, here to address the unwitting audience and promote his ideas. The audience is asked to believe that this is really happening and is even encouraged to shut the man up when people in the auditorium begin to shout at him. But what begins as super-realism is abruptly cut short when the drumbeat freezes the action. The actor playing Marcos Cortez and a woman from the audience who is now onstage become themselves, not the characters they just were, and introduce the production. This juxtaposition sets the style of the documentary and asks the audience to continually remember that the people onstage are actors demonstrating these events. "Hopefully," writes Martha Hernández, a member of the group, "the people will take an objective view of the presentation."[25]

Once the "demonstrators" have gathered on the stage for the opening song, they never leave. When not in the action they sit on the sidelines, making minimal costume or prop changes and watching the action. They observe the events as intently as the audience does, and when something is funny, they laugh too. All of the actors wear a basic costume of denims and workshirts, and the actresses wear similar trousers with black leotard tops. Changes in blouses, shawls, hats, or shirts define a new character as each demonstrator assumes a variety of roles. There is no preparing for a characterization behind the scenes in this production, since the actors have to plunge right into whatever they are demonstrating as soon as they enter the acting area. They are like members of a team, sitting at the side, cheering their comrades on, and participating when necessary.

With the presentational style of the production established, the demonstrators are free to move in and out of characters without explanations or excuses. Even within a scene, an actor might freeze for an instant, drop his character, and then deliver a quote that makes a political comment on the ensuing action. Once the quote is delivered, the actor reassumes the character and continues as before. There are no scene changes, no lighting adjustments, as the actors change before the audience's eyes after the opening song, moving on to the demonstration: they become *campesinos* picking tomatoes. The musical narrative and the pantomimed actions define the situation in a simple, effective mimetic action. In a later scene that depicts the priest exhorting the people not to follow Chávez, the parishioners, who are on their knees, turn toward the audience when the Mass ends and become *campesinos* picking the crops once again. The workers are still bent over, drawing an analogy between spiritual and material enslavement.

When the actors demonstrate a role, the style of acting is not exaggerated or stereotyped but is based on the actor's interpretation of how the character might react. Interviews with the actual persons involved in the Parents' Committee gave the members of the company definite characters to emulate, but few of the antagonists were ever observed. Thus, the actors' interpretations of the villains of the piece came from their own and the director's impressions rather than from actual observations. Careful scrutiny of the acting styles reveals a progression from realistic to stereotypical, with the protagonists portrayed as realistically as possible. The town gossips are also portrayed faithfully but with as much humor as possible, creating a caricature of these observers of life in Guadalupe; it is almost as if they were a chorus, somewhat outside the action. Their dialogue and manner provide the basic comedy in this otherwise serious production, attracting the audiences' attention as they push the action forward with their exposition. The audience does not see the antagonists of the town until the last two scenes, and they are all portrayed with transluscent plastic masks that give them an air of anonymity or facelessness, which is a comment in itself. Separated from the audience by these masks, the characters are depicted with a certain amount of exaggeration and become the symbolic villains of *any* barrio.

Guadalupe elaborates upon a series of events documented by the federal government, which brings the situation very close to home. If anybody in the audience doubts the validity of the piece, the Teatro members give that person a copy of the "Report," which they have available at every performance. But it is more important for the Teatro that the audience realize that the events in Guadalupe are not unique. Throughout the production, they are reminded that what they are witnessing is happening in every barrio in the nation. The quotes that introduce each scene and those that are inserted within the action add the documentation, however brief, that keeps the audience aware of the veracity of the incidents.

In creating this docudrama, the Teatro felt that it should employ certain features of Brechtian theory that would convert the theater into a lecture hall, a place where the audience would be asked to pay careful attention to the politics behind each action. Because the actors were also the creators of this piece, they had a clear understanding of why the characters were taking certain actions, making certain decisions, and what the consequences of those choices were. The Brechtian influences can be seen in the episodic structure, the quotations, the presentational attitude that included the audience from the beginning, the constant presence of the actors, and the political base for the work itself. The demonstrator style of acting was also a direct influence of the German dramatist, inspired by his writings about "a new technique of acting."[26] The detachment of the actors as demonstrators, stepping in and out of characters, helped them maintain the sense of critical observation that they hoped the audience would also adopt.

In an interesting article that discusses Chicano theater as a "popular image," Juan Bruce-Novoa and David Valentín argue that Chicano audiences differ greatly from the middle-class German public Brecht was attempting to "distance" with his *Verfremdungseffekt*, the often cited "alienation effect."[27] These two critics feel that the Chicano audience is already distanced by an unfamiliarity with and even mistrust of theater and needs, on the contrary, to be persuaded by the theater group that it can be trusted before a meaningful exchange can occur.[28] Bruce-Novoa and Valentín feel that *Guadalupe* is an excellent example of a theatrical piece that approaches its audience with a clear understanding of the Chicano experience. Rather than being perceived as "outsiders" who have come to tell the community what its problems are and offer some solutions, the members of Esperanza impress these critics as capable of reaching their audience through *Guadalupe*. By literally coming out of the audience, as well as by presenting characters that the audience knows are based on truth, they feel that the troupe establishes itself as "not only on the side of the Chicano audience, but part of it."[29]

To Bruce-Novoa and Valentín, *Guadalupe* encourages an "investment of trust and emotion" that they feel is "anathema in Brechtian theatre."[30] Yet, the Teatro was not attempting to create a piece that was so objective as to be emotionless, for the members understood their audience's sensitivity to the issues portrayed and knew that even Brecht's theater could pull at the heartstrings, no matter what he theorized. An audience needs some sort of emotional attachment to the characters and events demonstrated, and *Guadalupe* gives them this. As Bruce-Novoa and Valentín have suggested, the characters onstage are too real to a Mechicano audience to be ignored, and certainly their problems are the same. Curiously, while these two critics appreciate *Guadalupe* for its "non-Brechtian" technique, Ellen McCracken feels that the audience is "encouraged to keep its eyes on the unfolding narration rather than on the finish because 'Guadalupe' begins with its own ending," a direct reference to her Brechtian analysis of the docudrama.[31]

McCracken also feels that "empathy is replaced by a conscious questioning of our reactions to the scene; emotions take a back seat to productive thinking" in *Guadalupe*.[32] Though this may seem to contradict the other two critics, both observations are correct about what the Teatro was attempting to do. McCracken recognizes the obvious Brechtian influences, and appreciates their intent, while Bruce-Novoa and Valentín praise the piece for becoming one with its Chicano audience, the "popular image" positively reflected. There is no hiding the emotional appeal in *Guadalupe*, but what might have become mired in melodramatic supplications is controlled by a careful placement of the most visceral scenes toward the end of the documentary. Scene Ten turns the auditorium into a classroom in which a little girl who is attempting to give a report about the Virgin of Guadalupe, after whom she is named, is humiliated and completely devastated by the insensitive teacher. The audience is left with feelings of hatred toward the teacher, for he has not only denied the little girl her name and language but has also insulted the Virgin. This is immediately followed by a scene that depicts a local drug addict trading his wife for a fix, once again unleashing anger and frustration at this literal rape.

Both of the preceding scenes are portrayed realistically and contrast with the next scene, which presents the members of the School Board in masks, planning the evening with Marcos Cortez, while the Parents' Committee is gathered at the opposite side of the stage discussing strategy. The anger inspired by the two previous scenes is now directed at those in power, the representatives of the economic structure that perpetuates the conditions, and the audience is helped to understand the connection. The focus shifts quickly from side to side in a presentational technique that forces the audience to think about what is being said. They have already seen what happened at the meeting and are now compelled to analyze the forces behind that event.

The ultimate success of *Guadalupe* depends on its effect on the audience and the impact it had on social change. Audiences throughout the Southwest reacted with sincere appreciation for a dramatization that seemed to be directed at them alone, a reflection of what had happened or was still happening to them. In Mexico the audiences watched the production with an intense curiosity, for they were fascinated by those Chicanos presenting their reactions to life "pa'l otro lado" ("on the other side [of the border]"). The teatro members had translated as much of the dialogue as possible into Spanish, and when they held discussions with the audiences after each performance, they discovered that the Mexicans were astounded by what they had seen. When the actors asked them if they would still like to come to the United States, the answer was usually "Sí." *Guadalupe* may not have dissuaded its audiences from seeking a better life in this country, but it did open their eyes to the kinds of problems that plagued their relatives to the north.

More important than the popular and critical success *Guadalupe* enjoyed were the changes brought about by the production. In Guadalupe itself the docudrama was received with intense gratitude, and the members of the Parents' Committee were encouraged to continue their struggle. The fact that a teatro had elected to dramatize their plight gave them a renewed hope and determination to succeed.[33] Educators of Mexican-American children in different cities were moved by *Guadalupe* to call for more bilingual programs, teachers, and materials. Parents were reminded that the schools were supposed to be at their disposal and for the benefit of their children, and they were encouraged to organize where necessary.[34] And most importantly, the production educated many people who were unaware of the problems exposed.

One of the Teatro's most memorable performances during its two-month tour of Mexico took place in a little *ejido* (village where the land is farmed in common) in the lush jungles of Veracruz. The troupe was invited to participate in a celebration dedicated to the expropriation of lands for the peasants. The Teatro accepted the invitation and eagerly travelled to the remote village, which had no electricity and seemed like a return to the nineteenth century. The community treated the members of the Teatro as guests of honor, and after their performance of *Guadalupe* hundreds of campesinos joined the local organization of farmworkers that was working to improve their condition. The production had obviously struck a responsive chord with the hard-working villagers, who could relate to the problems presented. Even in Mexico, *Guadalupe* had made a considerable impact, advocating social action as an alternative to resigned acceptance of the status quo.

Guadalupe is a fitting conclusion to this chapter, for it reveals all of the forces that have worked against the educational and economic advancement of the Mechicano. From the two-character *High School Counselor* to the episodic documentary, the issues become more complex, reflecting the evolving dramatic structures that the different pieces represent. Although the four works in this chapter share the same general objective—expose the schools and/or local government—the separate manifestations of that intended purpose reveal similarities as well as differences. The greatest differences are between the *actos* and the documentary, especially in reference to the process that created each and the resultant structure of the two forms. The four works share a presentational format, though the acting techniques differ—the docudrama counterposing the realistic and the caricature, the unmasked with the masked.

The three *actos* are the products of personal observations and intimate reactions by their collective creators, while *Guadalupe* is based on documented incidents embellished by the troupe's contributions. The improvisations that led to the three *actos* were limited only by the participants' imaginations and experiences, for they were inspired by the actors' responses to the issues involved. The conclusions to these works were not bound by historical fact; therefore the actors developed their own solutions to the thematic problems. But by beginning with the virtual ending of the story, the documentary immediately defined its limitations; the conclusion was determined by the facts. Thus the *actos* were born of present experiences and personal recollections, while the documentary examined an historical event. All four works share the same conflicts and ultimately the solutions are the same: improve the quality of education.

In the two-character *acto* that begins this chapter, there is one protagonist and one antagonist, each with his/her clearly defined objective: go to college/keep the Chicano out of college. The *acto* is simple, direct, and exposes only one aspect of the educational suppression of the Mechicano. There is usually a sharp contrast between the two characters, the students being portrayed sympathetically and the counselor presented as a stereotypical parody or caricature. This *acto* must be brief, for the plot is limited and it might otherwise become a dramatized lecture rather than a concise revelation. The solution is clear, and the ending always shows the student victorious or at least on the road to victory. Through a vicarious triumph, the audience is encouraged to follow the example that has been set, should the occasion arise. As in the works that follow, the observers are urged to "fight for your rights."

The singular villain in *The High School Counselor* is amplified in *No saco nada de la escuela* to include three teachers as well as the ubiquitous sellout, Monty. This representative *vendido* is significantly given a "white bag" by President Nixon, who symbolizes the national power structure. The *acto* blames the teachers as well as the federal government for the failures of the educational system and implies that the assimilated Mexican Americans are also to blame for not bringing about change.

El alcalde identifies the mayor and his two "tokens" as the villains; they collectively represent the local political system of graft and corruption. In contrast to the two previous *actos*, which had individual protagonists, *El alcalde* presents the *pueblo* as a collective unit, nameless and all-inclusive of the Latino population in the area. This *acto* tells us that everyone suffers because of poor education and it attempts to reinforce a Pan-Americanism that is unique to its region.

In contrast, *Guadalupe*'s villains are numerous and are identified by their sociopolitical standing and economic position. The same sellout who calls on the *pueblo* in the Midwestern *acto* appears in the docudrama, but this time with a name and with an immediately identifiable character: he is on the side of the enemy from the start and is only the first of many other villains to come. The teachers from *No saco* return to plague Guadalupe, joined by representatives of the town's controlling interests. There are some villains we never see, such as the outside drug dealers, but the majority make an appearance, from Marcos Cortez to the priest. The *pueblo* is not an identifiable group of parents; it is represented by Moreno and Virgie on the side of social justice and the town gossips as indicators of the general apathy of the community.

All of the *actos* except for *The High School Counselor* share a similar character type: the sellout.[35] It is significant that the sellout continually appears in Chicano dramas, for he fascinates as he repels and reminds the audience that solutions are as possible at home as in the schools or bureaucratic offices. But the *vendido* is never the ultimate villain, for the real power resides in those who have created him and use him for their purposes: the teachers and schools, the mayor, the school board. Because these Mexican Americans are as much victims as villains, the three works do not lay the blame totally on them. They are being used by "The System" and are portrayed as people lost to the cause, but not forgotten.[36]

Structurally, *Guadalupe* is the most complex of the four works, each scene leading to the next as the characters and incidents develop. Some of the scenes can stand alone as vignettes of life in Guadalupe, but the optimum effect is achieved only by a presentation of the whole. Because *No saco nada de la escuela* is really three *actos* connected thematically, each scene could conceivably be presented as a separate *acto*. However, the triumphant conclusion to the final scene is important to the *acto*'s message and offers a solution to the problems presented in all three scenes. In contrast, there is no victory at the conclusion of *Guadalupe*. Three of the defendants are sentenced to jail, and after an appeal from Virgie urging the audience not to be intimidated, a song calls for solidarity and the docudrama is quickly over. There are no easy solutions to the problems exposed in *Guadalupe*, though the Teatro hopes that its audiences will be inspired by the example of the parents and children of that little town. As demonstrators, the Teatro members stand before their audience and call for organized resistance to oppression in the schools, churches, and community services.

By design, the *actos* are based on a comic portrayal of a serious situation, while the docudrama limits its comedy to the two scenes with the town gossips. There is some humor in other scenes, but generally *Guadalupe* is very serious, focusing the comedy on the only caricatures in the piece. The villains wear masks, but they are not comic. They are almost anonymous, and they are played with a sense of angry determination rather than as stereotypical bunglers. We can laugh at the chorus of gossips, for they remove themselves from the action and do not display the urgency of Moreno or Virgie. We can also laugh at the stereotypical teachers in *No saco*, but the educators in *Guadalupe* strike a chord of anger with their psychological brutality. The "Report" told of physical abuse of the children, but the Teatro chose to demonstrate what could be even more destructive than a slap across the face. There is no exaggerated pencil to prod the students as in the first scene of *No saco*, though the same result is intended by the teachers: to humiliate the child.

In 1975, a critic observed that *Guadalupe* ". . . probably has the most demanding roles of any acto . . . ,"[37] identifying another major difference between the documentary and the *acto* form. For the acting style required in *Guadalupe* removes it from the *acto* genre altogether, calling for well-defined characers as well as caricatures and faceless villains. Because none of the characters are exaggerated beyond reality, the acting has to be technically proficient and is, indeed, more demanding than an *acto* would call for. The documentary technique requires a very skilled troupe of actors in order to be successful, while the *acto* can be produced by an inexperienced teatro. The technique of demonstrating the characters, stepping in and out of different roles with ease, dictates a realistic reflection of the community and calls for more than personal observation from the actors. Certainly, an *acto* like *No saco nada de la escuela* requires a certain amount of stage presence and actor vitality—what so many critics have noted when describing teatros—and it is possible to produce this Valdezian *acto* poorly. However, no matter how inexperienced the actors, the basic message always gets across. But it would be much easier to ruin the documentary with poor direction and insufficient training.

From the broad strokes of exaggeration in the *acto* to the realistic re-creations of characters in the documentary, the four works in this chapter effectively dramatize what their creators felt compelled to say. While the Santa Barbara troupe hoped to encourage the audience to maintain an objective view of the incidents unfolding on stage, it also recognized the fact that subjectivity permeated the very core of its investigation. In fact, none of the works is devoid of subjective opinion, for they are all the consequences of an angry, determined desire to set things straight.

Each of the works discussed in this section is as valid today as when it was created, for the changes advocated have too often been ignored by the people in a position to effect them. The teatros will continue to address these vital issues, for they understand that education is a very necessary step in the advancement of the Mechicano. The four dramatic efforts may serve to inspire other *actos*, plays or docudramas that express the same concerns, guided by the motivation behind all the works examined in this book: to educate as well as entertain.

El Teatro Campesino performing *Mundo* by Luis Valdez, 1980.
Photo: © Ricardo Martínez

Chapter Five

JUSTICE: ON THE STREETS
AND IN THE COURTS

With Liberty and Justice For Some

"Drive up to the gate, unload your stuff, and then park in the lot to the left," the voice from the gun tower tells the first van. "Somebody will be there to check you in." With the dull grey walls of the prison-fortress looming behind them, the drivers of the two university vans do as they are told, unload the props and people and wait for a prison official to admit them. None of these students has ever been in a prison and the dramatic entrance procedure impresses them with its implacable separation between the men inside and the society from which they have come. After passing through a series of doors and chambers, the teatro members find themselves in a maximum security federal prison, already shaken by the experience. They have been invited to perform by a group of Mechicano inmates, who respond with eager enthusiasm to their program of *actos*, songs, and Mexican dances.

The *actos* deal with some of the problems faced by Mechicanos in 1970: inadequate housing, schools, and employment. The prisoners respond to what the troupe is trying to say; they are experiencing society's retribution for having been born to the wrong family, the wrong class, or the wrong color and the *actos* are no surprise to them. There they sit, these victims of all that the *actos* are attempting to dramatize, and the actors feel a sense of irony that they are performing for them. Yet, although these students have found their way to academia and a promising future that few of these men will ever have, their backgrounds are similar and the prisoners can sense this.

When the teatro members first decided to accept the invitation to perform at the prison, they immediately resolved to present *actos* that reflected their own experiences rather than to create material based on prisoners' comments. Everyone in the teatro knew someone who had been in prison, but none could transform that limited information into an *acto*. Before, during, and after this first presentation, however, the teatro members were made aware of the need for *actos* and plays that would address the specific situations that resulted in a disproportionate number of Mechicanos in prisons. This was the first of many prison performances for this teatro and, like all the other troupes that would perform in prisons, the members of the group would always be impressed with the basic humanity of the men who so eagerly awaited them. They left the confines of that federal institution feeling somber yet fulfilled. They knew they could not be overwhelmed by pity for the prisoners. They had to maintain an objective view of the differences between the Mechicanos on the inside and those on the outside.

Beyond the poverty, broken homes, and dropping out of schools and society, the prisoners had all confronted the unyielding judicial system that sentenced them to prison. Talking with inmates, the actors felt that many of the men could have been victims rather than culprits, having suffered their fate at the hands of a biased justice. "Why are these men in prison," the actors asked themselves, "while we are at the university?" The works discussed in this chapter attempt to answer some of the questions raised by that prison performance. They focus on justice and the processes by which Mechicanos are tried, both on the streets and in the courts, and are concerned with two forms of justice: justice that reflects the aspirations of the Mechicano and justice that serves the interests of the dominant society at the expense of the Mechicano. As might be expected, the two forms of justice are not viewed equally by the groups involved; what is justice in the eyes of the police is interpreted as injustice by the Mechicano.

In an article about the administration of justice in a California county, Hisauro Garza concluded that Chicanos are treated differently by the courts "generally as a consequence of the dominant-subjugated group context, and more specifically as a reslt of discrimination."[1] It is a common barrio belief that Mechicanos are treated badly by the judiciary, from the first confrontation with the police to the last day in court or confinement and beyond. This attitude is not unique to the present-day Chicano Movement but has its roots in the earliest disputes between the Mechicano and the law in the Southwest.

Dramas that expose relations between the Mechicano and the courts prior to the 1960s are rare. One scholar, Tomás Ybarra-Frausto, learned of an early twentieth-century teatro from an interview with a former member of the troupe, Marcus Glodel, in 1973.[2] Glodel told Ybarra-Frausto that the Cuadro México-España, of which he had been a member, toured California, Texas, and Arizona from 1920 to 1927, performing a variety of productions for the Spanish-speaking communities.

The troupe was one of the first political Chicano theater groups in this century, for it decided to challenge the judicial system and atempted to organize the Mechicanos with a play entitled *La vida y proceso de Aurelio Pompa* (The Life and Sentence of Aurelio Pompa).[3] Aurelio Pompa was a Mexican immigrant who became the central figure in a political trial during the 1920s. Unjustly accused of killing an Anglo, Pompa's fate seemed certain if nothing was done to counter the false charges. The play was a three-part dramatization of Pompa's life, beginning with his crossing to this country, elaborating upon his humanitarian activities, describing his trial, and concluding with his hanging. The play was performed while Pompa was actually on trial, adding a note of urgency to the situation. After each performance, members of the company would pass a petition through the audience seeking the governor's intervention on Pompa's behalf. Unfortunately, Pompa was ultimately convicted and hanged, but the efforts of the Cuadro México-España are evidence of an early teatro's political involvement against an obviously biased system of justice in the Southwest. *La vida y proceso de Aurelio Pompa* foreshadowed the works of later teatros in the 1960s and 1970s.

In 1968, Guadalupe Saavedra, a poet, community organizer, and teatro director, founded the Teatro Chicano in East Los Angeles—another response to the Teatro Campesino's example. Although the group did not last long, Saavedra published a brief *acto* entitled *Justice*, which demonstrated his anger at the power structure and urged the people to fight police violence with equal violence.[4] The *acto* sets up the typical construct of humble Mechicano versus oppressive landowner, the latter personified by Honky Sam and his dogs. Honky Sam uses his dogs to control the people, who are advised by the "Voice of God" to organize. For every person the dogs kill, a dead dog is found the next morning until Honky Sam is subdued by the people's efforts. The dogs represent the police and Saavedra's acto was a direct response to police violence in East Los Angeles—indiscriminate killings that continue today.[5]

After the people in this *acto* have successfully fought the powers of oppression, a group gathers around a woman in labor. The "child" is born, and it turns out to be a picture of Che Guevara, which the mother cradles as if in a Nativity scene. As Bernard Dukore has observed, this *acto* suggests that society must be transformed by revolution, "perhaps along socialist lines."[6] Unlike the Teatro Campesino and the nonviolent tactics of the Chávez union, Saavedra felt that nonviolence was not a viable strategy against the abuses of the police and governmental forces. In his poem entitled "Dilemma of a Revolutionary Poet," he succinctly expresses his sentiments about barrio battles, the theme of *Justice*:

> Words will not stop bullets;
> Rhymes offer no protection from a racist club.
> Metaphors are useless weapons against brutality,
> And
> Adjectives will not prevent my being slaughtered,
> So
> As a pastime
> I collect bullets.[7]

In 1970, Francisco O. Burruel, a native of Tucson, Arizona, published a brief two-scene play entitled *The Dialogue of Cuco Rocha*.[8] This play is a realistic dialogue between Cuco Rocha, an incarcerated Chicano activist, and Captain White, a prison guard. Rocha, sentenced to twenty years for his political activism, is being transferred to another prison and the guard has come to play a final chess game with him. The dialogue is carefully drawn to demonstrate the playwright's belief that the Mechicano cannot be suppressed by the courts, although Capt. White and those like him refuse to understand why there is a Chicano Movement at all. Neither of the two men is a stereotype but are intelligent, realistic characters who find themselves in conflict over right and wrong. Though the two are not friends, they are able to communicate on a fairly intellectual level, generating a strong interest in their discourse. The symbolic chess game is perhaps a bit simplistic, but the playwright does not let it get in the way of the dialogue. There is one allusion to the Chicano as a pawn, but generally the men do not concentrate on the game while they engage in verbal battle over the Chicano's right to organize against the system.

The first scene ends when Rocha is taken away and the next and final confrontation occurs fifteen years later, after Rocha has finally won an appeal. White is now the warden of the prison and the two meet a final time. The Chicano is still an activist; although he suffers from rheumatism, he will go back to his community to experience the harvest of the movement he had fought for in the past. "I think I'll just grow old and watch my people become lawyers, doctors, and school teachers," he tells the warden, indicating that this is the playwright's revolution in the making. In both scenes, White has an air of uncertainty about his adversary's activities, as if he felt conscience-stricken about the suppression of the Chicano. Burruel clearly does not sympathize with this symbol of Anglo domination over the Chicano, but he has nonetheless given us a role that is three dimensional rather than one-sided and flat. Although he represents the villain, White is just as human as the other man and is perhaps as much a victim of the system as Cuco Rocha.

Cuco Rocha represents all Mechicanos, with the obvious reference to cucaracha, or cockroach, a common literary metaphor for La Raza. Rocha tells the guard that his name represents "The Mexican-American people," not just an individual, leaving no doubt in the audience's mind about the symbolism. Unlike Saavedra's *Justice*, *Cuco Rocha* suggests that change will be brought about within the system, by educating Chicanos, who will return to their barrios armed not with bullets but with the training to function in the dominant society while being able to recognize the problems in the Chicano community.

The fact that Rocha is finally released after fifteen years indicates the playwright's belief that change will not come about overnight as Saavedra expressed in his *acto*. In both cases "justice will prevail," but it will be administered by the people themselves in *Justice* and by an enlightened court in *Cuco Rocha*. Saavedra's visceral approach, which appeals to the audience's emotions, is the opposite of the realistic dialogue in Burruel's play, which calls for reason rather than violent confrontation. Both attitudes were prevalent in the first stages of the Chicano Movement, although the mood of the period usually inspired the *acto*'s solution: violent overthrow by any means necessary.

These three brief dramatic expressions serve as historical prefaces to the three major works that are the focus of this chapter: *Trampa sin salida* by Jaime Verdugo, written in 1972; *Las many muertes de Richard Morales* by Carlos Morton, produced in 1976; and *Zoot Suit* by Luis Valdez, presented in 1978 and 1979. The first is an *acto*, the second a documentary, and the third an eclectic mixture of the forms Valdez had used previously—*acto, corrido, mito*—and the realistic play combined with documentary.

The first two productions deal with the Chicano at the mercy of the police who take justice into their own hands, and the final play presents a picture of racist justice in 1944. In all cases, the Chicanos are presented as rather helpless scapegoats for a system of discrimination and undue process. The works can all be categorized as exposures of the problem, intent on analyzing the conditions that have led to the judicial suppression of the Mechicano rather than finding a particular solution.

Trampa sin salida (Trap Without Exit) was first produced by Teatro de la Esperanza in 1972 and was subsequently presented by various teatros throughout the Southwest after its publication in 1973.[9] Like Saavedra's *Justice, Trampa sin salida* was written by a single playwright, not a collective. This *acto* is important to this study because it begins to investigate the pachuco and his relationship to his family, his friends, and his enemies: sociologists, employers, and police. The *acto* was written in response to the apparent murders of Chicanos in the Los Angeles County Sheriff's jail—deaths reported as suicides under very strange circumstances. It appeared that the sheriffs had taken justice into their own hands and Verdugo's script attempts to dramatize that theory.

Las many muertes de Richard Morales (The Many Deaths of Richard Morales) was written by one of the most prolific Chicano playwrights, Carlos Morton, with the collaboration of fellow graduate students at the University of California at San Diego. The group was given the task of creating a documentary about a pressing issue and chose to dramatize the events surrounding the death of a Chicano in Texas at the hands of a local police chief. The incident had aroused the indignation of the Mechicano community. An article in the *New York Times* triggered Morton's imagination and inspired him to investigate the matter for the group project. It appeared that little had changed since the days when the Texas Rangers could kill Mexicans indiscriminately, for the policeman was found guilty of aggravated assault and sentenced to two to ten years in prison.

The resultant documentary is a forceful retelling of the incident and it condemns the sheriff, his family, and the entire judicial system. Dual justice was dispensed, first by the officer, who believed he was ridding the community of a bad element, and second by the court, which in effect vindicated the sheriff's actions.

Zoot Suit dramatizes the Sleepy Lagoon murder trial of the early 1940s in Los Angeles, bringing to life an era of anti-Mexican sentiment that most historians have chosen to ignore. The central figure of the play is the leader of a group of Chicano youths who were accused, tried, and convicted of murdering another young

Chicano at a local gathering spot called the Sleepy Lagoon. Although the boys were eventually acquitted of any crime, the play brings to light an historical event that must not be forgotten, for the injustices portrayed are with us still. *Zoot Suit* is consummately important; it is the first Chicano play to reach the professional stages of both Los Angeles and New York, ushering in a new era for the man who initiated the contemporary Chicano theater movement: Luis Valdez.

Salsipuedes—Get Out If You Can: *Trampa sin salida*

Jaime Verdugo was a student at the University of California at Santa Barbara in 1971 when he wrote *Trampa sin salida* for a Chicano theater class taught by the director of El Teatro de la Esperanza. Originally, Verdugo intended to research what sociologists had written about the pachuco, but he soon realized that his own experiences while growing up in East Los Angeles were enough to inform his brief *acto*. The young playwright wanted to expose some of the daily problems faced by urban *vatos locos*, especially the police brutality to which these young Chicanos were often subjected. The Los Angeles County Sheriff's Department claimed that the pachucos had committed suicide in their jail cells, but Chicano newspapers and magazines reported that the deaths were undoubtedly murders.[10] Few political activists believed that the pachucos had actually taken their own lives, prompting Verdugo to depict two sheriff's officers beating an innocent young Chicano to death.

Born in Tijuana, Mexico, in 1952, Verdugo was brought to the United States by his family when he was eight years old and was raised in Los Angeles, which has the nation's largest concentration of Mechicanos. Growing up in urban conditions that perpetuate the pachuco syndrome, Verdugo later transferred his observations of street youth to the stage and created a sympathetic view of these much maligned young men. The published script also reflects the influences of the director and designer, calling for the use of masks, identical costumes, and constant movement in one direction, as if the characters are all on a one-way street. Verdugo was an actor with the Santa Barbara troupe before his work was published and he performed in the *acto*, experiencing his creation from both sides of the footlights before committing the script to the printed page. As with most scripts created for a teatro, *Trampa sin salida* is the product of the playwright's vision coupled with the collaboration of the director, designer, and other actors.

Like their predecessors, the legendary zoot suiters of the 1940s, contemporary pachucos affect a certain dress that immediately distinguishes them. Verdugo's script notes this; he agreed with the director and designer that this similarity of appearance should be exaggerated to the extreme in the *acto*. Therefore, the pachucos all wear the same costume of black shoes, khaki pants, suspenders, and white T-shirts. Their masks are all modeled from the same mold, giving them a carbon-copy likeness inspired by reality itself. Before closer scrutiny, these young Chicanos do appear to look alike. One of the pachucos in the opening scene mistakes his friend for an enemy, emphasizing the playwright's comment on the pachucos' propensity for affecting identical styles of clothing and mannerisms. The fact that the pachucos all look alike also stresses the *acto*'s suggestion that their suffering is equal and offers a composite vision of the pachuco through more than one protagonist. The pachucos are presented as common enemies, but they must join forces against a greater adversary in the end.

The *acto* is appropriately titled *Trampa sin salida* since it depicts the trap that the pachuco finds himself in—avoided by those who fear him and challenged by peers and enemies alike. The metaphoric "trap without exit" runs down a one-way street to nowhere, as the various representatives of the *vato loco* type fight their daily struggles for survival. It is a brief but dramatic statement that has been produced by teatros and students throughout the Southwest. It is especially popular among the young Chicanos whose reality it reflects, attesting to the truth of the depiction. Performed on a bare stage, with simple costuming and a cast of six major characters, Verdugo's script can easily be staged by a group of ten actors. All that is needed to set the scene is a one-way sign hung at center stage on a simple backdrop that frames the action. The rest is left to the audience's imagination. The use of masks accents the *acto* tradition of *commedia dell'arte* performance style and also enables the actors to play more than one role if necessary.

There is no real plot to Verdugo's *acto*; it is a series of scenes presenting various pachucos' confrontations with the forces around them. Little Ray is the central figure; we find him always on the street and always in conflict with another character as the playwright explores some of the conditions that have helped to form the pachuco's personality. The forces Little Ray confronts include his mother, his friends, other pachucos who are his adversaries, and a sociologist who uses him for a study of pachucos.

Both Little Ray and the other characters he confronts are continually walking down the one-way street, from stage left to stage right, around the backdrop, and back again. This movement, which runs from the audience's right to left, contrasts with the eye's normal pattern of left to right, creating a visual jarring that is intentional. None of the characters can get off this track and their movement against the normal eye pattern intensifies the impact of their trap. Sometimes it seems that they are about to reverse the pattern, but any hopes for escape are soon thwarted. When he is confronted by the voices of prospective employers, Little Ray freezes for a moment, only to continue down the one-way street when he is rejected.

After Little Ray and hs friend Jessie have been in a fight with other pachucos, Jessie suggests that they get involved in the Movement and help each other rather than destroy their own kind. The focus then shifts from Little Ray to Jessie's fate at the hands of the officers, who kill him in a slow motion beating. After unsuccessful attempts to find out what has happened to his friend, Little Ray reads an article in the newspaper stating that Jessie had committed suicide in his cell. According to the article, stolen goods had been discovered in Jessie's car. "A quién creen que hacen pendejos" ("Who do they think they're fooling"), he asks quietly, "ni tenía carro" ("he didn't even have a car"), and the *acto* is over.

The Teatro de la Esperanza produced this *acto* with *commedia dell'arte* techniques, but it is a serious statement, not a comic exposure of a problem with a rousing solution offered at the conclusion. The confrontations serve to define certain conditions by pitting characters against each other and against the audience itself. The opening lines are delivered to the audience in order to include them in the action. When an antagonistic pachuco comes on later in the *acto*, he actually threatens the public, pulling back with a grin the moment he has made them apprehensive about his presence.

After the two major pachucos decide to get involved in the Movement, another pachuco named Johnny comes on, declaring that he is now politically involved. When Little Ray enters, he and Johnny immediately draw knives. Johnny has just proclaimed his allegiance to his own people, but the moment a former adversary who looks exactly like him enters, the two supposed converts have to be dissuaded from fighting by a Chicana who calls to them from the audience and convinces them to work together. She is the only character in the *acto* who does not wear a mask, and she emerges from the audience calling for Chicano pride and unity in a brief statement that is directed as much to the audience as to the other characters. By having the pachucos verbally and physically threaten the audience members, Verdugo forces the latter to study their own responses to the pachuco type. Little Ray tells his mother: "As I walk by the streets people move out of my way. They're scared of me" (17).[11] When any of the characters confronts the audience seated before him, the audience feels a certain apprehension, which has its roots in the very conditions the characters are talking about. The air of mystery and fear surrounding the pachuco can be his protection as well as his nemesis, according to Verdugo's analysis.

These pachucos are the victims of each other's and society's categorizations, and the audience members are urged to confront their previous impressions of the pachuco. Because of the conventions of the *acto* form, we only learn a limited amount of information about the pachuco, but Verdugo's characters inspire more than a casual appraisal. Behind the costumes and the masks, these young Chicanos are very human—misunderstood members of a misunderstood minority fighting for survival the only way they can.

Verdugo's pachucos are streetwise and enterprising, not easily duped by police tactics or academic routines. When the sociologist asks Little Ray to answer some questions for a study of pachucos, the latter quickly realizes that the correct answers will earn him ready cash. The sociologist wants his subject to fit his particular definition of what a pachuco is and for every "yes" answer he gives him a dollar bill. In response to a particularly inept question, Little Ray replies: "A yes answer will cost you ten dollars" (19). When the academic balks, the pachuco takes the money out of his hand, aware that the man's fears overcome his frugality. The other characters are also wise to what is happening around them. When pitted against the sheriffs, Jessie knows that he is being framed. He is an innocent victim of repression who pays with his life. His friends know that he has been murdered, but they can do nothing about it.

The language in *Trampa sin salida* reflects the usual mixture of Spanish and English, with a touch of *caló*, the argot of the pachuco. When communicating with one another, the pachucos speak "Spanglish," switching from Spanish to English as the mood demands. When Little Ray confronts the various people in his life, his language pattern adjusts to fit the situation and the person. He speaks mostly Spanish to his mother, who speaks no English, and addresses her with respect. When confronted by the sociologist, Little Ray speaks to him in English, reserving his Spanish for derogatory remarks that the Anglo character cannot understand. The Mechicano audience members know what he is saying and can share in the joke, enjoying a feeling of linguistic superiority that the playwright intends. In the killing scenes, however, Jessie retorts to the sheriffs in Spanish, exacerbating the distinctions between them and bringing about his doom. It is as if the officers are punishing him for being able to communicate in a language they cannot understand.

Verdugo chose to have his characters speak a very vulgar language, emphasizing four-letter words with the frequency common on the streets. After this language was censored for a local high school performance, the Teatro members chose to temper the harsher epithets for community audiences. The message, they discovered, was more important than the language. A few years later, two reviewers who read the published script commented that the *acto* "depends excessively on impressionistic words that lose their impact due to constant repetition."[12] When performing before a university audience, the Teatro did not alter the language because the group felt that the "fucks" and "shits" were a true reflection of barrio realities that college audiences could appreciate. But the criticism of the "impressionistic language" is an important comment from a community viewpoint and cautions producing groups to forgo such verisimilitude on community stages.

Pachucos have created an extensive vocabulary of their own, but Verdugo limits his characters' use of *pachuquismos* or *caló*. He knew that his audiences would not be composed solely of pachucos, who could understand their own patois, and he therefore avoided conversations that would be accessible to them alone. Terms such as *ese* (used to refer to another person) and *orale* (loosely translated as "right on") give the pachuco characters a hint of linguistic authenticity and make the dialogue understandable to the majority of bilingual audiences.[13] Rather than converse excessively in English, Verdugo's pachucos communicate in just enough Spanish to give them credibility as street youth. Perhaps because they were so delighted to see themselves portrayed sympathetically onstage, the pachucos who saw *Trampa sin salida* never complained that the language was not realistic, even though their own speech was peppered with much more *caló*.

Language is also used for comic effect. To enhance the *commedia dell'arte* style of the production, the characters of both the mother and the sociologist are exaggerated and their farcical behavior is heightened by their speech. Angry because she cannot do anything to counter what is happening to her son, the mother storms about and then surprises the audience with a vulgar phrase in Spanish in reference to her son's teacher: "*¿Pos quién chingados se cree que es—la mamá de Tarzan?*" ("Well, who the fuck does he think he is, Tarzan's mother?") (17). The intended effect is to shock the audience while making a ridiculous reference to the popular comic strip character. For community performances, the Teatro usually substituted a milder term for *chingados*. The reaction from the audience was the same: laughter at the comparison.

The confrontation with the sociologist is also intended to arouse laughter by contrasting an ape-like scientist with an intelligent pachuco. When the would-be expert on barrio realities asserts that Little Ray obviously has all the sex he wants because he lives in the barrio, three Anglo girls come running onto the stage, begging for a turn in the pachuco's arms. The sociologist's inference that barrio women are sexually promiscuous is offset by the appearance of the blond-wigged characters, sometimes played by the men in the company to heighten the farce.

Farce is reserved, however, for the first portion of this *acto*; after the sociologist leaves, the transition to the major premise is made: the confrontations with other pachucos and the sheriffs. Having witnessed Jessie's cruel death, the audience is urged to sympathize with the plight of the pachucos at the hands of Anglo justice. Although Little Ray is the central figure of this *acto*, it is his friend who is killed, which diverts the focus to another character. This enhances the playwright's premise that these pachucos not only look alike, but are individuals whose personal sufferings are felt by the collective. There is no single hero; they are all victims, for any one of these pachucos could have died at the sheriffs' hands. The officers think that they can get away with another murder by labelling the death a suicide, though the people in the barrios know otherwise. To add to the pathos of Jessie's fate, Verdugo cuts short what appears to be an awakening of social consciousness by dealing the death blow to a politically aware pachuco. For those left behind, however, the only solution is to organize against such repression.

Although the *acto* does not offer a direct solution to the killings, the Chicana who comes from the audience urges the pachucos to practice *carnalismo* (brotherhood) instead of *chingazos* (fighting) among each other. Her appeal is made before the sheriffs kill Jessie rather than after his death, which plays on the audience's emotions by suggesting a solution and then snatching it away with Jessie's demise.

The raised fist and shouts of "Chicano Power!" of earlier *actos* are replaced by a simple, almost whispered response as the two pachucos silently leave the stage at the end of the piece, still on that one-way street. The suggestion that these pachucos can become political activists is somewhat idealistic, but the emotional appeal of the ending is that it urges the audience not to be fooled anymore. As in the work to be discussed next, the *acto*'s major purpose is to expose the problem; the solution is still a dream in the 1980s.

Tampering With the Evidence: *Las many muertes de Richard Morales*

Carlos Morton was born in Chicago, Illinois, in 1947, the son of first-generation Mexican-American parents. His paternal grand-father's original surname was Pérez, but after he migrated to the Midwest in the first part of this century, he discovered that his name was a liability when looking for employment. "He saw a billboard advertising Morton Salt," the playwright recounts, "and decided that 'Morton' must be a good American name."[14] Years later, the older Morton's grandson would acknowledge his cultural heritage and become one of the most prolific Chicano playwrights in the country.

Reared in the Midwest, Morton entered the University of Texas at El Paso in 1970, eager to discover his ties with the Southwest, Mexico, and Latin America. The young writer realized that he would have to see as much of the world as he could if he was to re-flect humanity's many faces, and he began to travel whenever possible. He majored in English and periodically abandoned his formal studies to see the world while continuing to write and publish short stories and poems.

Morton entered college at the height of the burgeoning Chicano Student Movement and was inspired by his love of theater to write his first play, *Desolation Car Lot*, in 1973. It was produced by Chicano students at Texas-El Paso for a 16th of September celebration and launched the young writer on a theatrical career. Although he would continue to write in other genres, Morton was continually drawn to the stage. In 1974 he published *El jardín* (The Garden), a Chicano version of the Fall of Man.[15] The developing playwright attended the Fourth National Chicano Theater Festival in June of 1973 and met teatro troupes from all parts of the United States and from Mexico. He began to study the growth of Chicano theater more closely and observed various teatros in action in order to understand their creative processes and dramaturgical styles. He became a travelling playwright who toured from group to group, learning what he could about Chicano theater.

After living with the Teatro Campesino for a brief spell, Morton published his next play, *El cuento de Pancho Diablo* (1976), dedicating the play to Valdez' troupe.[16] This raucous comedy is actually a sequel to *El jardín*; its premise is based on what would happen if the Devil retired from Hell and came to Earth to live. Perhaps because of the spectacle and the very large supporting cast of saints and sinners, devils and whores, this is his only unproduced play. Morton completed his B.A. in English at El Paso in 1975 and entered the Master of Fine Arts program in playwriting at the University of California at San Diego in 1976. While still a graduate student, he published *Las many muertes de Richard Morales*[17] and witnessed productions of two other plays: *Lilith* and *Los dorados*. After completing the M.F.A. in 1978, he published the sequel to *Los dorados, Rancho Hollywood* (1979).[18]

Lilith is a play based on the Biblical character of the same name who preceded Eve as Adam's first wife. This play, developed with a group of graduate students, proposes that the traditionally biased accounts of woman's deeds need to be reappraised. *Los dorados* was a street theater piece that toured San Diego County, giving a Chicano account of the discovery of California. *Rancho Hollywood* is an episodic account of California history from the Gold Rush to the present, employing the metaphor of Hollywood stereotypes to demonstrate how certain images of Chicanos, Blacks, and Native Americans have been perpetuated.

In 1979, Morton joined the San Francisco Mime Troupe as a playwright in residence, helping to develop the group's summer production entitled *Squash*. It was a collaborative process that was a new experience for the dramatist. In his previous writing, Morton had worked alone or had written his scripts for a particular group that would read the dialogue, critique it, and send him back to the typewriter for the revisions that he and the director felt necessary. The Mime Troupe, on the other hand, has a long tradition of collectively creating a piece without identifying a particular playwright's contributions. "It is a very humbling experience," relates the dramatist, "but a valuable one as well."[19]

While still working with the Mime Troupe, Morton began to revise *Las many muertes de Richard Morales* for a production by the Bilingual Foundation of the Arts in Los Angeles. Thus, in the fall of 1979, he was spending time in San Francisco, working with the Mime Troupe, in Los Angeles, re-writing for the Bilingual Foundation, and in Berkeley, teaching a course on Chicano Theater. Teatro Chicano had become a way of life for this wandering playwright, whose plays had been produced by teatros, drama departments, and Chicano Studies students from coast to coast. No other playwright besides Luis Valdez has been as active and prolific as Carlos Morton. He might be termed a one-man teatro, expressing a vision of the Chicano that is informed by his own experiences and his observations of the world around him.

Morton's first assignment in San Diego was to create a documentary in collaboration with a student director and a cast of four actresses and six actors. While searching for a topic, an article that had appeared in the *New York Times* in the summer of 1976 came to Morton's mind. The article began:

> CASTROVILLE, Tex., Aug. 13—Eleven months ago on a moonlit gravel road five miles west of town, Frank Hayes, the 52-year-old Castroville Police Chief, put the barrel of a sawed-off 12 gauge shotgun under the left armpit of Richard Morales and pulled the trigger.[20]

The article went on to report that Hayes was later convicted of aggravated assault and sentenced to two to ten years in prison. His wife, who had transported the body four hundred miles and buried it, was placed on one year's probation and fined $49.50 in court costs. Neither the daughter, who had helped the mother transport and bury the body, nor her boyfriend, who was at the scene of the death, were charged. The article told of efforts by local Chicano leaders to have the case investigated by the Justice Department, though this was only one of many such deaths at the hands of Texas police.

Here was an ideal topic for a documentary and Morton began to research the case, corresponding with Chicano publications in Texas that had been critical of the entire affair. Bennett McClellan, the student director, was also enthusiastic about the play and worked closely with the playwright to guide the staging and the character and plot development. Although the script is Morton's, the collaboration of his fellow students was an essential part of the finished product. Morton was working with a company composed of one Chicano, two Black and seven Anglo actors. This group differed from the usual teatro in its racial composition as well as in the fact that all of the members of the group were graduate students in drama with extensive backgrounds in theater. Luckily for the playwright, the group immediately became a cohesive unit, sympathetic with the message of the play and intent on making an effective state-ment. While the majority of the actors were not Chicanos, their sin-cerity and acting acumen overcame any linguistic shortcomings they demonstrated when speaking the few Spanish lines.[21]

In keeping with the documentary structure and form, *Las many muertes de Richard Morales* is written in a presentational style, with a narrator who moves in and out of the scenes, commenting on the action and characters and describing the various settings. There is no scenery required. A simple sawhorse and two milk crates suggest a car, a courtroom stand or chairs, and other set props as needed. A length of pipe that serves as the shotgun leaves much to the audi-ence's imagination. Once again, this is a very portable play, an ideal vehicle for economical production. To open the play, the company recites "Case open!" in unison from offstage, immediately establish-ing a courtroom atmosphere. The narrator steps to the center of the stage to deliver the opening address that repeats the introductory lines from the *Times* article. The remainder of the plot unfolds the events that led up to the trial, culminating with the sentencing of the major antagonist, Hank Frayes. (Except for Richard Morales, all of the characters' names have been altered, though the real-life counterparts are obvious.) There is no attempt to hide the bias of the company or the documentary: The police chief is guilty of first degree murder, even if a Texas court feels otherwise.

The playwright's research beyond the *Times* article enabled him to enhance the basic plot by giving the characters certain traits that remove them from a newspaper reporter's black and white portrayal. Hank Frayes is shown to suffer constant pain from gunshot wounds received during a robbery a few years before, and an early scene reveals that Morales had previous confrontations with the police. In other words, they both have a past and exhibit weaknesses and strengths that prevent them from being simple "good guy versus bad guy" types. There are moments when the police chief is very human, eager to provide his daughter with the best of everything, though his determination to "kill me a Mescin" shows the insidious side of his nature and identifies him as a villain. The two opposing figures of Morales and Frayes are each supported by their wives; María Morales, however, is at a disadvantage and is rather helpless once her man is dead. In contrast, Doris Frayes immediately sets out to bury the body when her husband announces that "nobody will believe it was an accident." María can only plead for justice in the courtroom, while the policeman's wife contributes to the travesty with grim determination. Each scene demonstrates how helpless the

Chicanos are when confronting the wall of racism that has made it possible for police officers to shoot Mexicans with impunity. Not all of the Anglo characters are villains, however. The deputy policeman sympathizes with Morales and tries to stop the murder, and the chief's daughter Joan is an unwilling accomplice to her mother's burial mission. Rather than create an entire family of macabre villains, the playwright adds an interesting stroke to the daughter's characterization, which is of his own devising. After having driven four hundred miles to bury the body, the women are returning to Castroville when they are apprehended by the homicide detectives. When the officer asks them to open the trunk, Joan loses her control and claims she is Richard Morales. Nearly hysterical, she tells the officer: "We got worms in the trunk . . . and vultures in our eyes!" (42). It is a terribly tense moment and a very interesting portrayal of a human being under stress. We do not necessarily become sympathetic to the daughter for this weakness, but we have to acknowledge her basic humanity.[22]

We learn about the characters through their interactions with one another and what they say directly to the audience when interrogated by the narrator or one of the lawyers. The narrator also elaborates upon the characters' personalities, though this type of exposition is judiciously kept to a minimum. By limiting the narrator's remarks to interjections and brief introductions that add insight rather than simple facts, Morton does not allow this play to become a dramatized lecture. The narrator is an essential element in the work, maintaining a tone of almost clinical observation as she moves the action forward. She is at once bailiff and interrogator for the prosecution, determined that the audience should witness the events as the playwright sees them. At times, Martin Willard, the attorney for the defense, assumes an almost judicial stance, demonstrating his apparent collusion with the figure of justice, whom we never see. Seated at the sidelines, the company assumes the voice of the judge and recites his admonishments in unison to the Chicano lawyer, Roel Saldívar. This collective voice resounds with all the sonority of a hollow courtroom. When addressing the judge, the characters look toward the back of the auditorium, above the audience's faces, at the invisible presence. When speaking to the jury, the lawyers address the audience members, embracing them with their pleas and urging them to make the right choice.

Richard Morales dies three times in the play that bears his name. His execution-style murder is re-enacted at the opening of the play after the narrator has given the first line. He is killed again within the unfolding action of the plot itself. We do not actually see his death a third time, but the trial is a constant reminder of his murder. By titling the play "The Many Deaths of Richard Morales," Morton is also commenting on the fact that this is not a singular event. Although the focus of the play is on Texas justice in regard to Mechicanos, the later version of the script takes into account police killings in all parts of the Southwest. The first script ends with the Chicano lawyer recounting similar cases in other parts of Texas, while the revised version lists the names and ages of Chicanos killed by policemen in several states.[23]

This emotional appeal brings the documentary to a close, urging the audience to side with the deceased and his family rather than with the defendant and those who uphold his actions as just. There is an ironic conclusion to the proceedings as we learn that Frayes's daughter eventually married her boyfriend, in effect perpetuating the species. The script does not mention María Morales' fate, but we must assume that she gave birth to Richard's child, another infant born to the culture of poverty. It is a continuation of the conditions that spawned Morales' situation in the first place, and the prospects for his child's escape from a similar fate seem dim indeed. On the other hand, the Frayes family lost the battle but won the war, for the father received a sentence that angered the Chicanos because of its leniency. "This is Texas-style justice," the play tells us, and we are outraged at the sense of helplessness that pervades the conclusion. As in *Trampa sin salida*, the problems have been exposed, yet there is little the audience can do.

When Saldívar tells the court that he is going to ask for a Justice Department investigation, a possible rectification is suggested, even though it is seemingly a gesture that will have no productive outcome. In fact, three years later, due to the efforts of the real lawyer, Rubén Sandoval, a federal judge sentenced Hayes to life in prison and committed his wife to three years behind bars. Both the battles and the war were eventually won, but the dead Chicano could not be brought back to life. Nonetheless, it was a rare victory for the Mechicanos of the area and was the first time a law officer in Texas was convicted on civil rights charges.[24] The revised version of the play includes the altered conclusion to the trial, but it still remains an angry re-creation of the murder and the first trial. In the years between the original production and the revisions in 1980, many more Chicanos had died while in the custody of the police, and the intervention by the Justice Department was still the rare exception to the rule.

Although the first version of the Morales play has been super-annuated by recent developments, it is still an excellent example of a documentary about an actual police murder and subsequent trial. By basing the play on newspaper accounts of the Morales case, Morton demonstrates how the mingling of fact with a little embel-lishment can create a very effective dramatic statement. The news-paper articles provide the characters, the plot, the conflict, and the conclusion, while the playwright gives the events dramatic interest. The documentary form allows the author to move quickly from scene to scene as he portrays the people and the incidents involved. Ultimately it is not Hank Frayes who is on trial, but the trial itself, for the playwright asks the audience to consider the process that led to a verdict of "aggravated assault."

The playwright's premise that the police chief murdered Richard Morales was based on an angry assumption that he was guilty. In reality, no one actually saw Frank Hayes kill the victim and his tes-timony as quoted in the play claimed it was an accident. But by demonstrating the killing as he envisions it, the playwright imme-diately sets the audience's imagination into motion and arouses its indignation. As the events and characters unfold, it seems only natural that Frayes should kill Morales, for he has little regard for the man's life; he repeatedly threatens him and even tells him, "I killed a Mexican before and I'm fixing to kill another one" (36) in front of witnesses. By the time the courtroom dialogue reveals the fact that no one actually witnessed the death, the audience already has a visual image of Frayes murdering Morales and few can doubt his guilt. Still, Frayes's guilt becomes a matter of opinion, for even the Justice Department did not convict him of murder, but rather of violating Richard Morales' civil rights. The playwright makes an impressive case against his villain, and while there may be those who feel that he was innocent, most barrio residents would agree that it was premeditated murder. *Las many muertes de Richard Morales* confirms their belief and effectively questions the process of justice.

The final play to be discussed in this chapter also questions the judicial process as it examines another historical event and takes its audience to the era of the zoot suiters of the 1940s. Valdez' dramatic step into Chicano history reveals the fact that there have been strug-gles in the past, while Morton's play reminds us that there are many battles in the future.

The Ultimate Pachuco: *Zoot Suit*

For years, Luis Valdez had looked upon the professional stage as a platform Chicano theater should avoid. "Will Broadway produce a Chicano version of *Hello Dolly* now that it has produced a Black one?" he asked in 1971.[25] As a leading figure in the Alternative Theater Movement of the 1960s, Valdez viewed the Broadway stage as pure commercialism, to be avoided by any truly political theater company. Broadway was and is big business and Valdez felt at the time that neither he nor his group would benefit from any association with professional producers and Equity contracts. Nor were any offers forthcoming, given the fact that political theater has seldom been an attraction on the Great White Way. The Teatro Campesino was a frequent visitor to off-Broadway houses; it even received an Obie in 1968 for "creating a worker's theater to demonstrate the politics of survival."[26] But Broadway houses and professional costs were anathema to Valdez and his troupe in 1971.

Riding on the popular success of *La gran carpa de los rasquachis* (The Great Tent of the Underdogs) in 1974, three years after he had produced *Dark Root of a Scream*, Valdez told this author that he would never write a play again.[27] *Carpa* was a magnificent product of collective creation under Valdez' guiding genius. Both its success and the resulting notoriety caused him to pause and reconsider his creative processes. He had not written a script independently since *Dark Root of a Scream*, and he felt that the individual playwright must give way to the group process. In addition, because of the number of projects the Teatro Campesino had undertaken, he never had time to write. The group had recently purchased forty acres of land on a sloping hill overlooking the rural community of San Juan Bautista in central California. Valdez looked forward to building a complex of offices, rehearsal spaces, studios, and housing for his extended family. He was also chief administrator of a growing business that included a publishing house, record and film distribution, and the yearly tours that generated the group's major income.

But by 1976 Valdez had again grasped the playwright's pen to write a realistic play, *Fin del mundo* (to be discussed in the next chapter). The author was pleased with his script, but confided that the members of his troupe, accustomed to the broad *acto-carpa* style of acting, were having trouble with the portrayals required for this realistic work. It was then that Valdez told this author that he was going to write a play about the "Zoot Suit Riots" of the early 1940s and produce it at the Mark Taper Forum in Los Angeles. "It will

probably go to Broadway," he said, "because we have to spread beyond the audiences we have been reaching."[28] He now agreed that
teatro had become theater for the already initiated and that the time
had come to seek a larger, more varied public. Certainly, the Teatro
Campesino was internationally known and the troupe had been seen
by scores of people on television, but Valdez, the visionary, understood the need for a more professional attitude in Chicano theater.
Continuing that conversation, he said,

> You know, I'm tired of having our group perform for some dis-
> organized student organization that can't generate enough publicity
> to gather an audience . . . The Teatro was supposed to perform in
> some little town, and when they arrived, the people said: "We
> didn't know you were coming, man. . . ."

We laughed about the reality of that scene, for it had happened
to many groups in different places. The Chicano Movement was
grinding to a halt it seemed, lost in philosophical debates that had
been parodied by teatros in such works as the Campesino's *Militants*
and Teatro Mestizo's *Cuatro años de colegio* (Four Years of College).[29] The "Revolution" was over, said the critics of the Movement,
when campus organizations could not decide upon a name for their
group much less the direction or political stance they should take.
Disorganization plagued all aspects of the Movement, including
the teatros. People who were truly serious about their work in theater
were often frustrated in their efforts by undisciplined aficionados
to whom teatro was a thing of the moment.

Although the Teatro Campesino is a professional theater company, Valdez, as a director, realized during rehearsals for the 1976
version of *Fin del mundo* that some of his actors lacked the breadth
of those exposed to a variety of acting experiences. He was ready
to work with a different breed of professionally trained actors, both
Chicano and Anglo. "There are a lot of talented Chicano actors
and actresses in Los Angeles," Valdez remarked, "and they've never
had a chance to be in a real Chicano play or movie." He knew that
if his plans succeeded, the play he envisioned would be the first of
its kind on either side of the continent. A professionally produced
play, written, directed, and performed by Chicanos about their own
struggles had never been achieved. It was a totally new direction for
Valdez and was a natural step in the evolution of his Teatro and in
his own commitments as a playwright and director. That 1976 conversation became a reality when *Zoot Suit* opened at the Mark Taper
Forum in Los Angeles two years later.

The move to the professional stage was a conscious act for Valdez and came as no surprise to anyone who had spoken with him over the years. At an early meeting of teatro directors in 1971, he had advised the teatros to seek a professionalism that would attract the public in the same way their favorite Mexican enertainers did. By going to Hollywood and then New York, Valdez was telling other teatros: ". . . it's a career, a serious one. Not just the money—that's the base level—but a profession. . . . Playwrighting is a noble profession."[30]

Gordon Davidson, the artistic director of the Center Theatre Group in Los Angeles, had long been interested in producing theater for the Mechicano community. The Teatro Campesino performed *La gran carpa de los rasquachis* in the Group's Mark Taper Forum in 1974 and attracted a large number of Mechicanos who would otherwise never have attended this prestigious theater in Los Angeles' imposing Music Center. Special public relations efforts were conducted in the barrios of Los Angeles and busloads of students and community members ushered in a new audience for the Forum's "New Theatre for Now Series." The *Carpa* was billed as a work in progress, part of a series of new plays, and the production pleased the public and critics alike. It was Valdez' first exposure to Davidson's company as well as the Center Theater Group's first experience with a Chicano theater group and its audiences. Both sides were pleased with the result of the alliance. When Davidson decided to investigate the possibility of producing a Chicano play, he turned to Luis Valdez.

Davidson was interested in theater that reflected our society's minority cultures and had engaged anthropologist Kenneth Brecher to oversee productions of this nature. Valdez suggested a play about the zoot suiters of the 1940s, and both Davidson and Brecher responded enthusiastically.

With a grant from the Rockefeller Foundation, Valdez and members of his toupe researched the events surrounding the Sleepy Lagoon murder trial and found that "what we came up with isn't a Chicano play, like the ones we do at San Juan Bautista. It's an American play."[31] It was another form of the indigenous theater Valdez had become known for. In this case the play was native to Los Angeles rather than to Mesoamerica. By terming it an "American play," Valdez was in effect telling his prospective audiences: "We've been considered different long enough. Now it's time to see the Chicano not as separate from this society, but as an integral part of it." Los Angeles, which has the largest concentration of Mexicans outside of Mexico City, was the perfect birthplace for a work that effectively dramatized an important episode in Mechicano history.

After months of research and writing and weeks of rehearsal and anticipation, tickets went on sale for the premiere of *Zoot Suit* in April 1978. Everyone involved in the production knew that there was great community interest in the play, but when it sold out its ten-day run in less than two days, the reality struck home: Chicanos wanted to see plays about themselves. Tickets to the performances became prized possessions as people clamored to see what *Zoot Suit* was all about. Even before opening night, the producers knew that they had struck a chord in the Chicano community that had only begun to vibrate.

The initial version of Valdez' vision of the Chicano in the 1940s was immediately hailed as a milestone in the American theater, although most of the critics agreed that the work in progress needed more developing and polishing. No matter how critical or cautious the reviewers were, however, the audiences were undaunted in their enthusiastic responses to the production. They laughed and cheered, cried and hissed, commenting upon the action as it unfolded before them. Those who had lived through the period being dramatized were moved by the representation, for they understood what it meant to be a Mechicano in this country in 1942. Audiences were divided between the subscribers—basically a white, theater-going public—and the Mechicanos—most of whom had never been to the Forum or any other legitimate theater to see a play. Many of the non-Spanish-speaking members of the audience felt left out when others laughed at the jokes in Spanish or *caló*, but they joined the cheering crowds who jumped to their feet at the end of each performance.

Something beautiful and strange was happening on that stage while Anglo and Chicano heroes and villains marched across Valdez' panorama of Los Angeles and the nation in the early 1940s. The play focused on the Sleepy Lagoon murder trial, concentrating on the leader of a group of young Chicanos who were virtually railroaded on charges of murder. As the defense lawyer says in the trial scene, "The only thing the prosecution has been able to prove beyond a shadow of a doubt is that these boys are Mexican!" The play mingled fact and fantasy, drawing on documentation and the playwright's imagination, to create a collage of events presented in the eclectic style that is Valdez' trademark. He combined elements of the *acto, corrido, carpa,* and *mito* with Living Newspaper techniques to dramatize a Chicano family in crisis.

Zoot Suit opened with the boys' release from prison and then flashed back to recall the events that had led to their imprisonment. Interwoven with this main thread of action was a developing love affair between the leader, Henry Reyna, and the Marxist Jewess who led the Defense Committee, Alice Springfield. Valdez also included other themes and unnecessary characters that tended to cloud the issues, and confusion surrounded his version of the death of the Chicano at the Sleepy Lagoon. The play seemed to grope about for an effective ending. Nonetheless, Valdez had stepped onto the professional stage with grace and confidence. The producers could not ignore the response of the public or the critics and selected the play to open the regular subscription season for a six-week run beginning the following August.

While the production was still enjoying its initial success, talk began about a Broadway production, a motion picture, a touring company, and other possible consequences of that triumph. But before any of these options could be considered, the playwright had to return to his typewriter and resolve the problems in the script. Valdez told this author, "Directing it was a breeze compared to the writing. Writing it was hell."[32] This was no longer a Chicano theater troupe leaving San Juan Bautista with a freshly typed revision and rehearsing on the road. Now there were union contracts, established runs, and opening nights that could not be avoided or postponed. Valdez could no longer substitute another *acto* if this one was not working. The pressure might have stopped a lesser man. Painfully, he rewrote and recast, while the others on the production staff revised their initial visions as the opening approached.

When tickets for the August production were about to go on sale, the newspapers began to publicize that "On July 30, 1978, the Second Zoot Suit Riot begins"—and it did. The play again sold out in record time and this prompted the Center Theater Group to begin looking for another space. "Zoot Suit fever" had hit Los Angeles once more and though the advertising campaign might have been considered offensive by some, those who understood the nomenclature appreciated the metaphor: the ad was a celebration of a people gathering to buy tickets to a play that spoke to them. Opening night again inspired a standing ovation, as would every subsequent production of the play in Los Angeles.

Valdez had trimmed the play considerably and focused more clearly on the people and events surrounding the trial. Gone were the superfluous characters and situations that had plagued the earlier version, replaced by a plot line that was clearly directed to the final scene. Changes in the casting helped create a stronger vision of the characters and newly choreographed dances and songs added to the spectacle considerably. The original set was altered to a slicker version, substituting clear plastic floors and invisible walls for the original wagon settings and barrio textures. Instead of the partial walls and movable furniture that rolled on in the first version, the designers and director chose to use stacks of newspapers as chairs, the judge's bench, and other set props. In a backyard scene, instead of taking clothes off the clothesline, the mother removes newspapers, folds them, and places them in a laundry basket.[33]

The burlap backdrop of earlier Campesino productions was replaced by a twenty-foot high blowup of the *Los Angeles Herald Examiner* carrying the headline "American Bomber Victim of Jap Raider" and a composite of other articles relating to the war abroad and the "wars" at home—the "Zoot Suit Riots." It was a Valdezian indictment of the press, which had helped create and perpetuate the racist hysteria of the period. As in the allegorical *actos*, a character named The Press continually debates the issues involved in this period of Los Angeles' history. In the trial scene, The Press becomes the prosecutor; he begins his comments to the court with, "The Press will prove beyond a shadow of a doubt—I mean the *prosecution* will prove . . ."—and the point is made.

From its opening scene, *Zoot Suit* is the product of all that Valdez had done before. The houselights dim, swing music of the 40s comes on, and a three-foot switchblade cuts through the huge newspaper. This is followed by the entrance of a zoot suiter, who is simply El Pachuco, the archetypal predecessor to the *vato loco* we have seen before on teatro stages. But this pachuco, dressed in his finest, strutting with a cocksure stance that seems to defy gravity, is unlike the previous types Valdez has dramatized. Like his switchblade, he is much larger than life; he makes a theatrical statement none of the critics can dismiss no matter what they think of the play.

After he surveys the spectators with a "What the hell are you looking at me for?" glance, El Pachuco tells them: "It is the secret fantasy of every *vato* to put on the zoot suit and play the part of the pachuco." This brings cheers from the contemporary *vatos* in the audience who share this fantasy. The others listen carefully as this figure from the past reveals the playwright's purpose in this "construct of fact and fantasy": to reveal a period in our history that is generally neglected in the history books.

From his opening narrative to the close of the play, El Pachuco has the audience in his grasp, commenting upon the action and occasionally stopping it like La Muerte did in *Soldado razo* in order to remind the audience that they are in a theater. El Pachuco is Henry Reyna's alter ego, his pachuco-half that sometimes keeps him from doing things he otherwise would, such as saying "thank you" to his lawyer. At other times he provokes Henry to do a deed he might have avoided. During a moment of intensity, when Henry yells out in anguish at his hounding subconscious, El Pachuco tells him, *"Orale pues, buey,* don't take the play so seriously!" The Pachuco's continual comments to Henry are calculated to break moments of tension with humor or skepticism. When the police are questioning Henry about his involvement in the alleged murder, The Press is behind them reading actual headlines from newspapers of the day. Quoting from a report to the grand jury, The Press refers to the zoot suiters as descendants of "bloodthirsty savages who sacrificed human beings." El Pachuco quickly interjects: *"¡Pues ponte las plumas, que ya te van a chingar!"* ("Well, put on your feathers, 'cause now they're gonna fuck you!").[34]

Valdez continually plays with his audience, poking at them with many barbs: emotional, comic, tragic, sardonic. After the climactic ending of the first act when the boys have been found guilty of murder and sentenced to life imprisonment, all leave the stage except for El Pachuco. He surveys the audience slowly, strutting to center stage where he can capture their attention with a mere glance. With a "Whadya think of *that* shit" look, he says: "Now we're gonna take a little break . . . so you can take a leak." Moments before, the audience was suffering for the families and the obviously innocent Chicanos; now their laughter is released at this mundane yet practical suggestion.

While the first act focuses on the trial and the events leading up to it, the second act finds the boys in jail while the Defense Committee works to free them. The rather maudlin romance between Henry and Alice in the first version is here replaced by a sensitive portrayal of an imprisoned man and his only link with the outside world—Alice. She is reluctant to get emotionally involved, but nonetheless their visit ends with an embrace and a kiss that is as tentative as Henry's hopes for freedom. Eventually the boys are freed, but what might have become a happy ending is channeled into a collage of possible conclusions to Henry's story. Each character surrounding the central figure of Henry addresses the audience with different versions of what happened to him: "He married and had three children"; "He died of the tragedy of his own existence"; "He overdosed a few years later." Other possibilities are thrown at the audience, reminding it that this character from the past still lives. The play's message calls for the audience to reappraise its attitudes and secret fantasies as it leaves the theater amid contemporary versions of historical personages.

In a climactic moment, after having been stripped by a group of sailors, El Pachuco is left in a loincloth, lying on the ground. Humiliated before the audience, no longer protected by the costume that distinguishes him, El Pachuco rises slowly, regains his dignity, and walks off the stage, a reminder in his nakedness of his *indio* ancestors. It is only a moment in this epic play, but it conveys that overriding ability to survive that has been postulated in all of Valdez' works. The pachuco—the symbol of fear, mistrust, and secret fantasies of defiance—permeates the minds of those in the audience. During a scene in the prison, Henry and another character are about to get into a fight when El Pachuco stops him with: "That's exactly what the play needs right now: two Mexicans killing each other! Everybody's watching, *ese* . . . that's what they came to see." Mechicanos and Anglos alike have probably wished at some point that "those pachucos would just kill each other off." They may laugh at El Pachuco's statement, but they may also, hopefully, consider the truth behind it.

After quickly selling out its initial run at the Forum, *Zoot Suit* moved to a larger theater in Hollywood, the Aquarius, six weeks later. Audiences lined up to buy tickets and the Center Theater Group signed a contract with the Shubert organization to open the play in New York the following year. While the play continued to run in Los Angeles with a largely new cast, the original cast went to New York and opened the production on March 25, 1979. Preopening publicity heralded the first Latino play on Broadway as a major event, and relatives, friends, and teatro aficionados flew to New York for the occasion.

The audience loved the production; the New York critics did not. Sylvie Drake, who has followed Valdez' evolution closely since he first began the Teatro Campesino, was present that opening night and thought the production was at its best, fitting "neatly into the stage of the Winter Garden, with an assurance and focus refined well beyond all three of the previous L. A. versions."[35] However, her initial statement about the New York opening provides an ironic metaphor for the production:

> Smooth as El Pachuco's reet pleat, slick as the mocking feather in his broad-brimmed hat, "Zoot Suit" skidded onto Broadway

Sunday with all the sass of a high school dropout clamoring for admission to an Ivy League college.

. . . admission was not granted.[36]

Ironic, because pachucos, as we learned in *No saco nada de la escuela*, are high school dropouts, as were a majority of Chicanos until quite recently.[37] Ironic, because few Chicanos have been admitted to Ivy League colleges. And finally, ironic because the "skid" Ms. Drake refers to suggests a stop, as if that were the production's ultimate destiny. It was not. While the play was breaking records in Los Angeles and Valdez was preparing for the move to Broadway, he told this author that New York was only another step in the course the production had to take.[38] Responding to the New York critics, Valdez told an interviewer:

> The play is still an enormous success in Los Angeles; it's going to do phenomenal business throughout the Southwest and Latin America, and it's going to continue to run in the great cities of America whether the critics like it or not.[39]

Zoot Suit lasted four weeks on Broadway while the producers attempted to recruit the Hispanic and Black audiences that might not be dissuaded by the largely negative press. Publicity campaigns were conducted in Latino neighborhoods, but the appeal failed to overcome the high cost of survival on the Great White Way. Most productions greeted with the notices *Zoot Suit* received close in a few days, yet this pachuco of the theater held on, determined to make its mark. The major New York critics called *Zoot Suit* "overblown and undernourished";[40] "a great deal of loose material draped over a spindly form";[41] "simplistic . . . poorly written and atrociously directed";[42] and "bloodless rhetoric."[43] There were positive reviews as well, but in the commercial arena of skyrocketing ticket prices few productions could overcome such condemnation.

Years before the Broadway experience, Valdez had written that the teatros must never get away from La Raza. "Without the *palomía* [populace] sitting there," he said, "laughing, crying and sharing whatever is onstage, the teatros will dry up and die."[44] Although he was speaking figuratively about the importance of reflecting the Chicano's reality, there was something prophetic in the statement. After the New York run, Valdez likened his play to the pachucos who went to the Hollywood Palladium dressed in their finest in the 1940s and were sometimes admitted, though often they were not. Today, Broadway is the Palladium of the theater world and *Zoot Suit* the pachuco who is not accepted. In Valdez' words: "The Pachuco himself is stripped . . . just as *Zoot Suit* has been stripped. But that doesn't take away its dignity. He still stands and *Zoot Suit* will stand."[45] The play continued to run in Los Angeles while plans were made for a national tour and Valdez began the task of transforming a theatrical spectacle into a screenplay. The New York experience had been a challenge from the start; although the play did not fulfill the hopes of its producers and creators, it had made an impact. Like the sleekly dressed pachuco, *Zoot Suit* could not be ignored. Critics might laugh at its bravado, scorn its audacity, and cry for a statement they could better understand, but they could never change this child of the barrios into what they termed "good theater." As Valdez had expected, the Hispanic and Black audiences in New York understood his play perfectly. El Pachuco was as much their symbol of defiance as he was the Chicanos', for he stood before his audience and declared himself a member of this society, whether society wanted him or not. "This is a cultural stand," Valdez told an interviewer in New York, "and America has got to come to grips with it. Because we're not going to go away."[46]

That *palomía* Valdez had written about in 1971 was still enchanted with his theatrical statements, and the impact he and his troupe had made on the Chicano Movement would continue to mold the direction for other teatros. The Teatro Campesino would continue to perform in this country and abroad; *Zoot Suit* would pack the houses in every major center of Mechicano population. Luis Miguel Valdez, the man who had started a national theatrical movement, had gone full circle. From political street theater to cultural and spiritual revolution to professional playwright and director, Luis Valdez remained constant to his initial purpose. His theater entertained as it educated; it was didactic, yet born of a basic human spirit that had endured the criticisms of both the politicians and the aesthetes. Valdez' world encompasses more than most of his critics can comprehend. As he continues to place his characters on stages that reflect his own people, this contemporary man of the theater will prevail.

Arturo Madrid-Barela concludes his engrossing study of the pachuco in literature with the following:

> The Pachuco must be viewed and understood in human terms, as someone with human aspirations and human desires, full of strengths and weaknesses, consistencies and inconsistencies, contradictions and complexities, like all Mexicans, like all Americans, like all human beings.[47]

Each of the central characters in the plays in this chapter can share Madrid's definition, for they are, indeed, very human portrayals. The masked pachucos in *Trampa sin salida* are the least developed, yet they demonstrate characteristics that enable us to see them as more than simple stereotypes. Richard Morales, though not described as a pachuco, has a working class background like the others and a record of confrontations with the police that relate him to the youths in the other plays. He is certainly a product of barrio poverty—a school dropout who struggles to exist from job to job. Henry Reyna is the most complex of these characters, with an alter ego to express his inner thoughts and conflicts. This complexity makes him the most difficult character of the three to understand.

For each of these men, the strugle to survive is a daily burden. Little Ray will not be hired by racist employers; Richard Morales works in the fields or in construction jobs when he can find them; and Henry Reyna enters prison as a boy only to return to society's disdain as an ex-offender. There is no talk of employment in *Zoot Suit*, but it is obvious that neither Reyna nor his companions will become members of the middle class. Reyna is the only one of these protagonists to escape an untimely death, yet his play ends in uncertainty and the script does not really tell us what becomes of him. The feeling is conveyed that his future is not very bright after suffering a prejudiced trial and unjustified imprisonment. Like the other protagonists, Henry is doomed from the start. "The real Henry died some years ago," Valdez told an interviewer in 1978, continuing: "His lawyer said he died of the trauma of his own life. Just wore out."[48]

Although the playwrights try to demonstrate the basic humanity of their characters, each author seems to agree that the men are seen as threats by the authorities, guilty because they are Chicanos. María Morales tells the court: "You're so certain that because he had these new things, that naturally they were stolen." She knows that no amount of legal assistance will alter preconceived ideas. There is no trial at all in *Trampa sin salida*, for there were no reprisals for the deaths reported as suicides. The Hank Frayes trial comes too late to save the life of Richard Morales; the Sleepy Lagoon trial is eventually overturned by a higher court although the damage has already been inflicted on the seventeen youths who go to prison. In each of the works, the playwrights are asking the same basic question: "Why is this happening to Chicanos?" The question could, of course, be asked about other groups, but the focus is on the Mechicano in these works. The authors concentrate their vision on their own people. For each of the playwrights, the focus of that dramatic lens reveals the same answer: racism.

None of the works in question offers a solution to the basic problem of racism. As Chicanos themselves, the playwrights know what it is to suffer discrimination for the color of their skin. Anger over past or present confrontations with bigotry rears its head in each of the works. By presenting their protagonists as complex human beings who suffer pain, anxiety, and desires like everyone else, the playwrights urge their audiences to sympathize with their causes. Little Ray looks directly at the audience and says, "I'm of flesh and bones like every one of you," as he searches for a solution to his plight. Yet none of these figures will beg for sympathy. Richard Morales does not go quietly to his doom, but shouts at the police chief: "You *rinche* (pig), put that gun away, put it down. I'll fight you." Nor will Henry Reyna, with his alter ego standing by, accept a lawyer's offer of assistance, since the lawyer is an Anglo and must therefore be the enemy.

Because the Chicanos are presented as the victims of racist employers, policemen, judges, and juries, any anti-white sentiments they express are seen as justifiable. In every instance, the Chicanos respond to discrimination rather than initiating it, reacting to negative treatment by Anglos who are always in a position of power. But the Chicanos are not meek lambs who turn the other cheek, for they are also capable of hating whites. Racism, the authors tell us, begets racism. If the Anglos who have the power to hire and fire are motivated by anti-Mexican sentiments, they are the initiators of the vicious circle of hate.

Of the three works in question, *Zoot Suit* is the most sympathetic toward the non-Hispanic characters, demonstrating the sincere efforts of the lawyer and the leader of the Defense Committee. "I want the audience to go away from this play feeling good," Valdez told this author, and the public did just that.[49] Both Chicanos and non-Chicanos jumped to their feet at the conclusion of the Henry Reyna story, for they had witnessed a struggle and a victory.

There is the danger that some audience members might see the events in *Zoot Suit* as history rather than as a reflection of today's realities, forgetting that police shootings and racist judgments are still commonplace in any city. Each of these plays ends tentatively because the problems will continue, no matter what the present victories. The courtroom conquests inspire hope, but for those who look at each of these works the message is clear: On the streets and in the courts, the battles will continue.

The courtroom scene of *Zoot Suit* by Luis Valdez, Mark Taper
Forum, 1978. *Photo: © Ricardo Martínez*

Chapter Six

THE CHICANO AND HIS COSMOS: REACHING FOR THE STARS

The Indigenous Roots of Chicano Theater

The Mechicano has an uninterrupted tradition of Christian folk drama that reaches back through the ages to the Spanish conquest of Mexico in the sixteenth century. For Luis Valdez, any study of Chicano theater must include not only the spiritual dramas of the Christian faith but the sacred ritual dramas of the Aztec and Maya as well, thus extending the tradition further back in time.[1] Although the majority of Chicano playwrights and teatros are concerned with secular issues, some have examined the Mechicano's spirituality, continuing a pattern that is firmly rooted in the culture of the barrio and the faith of the people.

If the Chicano is a descendant of the Mexican mestizo, who is of both European and indigenous ancestry, then it seems appropriate to investigate European and native cultural and spiritual foundations in an effort to understand Chicano spiritual theater. Most important to this study is the progression from native ritual to Christian drama, for it demonstrates the vital role played by theatrical presentations in the colonization and subjugation of the indigenous peoples of Mexico and the Southwest. The didactic theater of the Teatro Campesino and all the other troupes that developed after 1965 is directly related to the Spanish religious dramas that were imposed upon a thriving culture of rituals, dances, songs, and myths. But while the *actos* of the teatros attempt to portray social injustice, the early Spanish friars used their dramatic messages not to liberate but to indoctrinate and conquer. Today's teatros are following a missionary tradition, but with a totally different purpose.

When the Spaniards arrived in Tenochtitlán (Mexico City) in

1519, they encountered a culture that rivaled that of the great cities of Europe at the time. The militaristic Aztecs, known as Mexica, had built a grand city in the middle of a lake and had achieved a stunning architecture and other cultural accomplishments. Temples rose above the central plaza like little mountains dedicated to the gods and busy priests conducted daily sacrifices and ceremonies in honor of the highest diety, Huitzilopochtli, God of the Sun. The Aztec pantheon was a complex assortment of anthropomorphic gods and goddesses who often demanded human blood in order to protect the harvests and the seasons they represented. The Aztecs created myths around each of the dieties. Celebrations in their honor often included dancing, singing, and god-impersonations that recall the birth of tragedy in Greece.[2] But while the ritual beginnings of Mexica drama compare with Attic rites, the analogy is not complete because the arrival of the Europeans ended the Mexica rituals.

Aside from the inherent drama of a human sacrifice, the rituals contained dramatic elements that might have developed further if the Conquest had not effectively terminated them. In an interesting analysis of the sacrificial rituals, Willard C. Booth has divided their action into three parts, which he calls the "incarnation," "sacrifice," and "epiphany." He notes that there was sometimes an optional "agon" or struggle that preceded the sacrifice and added a dramatic note of conflict to the scenario.[3] In Booth's analysis, the epiphany is a symbolic reincarnation of the god-impersonator whose heart is torn out in the climax of the ritual. The god is reincarnated through decapitation, flaying of the body, communion with the flesh of the god, or the selection of a living successor who will portray the god until it is his turn to shed his blood for the good of the populace.

If this sounds ghastly to the modern reader, the Spanish soldiers who first witnessed the sacrifices were appalled and sent reports to Spain that quickly circulated throughout Europe, painting a picture of pagan savages eating the flesh of human beings. Although no amount of rationalizing will justify the killing of human beings, it is important to remember that the sacrificial victims were not being punished but were considered living symbols of the gods; the greatest honor for them was to die on the sacrificial stone.[4]

The myths that fostered these ritual sacrifices were tales of conflict and triumph. The birth of Huitzilopochtli and the many adventures of Quetzalcóatl are dramatic narratives that may have found their way into the repertories of roving troupes of actors called *tlaquetzque* ("those who made things stand out").[5] These small bands of players toured the villages and cities, performing in the marketplaces and plazas like the *commedia dell'arte* troupes in Italy and the travelling companies in Spain. The *tlaquetzque* were the ancient predecessors of Chicano teatros in the United States; while little is known about them, they demonstrate the existence of theatrical activity beyond the rituals of the sacrifices. Using the traditional myths for their scenarios, the *tlaquetzque* brought the stories to life, re-enacting poems and legends that everyone knew. Their themes seem to have been transitional between the sacred and the profane, although the myths they dramatized upheld the people's firm belief in the cosmic order.

Further to the south and east of the Mexica empire, the various Maya peoples built incredible ceremonial centers during the six hundred years between A.D. 300 and 900. When the Spaniards arrived several centuries later, the descendants of these ancient astronomers fought fiercely against the colonizers, resisting total submission to this day.[6] The restored temples at Chichén Itzá, Palenque, Uxmal, and Bonampak in the Yucatan peninsula are only a few of the hundreds of ceremonial centers of this people, who mysteriously vanished long before the rise of the Mexica. Whether the early Mayas had a spiritual theater is uncertain, though likely, but their descendants left us the only extant example of a pre-Columbian ritual drama. Entitled *Rabinal Achí* (The Warrior of Rabinal), this Maya-Quiché dance-drama has been hailed as a "pagan tragedy" by T. B. Irving[7] and compared to the Greek classics in form and structure by Richard E. Leinaweaver.[8]

Rabinal Achí revolves around the capture, interrogation, and sacrifice of Quiché Achí, the Warrior of Quiché, an adversary of the people of Rabinal. This drama is a series of dialogues between the two major characters, with occasional interjections from other figures, spoken to the continual accompaniment of a drum. A chorus of warriors dances periodically within the action, adding to the ritual format. The major action involves discovering why the Quiché warrior must die on the sacrificial stone. The play reveals that the antagonist is a wizard who has transgressed against his captors, and his sacrifice seems to be a symbolic purgation of the evil he represents. There is always the feeling that the captured warrior is free to run, though he does not, for he knows that he must participate in this cosmic communication with the gods.

Rabinal Achí is performed periodically in the Guatemalan provinces and reports of a production in 1955 affirm the spiritual nature of the piece.[9] Sacred rites accompanied the preparations for the performance and participants and audience alike were filled with a religious fervor that only suggests the original effect four hundred years ago. The script was first committed to paper by a missionary who transcribed it in the nineteenth century, but its structure and content have been identified as authentically pre-Columbian by several scholars.[10] The repetitious language and symbolism of the play and the ending of the action with a human sacrifice are evidence that it must have been initially produced before the arrival of the Spaniards. That the play is still being produced in the twentieth century is proof that, for the Maya-Quiché at least, indigenous ritual was in competition with colonial Catholicism.

The early Spanish friars quickly noted the natives' propensity for ritual drama and spectacle and began to produce Christian plays soon after their arrival. The priests initially presented rudimentary pantomimes of the differences between Heaven (up) and Hell (down) until they had mastered the native tongue. The missionaries must have been busy evangelizing the Spanish soldiers as well since the first recorded mention of a dramatic presentation after the Conquest notes that a version of the Christmas play *Los pastores* (The Shepherds) was performed in Spanish for the soldiers in 1526.[11] It did not take the friars long to learn the Mexica language and by 1533 they directed the natives in a Nahuatl version of *El juicio final* (The Last Judgment).[12] This play involves the downfall of Lucía, who chooses the life of a prostitute rather than that of the Church and is finally condemned to everlasting torment in Hell. The play is a Spanish *auto sacramental*, which combines the medieval mystery and morality play structures and includes earthly beings, allegorical figures, and saints and angels. This play was an important lesson for both the natives and the Spanish soldiers, whose conjugal lives were often not blessed by the Church.

These Spanish dramas employed as much spectacle as possible and the effects must have been exciting and terrifying for the audiences. The climax of *El juicio final* is a torture scene in which Lucía is surrounded by flames and serpents and pitifully bemoans her sinful life as she is taken off, accompanied by fireworks and devils blowing horns. The use of serpents as symbols of punishment and death was probably somewhat confusing to the Mexica, who believed the serpent meant life; futhermore, the Feathered Serpent represented their redeemer, Quetzalcóatl. The friars knew this and did as much as they could to re-educate the natives in the Christian symbols. In *El juicio final* the Church is the mother and the depths of the earth represent everlasting torment and punishment. The stage directions indicate that the Antichrist wears "the cloak of the wicked," which was usually a duplicate of the robes worn by the Mexica priests before the Conquest. In other plays, the devils are also dressed as Aztec priests in an attempt to make these once proud members of society appear wicked and despicable.

The Spanish missionary-producers were unrelenting in their didactic purposes. In 1539 they presented *El sacrificio de Isaac* (The Sacrifice of Isaac), which was an excellent choice for a people given to human immolation.[13] This story from the Old Testament had been produced in Spain and was translated into Nahuatl for the Tlaxcalan celebration.[14] The Biblical version of Abraham's test is basically a lesson in obedience to God. It is also a demonstration that the Judeo-Christian God does not demand human sacrifice. In the Old Testament version of the sacrifice, the entire story is told in only fourteen verses. God orders Abraham to offer his son on a mountain; the old man obeys without question until an angel appears and tells him to spare his son and offer a ram in his place. In the original Spanish play, other situations and characters were added in order to expand upon the theme and give it more interest. To avoid a completely serious presentation, the Spanish priests included a comic servant and a celebration as the opening scene. It was not until the middle of the play that the order to sacrifice Isaac occurred.

In contrast to the lively Iberian rendition of God's cosmic joke, the friars who chose to transfer the lesson to Mexican soil allowed no time for comedy. Instead, the characters are portrayed in almost somber tones. There is but one purpose here and the play is relentless in its appeal. According to the Bible, Abraham had a mistress, Hagar, and a bastard son, Ishmael, but in the friars' version these two were merely slaves in the house of Abraham. The dramatist-priests could hardly present the noble Abraham with a mistress and a bastard when they were fighting a losing battle against this common practice every day. To further denigrate indigenous beliefs, the priests portrayed Hagar and Ishmael as the antagonists and made them sun worshippers.

El juicio final and *El sacrificio de Isaac* are only two examples of the religious plays the missionaries produced for their audiences, but they exemplify the alterations the friars made in order to begin more effectively the long and grueling task of converting the natives.[15] The priests always made the messages clear and simple, sometimes using subtle devices calculated to present the natives in an inferior light while the more detestable Mexica practices were blatantly criticized. The Spaniards and natives created a distinctly mestizo drama that has gone largely unnoticed in the annals of theater history. The plays that have survived are important in the study of the evolution of the mestizo-Chicano psyche as well as in the development of Mexica-Mexicano-Chicano theater. It was not through theater alone that the Spaniards succeeded in colonizing the peoples of the New World, but their theatrical exercises served a definite purpose not unlike that of Chicano theater today: to alter people's way of thinking.

Northward to Aztlán

Almost a century after the conquest of Mexico, Spain looked to the north for more lands to call her own. Aztlán, the vast northern reaches of New Spain, beckoned to the colonizers with hints of cities of gold and other Shangri-las there for the taking. In 1598 the Crown granted Juan de Oñate, a Zacatecas millionaire, extensive privileges in what is now New Mexico. He immediately organized an expedition of colonists and set out to make the mythical land of the Aztecs' origin a part of the king's great empire. Oñate's party is noted for having produced the first European play in what is now the United States on April 30, 1598.[16] Three months later, at what is now Santa Fe, New Mexico, they performed the second play produced in the territory, *Los moros y los cristianos* (The Moors and the Christians).[17] Though we know very little about the first play, both of these productions serve to demonstrate a strong interest in dramatic presentations from the beginning of the Spanish intrusion into the North.

The missionary dramas that played a part in the colonization of Mexico became an equally useful didactic tool in Aztlán. The same Spanish plays that had been adapted to the Nahuatl language and culture found their way to New Mexico soon after Oñate's colonizers first performed their amateur productions. Like the productions in Mexico, these plays included the indigenous ritual elements of outdoor spectacle, masks, and scenery. Perhaps because New Mexico was the first area of Aztlán to be settled by the Spaniards and because of its relative isolation, the Christian theatrical tradition is richest in this state; nevertheless, productions of Spanish religious plays can be found wherever there are descendants of Mexico. Whether Roman Catholic or Protestant, Spanish-language churches are still performing plays and pageants that were first presented by the Spanish missionaries centuries ago.

The plays most often seen in the churches of Aztlán are Christmas or Easter presentations. *Los pastores* is one of the most widely produced Spanish religious plays in the United States, with a strong concentration of scripts found in New Mexico.[18] Other themes that have been dramatized in barrio churches include the Old Testament stories of Adam and Eve and Cain and Abel and the Easter Passion play.[19] One of the most popular religious folk plays today is a dramatization of the appearance of the Virgin of Guadalupe, *Las cuatro apariciones de la Virgen de Guadalupe* (The Four Appearances of the Virgin of Guadalupe). Originally created in the latter half of the sixteenth century, this play quickly became an important representation of the Virgin Mother, who was to become the patron saint of Mexico. Four centuries later, this work continues to attract the faithful and has become a part of the repertoire of some Chicano theater groups.

The Teatro Campesino first presented its version of the Guadalupe play, *La Virgen del Tepeyac* (The Virgin of Tepeyac), in December 1971. Some critics saw this as a political digression for the group, but Valdez felt that the play would enable his teatro to reach an audience that was more inclined toward spiritual matters than political realities.[20] He envisioned reaching a public that had been ignored by the political trend of the movement he had inspired. The Teatro Campesino was still new to its rural community of San Juan Bautista and this humble folk drama could demonstrate the group's spiritual foundations to the local residents. The Teatro did not miss an opportunity to make a political comment about the early Spanish missionaries, however, and opened the play with a theological debate over whether the Indians were "human" enough to be baptized.[21]

The purpose of the Teatro's presentation was to honor the Virgin and to reaffirm the members' faith, as well as to remind the audience that their ancestors were once considered unworthy of baptism. San Jose's Teatro de la Gente and the Teatro Mestizo of San Diego were among other teatros to recognize the need to move beyond their politically aware audiences to the more conservative, religious crowds that thronged to the church presentations. The people's deep tradition of religious theater could not be ignored.

Although it is not a conscious descendant of the Adam and Eve plays, Carlos Morton's *El jardín* (The Garden) is a Chicano version of the Fall that alters the story in order to make a statement to today's Chicano audiences.[22] Written in 1973, *El jardín* is a look at Judeo-Christian myths, which the playwright adjusts to suit the characters and conflicts of the period. Morton updates the familiar tale in order to present contemporary Chicano counterparts of Old Testament archetypes. His premise, quite simply, is this: What if Adam and Eve were Chicanos and God a rich early Californian? In the playwright's somewhat irreverent vision, the Serpent transforms before our eyes to become all manner of evil figures—from pusher to priest, from pimp to President Nixon. While Morton is critical of the Church, he ultimately upholds a Christian vision of the supreme diety as beneficent and worthy of respect. The Devil and God do not reconcile their differences, but the play ends with the two discussing possible alternatives to full-time residence in Hell.[23] Whereas *La Virgen del Tepeyac* alters only minor details surrounding the theme of the play, *El jardín* begins in the traditional Garden but quickly moves to a South Chicago urban barrio, thus leaving completely the realm of religious folk drama. Both plays, however, recognize the Mechicano's continuing concern with matters of the spirit and neither denies the basic faith of the people.

The importance of religion and spirituality in the lives of both the indigenous population and the colonized communities cannot be ignored, nor can we forget the role of didactic Christian drama in the cultural development of the Chicano. Today's teatros are the budding branches of a tree whose roots extend beyond man-made borders to encompass sacred rituals that reflect the universality of man's quest to understand the cosmos. The plays to be discussed in this chapter all come from the Valdezian/Teatro Campesino repertoire and represent the most important visions of the Chicano's spiritual quest.

Luis Valdez' *Bernabé* is a contemporary *mito* (myth) which like the early Biblical dramas mingles realistic characters with allegorical figures. *Bernabé* attempts to reconcile indigenous dieties with barrio realities in a form that explores a neo-Maya vision of the Chicano. The Teatro Campesino's *La gran carpa de los rasquachis* (The Great Tent of the Underdogs) was collectively created under the guiding hand of Luis Valdez. The *Carpa* has its moments of irreverence, but it culminates in a union of indigenous and Christian dieties calling for a return to the Golden Rule as espoused by the Mayas centuries ago.

To conclude the discussion, we turn to *El fin del mundo* (The End of the World). This work calls for a re-evaluation of the relationship between man and nature, and like *La gran carpa de los rasquachis* it is an assessment of man's diminishing faith in God. It is a very humorous yet serious portrayal of the Apocalypse, as Mother Earth runs out of natural resources and nations fight for what is left. With all the characters dressed in *calavera* (skeleton) costumes and skull masks, this sardonic dance of death reminds its viewers of their mortality, recalling the indigenous belief that death is life and life is death. For Valdez, there is no difference.

A Contemporary Myth: *Bernabé*

Luis Valdez first directed *Bernabé* in 1970, five years after the birth of the Teatro Campesino. This was the playwright's first *mito*, a term he chose to express the form and content of the play, and it ushered in a new period for the man who had formulated the *acto*. The change in terms reveals a change of thematic focus. Although the *actos* were collectively created, *Bernabé* is the product of Valdez' dramaturgy alone; it was his first attempt at playwrighting after the initial production of *The Shrunken Head of Pancho Villa* in 1963.

In 1971 Valdez discussed what he foresaw as the future of Chicano theater: "Not a teatro composed of actos or agit-prop but a teatro of ritual, of music, of beauty and spiritual sensitivity. A teatro of legends and myths."[24] Valdez described the genesis of the *acto* as taking place "through the eyes of man," while the *mito* was created "through the eyes of God."[25] Valdez, the constant seeker of truth, had begun to reach beyond the early Spanish religious theater to the ritual dramas of the Aztecs and Mayas.

For his first *mito*, Valdez chose to dramatize the transformation of a *loquito del pueblo* (village idiot) into a "child of the sun." If the *mito* was in fact written "through the eyes of God," that God was not the Judeo-Christian diety of barrio churches, but was instead the omnipotent Sun God, Huitzilopochtli, ruler of the cosmos. It was Huitzilopochtli who demanded human sacrifices, and Valdez becomes a modern interpreter of the sacred ceremonies atop the Mexica temples. Bernabé, the character for whom the play is named, is a universal symbol of innocence and purity who becomes the archetypal Chicano seeking his connection with Mother Earth, La Tierra. Bernabé is a character familiar to any barrio audience, for the people do not hide their abnormal children or adults in institutions. Although Bernabé is retarded, he commands our attention by his simplicity and honesty of purpose. As Valdez says in his introduction: "There is a central duality in the character of Bernabé: there is divinity in madness."[26]

Bernabé is a crippled farmworker, the only son of a pious, all-suffering mother who sees him as her single solace as well as her major burden. She is constantly scolding him and reminding him that he is her personal cross to bear. In the first scene, while they are walking down the barrio street under the noonday sun, the mother warns her son to avoid matters of the flesh with threats that the earth will swallow him up. She is the typical Roman Catholic *madre* who reflects a conservative theology. Her warning foreshadows the major action of the play, for Bernabé will indeed be swallowed up by the earth. Both the earth and the sun, whose heat is a constant presence, are stressed in the opening of the play, establishing the two major forces that Bernabé will later confront. The first part of the play is a realistic portrayal of barrio realities, setting the mood and establishing characters and individual objectives.

Economic survival is an important theme in the play's initial scenes. Money is the central force around which everything revolves except for Bernabé, whose only love is La Tierra. He talks to the earth as if she were another character, informing the others that he will someday marry her. To the normal characters, Bernabé's expressed desire is indicative of his mental state—he is crazy, after all. But when this realism is transformed into a fantastical vision of Bernabé's objective, the question becomes: "Who is crazy?"

Bernabé is a brief play, divided into seven scenes that lead to the transformation of the central figure. The setting is usually a stylized representation of a typical rural town, with the major action transpiring on the street. When the action shifts from outdoors to a prostitute's room, we enter Bernabé's mind and see the inner workings of his so-called distorted vision. Coaxed into an unwanted encounter with the prostitute Consuelo (literally, "solace"), Bernabé envisions his mother reprimanding him for commiting a sin. He has never had sexual relations with a woman; what would have been his loss of innocence is interrupted by his guilt and the appearance of his mother in Consuelo's garb. The two women merge in Bernabé's mind and the playwright lets the audience see the apparition. Bernabé flees from the hotel thinking he has killed his cousin in a skirmish and runs out to the fields. He hides in a hole he has dug in the earth, a mythic womb in which he has often masturbated in a symbolic copulation with La Tierra.

In this climactic scene in the fields Valdez takes us back in mythical and historical time. Bernabé's hole in the ground becomes larger than life and expands to include the audience within its protective walls. Bernabé is visited by allegorical figures that recall the Aztec gods and by figures from later periods in Mechicano history. First to appear is La Luna (The Moon), dressed as a 1940s zoot suiter, smoking a marijuana cigarette. La Luna is a detached and mythical figure whose very presence evokes a magnified vision of historical heroes. La Luna introduces Bernabé to his sister, La Tierra, who is dressed as an "Adelita," the name given to camp followers during the Mexican Revolution of 1910. The moon is a cool *vato* who speaks the language of the streets, but the earth is a revolutionary woman, aware of suffering and oppression. La Luna is Valdez' first re-creation of a mythical pachuco and foreshadows his later incarnation in *Zoot Suit*.

La Tierra questions Bernabé's love and asks him, "Well what makes you so macho? The smell of your sweat? The work you do for the patrón? I thought you were a Chicano!" (Steiner, p. 368). According to La Tierra the true Chicano will not let himself be manipulated by oppressive forces. "Are you Chicano enough to kill?" she asks this humble *campesino*, who is slowly gaining confidence and a masculinity that he did not have before. This Adelita, this vision from the past who encompasses both an indigenous deity (La Tierra) and an archetypal heroine from recent history, is forcing Bernabé to show an independence and assertiveness that will make him whole. Bernabé's response to the question of killing is still uncertain, for he has not committed himself to the ultimate sacrifice: his life for La Tierra's love.

El Sol is pleased with Bernabé and tells him that there were once men like him who respected La Tierra. "They saw what only a loco can understand," he tells our simple hero, "that life is death and death is life." In a ceremony that recalls the Aztec sacrifices to Huitzilopochtli, Bernabé gives his heart for La Tierra and becomes a natural man no longer crippled or retarded. When Bernabé promises to love his bride "unto death," she reveals a skull mask to him and the ritual is over. The last scene once again returns the audience to "reality," the barrio street, and we discover that Bernabé has died, his body discovered buried in his hole. In the "real world" Bernabé is presumably dead, the victim of a cave-in, but in the mythical world of gods and goddesses immortality is achieved by giving one's life.

It is his willingness to die that sets Bernabé apart from sane men. The innocence of madness, coupled with his instinctive respect for La Tierra, makes him a representative peasant whose death symbolizes the transformation from innocence to wisdom. His love for La Tierra reflects the Maya respect for all things natural, a philosophy that will greatly influence Valdez' later work. Bernabé dies in the so-called real world, but lives on in his spirit. The marriage with La Tierra is ultimately consummated in a manner that recalls the duality of Maya philosophy. Valdez told a group of teatro representatives a few years later that the Maya word for the phrase "to bury a body," *mucnal*, also means "to plant a seed."[27] To the Mayas they are the same thing, for death does produce life in the natural order of things.

Bernabé is in reality Valdez' myth. In the Aztec pantheon, Coatlicue, the earth goddess/virgin mother, gives birth to Huitzilopochtli, the sun. The moon, Coyolxauhqui, is the sun's sister. Valdez' dramatization of the sun as father and the earth and moon as children thus differs from the Aztec legends. In changing the sexes and relationships of this cosmic triumvirate, the playwright creates his own *mito*, based on his interpretation of the hero/quest myth. It is as if Bernabé could not want to marry the "mother of God" since that would be too presumptuous, but he can ask for the hand of the sun god's daughter. In the Nahuatl account of the birth of Huitzilopochtli, Coatlicue is merely the vessel for the virgin birth. But in Valdez' vision La Tierra is an activist who urges Bernabé to fight and die and even kill for her.

Teatro critic Betty Diamond believes that La Tierra is at heart "just a woman who wants only to be fought over and made love to,"[28] but the symbolic copulation is more than sexual; it is a holy consummation between man and earth that Valdez sees as a metaphor for becoming one with La Tierra. El Sol tells Bernabé that his daughter has been "fucked" many times, contrasting the act of lust and the quest for power with Bernabé's sincere love and respect for La Tierra. Throughout history, the play reminds its audience, man has violated the Earth by stealing her resources and destroying her natural beauties. By telling the humble *campesino* to give his life for La Tierra, Valdez makes a rather difficult request that contrasts sharply with the *actos'* original call to "join the Union." This is what separates this *mito* from the earlier *actos*: the solution becomes symbolic, couched in allegorical figures who represent natural forces. Bernabé's struggle represents an inner tension whose battleground is actually in the mind of each observer. The *acto* depends upon the sympathies of a politically aware audience, while the *mito* demands a spiritual understanding.

Valdez' script calls for anthropomorphic deities; they are not superhuman like the Greek gods but personas from barrio myths. The ubiquitous pachuco and the legendary Adelita are both figures of esteem and mystery to the people—both warriors, both misunderstood. They represent defiance against the system, whether the

Anglo-dominated society of the United States or the military forces of both this country and Mexico. The Adelita echoes Pancho Villa's struggle in Valdez' first play, transporting the Chicano back in time to a real revolution. Marijuana, which was the subject of the revolutionary song "La cucaracha," the musical motif for *The Shrunken Head of Pancho Villa* represents the defiance of La Luna as he smokes a marijuana cigarette with Bernabé.

Bernabé is the first *mito* to come from Valdez' pen, but the major theme of the play will be echoed in subsequent collective works, especially *El fin del mundo*. The later play looks more closely at how man has taken advantage of the Earth and lost the innocence of earlier times. By contrasting the human family with the cosmic order, Valdez points toward the Chicanos' greater understanding of their role in history as a people with a past and a heritage of myth. No one, not even the rich and powerful, can really own La Tierra, the main character tells us, for though men take from her in time they will all return to her eternal womb. In effect, the play tells us that the "real Chicano" will fight against the landowners for La Tierra and if need be will die for her. It is, after all, a metaphor for Zapata's famous decree: "The land belongs to those that work it."

The Return of Quetzalcóatl: *La gran carpa de los rasquachis*

The Fourth Annual Chicano Theater Festival was held in San Jose, California, in June 1973. As a climax to the week-long event, the Teatro Campesino had been chosen to present the final production. Valdez' company was very popular and the 2,000-seat auditorium was packed with a crowd of families, patrons, and supporters of the Festival who had gathered to see the Teatro's latest contribution to Chicano theater: *La gran carpa de los rasquachis*.

While the public entered the auditorium, the Teatro members were setting up a simple burlap backdrop, joking with members of the audience, and generally giving the appearance of very casual entertainment. The actors warmed up by doing gymnastics and inviting some audience participation. Once the Teatro was ready to perform, the actors gathered behind the backdrop for a moment as one of the musicians blew on a conch shell to open the proceedings. The loud, resonant tone of the conch shell immediately silenced the audience, who watched as a *calavera* dragged a Christ-figure carrying a cross onto the stage, followed by a jeering throng of executioners. All the while, drumbeats and music accompanied this religious spectacle. Suddenly, a devil entered the scene and began to preach the Christian faith.

The juxtaposition of Devil, Christ, and Roman Catholic proselytizer is typical Valdezian dramaturgy and points out its own contradictions. The audience loved this theatrical device and was immediately caught up in what was happening onstage. In swift fashion, the Teatro passed through generations of oppression and war by changing simple hand props and hats on the actor who was to become the major character, Jesús Pelado Rasquachi. The actor shifts from Roman sword to Renaissance rapier, through Mexican revolutionary rifle and bandolier, and ends up with a short hoe in hand and a look of utter confusion on his face. As played by Félix Alvarez, the character was totally engrossing, deftly moving from stance to stance while other actors changed his garb and the musicians sang his *corrido* in Spanish and English.[29]

The *acto, corrido, mito,* and *commedia* all came together in those first few moments of the play and continually flowed throughout the entire piece. The major action follows the trials of Jesús, who crosses the border from Mexico to find a better life. The action is explained bilingually through constant musical narration. The very name of the central figure immediately defines his social status and gives him an identity that is both Christian and poverty-stricken. The term *rasquachi* is another one of those words that defies translation, but it can be loosely interpreted to mean "underdog," "unsophisticated," or "funky" in contemporary English vernacular.[30]

La gran carpa de los rasquachis was the teatro's first full-length collective piece. Its use of techniques from the various forms Valdez had worked with before—swift, dance-like movement, changes of a hat or shirt, and continuous musical narrative—assures that the action is never boring or difficult to understand. Props are kept to a minimum and serve several purposes within the context of the plot. A vegetable shipping crate is transformed into a soapbox and then into a collection plate with the ease and simplicity of child's play. After Jesús marries, several children are born; the babies are represented by colorful little pillows with no semblance of human features to define them. These pillows are tossed at Jesús, yet the manner in which they are held suffices to explain what they are. Each of the children is baptized in "Saint Boss's Church" by an actor wearing a burlap robe and miter; his identification is painted on the robe and a large dollar sign on the miter.

In her astute analysis of the *Carpa*, Françoise Kourilsky has noted the significance of the rope motif in the action of the piece:

"In '*La Carpa*,' " she writes, "the objects actually 'play a role,' they are as important as the actors."[31] The French critic points out how the rope is used first to drag Christ, then is hung around the neck of the main figure and linked to his wife when they get married, thus continually reappearing as a symbol of oppression. The pruning shears and other simple hand props that immediately identify a character in the *actos* are now employed beyond their immediate definition and are transformed into symbols that can further define the message.

Jesús, who is continually oppressed by his employer, brings home his frustrations and takes them out on his wife and children. Although he is at the bottom of the ladder in the fields, he tries to be the master of his home and fails. His children go their separate ways: a daughter marries an Anglo and they ride off on his motorcycle, one son becomes a drug dealer, and the other becomes a crooked politician. When Jesús gets too old to work in the fields, he and his wife are left to apply for welfare. A *calavera* who has continually appeared in various guises becomes the lady at the welfare office and demands that Jesús repeat degrading statements after her: "You're Mexican"; he repeats, "I'm Mexican"; "You're dirty," "I'm dirty"; "You're a welfare bum!" Jesús can barely vocalize this last demeaning epithet and finally dies at the word "bum." The ever-present devil leans down over Jesús' corpse and asks: "Did you like the United Estates?" The dead man rises with alacrity, screams "NO!" and dances off the stage arm in arm with the devil.[32] The audience responds with laughter to this last commentary on what it is like to live in the "United Estates."

After Jesús and the devil have danced off, the *Carpa* demonstrates what happens to his two sons. The politician has become obsessed with power, although he claims to be for the people, and the drug pusher finds he must have more and more money. The latter finally kills the politician and the police kill the pusher—brother against brother and the system against them both. What is left? The fourth and final part of the play is announced by the familiar conch shell and is introduced as "The Salvation of Our People." The actor who originally played Christ enters as Quetzalcóatl, dressed in a magnificent robe and plumed headdress that contrast starkly with the *rasquachi* quality of the setting and characters. Quetzalcóatl, who was the Redeemer figure for all of Mesoamerica, becomes Valdez' symbol of hope for the people of Aztlán. It was this indigenous deity who taught the Toltecs fine arts, science, and the agricultural craft that would make them the leading nation of America long before Cortés or Moctezuma. Quetzalcóatl, the Feathered Serpent, represented God and man's duality. He promised to return before departing on a raft of serpents that flamed up into the sky to become the morning star, Venus.[33]

In the *Carpa*, Quetzalcóatl is tricked into getting drunk and losing control over his senses. People fight and kill each other, men oppress women, the rich oppress the poor, and all manner of evil resurfaces as Quetzalcóatl leaves, promising to return. Malevolent forces pursue the Chicano characters onstage to the sound of military music; suddenly the action is suspended and the Virgin appears, her beautiful blue mantle contrasting with the drab surroundings. She asks the people: "Have you forgotten that my son will return?"

Jesucristo-Quetzalcóatl comes back onstage to join the Virgin in reciting the Maya phrase "In lak'ech," which is repeated in Spanish: *Tú eres mi otro yo.* As one of these holy figures recites this Maya philosophy in Spanish, the other repeats it in English so that all will understand:

> *Tú eres mi otro yo* / You are my other self.
> *Si te hago daño a ti* / If I do harm to you,
> *Me hago daño a mí* / I do harm to myself:
> *Si te amo y respeto* / If I love and respect you,
> *Me amo y respeto yo* / I love and respect myself.

The music then swells into an indigenous "power song," *Mano poderosa* ("Powerful Hand"). At this point the opening-night audience jumped to its feet with thunderous applause. Many had tears streaming down their cheeks, for they were touched by this vision of an indigenous redeemer hand in hand with the Virgin Mother. Those who knew the lyrics sang along with the entire cast assembled onstage:

> *Mano poderosa* (Powerful hand)
> *De mi Dios amado* (Of my beloved God)
> *Bendice esta gente* (Bless these people)
> *Y a todo lo creado* (And all things under creation).

Guitars, drums, and other instruments joined in to create a moving musical finale to a very special moment in the history of Chicano theater.

It was difficult for anyone in the auditorium that first night not to feel touched by the presentation and its effect on the audience. Something that is usually reserved for churches and ritual sites had taken place in a university auditorium filled with community members. It was on this same campus that Luis Valdez had first seen his

Shrunken Head of Pancho Villa performed. He had returned almost ten years later to capture those present with this product of collective dramaturgy that was also the child of his spirituality. The piece would continue to undergo changes, but the overriding message of "In lak'ech" would still remain to urge the audiences to seek their own salvation through brotherhood and love. No one could deny the effectiveness of the presentation that night, but when it came time to evaluate it in political terms, the great debate began.

When Luis Valdez chose to dramatize his emerging neo-Maya/ Christian philosophy, he had to understand that both he and his Teatro would come under attack from other groups—certainly from the emerging Chicano leftists who were making their presence known in the Chicano movement as well as in TENAZ. The presentation in San Jose was the first exposure of the *Carpa* to the national organization; the leftist-inclined groups could hardly be expected to applaud a message of "In lak'ech" and "Wait for Jesucristo-Quetzalcóatl." "What about the problems of today?" they asked, angered that the leading Chicano theater company seemed to be losing its political perspective and proletarian origins.

As if he knew what the critics would say, Valdez had previously published a long poem in which he attempted to explain the new direction of his group. "Out of political necessity," he wrote, "El Teatro Campesino is turning toward religious theater."[34] He wrote of a "Cosmic Vision of our Indio ancestors" that would ultimately lead to the Chicano's liberation. He referred to *Bernabé, La Virgen del Tepeyac,* and *La carpa cantinflesca*[35] as *mitos* that had shown the way toward that cosmic vision, which he termed *Pensamiento serpentino* ("Serpentine Thought"), the title of his poem.

The poem begins:

> Teatro
>
> eres el mundo
> y las paredes de los
> buildings más grandes
> son
>
> nothing but scenery.[36]

"Teatro, you are the world; and the walls of the tallest buildings are nothing but scenery." Written in typical Chicano code-switching, Valdez' introduction sets the mood for the entire poem. He is telling us that his theatrical vision is larger than the barrios, the cities, and the nations from whence the Chicano came. His theater is the Calderonian *Gran teatro del mundo,* or "Great Theater of the Uni-

verse," in which man is only a small speck in the total picture. "We must all become NEO-MAYAS," he asserts.[37] He then relates the vision of "In lak'ech" that we see in the *Carpa* and extolls the Mayas for their ability to live by a creed that is reminiscent of the Christian Golden Rule.

Valdez' poem combines Christian with indigenous thought and answers his would-be critics:

> El indio baile [sic]
> He DANCES
> his way to truth
> in a way INTELLECTUALS will
> never understand.[38]

Valdez, a one-time advocate for Castro's Cuba, had begun to espouse spiritual solutions for a people who have more than enough spirituality and seldom enough to live on from day to day. The pragmatic, rational truth of the early *actos* was replaced by an ethereal sense of anti-intellectualism that of course angered the intellectuals even more. "But what about the people who are being oppressed by that very Church you speak about?" they demanded. Valdez reminded them that the Church in his *Carpa* was never idealized: it was called "St. Boss's Church" in answer to the Catholic hierarchy's historical collusion with the power structure in capitalistic society, especially in Latin America and the United States.

Pensamiento serpentino speaks of erasing racial distinctions and creating a common race of human beings who believe in the power of God within themselves. "You make your own hell or heaven," writes the poet/playwright, "and if you feel oppressed, then liberate yourself!"[39] The poem condemns Anglo intellectualization and upholds true belief as the only means of social, political, or cultural liberation. It is Valdez' explanation for his supposedly new direction, which had in fact emerged years before when he began to search for his identity. This "new philosophy" was nothing more than the natural evolution of Valdez' thought as he sought both his and his group's spiritual base. Members of the Teatro had to believe in what their mentor was thinking or they could not last in their tightly knit collective. Each member of the troupe set up individual altars and spent time meditating or praying for the creative force to propel them forward with the rest of the group. Those who could not follow in these spiritual footsteps eventually left the group.[40]

By opening the *Carpa* with a re-creation of an important Cris-

tian ritual, the playwright recalled a fundamental element in the Mechicano theatrical experience. But Valdez the visionary was not giving the people just what they wanted to see since his depiction of the Church as a greedy tool for the system was not always applauded by the more devout. The satiric jabs at the Church were tempered by the extremely reverent portrayals of Christ and the Virgin, who, Valdez knew, could never be caricatured. Priests are human, but the saints are not. Valdez has always walked a thin line between irreverence and piety, as only a man of spiritual understanding can.

No matter how respectfully the *Carpa* views the saints, the piece continually makes important political statements about the social institutions that surround the Chicano. Police brutality, political corruption, economic oppression, drugs—all of the problems of the barrio—are presented with quick, insightful commentary. The so-called revolutionaries of the *acto* entitled *The Militants* reappear in the *Carpa*, and this satiric comment on political machismo may have added to the critics' opposition.[41] Some saw this portrayal as a condemnation of the Movement itself and immediately set out to fight back with tooth and nail, if not with cross and sword.

No matter what the critics believed, something very special continued to happen on that stage and no amount of verbal or written criticism could deny that fact. At a presentation of the *Carpa* at the University of California at Santa Barbara the following year, a critic of Valdez' spirituality rushed to confront the playwright with his list of condemnations. After listening patiently to the young man's complaints, Valdez smiled at him and gave him a warm hug. No words from the spokesman of "In lak'ech," just a hug that left the perplexed antagonist speechless. Valdez was dancing his way to truth in a way no intellectual could understand.

La gran carpa de los rasquachis became the Teatro Campesino's major statement for the next five years. It toured the United States on several occasions and traveled to Europe in 1976 and again in 1978. As the Teatro evolved, so did its presentation of the *Carpa*, but the theme remained the same. Describing his Teatro's theatrical direction, Valdez told an interviewer in 1974:

> As a group, as people and as a theatre we are finally achieving a wholeness that our own colonization did not allow us to have in the past. Our acts are acts of human beings living and working on this earth, struggling together. . . . We are still very much the political theatre, but our politics are the politics of the spirit: not of the flesh, but of the heart.[42]

Valdez was speaking of a growing awareness that the Chicano could not remain nationalistic, tied only to an ethnic identity. He began to speak of himself and his company as human beings, not members of a minority group. His *Pensamiento serpentino* had spoken of a universal race of men and women who would find peace and harmony with the cosmos, and now he felt his group should reflect that universality.

Mechicano critics—usually contributors to campus newspapers that addressed Chicano students—were impressed by the *Carpa*'s style, but disappointed with its message. Writing in a now defunct Chicano newspaper at the University of California at Santa Barbara, Jorge R. González penned a response to Valdez' philosophy entitled "Pensamiento Serpentino: A Cultural Trampa [Trap] or Is the Teatro Campesino Campesino?" In his lengthy discussion, González was most critical of Valdez' reliance on indigenous culture and thought and of his dependence on spirit over matter. Although Valdez wrote and spoke of returning to "our Indio beginnings," González insisted that "We, for the most part, are no longer Indians culturally. Whether we like it or not, we have been deeply affected by Europe. We are Mestizos."[43] Of course, Valdez understood the fact that Mexicans and Chicanos are the product of European and Native American cultures, but *La gran carpa de los rasquachis* was his tour de force and there was nothing that could stop him from dancing.

In 1976, *La gran carpa de los rasquachis* was adapted for a special on National Educational Television and retitled *El corrido*. Valdez wrote the script and changed the opening scene with its devils and *calaveras* to a realistic representation of village farmworkers gathered in a labor contractor's truck, enroute to another day's labor in the fields. Valdez played the role of an older *campesino* who tells his own *corrido*, which becomes a staged vision of the original *Carpa* in a dreamlike setting. The action thus goes from reality to fantasy and back. The result is an effective transfer from stage to television screen. After Jesús' story has been told, the truck arrives at its destination and is greeted by striking *campesinos* waving the familiar *huelga* flag. The farmworkers climb out of the truck and join the picket lines.

The presentation of *El corrido* moved the *Los Angeles Times* television critic, Cecil Smith, to comment:

> This is an admirably successful attempt to corral within the dimensions of television's tiny proscenium the uproarious and joyful spirit that El Teatro Campesino . . . puts into its theatrical per-

formances. . . . Propaganda? Unquestionably. But it is also theater of a high order performed with enormous style and spirit."[44]

Once again, Valdez could look with pride at the accomplishments of his group, satisfied that *La gran carpa de los rasquachis* had reached hundreds of thousands—if not millions—of homes in the United States. A tour of Europe that spring led to another tour in 1978, making *La gran carpa de los rasquachis* the Teatro's longest-running collective effort. It is also the group's major achievement to date.

While the Teatro was evolving and producing *La gran carpa de los rasquachis*, it was also searching for other *mitos* to dramatize. The members of the troupe investigated the relationship between man and the cosmos, life and death, as the ancients might have seen them. This search resulted in their version of *El fin del mundo* (The End of the World), another *mito* that would go through changes like a serpent shedding its skin.

An Apocalyptic Vision: *El fin del mundo*

Like *La gran carpa de los rasquachis*, *El fin del mundo* went through various stages in its four-year evolution that began in 1974. Unlike the *Carpa*, some versions of *Fin* were written by Valdez alone, and others were the product of collective improvisations on his basic theme. As it evolved, *Fin* reflected the philosophy of its creators as well as the reactions of its audiences.

El fin del mundo was originally conceived as a production for the Teatro's yearly *Día de los muertos* (literally, Day of the Dead) celebrations, held in San Juan on or around November 2, All Souls' Day. The first version, like the earlier *Carpa cantinflesca*, was rather symbolic: a dance ritual rather than a drama or an *acto*. It celebrated the four directions of the universe and intermingled these with indigenous symbols and songs that the group felt all Chicanos would relate to because of their Indian ancestry. Perhaps the rural, land-working *campesinos* understood the message, but the majority of Chicanos, who are from the cities, left the play with a feeling of bewilderment. While the ritual was interesting at times, Valdez' anti-intellectualism was carried to the extreme, and even subjective analyses of the piece were often futile.[45]

This first version of *El fin del mundo* was based on a script by Valdez that the group subsequently expanded and changed as it toured. They returned from the tour with a production they could rightly call their own, although it lacked cohesion. The next version, performed in 1975 at the Seventh Annual Chicano Theater Festival in San Antonio, Texas, was easier to understand. The 1975 version of *Fin* was composed of four episodes that attempted to use indigenous symbols while dramatizing universal problems of violence and oppression with such characters as La Señora Plata (Mrs. Silver) and her son Goldie, rich landowners whose employees are called Cobre (Copper) and Fierro (Iron). It was an attempt to signify the elements and their relationship to one another and Mother Earth, but the symbolism was generally confusing. In her excellent analysis and detailed synopsis of this version, Betty Diamond discusses the dangers of collectively creating a piece that is based on a philosophy in which the participants are immersed:

> It becomes easy to forget that those outside the group, who do not know as much as you do, will not understand automatically the symbolism and the philosophy of a particular piece. . . . the symbolism of [*Fin del mundo*] is not consistent, and structural patterns are on occasion set up and then abandoned. It is possible that this looseness is the result of the number of people contributing to the work's creation.[46]

Audiences at the San Antonio festival recognized the sincerity and the entertaining quality of the presentation, but many expressed disappointment at what seemed a very ethereal direction for the troupe. This play, like the *Carpa*, denounced oppression, but the mixture of allegorical figures and contemporary situations left many people unsatisfied. Once again, the answer to oppression seemed to lie within the individual, and there were those who felt that the Teatro Campesino had strayed even further from its original purposes.

The third version of *El fin del mundo* ventured into the realm of realistic acting techniques and characterizations within the structure of an extended *corrido* written by Valdez. It is the *corrido* of one Raymundo Mata, called El Mundo in barrio vernacular. Raymundo signifies "king of the world" (*mundo* meaning "world" and *rey* meaning "king"). *Mata* means "kills," so that the full name may be rendered as "king of the world kills." This is an ironic image because it is Raymundo who is killed. The character of Mundo becomes the archetypal *vato loco* whose life and death are a metaphor for the prophesied end of the world in Christian and indigenous teachings.

The *corrido* is set before a backdrop of patchwork burlap and the setting itself is composed of agricultural packing crates, which are rearranged to form a meeting hall, street scene, cantina, packing shed, front porch, and car. During the transitions, the musicians sing the narrative while the set shifts before the audience's eyes. As in the *actos*, the public is constantly reminded that this is a theatrical event by the unselfconscious scene changes and constant narration.

The Valdez version of *El fin del mundo* toured the country in 1976 and was revised a fourth time. This next version, which this writer saw in October 1978, has elements of the realistic version but is more closely related to the *acto-corrido* style for which the Teatro Campesino has become known.[47] The 1978 edition was collectively created under Valdez' guidance and was directed by his multitalented sister, Socorro.

This version echoes an earlier one, for all the actors are dressed in basic *calavera* costumes consisting of black tights with the skeletal structure painted on them. The actors wear skull masks that have distinctive features as well as varied wigs and costume accessories to help distinguish characters. The effect is comic, with various *calaveras* traipsing about the stage, each one unique yet looking so similar. The setting is composed of a giant skeletal figure out of whose rib cage the characters enter and exit. Created by the Teatro's resident designer, Bob Morales, the setting of mammoth bones effectively contrasts with the *calavera* figures and manages to fill the stage without detracting from the action.

The 1978 version of the *mito* is also an extended *corrido* but is very different from the previous script written by Valdez. It is still the story of Mundo, but the situations in the previous versions have been changed. The acting style is once again the exaggerated technique of the *acto* and *commedia dell'arte*. As in *La gran carpa de los rasquachis*, the actors never leave the stage, and the ever-present musical accompaniment keeps the pace flowing as quickly or slowly as the mood requires. Like the previous version, this one begins with the sighting of a comet, which signals the end of the world. We are in Mundo's barrio, and we see his world coming to an end due to water and energy shortages that suggest that the "source" is drying up. The shortages of water, gasoline, and food at the time were indicators of the veracity of the prophecies. By dramatizing issues the people could relate to and whose implications they understood, the Teatro had judiciously responded to the criticisms of the earlier versions.

Mundo is unconcerned with energy shortages and continues to

live his life as if nothing were wrong. When he asks his girlfriend to make love to him, she says "I can't! I'm pregnant!" "How can you be pregnant?" he asks, "We haven't even done nothing yet!" "But I am," she replies. To which Mundo responds: "So what does that make me, San José?" The parallel with St. Joseph and the Virgin Mary is of course intentional. The girlfriend's name is Esperanza (Hope) and she becomes the archetypal Virgin Mother, whom Mundo agrees to marry. Just as they are about to "seal the bargain" by making love, rival gang members enter, and Mundo kills one of them after they have harassed him. The others leave, vowing revenge.

After various vignettes depicting the realities of high food prices and gas shortages, Esperanza's father gets Mundo to agree to marry his daughter. The wedding ensues; during the ceremony the rival gang members enter and shoot at Mundo but kill the bride instead. Other vignettes show inner-city looting and violence and the harassment of Mundo's family by the Migra (Immigration) officers on the street. "You're mojados (wetbacks)," the officer tells the grandparents; the grandmother replies, lifting up her dress, "Aquí tengo tus mojados, pinche gringo!" ("Here are your wetbacks, stupid Gringo!"). Mundo's parents fight, the father is put in jail, the mother is accosted by a rapist, the brother turns on to barbituates—all manner of societal decay confronts Mundo's microcosm of the larger society. He becomes a revolutionary and takes over a television station, demanding that his father be released from jail because he is a political prisoner. The officials send in a SWAT team, parodying the popular television police drama; this is followed by a summit meeting that includes the world's leaders. Jimmy Carter speaks, followed by Queen Elizabeth, Freud, Brezhnev, and Mao. The others acknowledge that Mao and Freud are dead, but succinctly add that in this *calavera* masquerade, what does it matter?

The world leaders begin to squabble over trivialities and their fight ends when the Bomb is dropped, effectively destroying the world. The *calaveras* all do a dance of death in front of a cardboard painting of a mushroom cloud. Suddenly the corpses come to life again and Esperanza gives birth to a little *calavera*. "He looks just like you," the grandmother tells the proud Mundo, and the audience laughs because they all do look alike. Racial distinctions mean nothing when the body's flesh is removed, and these farcical specters of Death are constant reminders of our mortality as well as our basic oneness. The parents name the baby Mundo, hinting that he is the savior of the world but never identifying this figure as either Christ or Quetzalcóatl. One of the *calaveras* steps forward and delivers the epilogue, enunciating the message that "La vida es muerte y la muerte es vida" ("Life is death and death is life"). The *corrido* ends with the breaking of a *piñata.*

El fin del mundo thus evolved through different stages, each reflecting the Teatro's commitment to its particular philosophy. Each version asked its audiences to look to themselves for salvation and to understand the relationship between man and nature, a relationship that changes drastically every day. In the 1978 version, the combination of *mito* and *corrido* demonstrates a message of respect for La Tierra, whose natural resources are not unlimited. As celebrated by the indigenous forefathers of these mestizo thespians, there is no difference between life and death, for the one leads naturally to the other. There is no end to the cycle, we are told, and we must look death in the face, prepared to make the transition from this world to the next just as the *calaveras* do.

In notable contrast to the earlier Valdez script of this *mito*, the 1978 version of *Fin* is presented in broad, farcical strokes, underlining the notion that these are *calaveras*, not people. The fantasy is undercut, however, by the fact that these dancing skeleton people *are* human underneath the tights and masks, further highlighting their comic vision of the world's end. The *calavera* who delivers the epilogue becomes an anonymous figure, almost preaching the message in a sermon-like format. We are once again reminded of the Spanish religious dramas and their didactic purposes, and we realize that this is, indeed, a modern morality play.

The wonderful Valdezian mixture of elements comes together in this piece like well-placed mosaics against a sharply defined black and white background. The skeleton figures, which might have gotten lost against the black background, are pulled out of obscurity by the dashes of color in costumes and accessories. The exaggerated bouffant wigs emerging from the skull masks serve to distinguish the characters with humor and style. The artwork of José Guadalupe Posada is an obvious influence in this piece. One of the Teatro's earliest posters is an enlargement of a Posada *calavera* frozen in a dance of death, and in this play that figure has come to life. The coordination of setting, costumes, and props is everywhere evident; cardboard houses, cars, and other settings are painted with a fine sense of craftsmanship. The juxtaposition of cardboard and beautifully painted effects gives the entire setting a feeling of "tasteful *rasquachi*," something the Teatro Campesino has mastered over any other group. In other hands the cardboard might have been poorly painted or ineffectively scaled, but in the hands of this thoughtful teatro everything fits into place. Cardboard, yes, but cardboard with class.

El fin del mundo recalls the Christian dramas that have been so popular in Mechicano communities for generations. The spiritual call that the Teatro Campesino is making with this piece is that of a contemporary morality play, with mushroom clouds instead of Hell's mouth to inspire awe and wonder in the audiences. If the *calaveras* are, indeed, symbols of humanity's basic oneness, then the Teatro Campesino is calling for a new age of liberation in which all people are considered equal. It is also a very individual message, a challenge to the heart as well as the mind. For some, the theme is overworked; for others it offers a positive attitude in the daily struggles for survival.

Luis Valdez and the Teatro Campesino are the leading perpetuators of the Mechicano's long tradition of religious theater. Although other teatros have dramatized such plays as *Las cuatro apariciones de la Virgen de Guadalupe*, no other group has been as consistently involved in spiritual drama as the Campesino. Above all, no other Chicano theater group has a spiritual guide with the directorial or dramaturgical leadership that the Teatro Campesino has. While other groups have also studied the historical evolution of the Mechicano and created works that call for an end to economic oppression, Valdez' group continually reminds audiences that the characters have a religious background as well. The desired effect is to deliver a theatrical sermon that calls for a political examination of the situation within a spiritual context. The dollar sign on "St. Boss's Church," the debate over baptizing the natives, the conference of the double-talking world leaders, and the recognition that it is the rich who have stolen from La Tierra—all of these aspects of the plays and more reveal a political stance that separates the Teatro Campesino from its predecessors in the churches of Aztlán.

Employing symbols that barrio audiences can easily relate to and recognize, these contemporary examples of Chicano religious theater are directed at a working-class audience, the humble folk who still believe in God and the Church. While some middle-class Chicanos may have abandoned their devotion to the teachings of the Church, the working-class public still reacts enthusiastically to a spiritual message. Indeed, no teatro or playwright has been bold enough to suggest to a barrio audience that there is no God, indigenous or Christian. But this same audience must not be patronized or condescended to. The people react with glee when the powers that have kept them subjugated are satirized.

Valdez has thus successfully blended critical commentary with ecumenical messages, reaching his audiences through their own devotion. As early as 1971, he was ready to proclaim his commitment to a ritual theater, for he knew that it would always be informed not only by the spirit, but by political consciousness as well. For Luis Valdez, as for the ancient Mayas, art, politics, theater, and science are all one:

> Teatro,
>
> eres el mundo
> y las paredes de los
> buildings más grandes
> son
>
> nothing but scenery.[48]

El Teatro Campesino performing *La gran carpa de los rasquachis*,
c. 1975-76. *Photo: Teatro Campesino*

AFTERWORD: THE MANY STAGES
OF THE REVOLUTION

From the Temple to the Arena

As we have seen, Chicano theater was not born full-grown in 1965 with the advent of the Chicano movement. Many of the themes that Chicano playwrights and teatros are addressing today have historical antecedents that should be recognized in order to better understand the present messages. Certainly, some knowledge of Aztec and Maya philosophy is essential to a study of the indigenous themes addressed by Luis Valdez, for although he manages the myths to suit his literary purposes, pre-Columbian thought permeates his vision of today's Mechicano. To know that a Mexican American acting company was dramatizing the plight of Aurelio Pompa long before the creation of the first *actos* by the Teatro Campesino is to understand that Chicanos have not been the "silent minority" they were long purported to be. Both the spiritual and political theatrical expressions of the Chicano inform the audience of a rich tradition, a past with a purpose.

Chicano theater *is* political, for it is a declaration of certain conditions that cry out for solutions in order to improve the Mechicano's situation in this country. As political theater, the creations of the many playwrights and teatros are decidedly non-commercial, more concerned with social justice than financial remuneration. Barrio performances are usually free or very modestly priced, with the traditional "passing of the hat" following each presentation. Teatros are certainly not adverse to economic independence, but they purposely remain apart from commodity theater in an effort to reach working-class Mechicano audiences. The older, more recognized teatros tour the university and college campuses, charging performance fees that often constitute the troupes' major income, but this minimal funding does not signify their commercialization. Several teatros receive state and federal subsidies, yet manage to retain their autonomy by not becoming wholly dependent on this kind of funding. No teatros are financially independent, unaligned with some sort of institution or federal program. Still, all of the teatros remain political, intent on promoting important changes in their communities.

While the focus of this book is on the works created by the more developed teatros, it must be remembered that all of them began as inexperienced troupes whose genesis was determined by a political cause rather than an artistic goal. The neophyte troupes remain the only true people's theaters, and the groups represented in this volume are the exception rather than the rule. The older teatros have survived to face the responsibility of maintaining a connection with their communities while reaching for professional performance standards. They have become travelling models for the other teatros, the groups that form the very foundation of the Chicano theater movement. The younger groups serve to stimulate the interest of both the participants and the audiences they serve, and the older teatros confirm that support.

It is clear that Luis Valdez and the Teatro Campesino have made the most important contributions to Chicano theater, beginning with the development of the *acto* and continuing through all the other forms and themes this partnership has addressed. The works of Valdez and his troupe permeate this book, often forming the very basis of the discussion. Few groups have gone beyond the initial format of the Teatro Campesino, and there is very little in the canon of Chicano dramatic literature that does not owe something to Valdez or his Teatro. All of the major themes in this study have been treated by Valdez as playwright, director, or both, but this eclectic visionary's contributions have yet to be recognized completely in his own country. Significantly, Valdez has never strayed too far from his indigenous roots. His theater is still a people's theater, and the people have responded with the highest approbation. Valdez' dramaturgy will live as long as the themes that he addresses remain vital.

One of the most telling facts revealed in this study is that most of the conditions exposed by the teatros remain unsolved and urgent. From the first farmworker *actos* to the urban themes dramatized by teatros and playwrights, little if any change has occurred. *Campesinos* continue to fight oppression; students are still placed in remedial classes because of the language barrier; police repression is rampant; drug addiction pervades the barrios; veterans of Vietnam have become invisible victims of that unwanted war; undocumented workers are still harassed by the INS and remain at the bottom of the economic ladder; pachucos continue to kill one another; Mechicanos are overrepresented in the prisons; *vendidos* ignore their less fortunate compatriots; politicians seek their own advancement; and Mechicanos still believe in Christian myth and dogma. Of course, it is difficult to document what changes have occurred due to theatrical presentations in the fields and factories. While audiences have often been moved by a teatro, the effects of that motivation are not always readily apparent. During the emotional rallies of the 1960s and early 1970s, spirits were raised and conditions exposed, but the audiences were usually the already initiated.

As Chicanos left the decade of the seventies behind them, a spokesman in *Time* (10/16/78) declared the eighties "the decade of the Hispanics." As the largest group of Hispanics in the country, Mechicanos will have to keep up the fight on all fronts for an improvement of their condition, inspired by the issues that writers, artists, and teatros continue to expose. If overall improvement has indeed been insignificant for the Mechicano, then the teatros and playwrights will have to analyze their methods and their means and perhaps work in other ways to bring about the changes they feel necessary. The most significant advances were achieved during the first few years of the Movement; by the mid-1970s the pace had slackened. With the fervor of those initial dramatists in cloaks and cassocks, atop sacrificial altars or in Christian temples, the teatros will have to assess their positive achievements and determine what new and different courses they will undertake in the arena of continuing struggle.

Expanding the Perimeters

One of the most important themes that still needs to be addressed by Mechicano dramatists is the condition of women in Mechicano society. Although teatros pride themselves on their familial structure and the constant presence of women as important contributors to the collectives, little has been said about the Mechicana in theatrical statements. Teatro Libertad's *Los pelados* effectively compares the drudgery of husband and wife and the incredible burden for the latter of managing a household, an alcoholic husband, and an outside job. Other plays discussed in this book make mention of the subservient position of the woman in the Mechicano household. However, there is only one play to date in the Chicano repertoire with a woman as the central figure caught in the web of societal structures and cultural pressures: Estella Portillo's *Day of the Swallows*. This play is in the style of poetic realism and was written by a woman, for women. Portillo is one of the few Chicana playwrights to have published her work, and *Day of the Swallows* establishes her as an important figure in Chicano theater.

Days of the Swallows has not been produced by a teatro, perhaps because it requires a rather complete setting for maximum effect. The author describes the very beautiful interior of the protagonist's home, a bright, feminine shelter away from the harsh world of men. The play is a period piece, set in a Mexican village that could be on either side of the border, in an earlier time. Portillo has structured her drama around the well-hidden passions of her central figure, who has carried on a lesbian relationship with a young woman she rescued from a whorehouse. With language as delicate as the lace the women weave, this play must be produced by very experienced actors, lest it appear to be a nineteenth-century melodrama Ultimately, *Day of the Swallows* is important for its realistic style, its language and imagery, and its uncommon theme. Homosexuality is a taboo subject for discussion in any barrio, and *Day of the Swallows* would be difficult to perform for a typical teatro audience. Portillo's play has been produced on campuses in California and Texas and has received much attention in Chicano literature courses. It should not long remain the singular example of a Chicana play.

No teatro or playwright has yet treated the middle-class Mechicano experience with sympathy, choosing instead to parody this segment of the culture. As teatros reach out beyond the initiated audiences they have traditionally addressed, they may choose to create dramas that have some appeal to members of this group, expressing their weaknesses but with a view to changing them in a positive way. Although an *acto* such as *Los vendidos* is rather harmless, it may alienate the butt of the joke if he or she is in the audience. It may be wise to present dramas or comedies that not only laugh at the middle-class mentality but show concern for the characters. The teatros and playwrights must learn to distinguish between the positive results of the progress they are advocating—financial security—and the negative aspects—cultural and political apathy. Most importantly, the teatros must enlarge their audiences by reaching beyond the political activists who are always at the rallies and performances to the many more people who are usually not present at either.

Zoot Suit proved that in Los Angeles, at least, Mechicanos from all walks of life were willing to pay to see professional theater dealing with their cultural, historical, and political experience. Audiences came to Los Angeles from all corners of southern California to see this play, people from East Los Angeles and Beverly Hills mingling together at this historic event. Any doubts about whether Chicanos would support theater of this kind were dispelled when the production lasted almost a full year. *Zoot Suit* became more than theater; it was an *event* that was supported by both Mechicanos and the non-Hispanics who jumped to their feet at the close of each performance. Working-class people sat next to season subscribers, each group experiencing distinct reactions, but neither ignored by the playwright. Valdez proved once and for all that the Chicano can produce a professional theater appealing to all people while not ignoring political realities.

As teatros attempt to expand their audiences, they will find that the working-class experience is not unique to the barrios, and they will begin to encompass other cultures in their dramas. Certainly, the themes treated by Chicano theaters are universal. Oppression knows no racial boundaries, and many of the works discussed in this book have Chicano as well as non-Chicano antagonists, though few present an Anglo protagonist. Ultimately, all of the characters are victims of the system exposed, be it the educational, judicial, economic or political system. But because the plays concentrate their efforts on the Mechicano exerience, there might be the inclination to perceive the problems as unique to this people. The teatros and playwrights must recognize the Mechicano within the broader context of the universal working class, remembering cultural distinctions but accepting the connection with other people. Some of the multiracial teatros have addressed the overall working class rather than the Mechicano alone and have consequently promoted a greater understanding among the groups represented.

By adapting plays to the Mechicano milieu, dramatists are revealing the similarities in working-class political goals, whether in Los Angeles, South America, or Brooklyn. Certain changes must be made in the scripts to accommodate the particularities of the Mechicano experience, but these alterations can be minimal, thus maintaining the intent of the original. This author's adaptation of Arthur Miller's *A View From the Bridge* in 1977 demonstrated how minor adjustments in the language and environmental references could transform a play about Italian immigrants into a statement about Chicanos and Mexican immigrants. Eddie Carbone became Eddie Carranza, and the play was moved from the base of the Brooklyn Bridge to the base of the Coronado Bridge in San Diego's Mechicano barrio. Local audiences were delighted that the play seemed written for them, although Miller had envisioned immigrants from another country. Miller's play is not a political tract but rather a common man's tragedy, and the adaptation purposely did not venture too far from the original intent. Still, the conditions affecting undocumented workers in the Southwest were clearly presented within the broader context of Eddie Carranza's personal disaster.

As Chicano playwrights develop their craft, they can learn a great deal by adapting dramatic literature from both the traditional and alternative theaters. Whether performed in English, Spanish, or a mixture of both, adaptations are one way of learning about the rigors of good dramatic structure. One need only look to Bertolt Brecht or Shakespeare to see how historical events, stories, and even other dramas have been adapted by the masters. A study of the versions of the Greek myth of Phaedra from Euripides to Racine to O'Neill shows quite clearly how a universal theme of incest and thwarted love can be dramatized for different audiences in different times.

Teatros might develop a repertoire of productions to be produced in a variety of styles and places: for the political events, an *acto*; for the university crowd, a portable production demonstrating another style; and for the resident company, a realistic play such as *Day of the Swallows*. Many of the regional theaters around the country have this sort of production schedule, reaching a diverse public with productions that vary from Shakespeare to *commedia dell'arte*, Harold Pinter to street theater in the schools. Teatro de la Esperanza experimented with a summer resident company in Santa Barbara in 1980, and the Teatro Campesino began plans the same year to convert a very large warehouse in San Juan Bautista into a spacious theater. Both were following in the footsteps of other regional theaters. Efforts such as these are becoming the trend as Chicano theater companies continue to attract larger audiences and expand their horizons.

It is imperative that barrio dramatists, actors, directors, and designers continue to develop their craft, learning through experimentation, experience, and some kind of formal training if possible. The yearly TENAZ festivals and symposiums have been very helpful to the emerging teatros, but they are of necessity too far apart in time to produce outstanding results. Younger teatros are exposed to the more developed groups for a week or two, taking workshops from them and learning from the critiques of their performances. But if they then return to a campus or community situation lacking the proper artistic direction and organizational administration, they find it difficult to continue. Some teatro members have gone to work with the Teatro Campesino and other groups and then have taken what they have learned back to their teatros, but such exposure is often limited to workshop productions of a few weeks. Helpful as this may be, it is obvious that much more training is necessary to make a lasting impression. In some instances, these interns become full-time members of another teatro, strengthening the host company but leaving a rather indignant teatro back home to suffer the loss of a member. If a teatro is to succeed, its members must learn from the experiences of those groups that have persisted; it must become more than an avocation for its members by developing directors, designers, actors, and playwrights who can meet the challenges of an evolving movement.

Securing the Resources

There are three methods of obtaining training in Chicano theater. The first is with a teatro that is independent of any institution. The second method is to work with a teatro that is affiliated with a university. The third approach is to enroll in a drama department that does not offer any exposure to Chicano theater. The third method is of course the least effective, although there are several people active in Chicano theater who did not receive any training in the form itself. Neither Luis Valdez nor the present author ever took a class in Chicano theater, for there were no such offerings before the late 1960s. It was a matter of adapting one's personal experiences to the study of world theater, employing the useful and discarding the unnecessary. Ultimately, the student of theater will later benefit from what he or she has learned, no matter what the origins of that training.

Without instructors who are either Chicano or interested in Chicano drama, few if any Chicanos are motivated to enter into the realm of academic theater. Economic factors are involved here, for as has been pointed out, the barrio child has not had the best educational training and is usually from a disadvantaged home. If the barrio Chicano is going to attempt to succeed at all, it will usually not be in theater but in what most parents prefer, no matter what their ethnic background: a stable profession. Unfortunately, very few people in this country are able to earn a living in theater. The study of drama has always been an unpractical pursuit, and most Chicanos cannot afford the luxury. Given the political nature of Chicano theater, it is not an economically secure profession at all. Just as most drama majors are pursuing a dream, so too are the Mexican Americans involved in theater, and many Chicanos will never experience that fantasy.

College-aged Chicanos who discover Chicano theater find that they are far behind the majority of theater students, who have usually been active in drama since their high school years or before. An early exposure to theater has prepared the major for the usual drama department fare: established classics, contemporary plays, and some experimental work, but little if any political theater. The politically active Chicanos may have some knowledge of sociopolitical concerns, but their dramatic training is sorely lacking, and their work exhibits that fact when they attempt to organize a teatro on campus. When they go to the drama department for help, they find that there are no Chicanos on the faculty and few Chicano students, if any. Though this pattern is repeated on campuses throughout the country, the more enterprising Chicanos get involved in the drama departments, learning all that they can, participating in productions, and working with a teatro on the side. The student lives a sort of double life, engaged in traditional theater as a student and in Chicano theater as an activist. It is a somewhat arduous way to get training, but for some of the survivors it has been the best solution to a difficult situation.

Several of the directors and playwrights represented in this book are the products of traditional theatrical training. All would agree that a diversity of dramatic exposures is vital to a greater understanding of Chicano theater, though they have elected to concentrate their efforts on Chicano theater in particular. These leaders are the predecessors of the second wave of Chicano theater artists, the students who entered the university during the 1970s, when a few drama departments began to offer courses in Teatro Chicano. Before Luis Valdez taught the first workshop in Chicano theater at Fresno State College in 1968, there had been no other courses of this kind in any institution of higher learning. In 1970, Valdez offered a workshop in Teatro at the University of California at Berkely, and the present author explored the same possibilities at the Santa

Barbara campus of the University of California. Other Chicanos and non-Chicanos who were interested in the genre began to teach classes in colleges in the Southwest, and by the late 1970s courses were being taught in California, Arizona, Texas, New Mexico, and Colorado. Sometimes these classes were offered by Chicano studies departments rather than drama departments, but in all cases Chicano theater was being analyzed, discussed, and experienced.

There are two kinds of teatros affiliated with universities: the groups that produce strictly Chicano works, and the teatros that perform traditional Hispanic plays or Broadway scripts in Spanish. Both types of group are valuable to the growth of Chicano theater, for they provide important training that can be carried over to the professional and semi-professional teatro. Teatro Bilingüe of Texas A & I University in Kingsville is a singular example of the traditional theater company. The group is directed by Professor Joseph Rosenberg, a Jewish-American married to a Mexican who has elected to concentrate his efforts on Spanish-language theater. The majority of students in the Teatro Bilingüe are Chicanos, and their productions are addressed to the Mechicano as well as the non-Hispanic. This group is an example of a teatro that performs the majority of its works in either Spanish or English, but not both. The troupe has produced and translated many Latin American plays and has toured in both the United States and Mexico. It is not the typical, unpolished student group usually associated with the teatro movement, but it nonetheless *is* Chicano. Teatro Bilingüe has produced works by Chicanos that address the particular experiences of the Mechicano; more importantly, the actors, directors, and designers that are graduating from Rosenberg's program are entering the Chicano theater movement. Two former members of Teatro Bilingüe joined the Teatro de la Esperanza in 1979, making very valuable contributions to this group.

The other type of university teatro is best exemplified by the Teatro Bilingüe de Sacramento at California State University, directed by Romulus Zamora from 1976 to 1980. In 1976, Zamora assumed the direction of the Chicano theater program developed on that campus by Elizabeth Ramírez the previous two years. With an interested core of students and with community support, Zamora staged original works as well as adaptations of Spanish and Mexican plays that he transposed to the barrio. Presentations of Lorca's *Bodas de sangre* (Blood Wedding), Sastre's *Muerte en el barrio* (A Death in the Barrio), and Emilio Carballido's *Yo también hablo de la rosa* (I, Too, Speak of the Rose) established this program's importance to the future development of Chicano theater. It was the most concerted effort anywhere in the country by a drama department and a Chicano director to produce teatro on a univeristy campus. Zamora's troupe included members of the community as well as students, creating an important link between the campus and the barrio. Manuel Pickett, a long time teatro participant and director/playwright, assumed the directorship of this program in 1980.

At the present time Chicanos are pursuing graduate studies in theater, teaching courses in teatro and/or directing Chicano productions. Until these students gain permanent faculty positions, however, the teatros they direct will have uncertain futures. In every case, the number of Chicano students who are drama majors is very limited, and the serious student often works side by side with the transient. As more Chicanos enter academic theater training programs in earnest, the quality of the productions will definitely improve. Obviously, the larger the percentage of Chicano students on campus, the greater the number of drama majors from that group. The fact that Rosenberg's program in Texas is extremely successful is due in large part to the great number of Mechicanos in the area.

Of course, it is hoped that the Chicano drama student will participate in all departmental productions, and some do. Generally, however, these students cannot compete with the more experienced non-Hispanic drama majors. Racial distinctions are also often a consideration: a dark-skinned, Indian-featured Queen Elizabeth is too much for some directors, who relegate the non-Anglos to servant's roles. This is, unfortunately, a reflection of the professional theater, but it leaves the non-Anglo drama majors with few opportunities to portray characters of their own background. The need for new Chicano scripts is pressing if Chicano actors are to gain the training they need. The Chicano actor who can pass for other ethnic types, especially European, will have greater opportunities in Anglo-dominated college productions, but most barrio Chicanos do not look like Anglos. Therefore the need is great for plays that Chicanos can call their own and that will serve as proving grounds for their talent.

The result of academic training as well as practical experience can be seen in many teatros. All of the present members of the Teatro Campesino are graduates of a drama department, another teatro, or both. The majority of members of the present Teatro de la Esperanza and Teatro de la Gente worked with other teatros before joining those companies. Although some are graduates of college drama programs, others in the two groups are not. Those members who have no formal training are limited to the teatro experience, lacking exposure to the classics and to other styles of theater. As the teatros develop their repertoires, they will be able to offer a broader training experience.

Each of these types of training available to the student of Chicano theater involves exposure to theatrical instruction that is only limited by the achievements of directors or instructors. This is to say that an apprenticeship with a two-year-old teatro will not equal the learning experience to be gained by participating with a ten-year-old troupe. A course of studies in a drama department that offers nothing in the way of Chicano theater will lack that particular experience, but the serious student of teatro can adapt quickly to the demands of an active Chicano theater company once he or she has graduated. With the proper tools in hand, many Chicanos with no background in Teatro Chicano have found that they have much to offer and learn while working with a teatro. And as the teatros become more financially independent, they may be able to offer more than a meager subsistence to their members.

Although some Chicanos are currently pursuing doctorates in theater, the total number of Chicanos with advanced degrees in drama is minimal. If the Chicano theater movement is to continue to develop, then the burden of responsibility rests with the few Chicanos in academic theater to recruit actively and to retain those who have the talent and determination to succeed in this field. Teachers trained in teatro techniques are needed at all levels if Mechicanos are to fully appreciate what they have to learn from their heritage as well as what they have to offer. The development of actors, directors, designers, and critics will not happen by itself, but only when Chicanos realize that they too have a theatrical statement to make and when they seize the opportunity.

Keeping the Revolution on Stage

While all of the issues addressed by teatros in the first fifteen years of the Chicano theater movement remain urgent today, advances have been made. Politicians at every level talk about the problems and their solutions, and the teatros demonstrate these same concerns for a public that appreciates their presentations. Audiences watch and listen as the many characters in the Chicano repertoire strut across stages from coast to coast, exposing conditions most of them already know about in a dramatic and different manner. People have been moved by teatro to boycott certain products, from grapes to beer, and all manner of social ills have been openly discussed. Many Chicano students have been motivated to go to college because of teatro presentations about that possibility, and once they arrive their education has been enhanced by their exposure to a teatro as participants or observers. Cultural ties are often renewed or discovered by Chicanos witnessing a teatro performance, and linguistic distinctions become an asset rather than a threat.

In its first fifteen years, the Chicano theater movement has reached millions, not only in the United States but in Latin America and Europe as well. The more far-reaching teatros have become cultural and political ambassadors for an ethnic minority that seemingly emerged from oblivion, leaping onto the public platform with fierce determination. In every instance, from the earliest *actos* to the professional productions, Chicano theater has made an impact that cannot be ignored. But despite all its travels across continents and oceans, Chicano theater is always most comfortable at home, in the barrio. Nothing can compare with the laughter, the tears, and the intense interest of a group of Mechicanos whose lives are being represented on the stage. Whether witnessing an *acto* about drug addiction or a spectacle about zoot suiters in the 1940s, Mechicanos know that the presentations are addressed to them by people who have suffered and triumphed just as they have. The language, the music, the characters, and the situations belong to the Mechicano audience in a way that no other media image can. Even Spanish-language radio, television, and films reflect Mexican reality or are Hollywood images in Spanish. Therefore Mechicanos have to turn to the stage for realistic, sympathetic portrayals of their daily lives.

And so it is that the plays discussed in this book can be read and analyzed by scholar and layman alike as sincere reflections of the Mechicano in this society. But, like all theater, the reader must go beyond the printed page and into that special arena for which the plays were written. Surrounded by the people whose experiences form the basis of the drama, the reader becomes a participant in the ritual, immersed in the sights and sounds, the noises and the silence as the audience watches the production with pride. As it evolves, shedding its skin like the Valdezian serpent, Chicano theater may change its forms, but it will never forget the struggles that its audiences have experienced, and those audiences will never forget Chicano theater.

NOTES

Introduction

[1]See two valuable papers by Fernando Peñalosa on this subject: "The Changing Mexican-American in Southern California," *Sociology and Social Research*, Vol. 51, No. 4 (July 1967); and "Recent Changes Among the Chicanos," *Sociology and Social Research*, October 1970. Both articles reprinted in Edward Simmen (ed.), *Pain and Promise: The Chicano Today* (New York: New American Library/Mentor, 1972), pp. 61-71, 72-78. In the 1970 paper Peñalosa pointed out that "One term referring to the Mexican American population which has now gained considerable ground among the more militant and more articulate leaders of this ethnic group is 'Chicano.' This term is used as a mark of ethnic pride and is considered preferable by those who stress its use for reasons among which are its popular origin and the fact that it was chosen by members of the group itself. That is, it was not imposed on the group by Anglo-Americans, as were such terms as 'Mexican American' or 'Spanish American' " (pp. 72-73).

[2]Stan Steiner and Luis Valdez (eds.), *Aztlán: An Anthology of Mexican-American Literature* (New York: Vintage, 1972), p. xxxiii.

Chapter One

[1]Stan Steiner and Luis Valdez (eds.), *Aztlán: An Anthology of Mexican-American Literature* (New York: Vintage Books, 1972), p. 218. "Venceremos Brigades" are organized yearly to send young people from the United States to post-revolutionary Cuba to meet the people, work with them, and generally get acquainted with the socialist government on the island.

[2]Luis Valdez, *Actos* (San Juan Bautista: Cucaracha Press, 1971), p. 5.

[3]*Lehrstuck* are described in John Willett, *The Theatre of Bertolt Brecht* (New York: New Directions, 1959), pp. 134-36.

[4]The term "agit-prop" stems from the political theater of Vladimir Mayakovsky in post-revolutionary Russia. For a discussion of his work, see Frantisek Deak, "The Agit-Prop and Circus Plays of Vladimir Mayakovsky," *The Drama Review*, 17 (March 1973), pp. 47-52. For a discussion of agit-prop in the United States during the 1930s, see Malcolm Goldstein, *The Political Stage* (New York: Oxford University Press, 1974), pp. 32-34.

[5]Valdez, *Actos*, p. 6.

[6]Bertolt Brecht, *Poems on the Theatre* (Suffolk: Scorpion Press, 1971), pp. 5-6.

[7]Luis Valdez, "Theatre: El Teatro Campesino," *Ramparts*, July 1966, p. 55.

[8]Valdez, *Actos.*

[9]Ralph J. Gleason, "Vital, Earthy and Alive Theater," *San Francisco Chronicle,* 4 May 1966, n.p.

[10]Beth Bagby, "El Teatro Campesino: Interview with Luis Valdez," *Tulane Drama Review,* 11 (summer 1967), p. 77.

[11]Valdez, *Ramparts,* p. 55.

[12]Valdez, *Actos,* pp. 7-19. All subsequent references to *actos* in Valdez' anthology will be given as page references in parentheses after each quotation.

[13]The *bracero* program was initiated after World War II in order to exploit cheap Mexican labor in the fields of the Southwest. For a brief description of this program and its problems, see Rodolfo Acuña, *Occupied America* (San Francisco: Canfield Press, 1972), pp. 168-72. For further documentation, see Ernesto Galarza, *Merchants of Labor* (Santa Barbara: McNally and Loftkin, 1964).

[14]Bagby, p. 78.

[15]Steiner and Valdez, p. 403.

[16]*El Plan de Santa Barbara* (Santa Barbara: La Causa Publications, 1970), p. 11.

[17]"Teatro Urbano," *El Teatro,* p. 2. NOTE: *El Teatro* was a publication of El Centro Campesino Cultural from 1970-71, when it became *El Teatro/EL TENAZ* in recognition of the founding of TENAZ, *El Teatro Nacional de Aztlán,* a coalition of Chicano theater groups formed in the spring of 1971. The issue cited here was the second number, released in the fall of 1970, though there is no date on the publication. Like so many Chicano publications of the period, this magazine is now a collector's item.

[18]From an interview with Ed Robledo in San Francisco, California, March 1979.

[19]From an interview with Adrian Vargas in the summer of 1978.

[20]*El hombre que se convirtió en perro* appears in English translation in the following anthologies: Francesca Colecchia and Julio Matas, *Selected Latin-American One-Act Plays* (Pittsburgh, PA: University of Pittsburgh Press, 1973), pp. 21-33; and Gerardo Luzuriaga and Robert S. Rudder, *The Orgy; Modern One-Act Plays From Latin America* (Los Angeles: UCLA Latin American Center, 1974), pp. 29-40.

[21]While participating on a panel for the small professional theaters category of the National Endowment for the Arts, I was surprised to see how many small theater groups in the United States do not pay their actors living wages. Financial troubles are not limited to the alternative theaters in this country but plague most companies.

[22]Elizabeth Ramírez, "The Annals of Chicano Theater: 1965-1973," unpublished M.A. thesis, University of California, Los Angeles, 1974, pp. 145-48.

[23]*Los pelados* (Tucson: Teatro Libertad, Inc., 1978). All references to the script will appear in parentheses after each quotation cited.

[24]The term *pelado* is so universally employed in the barrios that Teatro de la Esperanza of Santa Barbara, California, produced and published an *acto* by Felipe Castro entitled *Los pelados* in 1973, not to be confused with the Tucson production. Sylvia Wood, a member of Teatro Libertad, wrote me that "Perhaps we should have named it 'Los pelados de Tucson,' since there seems to be an abundance of pelados everywhere." *La gran carpa de los rasquachis* is discussed in Chapter Six of this book.

[25]*Los pelados,* pp. xv-xvi.

[26]Ibid., p. xvi.

[27]Juan Bruce-Novoa and David Valentín, "Revolutionizing the Popular Image: Essay on Chicano Theatre," *Latin American Literary Review*, 5 (spring-summer 1977), p. 44.

[28]Michele Keating, "Tucson Performing Arts Flóurish on Every Front," *Tucson Daily Citizen*, 24 July 1978, n.p. From correspondence with Sylvia Wood, Central Committee Chairperson, Teatro Libertad.

[29]Valdez, *Actos*, p. 4.

Chapter Two

[1]In the 1920s and '30s, Mexican troupes toured the Mechicano communities of the Southwest in presentations known as *carpas* (literally, "tents"), named for the portable theaters they performed in, and *variedades*, or vaudeville productions. These presentations included sketches about current topics as well as songs, dances, and other entertainment. See Tomás Ybarra-Frausto's brief discussion of these entertainments in *Los pelados* (Tucson: Teatro Libertad, Inc., 1978), xii-xiv.

[2]Teatro de la Esperanza's *La víctima* will be published by the University of California, San Diego, Chicano Studies Monograph Series in 1983, edited by the present author.

[3]This quote is from the author's notes of a TENAZ Director's Conference in San Fernando, California, 4 September 1971. The first conference had been held the previous April in Fresno, California, following the "Second Annual Chicano Theater Festival" the previous week.

[4]This and all other quotes are from an unpublished ms. of *The Shrunken Head of Pancho Villa* in the author's collection, copyright 1976 by Luis Valdez.

[5]*Radical Theatre Festival* (San Francisco: San Francisco Mime Troupe, 1969), p. 19.

[6]Sylvie Drake, "El Teatro Campesino: Keeping the Revolution on Stage," *Performing Arts*, September 1970, pp. 58-59.

[7]See the bibliography at the end of this book for articles on the first two years of the Teatro Campesino.

[8]All quotes from *Los vendidos* are from Luis Valdez, *Actos* (San Juan Bautista: Cucaracha Press, 1971), pp. 35-49.

[9]*Radical Theater Festival*, p. 40.

[10]*The Militants*, a five-minute *acto* by the Teatro Campesino, ridiculed the pseudo-revolutionaries who worried more about the outward trappings of the "real Chicano" than the sociopolitical and economic problems of the barrio. See Luis Valdez, *Actos*, pp. 95-98.

[11]See Jorge A. Huerta (ed.), *El Teatro de la Esperanza: An Anthology of Chicano Drama* (Santa Barbara: El Teatro de la Esperanza, Inc., 1973). For a detailed study of the evolution of this teatro, see Jorge A. Huerta, "The Evolution of Chicano Theater," unpublished Ph.D. dissertation, University of California, Santa Barbara, 1974, Chapters 4-6.

[12]Franz Fanon, *The Wretched of the Earth* (New York: Grove Press, 1968).

[13]Albert Memmi, *The Colonizer and the Colonized* (Boston: Beacon Press, 1965).

[14]For an argument against the theory of internal colonialism, see Mario García, "Internal Colonialism and the Chicano," *La Luz*, November 1974, pp. 27-28; and "Internal Colonialism: A Critical Essay," *Revista Chicano-Riqueña*, 7 (verano 1978), pp. 38-41.

[15]This and all other quotes from *La víctima* are from an unpublished ms. in the author's collection.

[16]Raúl Ruiz, "Teatro de la Esperanza y 'La víctima'," *La Raza Quarterly*, 2 (summer 1977), p. 19.

[17]Boleslaw Taborski, "Integration—Cooperation—Presentation: A New Formula for Avant Garde Festival," *The Theatre in Poland*, February 1979, pp. 13-14.

[18]Enrique Llovet, "Nuevas tendencias teatrales en Belgrado," *El País*, 12 November 1978, p. VIII.

[19]Upon witnessing *La víctima*, Barclay Goldsmith noted the influence of Brecht, commenting: "The sweep of scenes over several generations in a short theatrical time span and the use of such distancing devices as signs make this piece decidedly epic in the Brechtian sense." See Goldsmith's essay entitled "Brecht and Chicano Theater," in Joseph Sommers and Tomás Ybarra-Frausto, *Modern Chicano Writers* (Englewood Cliffs: Prentice-Hall, 1979), p. 173.

Chapter Three

[1]Aurelio M. Espinosa, "Los Comanches," *Bulletin of the University of New Mexico*, 1 (December 1907), p. 18.

[2]For information about *Los moros y los cristianos* and an English translation of the text, see T. M. Pearce, "Los Moros y Los Cristianos: Early American Play," *New Mexico Folklore Record*, 2 (1947-48), pp. 58-69.

[3]Aurelio M. Espinosa and J. Manuel Espinosa, "The Texans; A New Mexican Spanish Folk Play of the Nineteenth Century," *New Mexico Quarterly Review*, 13 (autumn 1943), p. 300.

[4]John Brokaw, in his article "A Mexican-American Acting Company, 1849-1924," *Educational Theatre Journal*, 17 (March 1975), p. 28, writes: "Such historical plays as *El Grito de Dolores, El Cinco de Mayo* (The Fifth of May), and *Los Héroes de Tacubaya* (The Heroes of Tacubaya) had special appeal to Mexican audiences on both sides of the border."

[5]Rodolfo Acuña, *Occupied America; The Chicano's Struggle Toward Liberation* (San Francisco: Canfield Press, 1972), p. 18.

[6]References to *El Alamo* are from an unpublished ms. in the author's collection, courtesy of Teatro de los Barrios, San Antonio, Texas.

[7]Ralph Guzmán, "Mexican-American Casualties in Vietnam," *La Raza*, I, 1 (1970), pp. 12-15.

[8]For a detailed account of the Chicano Moratorium of August 29, 1970, see Armando Morales, *Ando Sangrando* (Fairlawn, NJ: R. F. Burdick, 1972), Ch. VIII.

[9]This and all other quotes from *Vietnam campesino* and *Soldado razo* are from Luis Valdez, *Actos* (San Juan Bautista: Cucaracha Press, 1971). Page numbers are indicated in parentheses after each quote.

[10]Guzmán, pp. 12-13.

[11]Betty Diamond, *Brown-Eyed Children of the Sun; The Cultural Politics of El Teatro Campesino* (Ann Arbor, MI: University Microfilms [#77-28,242], 1977), p. 121.

[12]Dan Sullivan, "Teatros [sic] Goes Beyond Talent," *Los Angeles Times*, 23 September 1971, IV, p. 1.

[13]Valdez, *Actos*, p. 5.

¹⁴*The Shrunken Head of Pancho Villa* is discussed in Chapter Two. Luis Valdez' first *mito*, *Bernabé*, is discussed in Chapter Six.

¹⁵These and all other quotes from *Dark Root of a Scream* are from Lilian Faderman and Omar Salinas, *From the Barrio* (San Francisco: Canfield Press, 1973), pp. 79-98. The setting is described on pp. 79-80.

¹⁶*Dark Root of a Scream* was first produced at the Inner City Cultural Center in Los Angeles as part of a "Fiesta de los Teatros" from September 16-26, 1971. This was the first time and only instance of a TENAZ production outside of San Juan Bautista, California, home base of the Teatro Campesino after 1971. This ten-day effort brought together representatives from various teatros in the organization, and it proved successful but difficult to repeat. For a review of that production, see note 18, below.

¹⁷For more information about the legendary and historic Quetzalcóatls, see Miguel León-Portilla's two important books: *Aztec Thought and Culture* (Norman: University of Oklahoma Press, 1963), and *Pre-Columbian Literatures of Mexico* (Norman: University of Oklahoma Press, 1969).

¹⁸Dan Sullivan, "Homecoming of a Dead GI," *Los Angeles Times*, 25 September 1971, II, p. 8.

¹⁹For a brief but thorough history of Teatro del Piojo, see Blanca Estela Garza Martínez and Frank S. Martínez, "Teatro del Piojo: Un recurrido histórico," *Metamorfosis*, 2 (1979), pp. 8-15. See the same journal for an article about the genesis of Teatro Quetzalcóatl: Aurelia Betancourt, "Teatro Quetzalcóatl," pp. 16-19.

²⁰Jim Harmon, "Strong Stuff," *Pueblo Chieftan*, 14 September 1976, p. 2A. The mayor of Pueblo, Colorado, proclaimed Drug Awareness Day in honor of the Teatro's performance of *Manolo* there in 1976.

²¹The drug problem in the barrio is a very common theme for younger teatros to dramatize. Because the majority of groups do not publish their *actos* or plays, there are few printed references one can turn to. Liz Ramírez' M.A. thesis, "The Annals of Chicano Theater: 1965-1973" (UCLA, 1974), lists many teatros whose repertoires included *actos* about drugs. Notable productions over the years include: *El corrido de Juan Endrogado* by Teatro de la Gente, San Jose, California, 1973; *El Quetzal* by Adrian Vargas, Teatro de la Gente, 1979; *Angel Death* by Guillermo Loo, Teatro Primavera, Los Angeles, California, 1979; and *Who's To Blame?* by Teatro Obrero, Los Angeles, California, 1976. None of these works has been published to date. Teatro de la Esperanza's *Guadalupe*, discussed in Chapter Four, has a subplot dealing with a heroin addict, though the character is not significantly developed beyond an introductory acquaintance. The play's assertion is that the youth's alienation motivates his addiction.

²²All references to the script of *Manolo* are from Rubén Sierra, *Manolo, Revista Chicano-Riqueña*, 7 (invierno 1979), pp. 65-110.

Chapter Four

¹Rodolfo Acuña, *Occupied America* (San Francisco: Canfield Press, 1972), p. 147.

²Thomas P. Carter, *Mexican Americans in the Schools: A History of Educational Neglect* (New York: College Entrance Examination Board, 1970), pp. 16-23. For information on the educational achievement of the Mexican American in the

Midwest, see Gilbert Cárdenas, "Los Desarraigados: Chicanos in the Midwestern Region of the United States," *Aztlán*, 7 (summer 1976), pp. 179-81.

³Martin G. Castillo, "Statement of the U.S. Senate Sub-Committee on Executive Reorganization, Senate Bill 740, Inter Agency Committee on Mexican-American Affairs," quoted in *Aztlán*, 1 (spring 1970), pp. 24-25.

⁴See the discussion of San Jose's Teatro Urbano on pp. 28 and 30 of this book.

⁵*Report of the President's Task Force on Chicanos and the University of California* (April 1975), pp. 57-59. This report states: "Although only a small proportion of Chicanos enrolling as UC freshmen have been admitted through special action in the past five to eight years . . . The accumulated evidence indicates [that they] are completing University academic work at a satisfactory level and rate compared to Chicano and other students admitted regularly."

⁶Parker Frisbie, "Militancy Among Mexican-American High School Students," *Social Science Quarterly*, 53 (March 1973), pp. 867.

⁷See Luis Valdez' description of the *acto*, p. 16, Ch. One of this book.

⁸An *acto* dealing with the high school counselor developed by Teatro Mecha at the University of California at Santa Barbara in 1971 is in Jorge A. Huerta, "The Evolution of Chicano Theater," unpublished Ph.D. dissertation, University of California, Santa Barbara, 1974, Appendix D.

⁹Rodolfo Gonzales, *I Am Joaquín* (New York: Bantam Books, 1972).

¹⁰Though Luis Valdez has often stated that the Teatro Campesino never accepted federal or state subsidies prior to 1977, the student members of his group received support from federal financial-aid programs, which was an indirect help to the Teatro.

¹¹All references to and quotations from *No saco nada de la escuela* are from the script in Luis Valdez, *Actos* (San Juan Bautista: Cucaracha Press, 1971), pp. 66-94.

¹²For statistics on the number of Mexican Americans in service positions at the University of California, see the *Report of the President's Task Force on Chicanos and the University of California* (April 1975), pp. 135-65. This important study may well be representative of other large or small university systems and confirms the fact that in the California system, at least, "Chicano employees at the University tend to be rather heavily concentrated in blue-collar, non-managerial jobs" (p. 145 of same report).

¹³See Valdez, *Actos*, pp. 66-94.

¹⁴Teatro Desengaño del Pueblo disbanded at the end of 1979 when Professor Kanellos took a position at the University of Houston in Texas. Although the original teatro no longer exists, its members are active in community and professional theater in various parts of the country.

¹⁵Nicolás Kanellos, "Fifty Years of Theater in the Latino Communities of Northwest Indiana," *Aztlán*, 7 (summer 1976), pp. 255-56.

¹⁶Kanellos, p. 255.

¹⁷Kanellos, p. 261.

¹⁸For more information about the Teatro Chicano de Austin, see Elizabeth Ramírez, "The Annals of Chicano Theater: 1965-1973," unpublished M.A. thesis, University of California, Los Angeles, 1974, pp. 100-02. This teatro published one of its early *actos*, *Las avispas* (The Wasps), in *Revista Chicano-Riqueña*, 2 (summer 1974), pp. 8-10.

¹⁹Cross-feeding between teatros throughout the United States is very prevalent. Several present members of the Teatro Campesino and Teatro de la Esperanza,

for example, are originally from other teatros. Through TENAZ and its early festivals and other functions, a line of communication was encouraged. Some members of a teatro will work with another, more experienced group, such as Teatro de la Gente, and then return to the original troupe to share what they have learned. Others find that they prefer the new ambience and become permanent members of their new teatro.

[20]*El alcalde* is published in *Revista Chicano-Riqueña*, 2 (autumn 1973), pp. 2-9. References to the script are followed by page numbers in parentheses.

[21]*The Schools of Guadalupe. . . A Legacy of Educational Oppression* (Sacramento: California State Advisory Committee to the U.S. Commission on Civil Rights, 1973).

[22]Ibid., p. 42.

[23]This and all other quotes from *Guadalupe* are from a ms. in the author's collection. *Guadalupe* and *La víctima* will be published by the University of California, San Diego, Chicano Studies Monograph Series, in 1981 and 1983.

[24]"The Siege of Santa María de Iquique—A People's Cantata" was written and composed by Luis Advis; available on Paredon Records, P-1019. The cantata recounts a worker's strike in Chile in 1907, in which two thousand men, women, and children were killed by Chilean soldiers protecting the interests of foreign investors in the nitrate mines. Exiled Chilean musical groups have performed this beautiful cantata in many parts of the world, calling attention to the coup that overthrew the Allende government in 1973 and forming a spiritual alliance with the Chicano Movement in the United States.

[25]This quote is from an unpublished ms. in the author's collection by Martha Hernández, "Guadalupe: A Collective Creation," 1975.

[26]For discussions of Brecht's style of "epic theater," see Martin Esslin, *Brecht: The Man and His Work* (New York: Doubleday, 1961), pp. 120-46; John Willett, *The Theatre of Bertolt Brecht* (New York: New Directions, 1959), pp. 168-87; and Bertolt Brecht, *Brecht on Theatre* (New York: Hill and Wang, 1964), pp. 69-76. For a discussion of Brecht's "New Technique of Acting," see Brecht, pp. 136-47.

[27]For Brecht's observations on the *Verfremdungseffekt* or "alienation effect," see Brecht, pp. 94-96; 143-45; and 191-95.

[28]Juan Bruce-Novoa and David Valentín, "Revolutionizing the Popular Image: Essay on Chicano Theatre," *Latin American Literary Review*, 5 (spring-summer 1977), pp. 42-43.

[29]Ibid., p. 46.

[30]Ibid., p. 47.

[31]Ellen McCracken, "Guadalupe," *Educational Theatre Journal*, 27 (December 1975), p. 554.

[32]Ibid.

[33]One of the most interesting examples of changes brought about in Guadalupe was the hiring in 1976 of one of the Teatro de la Esperanza members, Martha Hernández, as a Bilingual/Cross-Cultural Specialist. Prompted by the "Report" and urged by the Parent's Committee, the Guadalupe School Board added six new positions in that category for the schools. This was an intriguing instance of a political theater's direct involvement in a community issue. Hernández had to eventually choose between her full-time teaching responsibilities and the demands of a teatro. After several years with the Teatro, she resigned from the organization in the summer of 1979 to continue her career in teaching. See Jorge A. Huerta, "El Teatro

de la Esperanza: Keeping in Touch with the People," *The Drama Review*, 21 (March 1977), pp. 37-46.

[34]After a performance of *Guadalupe* in East Los Angeles in 1974, a woman stood up to say: "I knew these things were happening in the schools around here a long time ago, but I didn't think they were still happening in other places." Suddenly, another woman stood up and shouted: "Señora, it's happening right now at Hillside School!" This exchange inspired the audience members to investigate their own situations, and the Teatro later learned that they had followed the example of the parents in Guadalupe and demanded a better education for their children.

[35]The counselor in *The High School Counselor* may be portrayed as a sellout Mexican American but is usually presented as an Anglo.

[36]*No saco nada de la escuela* makes the most complete analysis of the *vendido* syndrome and adds important insights about the sellout types discussed in Chapter Two by focusing on the assimilation process in the schools.

[37]Nicolás Kanellos, "Sexto Festival de los Teatros Chicanos," *Latin American Theatre Review*, 9 (fall 1975), p. 84.

Chapter Five

[1]Hisauro Garza, "Administration of Justice: Chicanos in Monterrey County," *Aztlán*, 4 (spring 1973), p. 137.

[2]Teatro Libertad, *Los pelados* (Tucson: Teatro Libertad, 1978), p. xiv. Information about the Cuadro México-España was also obtained in an interview with Professor Tomás Ybarra-Frausto in December of 1973, in Seattle, Washington.

[3]Though the script to this play is now lost, a popular *corrido* of the period gives the folk version of Aurelio Pompa's life and death. See Manuel Gamio, *Mexican Immigration to the United States* (New York: Dover Publications, 1971), pp. 103-07.

[4]Chicano magazines and journals that arose with the Chicano movement of the 1960s often told of police killings in the barrios. One example is the anonymously written "LAPD Murder Another Innocent Chicano," *La Raza*, I, 6 (n.d.—1971?), pp. 30-31.

[5]Reports of police violence continued throughout the 1970s and even major newspapers such as the *Los Angeles Times* began to report the incidents.

[6]Bernard Dukore, *Drama and Revolution* (New York: Holt, Rinehart and Winston, 1971), pp. 597-98.

[7]Bernard Dukore, *Documents for Drama and Revolution* (New York: Holt, Rinehart and Winston, 1971), p. 212.

[8]Francisco O. Burruel, "The Dialogue of Cuco Rocha," *El Grito*, 3 (summer 1970), pp. 37-45.

[9]Jorge A. Huerta, *El Teatro de la Esperanza: An Anthology of Chicano Drama* (Goleta: El Teatro de la Esperanza, Inc., 1973), pp. 12-27.

[10]For a novelized account of sheriffs' violence against Chicanos in Los Angeles during this period, see Oscar Zeta Acosta, *The Revolt of the Cockroach People* (San Francisco: Straight Arrow Books, 1973), Chaps. 8 & 9.

[11]This and all other quotes from *Trampa sin salida* are from the Huerta anthology cited above. Page numbers follow the quotes in parentheses.

[12]Francisco A. Lomelí and Donaldo W. Urioste, *Chicano Perspectives in Literature* (Albuquerque: Pajarito Publications, 1976), p. 61.

¹³For an example of the *caló* dialect in dialogue form, see Raquel Moreno, "El Milagrucho," *El Grito*, 4 (spring 1971), pp. 64-66. This brief dialogue is an extreme example of the Chicano's patois, and most people would need a glossary to understand it completely.

¹⁴From an interview with Carlos Morton in August of 1971, La Jolla, California.

¹⁵*El jardín* was published in *El Grito*, 7 (June-August 1974), pp. 7-37.

¹⁶*El cuento de Pancho Diablo* appeared in *Grito del Sol*, 1 (July-September 1976), pp. 39-85.

¹⁷*Las many muertes de Richard Morales* was published in *Tejidos*, 4 (primavera 1977), pp. 28-50.

¹⁸*Rancho Hollywood* appeared in *Revista Chicano-Riqueña*, 7 (invierno 1979), pp. 43-63.

¹⁹From an interview with Carlos Morton in September of 1979, Cardiff-by-the-Sea, California.

²⁰From the published script. All quotes from this play are from the script published in *Tejidos* and will be followed by page numbers in parentheses.

²¹While many Anglo reviewers of teatro performances are impressed with the "energy and commitment" of the actors in deference to their technical capabilities, I am curiously moved to praise the non-Chicano actors in this production for their "sincerity," not because of weaknesses in their acting, but because they were not Chicanos. A Chicano audience knows when an actor is unable to manage the Spanish language, and for some this is distracting. Because of this linguistic limitation on the part of the actors, the published script is written with few Spanish lines.

²²Although the original version of *Las many muertes de Richard Morales* only mentions in passing the fact that a Chicano informant "set up" the arrest, the later version develops this character, exposing a Chicano villain alongside the Anglo antagonists.

²³References to the revised versions of the Richard Morales play are kept at a minimum since the play was still undergoing rewriting as this book was being written. The focus of my discussion is on the original, published version unless otherwise noted.

²⁴Sean Mitchell, "Morales Case Taken to the Dallas Stage," *Dallas Times Herald*, 2 February 1979, p. 1-E.

²⁵Luis Valdez, *Actos* (San Juan Bautista: Cucaracha Publications, 1971), p. 2.

²⁶From the citation awarded the Teatro Campesino in 1968, on file in San Juan Bautista, California.

²⁷From an interview with Luis Valdez in the spring of 1974 in San Juan Bautista, California.

²⁸From an interview with Luis Valdez in the spring of 1976 in San Francisco, California.

²⁹Teatro Mestizo is a San Diego-based group that was formed in 1969 by students at San Diego State College. In 1974, this very active troupe collectively created a critique of the Chicano student movement entitled *Cuatro años de colegio* (Four Years of College). Nick Kanellos described this three-part *acto* as "a rollicking and biting satire" in the *Latin American Theatre Review*, 9 (fall 1975), p. 83. Teatro Mestizo continues to work in San Diego with a constantly changing membership of students and community members under the leadership of Marcos Contreras and Carolina Flores.

³⁰Tomás Benitel, "Facing the Issues Beyond 'Zoot Suit'," *Neworld*, 5/1 (1978), p. 37.

[31]Dan Sullivan, "Putting the Boomp into 'Zoot Suit'," *Los Angeles Times*, 16 April 1978, Calendar Section, p. 1.

[32]From an interview with Luis Valdez in October of 1978 in San Juan Bautista, California.

[33]In an interview with Eduardo Robledo, a former member of the Teatro Campesino, he recalled: "The use of newspapers as other objects came out of a summer workshop with Ron Davis in 1972. The mimetic images in 'Carpa' and 'Zoot Suit' are influenced by that workshop." San Francisco, California, March, 1979. The workshop Robledo refers to was the second annual TENAZ Summer Workshop held in San Juan Bautista, hosted by the Teatro Campesino.

[34]The exact quote comes from a report to the Los Angeles County Grand Jury of 1942 written by a Lt. Duran Ayres of the Los Angeles County Sheriff's Department. See the McWilliams Collection # 107 (Rare Books Section), folder 7, in the public affairs section of the UCLA Research Library. Reference is made to this document in Arturo Madrid-Barela, "In Search of the Authentic Pachuco: An Interpretive Essay," *Aztlán*, 4 (spring 1973), p. 34. Dr. Madrid's article is an excellent analysis of the pachuco in literature.

[35]Sylvie Drake, "Broadway Cool to 'Zoot Suit'," *Los Angeles Times*, 27 March 1979, IV, p. 1.

[36]Ibid.

[37]A look at the census reports for 1960 and 1970 reveals an improvement in the educational achievement of Spanish-surnamed people of Mexican descent, but the median is well below the national average.

[38]From an interview with Luis Valdez in October of 1978 in San Juan Bautista, California.

[39]"First Hispanic-American Show on Broadway: ZOOT SUIT," *New York Theatre Review*, 3 (May 1979), p. 23.

[40]Richard Eder, "Theatre; 'Zoot Suit,' Chicano Music-Drama," *New York Times*, 26 March 1979, Sec. C, p. 13.

[41]Ibid.

[42]Douglass Watt, " 'Zoot Suit' slithers in at the Winter Garden," *New York Daily News*, 26 March 1979, p. 21.

[43]Walter Kerr, " 'Zoot Suit' Loses Its Way in Bloodless Rhetoric," *New York Times*, 1 April 1979, Sec. D, p. 3.

[44]Luis Valdez, *Actos*, p. 4.

[45]"First Hispanic-American Show," p. 23.

[46]Ibid.

[47]Arturo Madrid-Barela, "In Search of the Authentic Pachuco," p. 57.

[48]Dan Sullivan, "Putting the Boomp," p. 69.

[49]From an interview with Luis Valdez in October, 1978, San Juan Bautista, California.

Chapter Six

[1]When I first told Luis Valdez that I was going to research the evolution of Chicano theater, he advised me to study the indigenous ritual theater of the Aztecs and Mayas. This was at the first Director's Conference in April 1971, Fresno, California.

[2]In his seminal chapter on pre-Columbian drama, Miguel León-Portilla states:

"There is even some indication that while acting out the myths, they had already begun to interpret them in different ways, searching for deeper significance, as happened also in the Greek theater." Miguel León-Portilla, *Pre-Columbian Literatures of Mexico* (Norman: University of Oklahoma Press, 1969), p. 103.

[3]Willard C. Booth, "Dramatic Aspects of Aztec Ritual," *Educational Theatre Journal*, 18 (December 1966), p. 423.

[4]According to the sixteenth-century Franciscan friar Bernardino de Sahagún, the Sun called the sacrificed warriors to live with him in a life of continual pleasure: ". . . never do they feel sad or experience any pain or sorrow, because they live in the mansion of the Sun, where there is an abundance of delights. . . . " Alfonso Caso, *The Aztecs, People of the Sun* (Norman: University of Oklahoma Press, 1958), p. 58.

[5]Miguel León-Portilla, *Pre-Columbian Literatures*, p. 109.

[6]Michael Coe, *The Maya* (New York: Frederick A. Praeger, 1966), p. 136.

[7]T. B. Irving, "Three Mayan Classics," *The University of Toronto Quarterly*, 20 (October 1950), p. 65.

[8]Richard E. Leinaweaver, "Rabinal Achí," *Latin American Theatre Review*, 1/2 (spring 1968), p. 11.

[9]Leinaweaver, ibid. It should be noted here that Maxine Klein has argued that the *Rabinal Achí* is not religious, though its very nature is a ritual born of spiritual beliefs and indigenous concepts of morality. See Maxine Klein, "Theater of the Ancient Maya," *Educational Theatre Journal*, 23 (October 1971), pp. 269-76.

[10]The following scholars believe the *Rabinal Achí* is authentically pre-Columbian: Juan José Arróm, "Raíces indígenas del teatro americano," *International Congress of Americanists, Selected Papers of the XXIXth* (New York: 1949, 1952), pp. 301-02; Leinaweaver, pp. 3-5; Marilyn E. Ravicz, *Early Colonial Religious Drama in Mexico* (Washington: Catholic University of America Press, 1970), pp. 24-25.

[11]Willis Knapp Jones, *Behind Spanish American Footlights* (Austin: University of Texas Press, 1966), p. 460.

[12]Hermenegeldo Corbató, "Misterios y autos del teatro misionero en Méjico durante el siglo XVI y sus relaciones con los de Valencia," *Anales del Centro de Cultura Valenciana*, 1 (1949), p. 7. For an English translation of *El juicio final* see Ravicz, pp. 141-57.

[13]Francis Borgia Steck, *Motolinia's History of the Indians of New Spain* (Washington: Academy of American Franciscan History, 1959), p. 167.

[14]A Spanish translation of the 17th-century Nahuatl version can be found in Francisco de Paso y Troncoso (ed.), *Sacrificio de Isaac, Auto en lengua mexicana escrita en el año 1678*, XII Congreso Internacional de Orientalistas (Florence: 1899). The only English translation of the Nahuatl version is in Ravicz, pp. 83-98. For the 16th-century Spanish version, see Leo Rouanet, "Auto del sacrificio de Abraham," *Colección de autos, farsas y coloquios del siglo XVI* (Madrid: Librería de Murille Alcala, 1901), I, pp. 1-21.

[15]For other examples of the early missionary dramas in Mexico translated into English, see Ravicz.

[16]Winifred Johnson, "Early Theater in the Spanish Borderlands," *Mid-America*, 13 (October 1930), p. 125.

[17]This play, mentioned in Chapter Three, is an outdoor spectacle celebrating the Spanish expulsion of the Moors.

[18]T. M. Pearce, "The New Mexican 'Shepherds' Play'," *Western Folklore*, 15 (1956), p. 77.

[19]See Charles B. Martin, *Survivals of Medieval Religious Drama in New Mexico* (Ann Arbor: University Microfilms, 1959), pp. 109-66, for accounts of the most popular religious plays in the southwestern repertoire.

[20]There are no published critiques of the Teatro Campesino's production of *La Virgen del Tepeyac* that reflect the criticisms alluded to here. The comments mentioned were verbal remarks within the ranks of the Chicano movement in general and the Teatro movement in particular.

[21]This debate is based on fact. For an interesting account of the problem see Lewis Hanke, *Aristotle and the American Indian* (Bloomington: Indiana University Press, 1959).

[22]Carlos Morton, *El jardín*, in *El Grito*, 7 (June-August 1974), pp. 7-37.

[23]As noted in Chapter Five, *El cuento de Pancho Diablo* is a sequel to *El jardín*. The later play brings the devil to earth as the owner of "the world's largest funeral parlor" when he resigns his post in Hell. Biblical figures mingle with saints and sinners, beggars and whores, in a zany comment on man's fallibility and God's complexity. See Carlos Morton, *El cuento de Pancho Diablo*, in *Grito del Sol*, 1 (July-September 1976), pp. 39-85.

[24]Luis Valdez, *Actos*, p. 3.

[25]Valdez, *Actos*, p. 5.

[26]Stan Steiner and Luis Valdez, *Aztlán: An Anthology of Mexican-American Literature* (New York: Random House/Vintage, 1972), p. 364. Scene Three from *Bernabé* appears in Spanglish in the Steiner-Valdez anthology, pp. 361-76. A complete version of this script in Spanish is published in Roberto Garza, *Contemporary Chicano Theatre* (Notre Dame: University of Notre Dame Press, 1976), pp. 30-58.

[27]From an informal discussion with Luis Valdez in the spring of 1973. Valdez was greatly influenced by the interesting treatise of Mexican anthropologist Domingo Martínez Paredez, *El Popol Vuh tiene razón* (México: Editorial Orion, 1968). In a controversial interpretation of the Maya classic, Dr. Martínez asserts that it is a scientific explanation of the creation of this planet. In reference to the word *mucnal*, Dr. Martínez states: ". . . MORIR es BAJAR, y esto es innegable, porque el cuerpo BAJA a la sepultura y a ésta se le llama MUCNAL—ENTERRAR MAIZ" (to die is to go down, and this is undeniable, because the body is lowered into the grave and this is called *mucnal*—to plant the corn. My translation), p. 153.

[28]Betty Diamond, *Brown-Eyed Children of the Sun; The Cultural Politics of El Teatro Campesino* (Ann Arbor: University Microfilms, 1977), p. 153.

[29]The *corrido* is a traditional Mexican folk ballad, telling of heroes and heroines, villains and conquests on either side of the border. See Américo Paredes, *With His Pistol In His Hand: A Border Ballad and its Hero* (Austin: University of Texas Press, 1958).

The term *corrido* was adapted by Luis Valdez and the participants in the first TENAZ Summer Workshop held in San Juan Bautista, California, in 1971. During this workshop, Valdez guided the participants in the creation of dramatic statements based on popular *corridos*. While a narrator sang the ballad, actors clad in stylized costumes and make-up would pantomime the action of the tale, occasionally speaking dialogue taken directly from the lyrics. This heralded another innovation for Valdez and the representatives of the various teatros who participated in the creation of the *corrido* form.

[30]The term *rasquachi* is a delicious word, bringing with it the Chicano's self-deprecating humor which allows him to laugh at himself and his surroundings. The term comes from the people, not the academies, and like the term "Chicano" has a meaning of its own. To call something *rasquachi* is to indicate a loving understanding of why it is so. "Perdona mi casa tan rasquachi" (Forgive my rasquachi home), one might be heard to say, connoting an attitude of personal attachment to that house; it may be humble, but it is theirs.

[31]Françoise Kourilsky, "Approaching Quetzalcóatl: The Evolution of El Teatro Campesino," *Performance*, 2 (fall 1973), p. 46.

[32]The devil figure is directly related to the *corridos* that preceded this creation, in which a pair of devils, one male and the other female, moved the action forward. The Devil has also been a popular character in the religious plays that have been produced in barrio churches for generations.

[33]For further definition of the Mesoamerican deity Quetzalcóatl, see Miguel León-Portilla, *Pre-Columbian Literatures of Mexico* and *Aztec Thought and Culture* (Norman: University of Oklahoma Press, 1963). For a contemporary interpretation of the Quetzalcóatl myth, see Anthony Shearer, *Lord of the Dawn* (Healdsburg, CA: Naturegraph Press, 1971).

[34]Luis Valdez, "Notes on Chicano Theater," *Chicano Theatre One*, 1 (spring 1973), p. 7.

[35]*La carpa cantinflesca* was an early version of *La gran carpa de los rasquachis*, performed several months prior to the 1973 edition of the latter. It was not a well-developed piece; its message was clouded by the symbolism that Valdez and his troupe were still working out.

[36]Luis Valdez, *Pensamiento serpentino* (San Juan Bautista: Cucaracha Publications, 1973), p. 1.

[37]Ibid., p. 3.

[38]Ibid., p. 7.

[39]Ibid., p. 12.

[40]See Carlos Morton, "The Teatro Campesino," *The Drama Review*, 18 (December 1974), 71-76.

[41]*The Militants* is a brief *acto* satirizing the so-called leadership of the Chicano movement of the late 1960s and early 1970s. The *acto* is published in Luis Valdez, *Actos*, pp. 95-98.

[42]Karen Stabiner, "El Teatro Campesino: Spiritualism Replaces Practical Politics," *Santa Barbara News and Review*, 17 May 1974, p. 14. For another, less negative response to *Pensamiento serpentino*, see Reyes Cárdenas, "Luis Valdez' 'Pensamiento serpentino'," *Caracol*, 2 (April 1976), p. 6.

[43]Jorge R. González, "Pensamiento serpentino, A Cultural Trampa or Is the Teatro Campesino Campesino?" Unpublished ms. in the author's collection.

[44]Cecil Smith, "Farmworkers' Folk Drama." *Los Angeles Times*, 4 November 1976, sec. IV, p. 18.

[45]In an interesting study of two Texas teatros, Theresa Hope Mason synthesized the reactions of the teatros' members to the indigenous symbols presented by Valdez' troupe:

> Members of both groups, Teatro de los Barrios, San Antonio, and Carnales en Espíritu, Austin, agree in their critique of the effect of Teatro Campesino's recent involvement with Mayan philosophy/religion. They note that the group's

actos were centered around dieties and symbols from Mayan mythology, which most Mexicanos cannot relate to. The result was that their performances became something to admire and appreciate, but as one member of *Barrios* put it, "The people didn't feel that the play involved them."
Theresa Hope Mason, "Teatro Chicano and Mexican Identity: The Case of Two Texas *Teatros*," unpublished M.A. thesis, University of Texas, Austin, 1977, pp. 25-26.

[46] Betty Diamond, *Brown-Eyed Children*, p. 207.

[47] The present author witnessed two performances of *Fin del mundo* in San Juan Bautista, California, 29 October 1978.

[48] Valdez, *Pensamiento serpentino*, p. 1.

BIBLIOGRAPHY

The following bibliography attempts to be as comprehensive as possible, particularly for the period from 1965 to 1980. The most important historical references are noted in Parts I, II, and III, but the bulk of the entries focus on the contemporary Chicano theater movement beginning with the Teatro Campesino and Luis Valdez in 1965. Because of the large number of articles dealing with this important group and individual, I have arbitrarily divided this category into three sections: 1965-70, 1971-80, and *Zoot Suit*. While it is difficult to separate the work of the Teatro Campesino and its creator/mentor Luis Valdez, *Zoot Suit* is Valdez' work, warranting a separate listing.

The remainder of the bibliography covers other teatros and playwrights and is divided into a general category, a section for festivals, and a final section for reviews of teatros and other Chicano productions. Many of the articles in the general category are brief descriptions of the groups concerned, but future scholars may want to refer to even these scant details in an effort to understand the movement they were part of. The section on plays in the general category is as inclusive as I could make it and does not attempt to distinguish between the "good" plays or *actos* and the "bad." Some of the plays listed are absurdly brief—the products of inexperienced playwrights searching for their methods—but they are included nonetheless as evidence of what was being written and even produced during this period.

Many of the references in this bibliography come from Chicano newspapers, journals, and other publications such as festival programs, some of which are no longer in print. Fortunately, some of the major Chicano research centers, such as the University of California campuses at Los Angeles, Berkeley, and Santa Barbara as well as the University of Texas at Austin, have good collections of these disappearing sources. A microfilm collection has also been started at many of these libraries in an effort to preserve these important documents for future generations. Most importantly, the library of the University of California at San Diego has agreed to store duplicates of all of my personal files, including most of the materials listed in this bibliography, in the "Archives of Chicano Theater." This will be one of the most thorough collections of its kind, carefully and conscientiously guided by librarian Edith Fisher, my long time colleague and friend.

Finally, I would like to offer my sincerest *gracias* to Professor Tina Eger, the bibliographer's bibliographer, who so kindly let me work from the galleys of her incredible volume, *A Bibliography of Criticism of Chicano Literature* (Berkeley: Chicano Studies Library, University of California, 1981). For even more references, the reader is advised to see her exhaustive compilation.

Of course, this bibliography owes its existence to the many teatros and individuals who shared their materials with me, especially the Teatro Campesino and Andrés Gutiérrez, whose files on his troupe are unequalled. To all of you dedicated scholars and artists, practitioners and observers, ¡Gracias!

I. Pre-Columbian Period

A. Books

Arias-Larreta, Abraham. *Pre-Columbian Literatures.* Los Angeles: The New World Library, 1964.

Garibay K., Angel M. *Historia de la literatura nahuatl.* México: Editorial Porrúa, 1953. 2 vols.

————. *La literatura de los aztecas.* México: Editorial Joaquín Mortiz, 1964.

————. *Panorama literario de los pueblos nahuas.* México: Editorial Porrúa, 1963.

León-Portilla, Miguel. *Pre-Columbian Literatures of Mexico.* Norman: University of Oklahoma Press, 1969.

————. *Aztec Thought and Culture.* Norman: University of Oklahoma Press, 1963.

Ravicz, Marilyn Ekdahl. "The Prehispanic Background for the Study of Colonial Drama." In *Early Colonial Religious Drama in Mexico: From Tzompantli to Golgotha.* Washington: Catholic University of America Press, 1970, pp. 1-25.

Rojas Garcidueñas, José J. *El teatro de Nueva España en el siglo XVI.* México: 1935.

Sten, Maria. *Vida y muerte del teatro nahuatl: El Olimpo sin Prometeo.* México: Sep Setentas, 1974.

Torres-Rioseco, A. "Teatro indígena de México." In *Ensayos sobre la literatura latinoamericana.* Berkeley: University of California Press, 1953, pp. 7-26.

B. *Journal Articles*

Arrom, José J. "Raíces indígenas del teatro americano." *Selected Papers of the XXIXth International Congress of Americanists.* Chicago: University of Chicago Press, 1952, pp. 299-305.

Bayle, Constantino. "El teatro indígena en América." *Lectura,* 52 (June 1946), 219.

Booth, Willard C. "Dramatic Aspects of Aztec Rituals." *Educational Theatre Journal,* 18 (December 1966), 421-28.

Garibay K., A. M., ed. "Poema de travesuras." *Cantares mexicanos,* fol. 67 r. (1952), 142-67.

Icaza, Francisco A. de. "Orígenes del teatro en México." *Boletín de la Real Academia Española,* t. II, cuad. VI (febrero 1915), 57-76.

Klein, Maxine. "Theatre of the Ancient Maya." *Educational Theatre Journal,* 23 (October 1971), 269-76.

Mace, Carroll E. "New Information About Dance-Dramas of Rabinal and the Rabinal Achí." *Xavier University Studies* (New Orleans), 6 (February 1967), 1-19.

Mérida, Carlos. "Pre-Hispanic Dance and Drama." *Theatre Arts Monthly,* August 1938, pp. 559-68.

Torre Revello, José. "Orígenes del teatro en Hispano-América." *Cuadernos de Cultura Teatral,* No. 7 (1937), 35-64.

C. *Plays*

Cid Pérez, José, ed. *Teatro indio precolombino: El Güegüence, o, Macho Ratón; El varón de Rabinal.* Madrid: Aguilar, 1964.

Rabinal Achí. Translated by Richard E. Leinaweaver. *Latin American Theatre Review,* 1 (spring 1969), 3-53.

Rabinal Achí; Teatro indígena pre-hispánico. Prólogo por Francisco Monterde. México: Ediciones de la Universidad Autónoma, 1955.

Villacorta, José Antonio. "Rabinal Achí, tragedia danzada de los quichés." *Anales,* 17 (1942), 352-71.

II. Mexican Colonial Period

A. *Books*

Alegre, Francisco Javier, S.J. *Historia de la Compañía de Jesús en Nueva España.* México: D. Carlos María de Bustamente, 1941.

Arrom, José Juan. *Historia del teatro hispanoamericano (Epoca Colonial).* México: Ediciones de Andrea, 1967.

Ballinger, Rex Edward. *Los orígenes del teatro español y sus primeras manifestaciones en la Nueva España.* México: Universidad Nacional Autónoma de México, 1951.

Corbató, Hermenegildo. *Misterios y autos del teatro misionero en Méjico durante el siglo XVI y sus relaciones con los de Valencia.* Anejo No. 1, *Anales del Centro de Cultura Valenciana.* Valencia: 1949.

Correa, Gustavo, et al. *The Native Theatre in Middle America.* New Orleans: Tulane University, Middle America Research Institute, 1961.

García Icazbalceta, Joaquín. *El teatro de Nueva España en el siglo XVI.* México: Luis Alvarez, 1935.

Horcasitas, Fernando. *El teatro nahuatl; epocas novohispanas y moderna.* México: UNAM Instituto de Investigaciones Históricas, 1974.

Mace, Carroll Edward. *Three Quiché Dance-Dramas of Rabinal, Guatemala.* Ann Arbor: University Microfilms, 1967.

María y Campos, Armando de. *Representaciones teatrales en la Nueva España (Siglos XVI al XVIII).* México: Colección La Máscara, B. Costa Amic, 1959.

Olavarria y Ferrari, Enrique de. *Reseña historia del teatro en México, 1538-1911.* México: Editorial Porrúa, 1961. 3rd edition, 5 vols.

Ravicz, Marilyn Ekdahl. *Early Colonial Religious Drama in Mexico: From Tzompantli to Golgotha.* Washington: Catholic University of America Press, 1970.

Rojas Garcidueñas, José J. *El teatro de Nueva España en el siglo XVI.* México: 1935.

Vetancourt, Fr. Agustín de. *Teatro mexicano: Crónica de la Provincia de Santo Evangelio de México, Menologio franciscano.* Primera edición facsimilar. México: Editorial Porrúa, 1971.

Warman Gryj, Arturo. *La danza de moros y cristianos.* México: Secretaria de Educación Pública, 1972.

B. Journal Articles

Caillet-Bois, Julio. "Las primeras representaciones teatrales mexicanas." *Revista de Filología Hispánica* (Buenos Aires), 1940, 376-78.

Girard, Rafael. "Una obra maestra del teatro maya." *Cuadernos Americanos,* 36 (1947), 57-138.

Irving, T. B. "Three Mayan Classics." *University of Toronto Quarterly,* October 1950, 61-68.

Jiménez Rueda, Julio. "La edad de Fernández de Eslava." *Revista Mexicana de Estudios Históricos,* t. II, núm. 3 (mayo-junio 1928), 102-06.

Johnson, Harvey L. "The Staging of Eslava's Coloquios." *Hispanic Review,* 8 (1940), 343-46.

Monterde, Francisco. "Pastorals and Popular Performances: The Drama of Viceregal Mexico." *Theatre Arts Monthly,* August 1938, pp. 597-606.

Oeste de Bopp, Marianne. "Autos mexicanos del siglo XVI." *Historia Mexicana,* 3 (1953-54), 112-23.

Pasquariello, Antonio M. "The Entremés in 16th-Century Spanish America." *Hispanic American Historical Review,* 32 (February 1952), 44-58.

Rodrígues Rouanet, Francisco. "Notas sobre una representación actual del *Rabinal Achí* o *Baile del Tun.*" *Guatemala Indígena,* II, No. 1 (Instituto Indigenista Nacional, 1962), 25-55.

Torres-Rioseco, José. "El primer dramaturgo americano." *Hispania,* 24 (1941), 161-70.

C. Plays

Autos y coloquios del siglo XVI. Prólogo y notas de José Rojas Garcidueñas. México: Universidad Nacional Autónoma de México, 1939.

Gillmor, Frances. "Spanish Texts of Three Dance-Dramas from Mexican Villages." *University of Arizona Bulletin,* 13 (October 1942), 3-38.

Hunter, William A. *An Edition and Translation of a Nahuatl Version of a Calderonian Auto Sacramental: El Gran Teatro del Mundo.* New Orleans: Reprinted from Publication 27, Middle American Research Institute, Tulane University, 1960, 105-202.

Johnson, Harvey L. *An Edition of Triunfo de los Santos, With a Consideration of Jesuit School Plays Before 1650.* Philadelphia: University of Pennsylvania, 1941.

Loubat, J. F. "Letra de la 'Danza de Pluma' de Moctezuma y Hernán Cortés con los capitanes y reyes que intervinieron en la conquista de México." Congrès Internacional des Americanistes, XIIe Session (Paris, 1900), 221-61.

Paso y Troncoso, Francisco del, trans. *Destrucción de Jerusalén: Auto en lengua mexicana. Biblioteca Nahuatl* 1 (1907), 130-77.

Ravicz, Marilyn Ekdahl, trans. *The Adoration of the Kings.* In *Early Colonial Religious Drama in Mexico: From Tzompantli to Golgotha.* Washington: Catholic University of America Press, 1970, pp. 119-40.

————, trans. *The Destruction of Jerusalem.* In *Early Colonial Religious Drama,* pp. 181-210.

————, trans. *The Final Judgement.* In *Early Colonial Religious Drama,* pp. 141-58.

————, trans. *How The Blessed St. Helen Found the Holy Cross.* In *Early Colonial Religious Drama,* pp. 159-80.

————, trans. *The Merchant.* In *Early Colonial Religious Drama,* pp. 99-118.

————, trans. *The Sacrifice of Isaac.* In *Early Colonial Religious Drama,* pp. 83-98.

————, trans. *Souls and Testamentary Executors.* In *Early Colonial Religious Drama,* pp. 211-34.

Tlacahuapahualiztli. Translated and edited by John H. Cornyn and Byron McAfee. *Tlalocán,* 1 (1944), 314-51.

III. Aztlán Before 1965

A. Books

Barsun, Helen. "Los Pastores, A Remnant of Medieval Drama in San Antonio." Unpublished M.A. thesis, English Dept., St. Mary's College (Texas), 1943.

Brewer, Fred Meza. "La Pastoría: A New Mexican Shepherds' Play." Unpublished M.A. thesis, Spanish Dept., Texas Western College, 1956.

Butts, Onna Barrett Mills. "The History of Los Pastores of Las Cruces, New Mexico." Unpublished M.A. thesis, History Dept., University of Southern California, 1937.

Campa, Arthur. *Spanish Religious Folk Theatre of the Southwest.* Albuquerque: University of New Mexico, 1934.

Englekirk, John E. "Fernando Calderón en el teatro popular nuevo-mexicano." *Memoria del segundo congreso internacional de catedráticos de literatura iberoamericana.* Berkeley: 1949, pp. 227-40.

Howard, Lyle. "Spanish Folkplays of the San Juan Basin (Colorado)." Unpublished M.A. thesis, English Dept., Western State College of Colorado, 1939.

Hunter, Mai Frances. "Los Pastores: Spanish-American Play of the Nativity Preserved in the Vicinity of Corpus Christi, Texas." Unpublished M.A. thesis, English Dept., Texas College of Arts and Industries, 1940.

Lea, Aurora (Lucero-White). *Literary Folklore of the Hispanic Southwest.* San Antonio: Naylor Co., 1953.

McCrossan, (Sister) Joseph Marie. *The Role of the Church and the Folk in the Development of the Early Drama in New Mexico.* Philadelphia: 1948.

Martin, Charles B. *The Survivals of Medieval Religious Drama in New Mexico.* Ann Arbor: University Microfilms, 1959.

Munroe, Edwin C. "The Nativity Plays of New Mexico." Unpublished M.A. thesis, English Dept., Texas College of Arts and Industries, 1940.

Simpson, Margaret Hall. "Padua Hills Theatre: An Experiment in Intercultural Relations." Unpublished M.A. thesis, Claremont College, 1944.

Smith, Tallant. "History of the Theatre in Santa Barbara, 1769-1894." Unpublished M.A. thesis, Drama Dept., University of California at Santa Barbara, 1969.

Waugh, Julia Nott. *The Silver Cradle.* Austin: University of Texas Press, 1935.

Wright, Corinne King. "Los Pastores: The Mystery Play in California." Unpublished M.A. thesis, English Dept., University of Southern California, 1921.

B. *Journal Articles*

Austin, Mary. "Folkplays of the Southwest." *Theatre Arts Monthly*, August 1933, pp. 599-606.

————. "Native Drama in New Mexico." *Theatre Arts Monthly*, August 1929, pp. 564-67.

————. "Spanish Manuscripts in the Southwest." *Southwest Review*, 14 (July 1934), 401-09.

Bach, Marcus. "Los Pastores." *Theatre Arts Monthly*, April 1940, pp. 283-88.

Brokaw, John W. "A Mexican-American Acting Company, 1849-1924." *Educational Theatre Journal*, 17 (March 1975), 23-29.

————. "The Repertory of a Mexican-American Theatrical Troupe: 1849-1924." *Latin American Theatre Review*, 8 (fall 1974), 25-35.

Campa, Arthur L. "Los Comanches: A New Mexican Folk Drama." *University of New Mexico Bulletin*, 7 (1942), 5-42.

————. "The New Mexican Spanish Folktheater." *Southwest Folklore Quarterly*, 5 (1941), 127-31.

————. "El origen y la naturaleza del drama folklórico." *Folklore Americas*, 20 (1960), 13-48.

————. "Religious Spanish Folk-Drama in New Mexico." *New Mexico Quarterly*, 1 (February 1931), 3-13.

————. "Spanish Religious Folktheater in the Southwest." *University of New Mexico Bulletin*, Language Series 5 (June 1934), 5-157.

Cosulich, B. "Yaqui Passion Play in Arizona; Primitive Religious Pageant at Barrio Pascua." *Travel*, March 1931, pp. 435-38.

Curtis, F. S., Jr. "Spanish Folk-Poetry in the Southwest." *Southwest Review*, 10 (January 1925), 68-73.

Englekirk, John E. "Notes on the Repertoire of the New Mexican-Spanish Folk-theatre." *Southern Folklore Quarterly*, 4 (1940), 227-355.

————. "The Passion Play in New Mexico." *Western Folklore*, 25 (1966), 17-33, 105-21.

————. "The Source and Dating of New Mexican Spanish Folk Plays." *Western Folklore*, 16 (1957), 232-55.

Englekirk, John E. "El teatro folklórico hispanoamericano." *Folklore Americas*, 17 (1957), 1-36.

Gillmor, Frances, ed. "Los Pastores Number: Folk Plays of Hispanic America— Foreword." *Western Folklore*, 16 (1957), 229-31.

Gipson, Rosemary. "The Mexican Performers: Pioneer Theatre Artists of Tucson." *Journal of Arizona History*, 13 (winter 1972), 235-52.

Gonzales, Rene Abelardo. "The Pastorelas of Rio Grande City and Hebbronville, Texas." *Folklore Annual of the University Folklore Association*, 4 & 5 (1972-1973), 10-22.

Hirshfield, D. "Los Pastores." *Theatre Arts*, December 1928, pp. 903-11.

Hood, Margaret Page. "The Devil, Saint Michael and the Hermit's Bottle." *New Mexican Folklore Review*, 1 (1946-47), 20-28.

Huerta, Jorge A. and Nicolás Kanellos. "Introduction." *Revista Chicano-Riqueña*, 7 (invierno 1979), v-ix.

Johnson, Winifred. "Early Theatre in the Spanish Borderlands." *Mid-America*, 13 (October 1930), 121-31.

Kanellos, Nicolás. "Fifty Years of Theatre in the Latino Communities of Northwest Indiana." *Aztlán*, 7 (summer 1976), 255-65.

———. "Mexican Community Theatre in a Midwestern City." *Latin American Theatre Review*, 7 (fall 1973), 42-48.

Kittle, J. L. "An Amateur Revives a Folk Play." *California Folklore Quarterly*, 5 (1946), 94-101.

Lummis, Charles F. "An American Passion Play." *The Land of Sunshine*, May 1896, pp. 255-65.

Michel, Concha. "Pastorela o coloquio." *Mexican Folkways*, 8 (January-March 1932), 5-30.

Pearce, T. M. "Los moros y los cristianos: Early American Play." *New Mexico Folklore Review*, 2 (1947-48), 58-65.

———. "The New Mexican Shepherds' Play." *Western Folklore*, 15 (1956), 77-88.

———. "Tracing a New Mexico Folk Play." *New Mexico Folklore Review*, 9 (1954-55), 20-27.

Place, Edwin B. "A Group of Mystery Plays Found in a Spanish-Speaking Region of Southern Colorado." *The University of Colorado Studies, Series A: General Studies*, 18 (1930), 1-9.

Rael, Juan B. "More Light on the Origin of *Los Pastores*." *New Mexico Folklore Review*, 6 (1951-52), 1-6.

Rapp, Mrs. I. H. "*Los Pastores* Is Gem of Miracle Plays." *El Palacio*, 11 (1921), 151-63.

Ribera-Ortega, Peter. "*Las Posadas*." *El Palacio*, 75 (winter 1968), 5-10.

Robe, Stanley L. "The Relationship of *Los Pastores* to Other Spanish-American Folk Drama." *Western Folklore*, 16 (1957), 281-89.

Steele, Thomas J. (S.J.). "The Spanish Passion Play in New Mexico and Colorado." *New Mexico Historical Review*, 53 (July 1978), 239-59.

Twitchell, R. E. "The First Community Theatre and Playwright in the U.S." *Museum of New Mexico and the School of American Research*, Santa Fe, 16 (March 1924), 83-87.

Van Stone, Mary R. "El Niño Perdido." *El Palacio*, 1933, pp. 163-65.

Ybarra-Frausto, Tomás. "Punto de partida." *Latin American Theatre Review*, 4 (spring 1971), 51-52.

C. Plays

Adán y Eva. University of New Mexico Bulletin, 5 (February 1934), 19-48.

Auto de Los Reyes Magos. University of New Mexico Bulletin, 5 (June 1934), 95-120.

Caín y Abel. University of New Mexico Bulletin, 5 (February 1934), 49-70.

Campa, Arthur L., trans. "Los Comanches: A New Mexican Folk Drama." University of New Mexico Bulletin, 7 (1942), 5-42.

_____. "Spanish Religious Folktheater in the Southwest (Second Cycle)." University of New Mexico Bulletin, Language Series 5 (June 1934), 5-157.

Cole, M. R., trans. Los Pastores: A Mexican Play of the Nativity. Memoirs of the American Folklore Society, 9, 1907.

Coloquio de pastores. University of New Mexico Bulletin, 5 (June 1934), 55-94.

Coloquio de San José. University of New Mexico Bulletin, 5 (June 1934), 11-54.

Espinosa, Aurelio M., trans. "Los Comanches: A Spanish Heroic Play of the Year Seventeen Hundred and Eighty." University of New Mexico Bulletin, Language Series 1 (1907), 1-46.

_____, and J. Manuel Espinosa, trans. "The Texans: A New Mexican Folk Play of the Middle Nineteenth Century." New Mexico Quarterly Review, 13 (autumn 1943), 299-309.

Espinosa, Gilberto, trans. Los Comanches. New Mexico Quarterly, 1 (May 1931), 133-46.

Howe, Charles E. B. A Dramatic Play Entitled Joaquín Murieta de Castill, the Celebrated California Bandit. In Five Acts. San Francisco: Commercial Book . . . Establishment, 1858.

Lea, Aurora (Lucero-White). En el portal de Belén. Santa Fe: Santa Fe Press, 1940.

_____. trans. and ed. New Mexican Folklore: Coloquio de los pastores, A Centuries-Old Christmas Folkplay. Santa Fe: Santa Fe Press, 1940.

El Niño Perdido. University of New Mexico Bulletin, 5 (June 1934), 121-54.

Van Stone, Mary R., ed. Los Pastores, Excerpts From an Old Christmas Play of the Southwest as Given Annually by the Griego Family, Santa Fe, New Mexico. Cleveland: Gates Press, 1933.

Van Stone, Mary R. and E. R. Sims, trans. Canto del Niño Perdido. Texas Folklore Society Publications, 11 (1933), 48-89. Rpt. in Spur of the Cock, ed. J. Frank Dobie. Dallas: Southern Methodist University Press, 1965.

IV. Teatro Campesino and Luis Valdez, 1965-70

A. Books

Anderson, Lola Marilyn Wheeler. "El Teatro Campesino." M.A. thesis, University of California/Los Angeles, 1970.

Cárdenas de Dwyer, Carlota. "The Development of Chicano Drama and Luis Valdez' 'Actos'." In Modern Chicano Writers, ed. Joseph Sommers and Tomás Ybarra-Frausto. Englewood Cliffs, NJ: Prentice-Hall, Inc., 1979, pp. 160-66.

Radical Theatre Festival. San Francisco: San Francisco Mime Troupe, 1969.

Santibáñez, James. "El Teatro Campesino Today and El Teatro Urbano." In The Chicanos: Mexican-American Voices, ed. Ed. Ludwig and James Santibáñez. Baltimore: Penguin, 1971, pp. 141-48.

Weisman, John. Guerilla Theater: Scenarios for Revolution. Garden City, NY: Anchor Press, 1973.

B. *Journal Articles*

Aaron, Jules. Review of sociopolitical theater incl. *La grande* (sic) *carpa de los rasquachis*. *Educational Theatre Review*, 27 (March 1975), 117-18.

"Actos." *New Yorker*, 19 August 1976, pp. 23-25.

Bagby, Beth. "El Teatro Campesino; Interviews with Luis Valdez." *Tulane Drama Review*, 11 (summer 1967), 70-80.

Cisneros, René. "*Los Actos*: A Study in Metacommunication." *Tejidos*, 2 (1975), 2-13.

Drake, Sylvie. "El Teatro Campesino: Keeping the Revolution on Stage." *Performing Arts Magazine*, September 1970, pp. 56-62.

"Guerilla Drama; Productions of the San Francisco Mime Troupe, Bread and Puppet, and California's Teatro Campesino." *Time*, 18 October 1968, p. 72.

Huerta, Jorge A. "Chicano Agit-Prop; The Early Actos of El Teatro Campesino." *Latin American Theatre Review*, 11 (spring 1977), 45-58.

Jiménez, Francisco. "Dramatic Principles of the Teatro Campesino." *Bilingual Review/Revista Bilingüe*, 2 (January-August 1975), 99-111.

"New Grapes; El Teatro Campesino Performs for Migrant Farmworkers." *Newsweek*, 31 July 1967, p. 79.

Steiner, Stan. "Cultural Schizophrenia of Luis Valdez." *Vogue*, 15 March 1969, pp. 112-13.

Valdez, Luis Miguel. "El Teatro Campesino." *Ramparts*, July 1966, pp. 55-56.

C. *Newspaper Articles*

Blevins, Winifred. " 'Peasants' Theater at Riverside." *Los Angeles Times*, 22 May 1968, n.p.

————. "Teatro Campesino 'Alive'." *Los Angeles Herald-Examiner*, 27 September 1969, sec. B, p. 9.

Delpech, Poirot. "Le Festival de Nancy à la recherche d' «autre chose»." *Le Monde* (Paris), 22 April 1969, p. 19.

Drake, Sylvie. "Teatro Campesino: Latin Troupe Stages 'Villa'." *Los Angeles Times*, 4 October 1969, sec. 2, p. 7.

Ferentinos, Nick. " 'Pancho Villa' Dramatic Triumph." (San Jose State College) *Daily Spartan*, January 1964, n.p.

Gleason, Ralph J. "On the Town: Vital, Earthy and Alive Theater." *San Francisco Chronicle*, 4 May 1966, p. 41.

Greig, Michael and Charles Howe. "*The Head*—Powerful." *San Francisco Chronicle*, 30 September 1968, p. 47.

Jones, David R. "Farm Labor: Viva el Picket Sign." *New York Times*, 30 July 1967, sec. 4, p. 5.

Kushner, Sam. "Comment: Campesino Culture." *People's World*, 4 May 1968, p. 6.

Mickelson, Donna. " 'The Shrunken Head' Triumph." *San Francisco Express Times*, 9 October 1968, n.p.

O'Connor, John J. "The Theater: Shades of the '30s." *Wall Street Journal*, 24 July 1967, p. 12.

Sullivan, Dan. "Chicano Group at ICCC." *Los Angeles Times*, 27 September 1969, sec. 2, p. 9.

————. "El Teatro Campesino at LACC." *Los Angeles Times*, 31 March 1969, sec. 4, p. 30.

Wasserman, John L. "The Man Behind El Teatro Campesino." *San Francisco Chronicle*, 2 May 1966, p. 60.

"Worker's Theater Leads Obie Winners." *New York Times*, 28 May 1968, p. 40.

D. *Plays*

La conquista de México. In *Actos*, ed. Luis Valdez. San Juan Bautista, CA: Cucaracha Press, 1971, pp. 50-65.

Las dos caras del patroncito. In *Actos*, pp. 7-19.

Los endrogados. Unpublished ms. in the author's collection, c. 1972.

The Militants. In *Actos*, pp. 95-98.

No saco nada de la escuela. In *Actos*, pp. 66-94.

La quinta temporada. In *Guerilla Street Theater*, ed. Henry Lesnick. New York: Avon Books, 1973, pp. 197-212. Also in *Actos*, pp. 20-34; *Guerilla Theater*, ed. John Weisman. Garden City: Anchor Press/Doubleday, 1973, pp. 21-32.

Valdez, Luis. *Bernabé.* In *Contemporary Chicano Theatre*, ed. Roberto J. Garza. Notre Dame: University of Notre Dame Press, 1976, pp. 30-58. Scene three in *Aztlán; An Anthology of Mexican-American Literature*, ed. Stan Steiner and Luis Valdez. New York: Vintage Books, 1972, pp. 361-76.

————— . *Dark Root of a Scream.* In *From the Barrio*, ed. Lilian Faderman and Omar Salinas. San Francisco: Canfield Press, 1973, pp. 79-98.

————— . *The Shrunken Head of Pancho Villa.* Unpublished ms. in the author's collection, c. 1971.

Los vendidos. In *Contemporary Chicano Theatre*, pp. 15-28. Also in *Guerilla Street Theater*, pp. 212-24; *People's Theatre in Amerika*, ed. Karen Malpede Taylor. New York: Drama Book Specialists, 1972, pp. 300-08; *Actos*, pp. 35-49; *Guerilla Theater*, pp. 42-54.

V. Teatro Campesino and Luis Valdez, 1971-80

A. *Books*

Bravo-Elizondo, Sergio. "Symbolic Motifs in Two Chicano Dramas." In *Selected Proceedings of the 1st and 2nd Annual Conferences on Minority Studies*, ed. George E. Carter and Bruce L. Mouser. La Crosse, WI: University of Wisconsin Institute for Minority Studies, 1975, pp. 47-54.

Cárdenas de Dwyer, Carlota. "The Development of Chicano Drama and Luis Valdez' 'Actos'." In *Modern Chicano Writers*, ed. Joseph Sommers and Tomás Ybarra-Frausto. Englewood Cliffs, NJ: Prentice-Hall, Inc., 1979, pp. 160-66.

Diamond, Betty Ann. *"Brown Eyed Children of the Sun": The Cultural Politics of El Teatro Campesino.* Ann Arbor: University Microfilms, 1977.

Goldsmith, Barclay. "Brecht and Chicano Theatre." In *Modern Chicano Writers*, pp. 167-75.

Rahner, Christiane Gertrud Martha. "The Background of Chicano Theatre and the Artistic and Political Development of the Teatro Campesino." Unpublished M.A. thesis, University of California at San Diego, 1980.

Taylor, Karen Malpede. *"El Teatro Campesino."* In her *People's Theatre in Amerika.* New York: Drama Book Specialists, 1972, pp. 293-96.

Valdez, Luis. "The Actos." In *Guerilla Street Theater*, ed. Henry Lesnick. New York: Avon Books, 1973, pp. 95-97.

Valdez, Luis. "Notes on Chicano Theater." In *People's Theatre in Amerika*, ed. Karen Malpede Taylor. New York: Drama Book Specialists, 1972, pp. 296-300. Also in *Actos*, ed. Luis Valdez. San Juan Bautista, CA: Cucaracha Press, 1971, pp. 1-4.

————. *Pensamiento serpentino*. San Juan Bautista, CA: Cucaracha Press, 1971. Also in *Chicano Theatre One* (primavera 1973), 7-19.

Wessel, David Steven. *The Quetzalcóatl Prophesy and Interpretation of "Reality is a Great Serpent" in Chicano Expression*. Ann Arbor: University Microfilms, 1977.

Yarbro-Bejarano, Yvonne. "From 'acto' to 'mito': A Critical Appraisal of the Teatro Campesino." In *Modern Chicano Writers*, pp. 176-85.

B. Journal Articles

Armas, José. "Teatro Campesino in New Mexico." *RAYAS*, 1 (May-June 1978), 3.

Bruce-Novoa, Juan. "El Teatro Campesino de Luis Valdez." *Texto Crítico*, 4 (mayo-agosto 1978), 65-75.

Cárdenas, Reyes. "Review of *Pensamiento Serpentino* by Luis Valdez." *Caracol*, 2 (April 1976), 6.

"Chicano Street Theatre at Inner City Playhouse." *The Hollywood Reporter*, 1 October 1971, p. 17.

Copeland, Roger F. "La carpa de los rasquachis." *Educational Theatre Journal*, 27 (October 1973), 367-68.

Delgado, José. "El Teatro Campesino." *Festival de Los Teatros Chicanos*, July 1977, pp. 24-26, 29.

Delucchi, Mary Phelan. "El Teatro Campesino de Aztlán/Chicano Protest Through Drama." *The Pacific Historian*, 16 (spring 1972), 15-27.

Franco, Abel. "Teatro Campesino: Change and Survival." *Neworld*, fall 1974, pp. 22-26.

Fuentes, Víctor. "Luis Valdez: De Delano a Holliwood." *RAYAS*, 2 (May-June 1979), 10.

Harrop, John and Jorge A. Huerta. "The Agitprop Pilgrimage of Luis Valdez and El Teatro Campesino." *Theatre Quarterly*, 5 (March-May 1975), 30-39.

Jiménez, Francisco. "Dramatic Principles of the Teatro Campesino." *Bilingual Review/Revista Bilingüe*, 2 (January-August 1975), 99-111.

Kourilsky, Françoise. "Approaching Quetzalcóatl: The Evolution of El Teatro Campesino." *Performance*, 2 (fall 1973), 37-46.

Moreno, Carlos. "The Rose of the Rancho." *TENAZ*, 1 (spring 1972), 3.

Morton, Carlos. " 'I am recreating our own reality': A Nuestro Interview with Luis Valdez." *Nuestro*, November 1977, pp. 30-37.

————. "El patrón, el patroncito y él: Félix Alvarez—A Mito Come True." *Festival de Los Teatros Chicanos*, July 1977, pp. 10-12.

————. "Platicando con Luis Valdez." *RAYAS*, 4 (July-August 1978), 11, 12.

————. "The Teatro Campesino." *The Drama Review*, 18 (December 1974), 71-76.

Pickett, Manuel. "El Teatro Campesino: A Development of Art Through a Growth in Political Ideology." *Praxis*, 5 (March 1980), n.p.

Shank, Theodore. "A Return to Aztec and Maya Roots." *The Drama Review*, 18 (December 1974), 56-70.

"El Teatro Campesino." *Chicano Theatre Two*, verano 1973, pp. 9-10.

"Teatro Campesino (Warm-Ups)." *Chicano Theatre One*, primavera 1973, pp. 22-23.

Valdez, Luis. "History of the Teatro Campesino." *La Raza*, 1, No. 6 (1970), 17-19.

_____. "Notes on Chicano Theatre." *Chicano Theatre One*, primavera 1973, pp. 7-19.

_____. "Notes on Chicano Theatre." *Latin American Theatre Review*, 4 (spring 1971), 52-55.

_____. "Pájaros y Serpientes/A Conversation with Peter Brook." *Chicano Theatre Three*, primavera 1974, pp. 36-44.

_____. "Pensamiento Serpentino." *Chicano Theatre One*, primavera 1973, pp. 7-19. Also in his *Pensamiento serpentino*. San Juan Bautista, CA: Cucaracha Press, 1973.

_____. "Teatro Chicano." *Caracol*, 1 (May 1975), 14-15.

C. Newspaper Articles

Aisenman, Leslie. "El Teatro Campesino." *Los Angeles Free Press*, 31 March 1972, sec. 2, p. 7.

Buenaventura, Enrique. "La búsqueda de la identidad: Carta abierta a Luis Valdez." *Sí Se Puede*, 15 August 1975, p. 9.

Christon, Lawrence. "From Delano Into a Mythic Realm." *Los Angeles Times*, 9 April 1975, sec. I, p. 32.

Drake, Sylvie. "Indio Holiday Pageant at the Fountainhead." *Los Angeles Times*, 14 December 1978, sec. IV, pp. 1, 31.

_____. "Life, Hope Under 'La Carpa'." *Los Angeles Times*, 15 October 1974, sec. IV, p. 10.

_____. "El Teatro Campesino Presents Triple Bill." *Los Angeles Times*, 27 October 1970, sec. IV, p. 13.

_____. "*Los Teatros* Curtain Rises." *Los Angeles Times*, 18 September 1971, sec. II, p. 9.

_____. "Watching El Teatro Campesino Grow." *Los Angeles Times*, 1 October 1973, sec. IV, p. 9.

Faber, Charles. "El Teatro Campesino—Two Views." *Los Angeles Free Press*, 25 October 1974, p. 18.

_____. "Theatre." *Los Angeles Free Press*, 25 October 1974, p. 19.

González, Jorge. "Theatre of Political Hope Contrasts Valdez's Work." *Santa Barbara News and Review*, 17 May 1974, p. 15.

Gussow, Mel. "Stage: Teatro Campesino in Brooklyn." *New York Times*, 28 April 1973, p. 21.

Jones, Welton. "Teatro Campesino Modest, Powerful." *San Diego Union*, 5 May 1975, sec. A, p. 13.

Kushner, Sam. "El Teatro Campesino—Two Views." *Los Angeles Free Press*, 25 October 1974, p. 18.

"Lively Theater in San Juan Reflects Chicano Experience." *San Jose Mercury*, 7 March 1972, p. 22.

Lowell, Sondra. "El Teatro Campesino, Chicano Street Theatre." *Los Angeles Free Press*, 24 September 1971, p. 21.

MacKay, Barbara. "Teatro Campesino Brings Art Home to Workers." *Denver Post*, 29 July 1976, sec. G, p. 61.

_____. "Teatro Conjures Up Vivid Bilingual Show." *Denver Post*, 28 July 1976, sec. C, p. 29.

"Mecha Sponsors Teatro Campesino." *La Gente* (UCLA), 7 febrero 1972, p. 4.

Nellhaus, Arlynn. "El Teatro Group Packs a Wallop." *Denver Post*, 20 August 1975, sec. F, p. 80.

Russell, Bruce, "Chicano Guerilla Theater." *Washington Post*, 14 November 1971, sec. H, p. 5.

Sainer, Arthur. "Chicanos at Chelsea." *Village Voice*, 26 April 1973, pp. 74, 80.

Smith, Cecil. "Farmworkers' Folk Drama." *Los Angeles Times*, 4 November 1976, sec. IV, p. 18.

Stabiner, Karen. "Peace, Calm in San Juan." *Santa Barbara News and Review*, 17 May 1974, p. 15.

————— , with Eric Mankin and David Ewing. "Teatro Campesino: Spiritualism Replaces Practical Politics." *Santa Barbara News and Review*, 17 May 1974, p. 14.

Sullivan, Dan. "Called on the Carpet by a Theater Guru." *Los Angeles Times*, 2 September 1973, Calendar, p. 1.

—————. "Eavesdropping on El Teatro." *Los Angeles Times*, 16 November 1973, sec. 4, pp. 1, 24.

—————. "For El Teatro, Home Is Where the Heart Is." *Los Angeles Times*, 11 November 1973, Calendar, p. 36.

—————. "Homecoming of a Dead GI." *Los Angeles Times*, 25 September 1971, sec. II, p. 8.

—————. " 'Rose' by El Teatro Campesino." *Los Angeles Times*, 8 July 1977, sec. IV, pp. 1, 7.

—————. "El Teatro Campesino in Halloween Program." *Los Angeles Times*, 3 November 1970, sec. IV, p. 9.

—————. "Teatros (sic) Goes Beyond Talent." *Los Angeles Times*, 23 September 1971, sec. IV, pp. 1, 29.

"El Teatro Campesino To Perform." *San Francisco Chronicle*, 12 February 1971, p. 45.

Weisman, John. "Chicano Pride Focus of Teatro Campesino." *Los Angeles Times*, 7 May 1971, n.p.

D. Plays

Huelguistas. In *Actos*, ed. Luis Valdez. San Juan Bautista, CA: Cucaracha Press, 1971, pp. 99-103.

Soldado razo. In *Actos*, pp. 131-45.

Valdez, Luis. *Los vendidos.* Unpublished video script in the author's collection, 1973.

Vietnam campesino. In *Guerilla Street Theater*, ed. Henry Lesnick. New York: Avon Books, 1973, pp. 225-49. Also in *Actos*, pp. 104-30.

La Virgen del Tepeyac. Unpublished ms. in the author's collection, c. 1972.

VI. Zoot Suit

A. Journal Articles

Benitel, Tomás. "Facing the Issues Beyond 'Zoot Suit'; An Interview with Playwright Luis Valdez." *Neworld*, 4 (1978), pp. 34-38.

Brecher, Kenneth. "Pageants to Play." *Westways*, May 1979, pp. 38-41, 66.

Chaillet, Ned. "Theatrical Gold in California." *Plays and Players*, 26 (March 1979), 16-17.

"Chicano Play A Coast Click, B'way Bound." *Variety*, 24 January 1979, pp. 1, 98.

Cizmar, Paula. "Luis Valdez." *Mother Jones*, June 1979, pp. 47-64.

"Conference in Shubert Alley." *The New Yorker*, 19 February 1979, pp. 29-31.

Dubois, Rochelle. "Zoot Suit—Back in Fashion." *Caracol*, 5, Nos. 11 & 12 (1979), 6-7.

Gill, Brendan. "Borrowings." *The New Yorker*, 2 April 1979, p. 94.

Giner, Oscar. "Theater in Los Angeles: Valdez' *Zoot Suit*." *Theater*, 10 (spring 1979), 123-28.

Gottfried, Martin. "Of Zoot Suits and Reet Pleats." *Saturday Review*, 26 May 1979, p. 59.

Huerta, Jorge A. "Zoot Suit: El Chicano Comes of Age en el jalewood." *Tenaz Talks Teatro*, 1 (summer-fall 1978), 9-11.

Kroll, Jack. "Heartbeats from the Barrio." *Newsweek*, 9 April 1979, pp. 85-86.

McWilliams, Carey. "A Play on History." *Westways*, May 1979, pp. 18-19.

Montoya, José. "Zootsuit Riots of 1943: The Making of the Pachuco Myth." *Somos*, June-July 1978, pp. 23-27.

Morton, Carlos. "The Many Masks of Teatro Chicano." *Latin American Theatre Review*, 12 (fall 1978), 87-88.

Murray, William. " 'Zoot Suit': The Triumph of El Pachuco," *New West*, 11 September 1978, p. 47.

Parker, Robert A. "The Pachuco World of Luis Valdez." *Americas*, August 1979, pp. 3-8.

Pennington, Ron. "Stage Review: 'Zoot Suit'." *Hollywood Reporter*, 26 April 1978, p. 14.

Pollarski, Santiago. "Crítica de Teatro." *El Tiempo de Nueva York*, 26 marzo 1979, n.p.

Prida, Dolores. "Broadway, Here We Come." *Nuestro*, April 1979, pp. 22-26.

Rodríguez, Rene and Rosemary A. Rodríguez. "*Zoot Suit*." *Somos*, June-July 1978, pp. 28-29.

Ryweck, Charles. "Stage Review: 'Zoot Suit'." *Hollywood Reporter*, 28 March 1979, n.p.

Simon, John. "West Coast Story." *New York Magazine*, 9 April 1979, p. 93.

Thompson, Thomas. "A Dynamo Named Gordon Davidson." *New York Times Magazine*, 11 March 1979, pp. 17-18, 95-100.

Torres, Luis R. "Thoughts on el Pachuco." *Performing Arts* (Mark Taper Forum), August 1978, pp. 6, 7, 8, 13.

Valadez, Kathy L. "Zoot Suit by Luis Valdez." *Somos*, June-July 1978, pp. 20-21.

Valdez, Luis. "First Hispanic-American Show on Broadway: *Zoot Suit*; Luis Valdez Talks About the Show, the Critics, the Audiences." *New York Theatre Review*, May 1979, pp. 22-23.

————. "From a Pamphlet to a Play." *Performing Arts* (Mark Taper Forum), August 1978, p. 4.

" 'Zoot Suit' Again Set For 1978-79 at New Theatre." *The Hollywood Reporter*, 9 May 1978, p. 17.

B. *Newspaper Articles*

Barnes, Clive. " 'Zoot Suit' Proves Moot." *New York Post*, 26 March 1979, pp. 71, 77.

Christon, Lawrence. " 'Zoot Suit' to Close in New York Sunday." *Los Angeles Times*, 26 April 1979, sec. IV, p. 28.

————. "Stage Review: 'Zoot Suit' at the Aquarius." *Los Angeles Times*, 19 October 1978, sec. IV, pp. 25, 26.

————. " 'Zoot Suit' on Film: A Tailor-Made Transition." *Los Angeles Times*, 3 March 1981, Calendar, pp. 1, 5.

Del Olmo, Frank. "The Cast Savors Its Own Victories." *Los Angeles Times*, 8 April 1979, Calendar, p. 63.

Drake, Sylvie. "Broadway Cool to 'Zoot Suit'." *Los Angeles Times*, 27 March 1979, sec. IV, pp. 1, 2.

————. "Stage Notes/Zooting to Broadway." *Los Angeles Times*, 12 October 1978, sec. IV, p. 21.

————. " 'Zoot Suit' at the Taper." *Los Angeles Times*, 18 August 1978, sec. IV, pp. 1, 18, 19.

————. " 'Zoot Suit': Invasion of Privacy?" *Los Angeles Times*, 29 November 1979, sec. IV, p. 28.

————. " 'Zoot Suit' Keeps Chin Up Despite Negative Reviews." *Los Angeles Times*, 8 April 1979, Calendar, p. 62.

————. " 'Zoot Suit': Tailor-Made as L.A. Theater." *Los Angeles Times*, 27 August 1978, Calendar, p. 54.

Eder, Richard. "Theater: 'Zoot Suit', Chicano Music-Drama." *New York Times*, 26 March 1979, sec. C, p. 13.

Feingold, Michael. "Truth in Melodrama." *Village Voice*, 2 April 1979, p. 89.

Gottschalk, Earl. " 'Zoot Suit' and Pride Are Opening on Broadway." *Wall Street Journal*, 23 March 1979, Leisure and the Arts, p. 1.

Grant, Lee. "In the Bidding for 'Zoot Suit'." *Los Angeles Times*, 18 September 1978, sec. IV, p. 8.

Gussow, Mel. "World of Pachucos in Musical 'Zoot Suit'." *New York Times*, 15 February 1979, sec. C, p. 14.

Kerr, Walter. " 'Zoot Suit' Loses Its Way in Bloodless Rhetoric." *New York Times*, 1 April 1979, sec. 2, pp. 3, 20.

La Garda, Velia. " 'Zoot Suit' Relives Sleepy Lagoon." *Voz Fronteriza* (UCSD), February 1979, p. 9.

McKay, Gardner. "Theater Review: 'Zoot Suit'." *Los Angeles Herald Examiner*, 28 April 1978, sec. B, p. 12.

Munk, Erika. "Cross Left." *Village Voice*, 2 April 1979, p. 88.

Novick, Julius. "N.Y. Critic's View of L.A. Theater." *Los Angeles Times*, 1 April 1979, Calendar, p. 60.

Overend, William. "The '43 Zoot Suit Riots Reexamined." *Los Angeles Times*, 9 May 1978, sec. IV, pp. 1, 4, 5.

Pezas, Evan A. "The Zoot Suiter in Greece: A Vision Out of Whole Cloth." *Los Angeles Times*, 1 October 1978, Calendar, p. 56.

"Play of Fact and Fantasy." *Newsday*, 26 March 1979, sec. C, p. 1.

Pollarsky, Santiago. "Crítica de teatro." *El Tiempo de Nueva York*, 26 marzo 1979, p. 17.

Riley, Clayton. "Death of an American Play." *Village Voice*, 7 May 1979, p. 44.

————. " 'Zoot Suit' On the Great White Way." *Los Angeles Times*, 3 June 1979, Calendar, p. 3.

Sharbutt, Jay. "Power and Peasantry Join To See If 'Zoot Suit' Fits Broadway." *The San Diego Union*, 18 March 1979, sec. E, p. 4.

Sullivan, Dan. "Putting the Boomp Into 'Zoot Suit'." *Los Angeles Times*, 16 April 1978, Calendar, pp. 1, 69.

———. " 'Zoot Suit' at the Taper Forum." *Los Angeles Times*, 24 April 1978, sec. IV, pp. 1, 11.

Vásquez, Richard. " 'Zoot Suit' Image Raises Chicano Consciousness." *Los Angeles Times*, 22 April 1979. Calendar, pp. 73,75.

Watt, Douglas. " 'Zoot Suit' Slithers In at the Winter Garden." *New York Daily News*, 26 March 1979, p. 21.

Weiner, Bernard. " 'Zoot Suit': A Play Tailored to Its Region." *San Francisco Chronicle*, 31 August 1978, p. 61.

Wetzsteon, Ross. "Agitprop Sitcom." *Village Voice*, 4 December 1978, p. 121.

Yarbro-Bejarano, Yvonne. " 'Zoot Suit Mania' Sweeps L.A., Moves Toward East." *In These Times*, 31 Jan.–6 Feb. 1979, p. 23.

" 'Zoot Suit' to Open New Taper Season." *Los Angeles Times*, 9 May 1978, IV, p. 11.

VII. Other Teatros, General

A. Books

Bravo-Elizondo, Sergio. "Symbolic Motifs in Two Chicano Dramas." In *Selected Proceedings of the 1st and 2nd Annual Conferences on Minority Studies*, ed. George E. Carter and Bruce L. Mouser. La Crosse, WI: University of Wisconsin Institute for Minority Studies, 1975, pp. 47-54.

Castellano, Olivia. "A Study of the Significance of Drama and Identity in the Chicano Social Movement." M.A. thesis, Sacramento State College, 1970.

Dukore, Bernard F. "The Brown Revolution." In his *Documents for Drama and Revolution.* New York: Holt, Rinehart and Winston, 1971, pp. 211-13.

———. "Interview with Tony Avallón." In his *Documents for Drama and Revolution*, pp. 221-25.

———. "Interview with Guadalupe de Saavedra." In his *Documents for Drama and Revolution*, pp. 214-20.

Goldsmith, Barclay. "Brecht and Chicano Theatre." In *Modern Chicano Writers*, ed. Joseph Sommers and Tomás Ybarra-Frausto. Englewood Cliffs, NJ: Prentice-Hall, Inc., 1979, pp. 167-75.

Huerta, Jorge. "Algo sobre el Teatro Chicano." In *Chicanos: Antología histórica y literaria*, ed. Tino Villanueva. Mexico: Tierra Firme, 1980, pp. 136-43. Rpt. in *Revista de la Universidad de Mexico*, 27 (febrero 1973), 20-24.

———. "Del templo al pueblo." In *La otra cara de México: Los Chicanos*, ed. David Maciel. México: Ediciones El Caballito, 1977, pp. 316-47.

———. "From the Temple to the Arena: Teatro Chicano Today." In *The Identification and Analysis of Chicano Literature*, ed. Francisco Jiménez. New York: Bilingual Press, 1979, pp. 90-116.

Mason, Theresa Hope. "*Teatro Chicano* and Mexican Identity: The Case of Two Texas *Teatros*." M.A. report, University of Texas, Austin, 1977.

Quiles, Víctor. M. "An Exploration Into Chicano Theatre." M.A. thesis, University of California, Santa Barbara, 1973.

Ramírez, Elizabeth Cantú. "The Annals of Chicano Theater. 1965-1973." M.A. thesis, University of California, Los Angeles, 1974.

Santibáñez, James. "El Teatro Campesino Today and El Teatro Urbano." In *The*

Chicanos: Mexican American Voices, ed. Ed. Ludwig and James Santibáñez. Baltimore: Penguin, 1971, pp. 141-48.

Serrano, Héctor M. "The Mexican-American and Dramatic Literature." M.A. thesis, University of Texas at El Paso, 1972.

B. *Journal Articles*

Altuna, Cecilia Cartwright. "Breve biografía de Ruben Sierra." *Metamorfosis*, 2 (1979), 4.

Alegría, Alonso. "El teatro chicano en California: Un teatro necesario." *Amaru* (Lima), 12 (June 1970), 29-30.

Betancourt, Aurelia. "Teatro Quetzalcóatl." *Metamorfosis*, 2 (1979), 16-19.

Bravo-Elizondo, Pedro. "El Teatro Chicano." *Revista Chicano-Riqueña*, 1 (otoño 1973), 36-42.

Brokaw, John W. "Teatro Chicano: Some Reflections." *Educational Theatre Journal*, 29 (December 1977), 535-44.

Bruce-Novoa. "El Teatro 'Chicano' de Alves Pereira." *Revista Chicano-Riqueña*, 3 (otoño 1975), 48-52.

————, and David Valentín. "Revolutionizing the Popular Image: Essay on Chicano Theatre." *Latin American Literary Review*, 5 (spring-summer 1977), 42-50.

Carrillo, Loretta. "Chicano Teatro: The People's Theatre." *Journal of Popular Culture*, 13 (spring 1980), 556-63.

Castañón-García, Juan. "Teatro Chicano and the Analysis of Sacred Symbols: Towards a Chicano World-View in the Social Sciences." *Grito del Sol*, 3 (January-March 1978), 37-49.

Chamberlain, Vibiana Aparicio. "Children's Teatro/The Implications of Birth and Death in Children's Teatro." *Chicano Theatre Three*, primavera 1974, pp. 30-35.

————. "Teatro de Niños: A Revolutionary Arm of Social Struggle." *Pláticas del Sexto Festival Nacional de los Teatros Chicanos*, 14-19 July 1975, pp. 9-10.

————. "Títeres y Teatro Chicano, Puppetry." *Caracol*, 2 (February 1976), 10.

Davis, R. G. "1971: Rethinking Guerilla Theatre." *Performance*, 1 (December 1971), 166-73.

"Documentary Theatre; A Collective Discussion by El Teatro de la Esperanza." *Pláticas del Sexto Festival Nacional de los Teatros Chicanos*, 14-19 July 1975, pp. 12-14.

Donahue, Francis. "Teatro de Guerrilla." *Cuadernos Americanos*, 32 (September-October 1973), 17-33.

"Entrevista con Enrique Buenaventura." *Chicano Theatre Two*, verano 1973, pp. 11-13.

Fuentes, Víctor. "Guest Editorial/Cultura Nacional y Conciencia Político-Social." *Chicano Theatre Three*, primavera 1974, pp. 1-2.

Gamboa, Erasmo. "Raíces." *Metamorfosis*, 2 (1979), 3.

García-Camarillo, Cecilio. "Platicando con Jorge Huerta." *RAYAS*, 3 (May-June 1979), 11-12.

Garza, Abel. "Teatro Chicano." *Caracol*, 2 (diciembre 1975), 19.

Garza, Sabino. "Teatro Chicano: A Creative Explosion." *Caracol*, 4 (March 1978), 3.

Huerta, Jorge. "Algo sobre el teatro Chicano." *Revista de la Universidad de México*,

27 (febrero 1973), 20-24. Rpt. in *Chicanos: Antología histórica y literaria*, ed. Tino Villanueva. México: Tierra Firme, 1980, pp. 136-43.

Huerta, Jorge. "Chicano Teatro: A Background." *Aztlán*, 2 (fall 1971), 63-78.

_____. "Concerning Teatro Chicano." *Latin American Theatre Review*, 6 (spring 1973), 13-20.

_____. "The Difference Between Teatro Chicano and Traditional Theatre." *Pláticas del Sexto Festival Nacional de los Teatros Chicanos*, 14-19 July 1975, pp. 7-8.

_____. "En torno." Chicano Theatre One, primavera 1973, pp. 2-6.

_____. "The Evolution of TENAZ." *Pláticas del Sexto Festival Nacional de los Teatros Chicanos*, 14-19 July 1975, pp. 3-6.

_____. "Seminario '78, August 11-13, Mill Valley, CA." *Tenaz Talks Teatro*, 1 (summer-fall 1978), 1-5.

_____. "El Teatro de la Esperanza: Keeping in Touch With the People." *The Drama Review*, 21 (March 1977), 37-46.

_____. "Teatros de la Gente." *La Luz*, August 1973, pp. 6-10.

_____. "TENAZ." *Festival de los Teatros Chicanos*, July 1977, pp. 28-29.

_____. "Where Are Our Chicano Playwrights?" *Revista Chicano-Riqueña*, 3 (otoño 1975), 32-42.

"Huerta y el Teatro Chicano en Nuevo Méjico." *Floreciendo*, 1 (February-March 1979), 5.

"L'implication ideologique du Théâtre Chicano/The Ideological Implications of Chicano Theatre." *International Theatre Informations* (Paris), spring 1975, pp. 22-27.

Kanellos, Nicolás. "Chicano Theatre to Date." *Tejidos*, 2 (invierno 1975), 40-46.

_____. "Folklore in Chicano Theater and Chicano Theater as Folklore." *Journal of the Folklore Institute*, 15 (January-April 1978), 57-82.

_____. "Los Teatros de la Raza." *Abrazo*, summer 1979, pp. 30-32.

Loo, Guillermo. "Organizing Teatro." *Pláticas del Sexto Festival Nacional de los Teatros Chicanos*, 14-19 July 1975, pp. 10-11.

Martínez, Blanca E., and Frank S. Martínez. "Teatro del Piojo: Un recorrido histórico." *Metamorfosis*, 2 (1979), 8-15.

Martínez, Douglas R. "Language and Folklore Alive in the Theater." *Agenda*, 8 (November-December 1978), 16-19.

"Los Mascarones." *Chicano Theatre Two*, verano 1973, pp. 18-19.

Miguelez, Armando. "Teatro Chicano." *RAYAS*, 6 (November-December 1978), 5.

"Miotroyo." *Chicano Theatre Two*, verano 1973, p. 27.

Morton, Carlos. "Los dioses y los diablos en el teatro Chicano." *Abrazo*, summer 1979, pp. 24-26.

_____. "An Interview With Jorge Huerta." *Somos*, August/September 1978, pp. 30-31.

O, Charlie de la. "El Chisme del Charlie." *Floreciendo*, 1 (abril-mayo 1980), 3.

_____. "Que Vivan los Teatros." *Floreciendo*, 1 (mayo-junio 1979), 6.

Pino, Frank. "El Teatro." *Revista Chicano-Riqueña*, 1 (otoño 1973), 11-13.

Prida, Dolores. "A New Act for Latino Theater." *Nuestro*, November 1977, pp. 22-29.

Reyes, Ruperto, Jr. "Teatro Chicano: A Political Art Form." *Chicano Times* (San Antonio, TX), 19 August-1 September 1977, p. 20.

Rodríguez, Alfonso. "Tragic Vision in Estella Portillo's *Day of the Swallows*." *De Colores*, 5 (1980), 152-58.

Rojas, Rogelio "Smiley." "Teatro Conference." *Magazín*, April 1972, pp. 16-17.

Rosenberg, Joe. "La Compañía de Teatro Bilingüe." *Educational Theatre Journal*, 30 (May 1978), 240-52.

—————. "The Emerging Chicano Drama." *Bulletin of the Southwest Ethnic Study Center*, 3 (September 1976), 1-4.

—————. "Experiments With Language in the Theater." *Design*, 82 (November-December 1980), 31-33.

—————. "Rehearsal Problems in Bilingual Theatre." *Latin American Theatre Review*, 11 (spring 1978), 81-90.

—————. "The Syntax of Dialogue: A Problem in Scholarship and Translation." *Theatre Southwest*, 6 (May 1980), 12-18.

—————. "Teatro Bilingüe." *Latin American Theatre Review*, 9 (fall 1975), 87-88.

Salinas, Judy. "The Image of Woman in Chicano Literature." *Revista Chicano-Riqueña*, 4 (otoño 1976), 139-48.

Serrano, Héctor M. "Teatro Chicano—Its First Decade." *Bulletin of the Cross-Cultural Southwest Ethnic Study Center*, 3 (March 1976), 1, 2.

Sierra, Rubén. "Autobiografía." *Metamorfosis*, 2 (1979), 5.

"El Teatro de Aztlán." *Chicano Theatre Two*, verano 1973, pp. 6-7.

"Teatro de los Barrios." *Chicano Theatre Two*, verano 1973, p. 8.

"Teatro Bilingüe." *Festival de los Teatros Chicanos*, July 1977, p. 30.

"Teatro Desengaño." *Festival de los Teatros Chicanos*, July 1977, p. 15.

"El Teatro de la Esperanza." *Chicano Theatre Two*, verano 1973, pp. 14-15.

"Teatro de la Esperanza." *Festival de los Teatros Chicanos*, July 1977, p. 27.

"Teatro de la Gente." *Chicano Theatre Two*, verano 1973, pp. 16-17.

"Teatro de la Gente." *Festival de los Teatros Chicanos*, July 1977, pp. 8-9.

"Teatro Libertad." *Festival de los Teatros Chicanos*, July 1977, pp. 4-5.

"Teatro Mestizo." *Chicano Theatre Two*, verano 1973, pp. 25-26.

"Teatro Mestizo." *Festival de los Teatros Chicanos*, July 1977, pp. 6-7.

"El Teatro Movimiento Primavera." *Festival de los Teatros Chicanos*, July 1977, pp. 22-23.

"Teatro Nacional de Aztlán." *Chicano Theatre Two*, verano 1973, pp. 32-33.

"El Teatro de los Niños." *Chicano Theatre Two*, verano 1973, p. 28.

"Teatro de los Niños." *Festival de los Teatros Chicanos*, July 1977, p. 15.

"Teatro Quetzalcóatl." *Festival de los Teatros Chicanos*, July 1977, pp. 20-21.

"Teatro Urbano." *Chicano Theatre Two*, verano 1973, p. 30.

"T.E.N.A.Z." *Chismearte*, 1 (fall 1976), 20-23.

"Theater in the Streets Presents 'My People, My Life . . .' Starring Spanish-American Residents of Santa Fe, New Mexico." *Vista Volunteer*, September 1968, pp. 16-25.

"Los Topos." *Chicano Theatre Two*, verano 1973, p. 29.

Torres, Luis. "The Arts: Hope Abroad." *Nuestro*, August 1979, p. 50.

—————. "A Profile of Jorge Huerta/A Look at the Status of Chicano Theater." *La Luz*, September 1976, pp. 17-18.

Vargas, Adrian. "Notes on Chicano Theatre." *Chicano Theatre Two*, verano 1973, pp. 20-24.

Velásquez, Jorge. "Teatro." *Caracol*, 1, No. 5 (enero 1975), 14-16.

"Workshop on Teatro Chicano." *Floreciendo*, 1 (febrero-marzo 1979), 5.

Ybarra-Frausto, Tomás. "Punto de Partida." *Latin American Theatre Review*, 4 (spring 1971), 51-52.

Zamora, Romulus. "*Yo también hablo de la rosa*; A Unique Bilingual Production." *Latin American Literary Review*, 12 (fall 1978), 91-94.

C. Newspaper Articles

"Chicano Historian Directs Teatro Production at UCSB." *Santa Barbara News-Press*, 7 May 1972, sec. D, p. 12.

"Chicano Theater." *San Francisco Chronicle*, 11 June 1973, p. 44.

Drake, Sylvie. "Chicano Theater Finds Its Voice." *Los Angeles Times*, 5 July 1970, Calendar, pp. 30, 32-33.

Huerta, Jorge A. "TENAZ: El teatro chicano." *Sí Se Puede*, 24 October 1975, pp. 6, 10-11.

Loper, Mary Lou. "Barrio Theater Run on a Shoestring." *Los Angeles Times*, 7 February 1971, sec. E, p. 4.

Mitchell, Sean. "Morales Case Taken to the Dallas Stage." *Dallas Times Herald*, 2 February 1979, n.p.

"Teatro Aztlán." *El Popo* (Cal. State Univ., Northridge), summer 1973, p. 5.

"We Are Sowers, And We Sow Seeds of Liberación. . . ." *El Chicano*, 15 February 1970, p. 3.

D. Plays

El alcalde. Revista Chicano-Riqueña, 3 (otoño 1973), 2-9.

Alurista. *Dawn. El Grito*, 7 (June-August 1974), 55-84.

Alves Pereira, Teresinha. *Andale, Rosana*. Bloomington: Backstage Books, 1973.

————. *Hey, Mex!* Bloomington: Backstage Books, n.d. (c. 1972).

Arias, Ron. *The Interview*. In *Nuevos Pasos: Chicano and Puerto Rican Drama*, ed. Nicolás Kanellos and Jorge Huerta. Gary: Indiana University Northwest, 1979, pp. 1-7. Special issue of *Revista Chicano-Riqueña*, 7 (invierno 1979).

Las avispas. Teatro Chicano de Austin. *Revista Chicano-Riqueña*, 2 (verano 1974), 8-10.

Barrientos, L. S. *The Mañana Show. Maize*, 2 (primavera 1979), 22-31.

Boyle, Virginia. *¡Zas! una comedia musical bilingüe*. Chicago: Coach House Press, 1979.

Burruel, Francisco O. *The Dialogue of Cuco Rocha. El Grito*, 4 (spring 1971), 37-45.

Cárdenas, Reyes. *A Destruction and Reconstruction of Santos Rodríguez. Caracol*, 3 (July 1977), 6-7.

Castro, Felipe. *Los pelados*. In *El Teatro de la Esperanza: An Anthology of Chicano Drama*, ed. Jorge A. Huerta. Goleta: El Teatro de la Esperanza, 1973, pp. 73-94.

Chávez, Mauro. *The Last Day of Class. El Grito*, 4 (spring 1971), 48-63.

Duarte-Clark, Rodrigo. *Brujerías*. In *El Teatro de la Esperanza*, pp. 39-62. Revised rpt. in *Nuevos Pasos*, pp. 9-18.

Durán, Ricardo. *Dos vatos*. In *From the Barrio: A Chicano Anthology*, ed. Lilian Faderman and Omar Salinas. San Francisco: Canfield Press, 1973, pp. 71-79.

Espinosa, Rudi. *Jailed. Tecolote*, 27 October 1971, p. 7.

García, Joey. *Juan's Epitaph*. In *El Teatro de la Esperanza*, pp. 5-11.

Garza, Juan Manuel. *El Polo. Caracol*, 4 (March 1978), 14-16.

————. *The Ultimate Touch. Caracol*, 3 (July 1977), 7-8.

Garza, Roberto J. *No nos venceremos*. In his *Contemporary Chicano Theater*. Notre Dame: University of Notre Dame Press, 1976, pp. 192-204.

Hernández, Alfonso. *Every Family Has One*. In his *The False Advent of Mary's Child and Other Plays*. Berkeley: Editorial Justa, 1979, pp. 53-129.

————. *The False Advent of Mary's Child*. In *The False Advent of Mary's Child*, pp. 1-52.

————. *The Imperfect Bachelor*. In *The False Advent of Mary's Child*, pp. 130-53.

————. *The Lemon Tree*. *El Grito*, 7 (June-August 1974), 38-43.

————. *The Potion*. *El Grito*, 7 (June-August 1974), 50-54.

————. *The Wedding Dress*. *El Grito*, 7 (June-August 1974), 44-49.

Huelga en Cristal. *Magazín*, May 1972, pp. 14-28.

Huerta, Jorge. *El renacimiento de Huitzilopochtli*. In his *El Teatro de la Esperanza*, pp. 98-125.

Landy, Lino and Ricardo López Landy. *La chamaca brava*. *Grito del Sol*, 1 (April-June 1976), 37-54.

————. *Jamanegs*. *Grito del Sol*, 1 (April-June 1976), 29-35.

León, Nephtalí de. *Chicanos: The Living and the Dead*. In his *Five Plays*. Denver: Totinem Books, 1972, pp. 43-90.

————. *The Flies*. In *Five Plays*, pp. 139-59.

————. *The Judging of Man*. In *Five Plays*, pp. 131-38.

————. *La muerte de Ernesto Nerios*. In *Five Plays*, pp. 17-42.

————. *Play Number 9*. In *Five Plays*, pp. 91-130.

Moreno, Raquel. "El Milagrucho." *El Grito*, 4 (spring 1971), 64-66.

Morton, Carlos. *El cuento de Pancho Diablo*. *Grito del Sol*, 1 (July-September 1976), 39-85.

————. *Desolation Car Lot*. Unpublished ms. in the author's collection, c. 1973.

————. *Los dorados*. Unpublished ms. in the author's collection.

————. *El jardín*. *El Grito*, 7 (June-August 1974), 7-37.

————. *Las many muertes de Richard Morales*. *Tejidos*, 4 (primavera 1977), 28-50.

————. *Rancho Hollywood*. In *Nuevos Pasos*, pp. 43-63.

Navarro, J. L. *In the Park*. In his *Blue Day on Main Street*. Berkeley: Quinto Sol, 1973, pp. 116-27.

Olvera, Joe, Leo Rojas and Raul Estrada. *A Barrio Tragedy*. In *Caracol*, 4 (March 1978), 16-22.

Ortiz, Rudy C. *Los mártires*. *Caracol*, 3 (June 1977), 18-22.

Panfila la curandera. In *El Teatro de la Esperanza*, pp. 28-38.

Los pelados. Tucson: Teatro Libertad, 1978.

Pérez, Reimundo. *Syndrome of an American Nightmare*. *De Colores*, 4, Nos. 1 & 2 (1978), 53-64.

Portillo, Estella. *Blacklight*. Unpublished ms. in the author's collection, 1980.

————. *Day of the Swallows*. In *Contemporary Chicano Theatre*, pp. 206-45. Also in *We Are Chicanos: An Anthology of Mexican-American Literature*, ed. Philip D. Ortego. New York: Washington Square Press, 1973, pp. 224-71; and *El Espejo*, ed. Herminio Ríos and Octavio Romano-V. Berkeley: Quinto Sol, 1972, pp. 149-93.

————. *Isabel and the Dancing Bear*. Unpublished ms. in the author's collection, 1977.

————. *Labyrinth of Love*. Unpublished ms. in the author's collection, 1980.

——————. Excerpt from *Morality Play*. *El Grito*, 7 (September 1973), 7-21.

Portillo, Estella. *Puente negro*. Unpublished ms. in the author's collection, c. 1979.

——————. *Sun Images*. In *Nuevos Pasos*, pp. 19-42.

Ramírez, Frank. *La bolsa negra*. In *El Teatro de la Esperanza*, pp. 63-72.

Ríos, Alberto Alvaro. *Rosete's Smile*. In *Hispanics in the United States: An Anthology of Creative Literature*, ed. Gary D. Keller and Francisco Jiménez. Ypsilanti, MI: Bilingual Review/Press, 1980, pp. 30-38.

Romano-V., Octavio Ignacio. *Mugre de la canción*. *El Grito*, 3 (winter 1970), 50-55.

Saavedra, Guadalupe de. *Justice*. In *Drama and Revolution*, ed. Bernard F. Dukore. New York: Holt, Rinehart and Winston, 1971, pp. 589-98.

Sierra, Rubén. *Articus and the Angel*. Unpublished ms. in the author's collection, c. 1978.

——————. *Manolo*. In *Nuevos Pasos*, pp. 64-109.

——————. *La Raza Pura, or Racial, Racial*. In *Contemporary Chicano Theatre*, pp. 59-101.

Solis, Annie, and Larry García. *It's Too Late to Understand*. *Caracol*, 4 (March 1978), 4-5.

de la Torre, Alfredo. *Las dos caras de la migra*. *Caracol*, 4 (March 1978), 6-13.

Tortilla Curtain; A Collective Play by Teatro del Piojo. Seattle: Editorial Ce Atl, 1980.

Verdugo, Jaime. *La trampa sin salida*. *Chicano Theatre One*, primavera 1973, pp. 33-43. Rpt. in *El Teatro de la Esperanza*, pp. 12-27.

Vigil, Evangelina. *El partido hipócrita*. *Caracol*, 3 (February 1977), 22-23.

VIII. Festivals

A. *Journal Articles*

Acosta, María. "Festival de los Teatros." *La Raza*, September 1973, p. 11.

Alvarez, Félix. "The Pacific People's Theatre Festival." *Tenaz Talks Teatro*, 1 (summer-fall 1978), 7-8.

——————. "Reorganizing TENAZ." *Chismearte*, 2 (winter-spring 1977), 51.

Bruce-Novoa y Carlos May-Gamboa. "El Quinto Festival de Teatros." *De Colores*, 2 (1975), 65-72.

Castillo, Susana D. "Cuarto Festival de Teatros Chicanos en San José, Califas." *Latin American Theatre Review*, 7 (fall 1973), 100-02.

——————. "Festivales de Teatro en América." *Latin American Theatre Review*, 8 (fall 1974), 75-89.

Ciccone, Oscar. "Festival de Teatro Chicano/Chicano Theater Festival." *Canto Libre*, 2 (invierno 1975-76), 32-34.

Copelin, David. "Chicano Theatre: El Festival de los Teatros Chicanos." *The Drama Review*, 17 (December 1973), 73-89.

——————. "TENAZ Festival IV." *Chicano Theatre Three*, primavera 1974, pp. 7-22.

Cumpián, Carlos. "Flor y Canto Festival: A Theater Review." *Abrazo*, summer 1979, p. 15.

——————. "Theatre Review: Teatro de los Barrios at Floricanto 3, San Antonio, June 14." *Caracol*, 3 (May 1977), 16.

"Fiesta de los Teatros." *La Raza*, I, No. 6 (1971), 8-16.

"The First Texas Bilingual Theater Festival" (photo essay). *Caracol*, 5, Nos. 11 and 12 (1979), 26.

González, Teresa. "Quinto Festival de los Teatros Chicanos/Primer encuentro latinoamericano." *Caracol*, 1 (September 1974), 3-7.

Kanellos, Nicolás. "Sexto Festival de los Teatros Chicanos." *Latin American Theatre Review*, 9 (fall 1975), 81-84.

Morton, Carlos. "El Mito del Midwest." *Latin-American Theatre Review*, 9 (spring 1976), 94-98.

————. "Notas de un festival." *La Luz*, January-February 1975, pp. 8-9.

————. "Primer taller de teatro latinoamericano." *Latin American Theatre Review*, 11 (spring 1978), 115-16.

Noriega, Raúl. "Festival de los Teatros de TENAZ." *Chismearte*, 2 (winter-spring 1977), 18-19.

Platt, José. "Teatro Festival of Engagé in East Los Angeles." *Latin American Literary Review*, 5 (spring-summer 1977), 145-48.

Purkiss, Bill. "Reflections of Festival III." *Chicano Theatre Two*, verano 1973, p. 31.

"El Quinto Festival de los Teatros Chicanos." *Chicano Theatre Three*, primavera 1974, pp. 3-6.

B. Newspaper Articles

Arias, J. "Festival de Teatros Held in San José." *El Chicano*, 12 July 1973, p. 3.

Cárdenas, Juan. "TENAZ Mini-Festival . . . Stage for Struggle." *El Popo*, March 1976, pp. 8, 9.

Crawford, Corine. "Festival Showcases Teatro de la Tierra." *Los Angeles Times*, 21 September 1971, sec. IV, p. 9.

Drake, Sylvie. "Teatros Festival Presented in Fresno." *Los Angeles Times*, 12 May 1970, sec. IV, p. 9.

————. "Teatros Reach Into Barrios." *Los Angeles Times*, 31 March 1972, sec. IV, pp. 1, 10.

Gonzales, Juan. "Teatros de las Américas in First Encounter." *El Tecolote*, 12 August 1974, pp. 1, 4-6.

"Group Boycott of Festival Limits Chicano Participation." *Voz Fronteriza*, November-December 1978, p. 8.

Hale, David. "On the Aisle: 'Chicanos' Meet: First Festival." *Fresno Bee*, 9 May 1970, sec. B, p. 5.

Lizárraga, Marcos. "Sexto aniversario: Festival de Teatros Chicanos." *Sí Se Puede*, 15 August 1975, pp. 9-10.

"El Octavo Festival de TENAZ/Eighth Annual TENAZ Festival." *Voz Fronteriza*, June 1977, p. 8.

"El Quinto Festival de los Teatros." *El Chicano*, 27 June 1974, p. 8.

Rojas Zea, Rodolfo. "Al grito de '¡Viva la Raza!', comenzó ayer en Teotihuacán el I encuentro latinoamericano." *Excelsior* (Mexico City), 25 junio 1974, A, p. 10.

Savage, Milton, "Chicano Festival Ends Strongly." *San Diego Union*, 11 July 1977, sec. A, p. 10.

"Teatros Agitators to Descend Upon Orange County Saturday." *Los Angeles Free Press*, 24 March 1972, sec. I, p. 30.

IX. Other Teatros, Reviews

A. Journal Articles

Brokaw, John. "*Dos peones por patroncito, Los venditos* (sic), and *El soldado razo.*" Review of a production by CLETA (Centro Libre de Experimentación Teatral y Artística) during the summer of 1973 in Mexico City. *Educational Theatre Journal*, 26 (March 1974), 108-10.

Bruce-Novoa. "Review of *Nuevos Pasos: Chicano and Puerto Rican Drama.*" *Latin American Theatre Review*, 14 (fall 1980), 108-10.

Coronado, Luis Carlos. "Teatro Esperanza en Portales." *Floreciendo*, 1 (May-June 1979), 6.

Fox, Lucía. "El Teatro de la Esperanza en East Lansing, Michigan." *Latin American Theatre Review*, 13 (spring 1980), 106-08.

Huerta, Jorge. "From Quetzalcóatl to Honest Sancho; A Review Article of *Contemporary Chicano Theatre.*" *Revista Chicano-Riqueña*, 3 (summer 1977), 32-49.

_____ . Review of *Early Colonial Religious Drama: From Tzompantli to Golgotha* by Elizabeth E. Ravicz. *Latin American Theatre Review*, 6 (spring 1973), 76-78.

_____ . Review of *Hijos: Once A Family* by El Teatro de la Esperanza. *Tenaz Talks Teatro*, 2 (spring 1979), 9-10.

_____ . Review of *Historias para ser contadas* by Osvaldo Dragún, performed by Teatro Bilingüe. *Educational Theatre Journal*, 29 (March 1977), 115-16.

_____ . Review of *El Quetzal* by Adrian Vargas, performed by Teatro de la Gente. *Tenaz Talks Teatro*, 2 (spring 1979), 10-11.

_____ . Review of *Los vendidos*, a film by El Teatro Campesino. *Hispania*, 59 (December 1976), 977-79.

McCaffrey, Mark. Review of *Los dorados* by Carlos Morton. *Latin American Theatre Review*, 12 (fall 1978), 89-90.

McClellan, Bennett E. "Performance Review: 'El Garden' (12/1/76)." *Latin American Theatre Review*, 10 (spring 1977), 77-79.

McCracken, Ellen. "*Guadalupe.*" *Educational Theatre Journal*, 27 (December 1975), 554-55.

O, Charlie de la. "Festival de los Teatros 'Rasquacho' del Pueblo." *Floreciendo*, 1 (febrero-marzo 1979), 4, 5.

_____ . "IV Festival de los Teatros Chicanos del Pueblo." *Floreciendo*, 1 (abril-mayo 1980), 6, 9.

"A Review of 'Silver Dollar': El Teatro Urbano en Florencia, N.M." *Floreciendo*, 1 (abril-mayo 1980), 11.

Rivas, Maggie. "Teatro Chicano Portrays Changing Roles." *Tejidos*, 2 (otoño 1975), 10-11.

"El teatro chicano de Austin." *Magazín*, October 1971, p. 43.

B. Newspaper Articles

Alarcón, Francisco X. "Teatro: Las many muertes de Dany Rosales." *La Opinión* (Los Angeles), 7 septiembre 1980, sec. 15, pp. 12-15.

Charest, Karen. " 'Theater of Hope' Deals With Problems of the Chicanos." *Santa Barbara News-Press*, 18 May 1972, sec. A, p. 19.

Cless, Downing. "Teatro de la Esperanza: 'Actos' of Chicano Culture." *Santa Barbara News and Review*, 19 May 1972, p. 12.

Cook, Robert M. "Chicano Theater: Drama of Streets and Fields." *Los Angeles Times*, 1 January 1979, sec. 2, p. 6.

Cuellar, Rodolfo. "Teatro de la Tierra 'Bernabé'." *Sacramento El Hispano*, 20 May 1975, pp. 1, 8.

Downey, Bill. "Casa de la Raza/Fine Theatrical Performance." *Santa Barbara News-Press*, 10 August 1972, sec. B, p. 2.

Drake, Sylvie. " 'Los Teatros' Curtain Rises." *Los Angeles Times*, 18 September 1971, sec. II, p. 9.

González, Jorge. "Chicano Theatre Explores Drama of Guadalupe Life." *Santa Barbara News and Review*, 24 May 1974, p. 20.

————. "Theatre of Political Hope Contrasts Valdez' Work." *Santa Barbara News and Review*, 17 May 1974, p. 15.

Hoxie, Connie M. " 'Hijos, Once a Family' is Artful." *Santa Barbara News-Press*, 18 June 1979, sec. B, p. 7.

McCloskey, Katherine. "Program is Bilingual; Teatro Esperanza Performances Fill Audiences With Pride." *Santa Barbara News-Press*, 13 August 1971, sec. B, p. 3.

Mitchell, Sean. "Morales Case Taken to Dallas Stage." *Dallas Times Herald*, 2 February 1979, sec. E, p. 1.

Moore, Jim. "Minority Theatre Branching Out: Increased Professionalism." *Los Angeles Times*, 11 May 1976, sec. 6, pp. 3, 5.

————. "Out of the Barrio, An Acto of Faith." *Los Angeles Times*, 13 October 1974, Calendar, pp. 44, 45.

Mora, Juan Miguel de. " 'Guadalupe'." *El Heraldo de México*, 7 July 1974, sec. D, p. 8.

Rizo, Joe. "El Teatro de la Esperanza." *Sí Se Puede*, 11 February 1975, p. 9.

Ruiz, Raúl. "Teatro de la Esperanza y *La víctima*." *La Raza Quarterly*, 3 (1977), 19.

Saville, Jonathan. "Modified Miller." *San Diego Reader*, 17-23 November 1977, pp. 19, 25.

Silver, Jon. " 'Guadalupe' Provides Educational Strength." *UCSB Daily Nexus*, 1 May 1975, p. 8.

Stabiner, Karen. "El Teatro de la Esperanza: Confronting Us with the Way Things Are." *Santa Barbara News and Review*, 7 February 1975, p. 18.

"El Teatro Challenges Audiences." *UCSB Daily Nexus*, 11 May 1972, p. 6.

"El Teatro de la Esperanza Features 'Brechtian Didacticism'." *UCSB Daily Nexus*, 18 May 1972, p. 5.

"Teatro Shows What's Happening in Guadalupe." *Sí Se Puede*, June 1974, p. 6.

Valenti, Grace. "Brilliant." *Santa Barbara News and Review*, 21 June 1979, n.p.

Villarreal, J. A. "Teatro Los Pobres Production Offers a Fine Evening of Entertainment." *El Paso Herald Post*, 8 November 1972, sec. D, p. 7.

INDEX

This index is divided into two sections: (a) titles of *actos*, plays, and songs, and (b) names and topics. The entries reflect the content of the text and the endnotes (pages 1-240); names and titles in the bibliography are not indexed.

A. Actos, plays, and songs

Alamo, El: Our Version of What Happened, 83, 84-86
Alcalde, El, 121, 134, 135, 137-140, 142, 150
Angel Death, 231, note 21
Bernabé, 49, 97, 98, 194, 195-199, 203
"Boda del piojo y la pulga, La," 39
Bodas de sangre, 223
Carpa cantinflesca, La, 203, 207, 239, note 35
Comanches, Los, 83-84
Conquista de México, La, 133
Corrido, El, 206-207
Corrido de Juan Endrogado, El, 35, 231, note 21
"Corrido de Rosita Alvirez, El," 73
Cuatro años de colegio, 175, 235, note 29
Cuatro apariciones de la Virgen de Guadalupe, Las, 193, 212
"Cucaracha, La," 52, 199
Cuento de Pancho Diablo, El, 168, 238, note 23
Dark Root of a Scream, 49, 97-103, 113-114, 117, 174, 231, note 16
Day of the Swallows, 218, 220
Desolation Car Lot, 167
Dialogue of Cuco Rocha, The, 158-159
"Dilemma of a Revolutionary Poet," 158
Dorados, Los, 168

Dos caras del patroncito, Las, 18-23, 24, 34, 44
Everyman, 96
Fin del mundo, 174, 175, 194, 199, 207-213
Gran carpa de los rasquachis, La, 37, 78, 174, 176, 194, 199-207, 208, 209
Gran teatro del mundo, El, 203
Guadalupe, 69, 71, 77, 121, 140-149, 150-151, 152, 153, 231, note 21; 234, note 34
Hello Dolly, 174
High School Counselor, The, 120, 121-127, 128, 133, 135, 149, 150, 151
Historias para ser contadas, 32
Hombre que se convertió en perro, El, 21-36, 44-45
I Am Joaquín [film], 129
Jardín, El, 167, 168, 193-194
Juicio final, El, 190, 191
Justice, 157-158, 159, 160
Lilith, 168
"Mano poderosa," 202
Manolo, 86, 103-118, 231, note 20
Many muertes de Richard Morales, Las, 159, 160, 168-173, 184, 185
Militants, The, 69, 175, 205, 239, note 41
Moros y los cristianos, Los, 84, 192
Muerte en el barrio, 223
No saco nada de la escuela, 120-121,

128-134, 135, 150, 151, 152, 182
Pastores, Los, 190, 193
Pelados, Los (Felipe Castro), 228,
    note 24
Pelados, Los (Teatro Libertad), 37-40,
    42, 43, 44, 45, 217
Pensamiento serpentino, 203-204, 206
Quinta temporada, La, 23-27, 34-40,
    69, 122
Rabinal Achí, 189-190, 237, note 9
Rancho Hollywood, 168
Sacrificio de Isaac, El, 191
"Santa María de Iquique,", 143, 233,
    note 24
Shrunken Head of Pancho Villa, The,
    13, 14, 47, 48, 49-60, 78, 79-80, 97, 98,
    111, 195, 199, 203
Soldado razo, 86, 87, 91-97, 101, 102,
    117, 180
Squash, 168
Tejanos, Los, 84

Theft, The, 13
Three Grapes, The, 23
Trampa sin salida, 159, 160, 161-167,
    172, 184, 185
Vacil '76, 36
"Valentín de la Sierra," 143
Vendidos, Los, 47, 48, 61-68, 69, 80,
    122, 131, 133, 218
Víctima, La, 47, 48-49, 68-81, 114
Vida y proceso de Aurelio Pompa, La,
    157
Vietnam campesino, 86-91, 94, 95, 97,
    115, 117
View From the Bridge, A, 219-220
Virgen del Tepeyac, La, 193, 194, 203
"Visions" (NET series), 142
Who's To Blame? 231, note 21
Yo también hablo de la rosa, 223
Zoot Suit, 41, 49, 50, 79, 159, 160-161,
    174-184, 185, 197, 219

B. Names and topics

acculturation, 52, 54, 61, 62, 121
activist, 1, 4, 8, 14, 29, 36, 47, 76, 77,
    86, 112, 118, 119, 138, 167, 219
acto, 2, 3, 12, 13, 14-18, 18-23, 23-27,
    28, 29, 30, 32, 33, 34, 36, 37, 38, 40,
    43, 44-45, 48, 49, 50, 51, 55, 61-68, 69,
    72, 78, 80, 84, 87-97, 86, 87-91, 91-97,
    101, 104, 116, 117, 118, 119, 120, 121-
    128, 129-134, 135, 136, 137-140, 141,
    149, 150, 151, 152, 153, 155-157, 159,
    160, 161-167, 174, 177, 178, 179, 187,
    195, 198, 200, 204, 205, 209, 215, 216,
    218, 220, 226
acto-corrido, 209
actor/demonstrator [see also perform-
    er/demonstrator], 71, 72, 75, 79,
    144-145, 146, 151, 152
actor/investigator, 33-35, 140, 141,
    142, 146, 152
Acuña, Rodolfo, 84, 119
adaptation, 32-35, 219-220
"Adelita," 197, 198-199
agit-prop, 15, 96, 195, 227, note 4
agribusiness, 22, 23, 43, 87, 90

Alamo (Battle of the), 83, 84-85, 86
alcoholic, 53
"alienation effect," 146-147
allegorical: *acto,* 25, 179; figure, 23, 24,
    27, 34, 87, 90, 116, 194, 196, 198, 208;
    situation, 19, 23, 31
allegory, 66
alternative theaters, 42
Alvarez, Félix, 200
Anglo-American [Anglo], 4, 5, 28, 30,
    47, 48, 50, 56, 59, 67, 76, 83, 84, 85,
    112, 115, 119, 120, 121, 128, 130, 131,
    133, 134-135, 137, 157, 159, 165, 166,
    169, 171, 175, 181, 185, 199, 201, 204,
    219, 224, 235, note 21
Apaches, 100
Aquarius Theater (Hollywood), 181
archetype, archetypal, 38, 59, 179
Arizona, 157, 223
assimilation, 47, 48, 60, 61, 122, 130,
    150
assimilationist, 4, 8, 131
auditions, 35

Austin, TX, 136
auto sacramental, 23, 190
Aztecs [Mexico], 29, 98, 102, 133, 187, 188-189, 191 192, 195, 196, 197, 215
Aztlán, 29, 68, 88, 96, 192, 193, 201

Baptists, 136, 137
Belgrade International Theatre Festival, 77
Berkeley, CA, 169
Beverly Hills, CA, 219
Bicentennial, 36
bilingual, 64, 72, 78, 91-92
bilingual education, 133, 138, 148
Bilingual Foundation of the Arts, 168-169
bilinguality, 6, 21, 71, 72, 73, 91-92, 94, 114-115, 133, 137, 164-165, 177, 200
Black-American, 28, 111, 121, 130, 131, 169, 182, 183
Booth, Willard C., 188
Bowie, James, 83, 85
bracero, 20
bracero program, 228, note 13
Brecher, Kenneth, 176
Brecht, Bertolt, 15, 16, 17, 18, 91, 95, 146-147, 220
Broadway, 42, 174, 175, 178, 181, 182, 223
Brokaw, John, 230, note 4
Brooklyn, 219
Bruce-Novoa [Juan], 38, 44, 146-147
Burruel, Francisco O., 158, 159

California, 30, 60, 68, 122, 127, 129, 156, 157, 168, 174, 219, 223
California Advisory Committee to the U.S. Commission on Civil Rights, 139, 140
caló, 6, 164, 165, 177
Campos, Estella, 78
Cantinflas, 18, 20
capitalism, 32, 70
Carballido, Emilio, 223
caricature, 38, 39, 44, 129-130, 145, 149, 150, 152
Carnales en Espíritu, 239, note 45
Carnalismo, 166
Carpa, 174, 177, 229, note 1
Casa de la Raza, La, 68-69

Castillo, Martín 6, 120
Castro, Felipe, 228, note 24
Castro, Fidel, 13, 14, 204
Castroville, TX, 169
Ce Acatl Topiltzin Quetzalcóatl, 98, 101
Center Theatre Group (Los Angeles), 176, 178, 181
Centro Campesino Cultural, 31, 129
Centro Cultural de la Gente, 31-32
Chávez, César, 1, 16, 22, 23, 26, 28, 30, 43, 48, 61, 110, 129, 141, 143, 144, 145, 158
Chicago, IL, 5, 167
Chicano Liberation Youth Conference, 29
Chicano Moratorium on the War in Vietnam (Fresno, CA, 1971),
Chicano movement, 14, 28-29, 30, 31, 48, 61, 119, 132, 133, 136, 141, 143, 156, 158-159, 163, 175, 183, 203, 215, 217
"Chicano power," 131, 166
Chicano student movement, 2, 28-32, 120, 167
Chicano Theatre One, 2
Chicano Theatre Two, 2
Child abuse, 35
Children, 44, 93-94, 107, 130, 137
Christ, 199, 200, 201, 205, 210
Christian folk drama, 187, 190-191, 192-193, 194, 212
Cinco de Mayo, 70, 142
civil rights movement, 28
Coatlicue, 198
collective, 36, 37, 48, 49, 70, 77, 78, 83, 91, 97, 166, 199, 204, 207
collectivity, 12, 14, 16, 18, 30, 34, 36, 38, 40, 43, 48, 64, 77, 104, 117, 131, 133, 134, 136, 137, 149, 168, 174, 194, 195, 203, 208, 209
Colonizer and the Colonized, The, 70
Colorado, 223
Comanches, 83-84
comedy, 18, 26, 40, 63, 89, 91, 101, 151
comic relief, 92
commedia dell'arte, 14, 130, 162, 163, 165, 189, 200, 209, 220
commodity theater, 42, 215
communism, 95

communist, 74
"communist threat," 75
corrido, 32, 34, 72, 142, 143, 159, 177, 200, 206, 208, 209, 211, 238, note 29
Cortés, Hernán, 202
cost of living, 38
costumes, 13, 25-26, 36, 71, 72, 79, 102, 145, 161, 162, 181, 195, 209, 211
courts, 8, 30, 49
Coyolxauhqui, 198
Crockett, Davy, 83, 85
Cuadro México-España, 157
Cuba, 13, 14, 204
cultural workers, 32, 35, 37, 42, 43
"culturally deprived," 134

dance, 39, 155, 179, 187, 188, 195, 204
dance-drama, 189-190
dance ritual, 207
Davidson, Gordon, 176
Davis, Ron, 13, 18, 236, note 33
Del Rey, CA, 61, 67, 129
Delano, CA, 11-14, 15, 18, 61, 126
"demystify," 78-79
Denver, CO, 29
deportation [see also repatriation], 20, 49, 70, 72, 76, 77, 78
Depression, 137
designer, 104, 161-162, 179
Día de los Muertos, 207
dialect, 114
Diamond, Betty, 95-96, 198, 208
director, 17, 30, 31, 32, 33, 42, 103, 104, 105, 134, 142, 161-162, 179, 209
docudrama [see also documentary] 69, 71-74, 78-79, 119, 121, 140-151, 152, 153
documentary [see also docudrama], 48, 49, 70, 71-74, 78-79, 140-151, 152, 153, 159, 160, 169, 170, 172, 173
draft (conscription), 88, 90, 91, 96, 105
Dragún, Osvaldo, 32, 33, 34
Drake, Sylvie, 181-182
dramatized lecture, 87, 150, 171
drug abuse/addiction, 35, 105, 106, 107, 109, 110, 111, 112, 113, 114, 116, 117, 148, 217, 226
drug dealer/pusher, 105, 115, 116, 151, 201

drug rehabilitation, 106, 108, 114
drugs, 104, 111, 112, 113, 115, 116, 140, 141-142, 144, 205
Dukore, Bernard, 158

East Chicago, IN, 134-135
East Los Angeles, CA, 86-87, 122, 157, 161, 219
economic system, 50, 59
education, 119, 120
educational system, 64, 121
Eighth Annual Chicano Theater Festival, 37, 77
epilogue, 95, 106, 113, 211
Euripides, 220
exposition, 19, 53, 97, 105, 146, 171
expressionism, 35, 55, 116
extended *acto*, 38, 120

Fanon, Franz, 70
fantastic, 34, 57, 59, 66, 67, 97, 98
fantasy, 39, 54, 60, 206, 211
farce, 14, 21, 34, 38, 40, 44, 87, 88, 89, 91, 92, 130, 165, 166, 210, 211
farm-labor contractor ("coyote"), 23, 24-27, 55, 56, 60, 62, 89, 206
feathered serpent, 97, 98, 100
film, 129
flashback, 108
flash-forward, 108
folk plays, 32
folk song, 75
folk theater, 1, 6
foreshadow, 54, 84, 91, 99, 196
Fourth National Chicano Theater Festival, 167, 199
fourth wall, 78
Fresno, CA, 91, 129
Fresno State College, 129, 222
Frisbie, Parker, 128
"Frito Bandito," 67

García, Joey, 69-70
García Lorca, Federico, 223
Gary, IN, 134-135, 140
Garza, Hisauro, 156
gavacho, 53, 54, 58
Gleason, Ralph, 18
Glodel, Marcus, 157
Gold Rush, 168

Goldsmith, Barclay, 36, 230, note 19
González, Héctor, 83
González, Jorge R., 206
González, Rodolfo ("Corky"), 129
grape boycott, 61, 88, 96
gringo, 56-57
grito, 52
Guadalupe, CA, 121, 139, 140-141, 142-149, 150-151
Guevara, Che, 158
Guzmán, Ralph, 90

Hayes, Frank, 169, 172, 173
Hernández, Martha, 144, 233, note 33
heroin, 86, 105, 106, 107, 108, 109, 110, 111, 112, 113, 114, 115, 142
Hollywood, CA, 66, 83, 85-86, 176, 181, 226
Hollywood Palladium, 182
homosexuality, 218
Hoover, President (Herbert), 71
housing, 38, 120
Houston, Sam, 85
Huelga, 13, 17, 22, 26, 27, 60-61, 109, 110, 206
Huitzilopochtli, 188, 195, 197, 198
human sacrifice, 101, 188, 190, 191, 195, 197

Ibsen, Henrik, 38
"illegal alien scare," 5, 70, 75
immigrants, 4, 29, 84, 100-101
immigration, 49
immigration officer, 49, 80
imperialism, 85
improvisation, 3, 12, 13, 14, 15, 16, 17, 19, 33, 69, 70, 123-127, 137, 140, 141, 149, 207
Indiana University Northwest, 136
"In Lak'Ech," 202, 203, 204, 205
inmates, 155
Inner City Cultural Center, Los Angeles, CA, 96, 231, note 16
I.N.S. (Immigration and Naturalization Service), 72, 74, 76, 77, 144, 217
internal colonialism, 60, 70
Irish American, 37
irony, 20, 21
Irving, T. B., 189

John Birch Society, 141
judges, 50
Justice Department, 169, 172, 173

Kanellos, Nicolás, 121, 134-137, 232, note 14
Kennedy, John F., 38
Kingsville, TX, 223
KNBC, Los Angeles, 66
Korean War, 74, 75, 95, 99
Kourilsky, Francoise, 200-201

language, 4, 5, 6, 7-8, 21, 40, 42, 57, 59, 62-63, 64, 65, 72, 73, 77, 78, 91-92, 94, 99, 114-115, 116, 131, 133, 148, 164-166, 177
Latin America, 2, 14, 34, 143, 223, 226
"law and order," 58
Lehrstücke, 15
Leinaweaver, Richard E., 189
lettuce boycott, 87, 88, 96
lighting, 79, 97-98, 104, 108, 109, 145
Living Newspaper, 177
Loo, Guillermo ("Billy"), 231, note 21
Los Angeles, CA, 5, 41, 66, 96, 160-161, 168, 169, 174, 175, 176-177, 178, 179, 181, 182, 183, 219
Los Angeles County Sheriff, 160, 161
Los Angeles Herald Examiner, 179
Los Angeles Times, 87, 206

machismo, 92
McClellan, Bennett, 169
McCracken, Ellen, 147
Madrid-Barela, Arturo, 183-184
makeup, 79, 92
Manhattan: see New York City
"Manifest Destiny," 50, 85
marijuana, 64, 99, 197, 199
Marines, 58
Mark Taper Forum (Los Angeles), 174, 175, 176, 177, 181
Martínez, Manuel, 31
Martínez Paredez, Domingo, 238, note 27
Marxist, 178
masks, 12, 13, 14, 18-20, 22, 44, 130, 138, 139, 146, 148, 149, 151, 161, 162, 163, 195, 197, 209, 211
Mason, Theresa Hope, 239, note 45

Maximilian, Joseph Ferdinand, 71
Maya, 187, 189, 194, 195, 197-198, 202, 204, 213, 215
Maya-Quiché, 189-190
M.E.Ch.A. (UCSB), 68
Mechicana, 217
Mechicano, 5, 6, 7, 8, 9, 15, 18, 31, 32, 33, 36, 40, 43, 45, 49, 50, 51, 52, 55-56, 59, 60, 61, 62, 66, 70, 77, 80, 83, 84, 85, 87, 88, 92, 95, 96, 113, 117, 119, 120, 121, 127, 128, 133, 135, 136, 140, 147, 149, 150, 153, 155, 156-157, 158, 159, 160, 161, 165, 172, 176, 177, 181, 183, 184, 187, 194, 196, 205, 206, 212, 215, 217, 218, 219, 220, 223, 224, 226
media, 2, 49, 56, 67, 72, 85, 96
melodramatic, 116, 147
"melting pot," 29, 47-49, 122, 132
Memmi, Albert, 70
Mesoamerica, 176
metaphor, 39, 54, 55, 63, 98, 159, 208
Mexica [Aztecs], 188-189, 190-191, 192, 195
Mexican-American War, 70
Mexican Revolution, 49, 52, 53, 57, 72, 73, 197
Mexico, 2, 5, 6, 20, 29, 34, 44, 45, 52, 56, 57, 65, 72, 73, 74, 75, 80, 142, 144, 147, 149, 167, 187, 192, 199, 200, 223
Mexico City, 135, 142, 177
Michigan, 122-123, 127, 128
"Migra," 76, 144, 210
Miller, Arthur, 219-220
missionary, 141, 190
missionary drama, 187, 190-192
mito, 97, 98, 101, 102, 103, 116, 117, 159, 177, 194, 195-199, 200, 207, 209, 211
Moctezuma, 133, 202
monologue, 20, 21, 92
Moors, 84
Morales, Bob, 209
Morales, Richard, 169, 170, 171-172, 173, 184
morality play, 23, 27, 190, 211, 212
Morton, Carlos, 159, 160, 167-170, 171, 172, 173, 193-194
Murieta, Joaquín, 53, 111
music, 31, 33, 34-35, 48, 51, 52, 55, 69,

72, 73, 75, 109, 116, 129, 143, 144, 145, 179, 195, 199, 200, 202, 209
mystery play, 23, 190
myth, 32, 41, 85, 101, 187-190, 193, 194, 195, 199
mythical, 49

Nahuatl, 190, 191, 192
narration, 34, 72, 73, 74, 85, 92, 147, 209
narrator, 36, 37, 50, 91, 92, 170, 171, 179-180
National Chicano Moratorium (Los Angeles, CA, 1970), 86-87
Nazi, 131
N.E.T. (National Educational Television), 142, 206
New Jersey, 136
New Mexicans, 83-84, 86
New Mexico, 84, 192, 193, 223
New York City, 161, 176, 181, 182, 183
New York Times, 160, 169, 170
Newport Folk Festival, 61
Nixon, Richard M., 132, 150, 194

Oakland, CA, 94
Old Testament, 113, 191, 193, 194
O'Neill, Eugene, 220
Oñate, Juan de, 192

pachuca, 132
pachuco, 50, 53, 54, 56, 62, 63-64, 65, 66, 67, 68, 98, 131, 132, 133, 160, 161, 162-165, 166, 167, 179-180, 181, 182, 183-184, 197, 198, 217
pachuquismos, 165
pamphleteering, 49
pantomime, 20-21, 90, 91, 92, 145, 190
parody, 26, 39, 48, 150
pelado, 37, 228, note 24
Pentagon, 88-89
people's theater, 3, 31
performer/demonstrator [see also actor/demonstrator], 16-17, 32, 43
Pickett, Manuel, 224
Pinter, Harold, 220
Plan de Santa Barbara, El, 29
Plymouth Rock, 29
pocho, 144
poetic realism, 218

Poland, 71, 77
police, 8, 30, 50, 53, 58, 66, 102, 105-
    106, 111-112, 115, 121, 140, 156, 157,
    158, 160, 161, 164, 170, 171, 172, 173,
    184, 185, 205, 217
politicians, 72, 85, 121
Pompa, Aurelio, 157, 215
Portillo, Estella, 218
Posada, José Guadalupe, 211
poverty, 57
priests, 50, 145
prison, 52, 53, 58, 60, 155-156, 160, 184,
    217
prologue, 39, 51, 52, 72-73, 105
props, 19, 20, 55, 71, 72, 85, 91, 145,
    179, 211
Puerto Rican(s) 2, 8, 121, 134-135, 136,
    138, 139, 140
Puerto Rican theater, 134
puppets, 133
pyramid, 87, 98, 102

Quetzalcóatl, 98, 99, 100, 101, 102, 103,
    188, 190, 201-202, 210

Rabinal, Guatemala, 189
Racine, Jean Baptiste, 220
racism, 84, 95, 101, 128, 129, 171, 185
racist, 56, 84, 120, 127, 160, 179, 184
Radical Theatre Festival (San Fran-
    cisco, 1968), 52
Ramírez, Elizabeth, 223, 232, note 18
Ramparts (magazine), 18, 95
rasquachi, 37, 200, 201, 211, 239, note
    30
Raza, La, 50
Reagan, Ronald, 63
realism, 19, 20, 35, 36, 44, 96, 105, 116
realistic, 3, 43, 44, 55, 78, 104, 105, 116,
    149, 159
recession, 70
religious theater, 1, 6, 9, 83, 135, 203,
    211
repatriation [see also deportation], 20,
    49, 70, 72, 76, 77, 78
revolution, 95
revolucionario, 62, 65, 66
Riqueños, 136, 139
ritual, 6, 187-190, 194, 195, 205, 207
ritual drama, 187, 188-190, 195, 212

Robledo, Eduardo (Ed), 31, 236, note
    33
Rockefeller Foundation, 176
Roman Catholic, 136, 192, 200
Rosenberg, Joseph, 223, 224
Ruiz, Raul, 77
Russia, 15

Saavedra, Guadalupe, 157-158, 159,
    160
St. Mary's University, TX, 103
Salazar, Rubén, 87
San Antonio, TX, 5, 83, 84, 127, 142,
    208
San Diego, CA, 37, 168, 169, 193, 220
Sandoval, Rubén, 172
San Francisco, CA, 14, 52, 168
San Francisco Chronicle, 18
San Francisco Mime Troupe, 13, 14,
    168, 169
San Joaquin Valley, CA, 25
San Jose, CA, 28, 30, 31, 32, 33, 34, 42,
    44, 193, 199, 203
San Jose City College, 31
San Jose State College, 12, 13, 28, 31
San Juan Bautista, CA, 61, 174, 176,
    178, 193, 207, 220
Santa Barbara, CA, 29, 68-69, 121, 140,
    142, 152, 161, 220
Santa Fe, NM, 192
Santa Maria, CA, 142
Sastre, Alfonso, 223
satire, 16, 18, 48, 69, 86
Saturday Review of Literature, 95
Saucedo, José, 69-70, 78
scapegoat, 66, 70
Schools of Guadalupe . . . A Legacy
    of Educational Oppression, The,
    140, 152
scrim, 102
Seattle, WA, 103, 104, 127
selective realism, 104
sellout, 8, 47, 54, 59, 62, 66, 67, 68, 122,
    133, 151
Senate Sub-Committee on Migratory
    Labor, 61
settings, 13, 19, 36, 38, 43, 55, 71, 72, 85,
    88, 91, 97, 98, 104-105, 107, 130, 142,
    145, 162, 170, 179, 196, 208, 211

Seventh Annual Chicano Theater Festival, 208
sex, 166
Shakespeare, William, 220
sheriff, 13, 20, 87, 166
Shubert Organization, 181
Sierra, Rubén, 86, 103-104, 105, 109, 110, 111-112, 113-114, 115, 116, 117
Sixth National Chicano Theater Festival, 83
Sleepy Lagoon murder trial, 160, 176, 177
slides (projections), 51, 52, 57, 129
Smith, Cecil, 206-207
social bandit, 51, 58
social realism, 43, 44-45, 54
social worker, 58-59
song, 28, 35, 61, 74, 75, 143, 155, 179, 187, 188
sound effects, 52, 79, 80, 92, 108, 109
South Chicago, IL, 194
Spain, 192
"Spanglish," 114, 164
Spaniard, 84, 133, 141, 187, 190-192
Stanford University, 17
State Department, 78
stereotype, 2, 23, 33, 34, 38, 51, 54, 63, 65, 67, 72, 100, 104, 112, 125, 135, 141, 145, 150, 151-152, 158, 184
street theater, 3, 15, 90
subsidies, 32
Sullivan, Dan, 96, 102
super-acto, 36, 38-40, 44-45
supernatural, 107
super-realism, 144
surreal, 97
surrealism, 55, 57, 78, 79, 96
suspense, 71, 91, 95
Sweden, 71, 77-78
symbolism, 32, 33, 35, 51, 52, 78, 208

tableau, 73, 74, 95, 98
Teatro Bilingüe (California State University, Sacramento), 223-224
Teatro Bilingüe (Texas A & I University), 223
Teatro Campesino, 1, 2, 3, 9, 12, 16, 18-27, 28, 29, 36, 37, 40, 41, 42, 43, 44, 45, 60-61, 64, 69, 72, 78, 86, 87, 91-92, 95-96, 97, 120, 122, 126, 128, 129-130, 131, 132, 133, 157, 158, 168, 174, 175, 176, 179, 181, 183, 187, 193, 194, 195, 199-200, 203, 204, 205, 206, 207-208, 209, 211, 212, 215, 216, 220, 221, 224
Teatro Chicano (East Los Angeles), 157-158
Teatro Chicano de Austin [Texas], 136, 232, note 18
Teatro de la Esperanza, 48, 67, 68-81, 114, 121, 140, 141-151, 152, 160, 161, 163, 165, 220, 223, 224, 231, note 21
Teatro de la Gente, 31-36, 37, 39, 40, 41-42, 193, 224, 231, note 21
Teatro de los Barrios (San Antonio, TX), 83, 84-86, 239, note 45
Teatro del Piojo, 103, 231, note 19
Teatro del Pueblo, 36
Teatro Desengaño del Pueblo, 121, 134-135, 136-137, 139, 232, note 14
Teatro Libertad, 36-45, 217-218
Teatro Mecha (UCSB), 68
Teatro Mestizo, 175, 193, 235, note 29
Teatro movement, 2-3, 30
Teatro Obrero, 231, note 21
Teatro Primavera, 231, note 21
Teatro Quetzalcóatl, 103-104, 110, 231, note 19
El Teatro/El Tenaz, 2, 228, note 17
Teatro Urbano, 28, 30
tenant's union, 39
TENAZ, 2, 50, 203, 220-221, 231, note 16; 232-233, note 19
TENAZ Summer Workshop, 238, note 29
Tenaz Talks Teatro, 3
Texans, 84
Texas, 20, 24, 44, 83-84, 85, 136, 170, 172, 223, 224
Texas Rangers, 160
Tezcatlipoca, 101
theater of workers, 36
Tijuana, México, 5, 161
tlaquetzque, 188-189
Toltec, 101, 201
tragedy, 18, 96, 188, 220
translation, 72, 77, 78, 114-115, 148
Travis, William, 83, 85
Tucson, AZ, 36, 37, 40, 44, 158

UFW (United Farmworkers' Union), 11, 12, 16, 17-20, 21, 22, 23, 26, 27, 30, 31, 41, 43, 48, 60, 61, 87, 109, 110, 129, 141, 144, 158, 198
"Uncle Sam," 95
undocumented worker, 5, 20, 36-37, 70, 144
unemployment, 38, 120
University of California at Berkeley, 222
University of California, San Diego, 70-71, 160, 168
University of California, Santa Barbara, 68, 161, 205, 206, 223
University of Michigan, 126
University of Texas, 136
University of Texas at El Paso, 167
University of Washington, 103
U.S. Army, 74, 115, 127
U.S. Commission on Civil Rights, 69

Valdez, Daniel (Danny), 22, 30
Valdez, Luis, 1, 2, 4, 6, 9, 11-27, 28, 30, 31, 39, 41-43, 45, 48, 49-60, 61, 64, 66, 67, 68, 78, 79, 80, 86, 87, 95, 97, 98, 99, 100, 102, 103, 111, 113-114, 115, 117, 126, 128, 129, 159, 161, 168, 169, 173, 174-184, 187, 194, 195, 196-199, 200, 202-207, 208-209, 210, 211, 212-213, 215, 216, 221, 222, 238, note 27
Valdez, Socorro, 209
Valdezian, 17, 152, 179, 194, 200, 211, 226
Valentín, David, 38, 44, 146-147
Vargas, Adrian, 31, 32, 33, 35, 36, 41-42, 231, note 21
Variedades, 229, note 1
Vasconcelos, José, 29
vato, 30, 50, 59, 64, 68, 98, 99, 100, 101, 161, 162, 197, 208
Venceremos Brigade, 14
vendido, 48, 50, 51, 54, 56, 58, 60, 62, 75, 81, 122, 132, 141, 150, 151, 217
Veracruz, México, 149
Verdugo, Jaime, 159, 161-162, 164, 165
Verfremdungseffekt, 146-147
veteran, veterano, 53, 86, 95, 104, 113, 117, 217
vida loca, 64

Vietnam, 49, 86, 87-91, 94, 95, 104, 105, 107, 109, 117
Vietnam "conflict," 8, 86-91, 97, 115-116, 118, 127, 130, 217
Vietnamese, 88, 90
Villa, Pancho, 51, 52, 53, 54, 57, 59, 62, 79, 199
Village Theater (New York City, NY), 60-61
Virgin of Guadalupe, 38, 147-148, 193, 202, 205

walkouts, 28
Washington, D.C., 28, 61
"WASP," 48
Wayne, John, 100
welfare, 53, 201
Winter Garden Theatre, 181
Wood, Sylvia, 228, note 24
worker's theater, 27, 28, 36, 40, 41, 42, 43, 45
working class, 4, 5, 7, 8, 18, 33, 36, 37, 40, 90, 95
World War II, 95, 99
Wretched of the Earth, The, 70

Ybarra-Frausto, Tomás, 157
Yugoslavia, 71, 77

Zacatecas, México, 192
Zamora, Romulus, 223-224
"Zoot Suit Riots," 174, 179
zoot suiter, 162, 173, 176, 179, 196, 226